D1617341

The Logic of American
Nuclear Strategy

BRIDGING THE GAP

Series Editors

James Goldgeier
Bruce Jentleson
Steven Weber

The Logic of American Nuclear Strategy:
Why Strategic Superiority Matters
Matthew Kroenig

The Logic of American Nuclear Strategy

Why Strategic Superiority Matters

MATTHEW KROENIG

OXFORD
UNIVERSITY PRESS

OXFORD
UNIVERSITY PRESS

Oxford University Press is a department of the University of Oxford. It furthers
the University's objective of excellence in research, scholarship, and education
by publishing worldwide. Oxford is a registered trade mark of Oxford University
Press in the UK and certain other countries.

Published in the United States of America by Oxford University Press
198 Madison Avenue, New York, NY 10016, United States of America.

© Oxford University Press 2018

Library of Congress Cataloging-in-Publication Data
Names: Kroenig, Matthew, author.
Title: The logic of American nuclear strategy : why strategic
superiority matters / Matthew Kroenig.
Description: New York City : Oxford University Press, [2018] |
Includes bibliographical references and index.
Identifiers: LCCN 2017035084 (print) | LCCN 2017058642 (ebook) |
ISBN 9780190849191 (updf) | ISBN 9780190849207 (epub) | ISBN 9780190849184 (hardcover)
Subjects: LCSH: Nuclear weapons—Government policy—United States. |
United States—Military policy. | Strategic forces—United States. | Strategy.
Classification: LCC UA23 (ebook) | LCC UA23 .K783 2018 (print) | DDC 355.02/170973—dc23
LC record available at https://lccn.loc.gov/2017035084

1 3 5 7 9 8 6 4 2

Printed by Sheridan Books, Inc., United States of America

Also by Matthew Kroenig

Author or Co-Author

A Time to Attack: The Looming Iranian Nuclear Threat

Exporting the Bomb: Technology Transfer and the Spread of Nuclear Weapons

The Handbook of National Legislatures: A Global Survey

Co-Editor

Nonproliferation Policy and Nuclear Posture: Causes and Consequences for the Spread of Nuclear Weapons

Causes and Consequences of Nuclear Weapons Proliferation

CONTENTS

PREFACE

In the fall of 2008, I was settling in to my first semester as an assistant professor in the Department of Government at Georgetown University and teaching a course in my area of expertise, titled "Nuclear Weapons in World Politics." Developing a new course is always challenging, and there were many memorable episodes from that first semester, but one in particular stands out.

I was discussing the requirements for successful nuclear deterrence and I explained to my students that once a country possesses a nuclear arsenal capable of a secure, second-strike (the ability to absorb a nuclear attack from an opponent and retain enough surviving warheads to respond with a devastating nuclear counterattack), then nuclear deterrence would hold. I also mentioned that, although academics are skeptical of the idea, many US policymakers believe that the United States's possession of nuclear superiority over a rival, even above and beyond a mere second-strike capability, also contributes to deterrence.

Inevitably, one of my smart and curious students asked why.

I did not have an answer.

The politics of nuclear weapons was my area of expertise. It was a major part of the reason why I was hired at Georgetown. I had received a Public Policy and Nuclear Threats fellowship from the National Science Foundation during graduate school at the University of California at Berkeley and I had just spent a year as a postdoctoral fellow at the Managing the Atom Project at Harvard University. I had previously served as a military analyst at the Central Intelligence Agency and a strategist in the Office of the Secretary of Defense, where I had worked on issues of nuclear weapons and deterrence. I had a book and several articles on nuclear issues in the pipeline, accepted for publication in top scholarly outlets. I vividly recalled the reams of scholarship I had read on nuclear deterrence theory. Yet, I could not call to mind a single, clear explanation for why a strategic nuclear advantage might translate into a geopolitical advantage. If anyone should have been able to answer this question, it was me. But I was at a loss for words.

I eventually offered something about how a more robust nuclear force might be relevant to counterforce targeting in the event of a nuclear war, but the answer was deeply unsatisfying, even to myself. I was determined to learn more.

This book is the result of that initial curiosity.

The writing of this book was made possible by many institutions and individuals. I am fortunate to teach at Georgetown University and I am grateful to Georgetown's senior leadership, Jack DeGioia, Robert Groves, Joel Hellman, Charles King, and Irfan Nooruddin, for providing me with a career at what I believe is the best institution in the world to be a political science professor. To my fellow international relations scholars at Georgetown, Anthony Arend, Andrew Bennett, Marc Busch, Daniel Byman, Victor Cha, Raj Desai, David Edelstein, Bruce Hoffman, Lise Howard, Robert Lieber, Keir Lieber, Charles Kupchan, Kathleen McNamara, Daniel Nexon, Abraham Newman, Nita Rudra, George Shambaugh, Elizabeth Stanley, Erik Voeten, and James Vreeland, thank you for setting a high bar and inspiring me to do better work every day.

In 2013, I accepted an affiliation as a senior fellow in the Brent Scowcroft Center on International Security at the Atlantic Council. Jon Huntsman, Frederick Kemp, Damon Wilson, Barry Pavel, and Magnus Nordstrom deserve credit for transforming the Atlantic Council from a small organization focusing on transatlantic issues into one of the largest, most diverse, and impactful nonpartisan foreign policy think tanks in Washington in less than a decade.

The book was completed with financial support from the Smith Richardson Foundation. Some of the work on this project was also conducted while I was on a Stanton Nuclear Security Fellowship at the Council on Foreign Relations in Washington, DC. For this opportunity, I am grateful to the Stanton Foundation; the Council on Foreign Relations; the Council's senior leadership, including Richard Haass and James Lindsay; CFR senior fellows Michael Levi and Micah Zenko; and the individuals behind the Council's fellowship programs, Janine Hill and Victoria Alekhine.

I benefited from feedback at a number of seminars where I presented earlier versions of this research. I thank participants at events at the American Political Science Association's 2009 Annual Meeting; The Center for Strategic and International Studies; Georgetown University; The George Washington University; Harvard University; the International Studies Association's 2013 Annual Meeting; Lawrence Livermore National Laboratory; Los Alamos National Laboratory; Michigan State University; Princeton University; the University of California's Institute on Global Conflict and Cooperation; the University of California at Los Angeles; Wilton Park; US Strategic Command; US Office of the Secretary of Defense; US National Security Council Staff; US Navy submarine bases in Bangor, Washington, and King's Bay, Georgia; Vanderbilt University; and Yale University.

For helpful comments on drafts of various parts of this book, I thank Victor Asal, Kyle Beardsley, Richard Betts, Philipp Bleek, Giacomo Chiozza, Jennifer Erikson, M. Steven Fish, Matthew Fuhrmann, Christopher Gelpi, Bruce Goodwin, Rebecca Davis Gibbons, Peter Henne, Robert Jervis, Paul Kapur, Michael Levi, Adam Mount, Abraham Newman, Robert Powell, Daryl Press, Marc Trachtenberg, Bob Vince, and two anonymous reviewers. My apologies to anyone I forgot.

I am indebted to William Hallisey, Anastasia Kazteridis, Miriam Krieger, Rebecca Kuang, Anthony Perisco, Sami Scheetz, Dane Shikman, Shannon Callahan Souma, Alexander Sullivan, and Michael Weintraub for helpful research assistance.

This book contains selections of material that have been previously published in other outlets, including *International Organization, Journal of Peace Research, Foreign Policy*, and *Survival*. I thank the editors of these outlets for the permission to draw on this material in the book manuscript.[1]

David McBride and his team at Oxford University Press did an outstanding job in helping me bring this book to press. I congratulate James Goldgeier, Bruce Jentleson, and Steve Weber on their editorship of the new Bridging the Gap Series. It is an honor to be among the first books included in what I believe could become one of the most exciting and important series in our field.

There are many individuals who have contributed to my development as a political scientist and a scholar. I could not have asked for a better friend or a more dynamic research collaborator on nuclear issues than Erik Gartzke. Giacomo Chiozza, Steve Fish, Michael Nacht, and Steve Weber, as you promised at my dissertation defense, you have remained my most trusted academic advisors throughout my career.

As always, thanks to my wonderful friends and family, including our newest addition, my beautiful daughter Eleanora. Finally, I am blessed to have married my best friend. Olivia, you make me happy, but more importantly, you make me a better person. This book is dedicated to you.

ABBREVIATIONS AND ACRONYMS

ALCM	Air-launched cruise missile
C4ISR	Command, control, communications, computers, intelligence, surveillance, and reconnaissance
CFR	Council on Foreign Relations
CPO	Causal process observation
CIA	Central Intelligence Agency (United States)
DEFCON	Defense condition (United States)
EMP	Electromagnetic pulse
GAO	Government Accountability Office
GDP	Gross domestic product
H-PAC	Hazard prediction and assessment capability
HEU	Highly enriched uranium
IAEA	International Atomic Energy Agency
IAEA AP	International Atomic Energy Agency Additional Protocol
IAEA BOG	International Atomic Energy Agency Board of Governors
ICB	International Crisis Behavior Dataset
ICBM	Intercontinental ballistic missile
ISR	Intelligence, surveillance, and reconnaissance
JCPOA	Joint Comprehensive Plan of Action (the Iran nuclear deal)
JPOA	Joint Plan of Action (the interim Iran nuclear deal)
KT	Kiloton
LOC	Line of control
LRSO	Long-range standoff weapon
MRBM	Medium-range ballistic missile
MAD	Mutually assured destruction
MCT	Militarized compellent threat
MIRV	Multiple independently targetable reentry vehicle
MT	Megaton

NATO	North Atlantic Treaty Organization
NPT	Treaty on the Nonproliferation of Nuclear Weapons
NSG	Nuclear Suppliers Group
PLA	People's Liberation Army (China)
PNE	Peaceful nuclear explosion
PNI	Presidential Nuclear Initiative
GLCM	Ground-launched cruise missile
SAC	Strategic Air Command
SLBM	Submarine-launched ballistic missile
SLCM	Submarine-launched cruise missile
SRBM	Short-range ballistic missile
SSBN	Subsurface ballistic nuclear (submarine)
T-LAM	Tomahawk land-attack missile
UELE	Use 'em or lose 'em
UN	United Nations
UNSC	United Nations Security Council

The Logic of American
Nuclear Strategy

Introduction

Nuclear weapons have returned to the center of politics among nations. For half a century during the Cold War, nuclear forces were fundamental to the bipolar, strategic competition between the United States and the Soviet Union, but they temporarily receded into the background in the post–Cold War period. For the quarter century between 1989 and 2014, many viewed nuclear weapons as nothing more than Cold War relics. By 2009, serious people even debated whether complete nuclear abolition was within reach.[1] It is now becoming clear, however, that this sustained de-emphasis on nuclear weapons was not achieved because humanity had somehow become more enlightened.

Rather, nuclear weapons remain the ultimate instrument of military force and they are still, therefore, essential tools of great power political competition. Such great power rivalries were muted when the United States emerged as the world's unipolar power at the end of the Cold War and Washington overawed any potential peer competitors. The adversaries it did face in the 1990s and 2000s, such as Serbia, Afghanistan, Iraq, and Al Qaeda, did not possess nuclear weapons and the US nuclear arsenal was not directly relevant to the asymmetric security challenges these enemies posed.

But great power political competition has returned, and with it, the salience of nuclear weapons in world politics. In 2014, Russian President Vladimir Putin invaded Ukraine and, in the following year, intervened in Syria. In a bid to deter NATO intervention, Putin has made explicit nuclear threats and has brandished nuclear weapons at a level we have not seen since the end of the Cold War.[2] China has become more aggressive in East Asia, claiming contested territory from US allies through military coercion. In the event of great power war in East Asia, there is a real risk of nuclear use.[3] Kim Jong Un in North Korea continues to conduct nuclear and missile tests and engage in nuclear brinkmanship against the United States. Moreover, these countries and others are taking steps to ensure they have the nuclear capabilities to support their nuclear strategies. In recent years, Russia, China, India, Pakistan, and North Korea have all expanded and/or modernized their arsenals. Indeed, Yale political scientist Paul Bracken has argued that we are entering a "second nuclear age."[4]

These developments demonstrate that nuclear weapons (despite the fond hopes of many) will likely remain an important feature of international politics for years to come. They also raise an important and enduring question with renewed relevance: what kind of nuclear strategy and posture does the United States need to protect itself and its allies in this new nuclear age?

According to a widespread and long-standing academic conventional wisdom, the answer to this question is straightforward: the United States needs a secure, second-strike capability.[5] In other words, it must maintain a nuclear force capable of absorbing an enemy nuclear attack and retaining enough of a surviving force to retaliate with a devastating nuclear counterattack. So long as the United States (or any other nation) retains such an assured retaliation capability, scholars argue, no sane leader would intentionally launch a nuclear attack against it, and nuclear deterrence will hold.

These arguments are logical and persuasive, but, when compared to the evidentiary record, they point to an important puzzle. Empirically, we see that the United States has consistently maintained a nuclear posture that is much more robust than a mere second-strike capability. It possesses thousands of nuclear warheads, counterforce targeting policies and capabilities, missile defenses, and has more generally shown a recurring interest in military nuclear advantages over rivals.[6] For example, during the Cold War, officials in Washington feared possible bomber and missile gaps with the Soviet Union and, in 1963, US President John F. Kennedy vowed to build a nuclear arsenal "second to none."[7] Even after the Soviet Union achieved numerical parity with the United States in the mid-to-late 1970s, Washington continued to search for military nuclear advantages with its "countervailing" strategy.[8] And, at present, US officials and experts on both side of the aisle argue that the United States must retain a clear numerical superiority over China.[9] As then–Secretary of State Hillary Clinton put it in 2010, "we'll be, you know, stronger than anybody in the world as we always have been with more nuclear weapons than are needed many times over."[10] And, in 2016, US President Donald Trump said, "If countries are going to have nukes, we're going to be at the top of the pack."[11]

How do we make sense of this contradiction? Scholars argue that nuclear capabilities above and beyond a second-strike capability do not matter, but policymakers often behave as if they do. Leading academic deterrence theorists have noted the gap between theory and policy and have consistently concluded that the explanation is simple: policymakers are wrong. Perhaps most notably, Robert Jervis penned a foundational book on this subject titled *The Illogic of American Nuclear Strategy*.[12]

Social science aims to explain the world around us, but existing theories do not help us understand empirical patterns of US nuclear strategy.

This book takes a different approach. Rather than dismiss it as illogical, this book explains *the logic of American nuclear strategy*. It argues that military nuclear advantages above and beyond a secure, second-strike capability can contribute to a state's national security goals. This is primarily because a robust nuclear force reduces a state's expected cost of nuclear war, increasing its resolve in high-stakes crises, providing it with coercive bargaining leverage, and enhancing nuclear deterrence.

This book defines a robust nuclear posture as a nuclear force larger and more sophisticated than a secure, second-strike capability, with capabilities designed to limit damage in the event of nuclear war. Nuclear superiority is defined as a military nuclear advantage over an opponent and it is operationalized according to a state's expected cost of nuclear war. Nuclear superiority is a situation in which a state's expected cost of nuclear war is lower than that of its adversary (even if the expected cost is high for both sides). As we will see later in this book, a state's relative vulnerability to nuclear war is closely linked to the balance of nuclear capabilities between states, and "nuclear superiority" will, therefore, be used interchangeably with the terms "favorable nuclear balance of power" and, following past scholarship, "military nuclear advantages."[13]

The argument of this book draws on well-developed bodies of scholarship on nuclear strategy and nuclear deterrence theory and brings them together to form a new synthesis. In so doing, it provides a novel theoretical explanation for why military nuclear advantages can result in international political advantages. From nuclear brinkmanship theory, this explanation draws on the idea that even if sane leaders are unwilling to intentionally launch a nuclear war, they have time and again shown themselves quite willing to risk one. Deterred from engaging in direct combat, nuclear powers attempt to coerce opponents by playing games of brinkmanship.[14] They initiate or escalate crises, intentionally raising the risk of nuclear war in an attempt to force less resolute adversaries to capitulate. According to nuclear brinkmanship theory, therefore, the nuclear revolution transformed international politics from a competition in military capabilities to a "competition in risk taking."[15]

From the nuclear strategy literature, this explanation borrows the insight that the nuclear balance of power affects nuclear war outcomes.[16] Of course, the primary goal of nuclear strategy should be to prevent nuclear war. But if, God forbid, a war were to occur, analysts have argued that the United States should seek to limit the damage to itself and its allies to the greatest extent possible and a robust nuclear posture contributes to its ability to do so.[17]

The central theoretical argument of this book, which I label the *superiority-brinkmanship synthesis theory*, brings these strands of scholarship together to argue, quite simply, that military nuclear advantages increase a state's willingness to run risks in international conflicts. A robust nuclear posture reduces a state's expected cost of war, increasing its resolve in international political disputes, and thus providing it with a coercive advantage over states more vulnerable to a nuclear exchange. When political conflicts of interest emerge, nuclear inferior opponents are less likely to initiate a military challenge and more likely to back down if the crisis escalates.

In more colloquial terms, the logic of the argument is simple: in a game of chicken we might expect the smaller car to swerve first even if a crash would be disastrous for both.

The idea that nuclear superiority is useful because it allows states to run greater risks in games of nuclear chicken might sound dangerous, but scholars and practitioners have long accepted that brinkmanship in high-stakes crises is an inevitable feature of the nuclear era. As Stanley Hoffman writes, the nuclear age is characterized by "the substitution of crises for wars."[18] In the words of former US Secretary of State John Foster Dulles, "The ability to get to the verge without getting into the war is the necessary art. . . . If you try to run away from it, if you are scared to go to the brink, you are lost."[19] Robert Jervis also recognized that "states are under especially great, and especially contradictory, pressures. War must be avoided, but . . . the other side's need to avoid war can be used for leverage."[20]

This logic of nuclear competition is universal, but there is good reason why the United States, arguably more than any other nation, has shown a strong and recurring interest in the maintenance of a robust nuclear force. Washington, unlike other nuclear powers, does not merely attempt to deter attacks against its homeland. Rather, it also extends nuclear deterrence to over thirty formal treaty allies in Europe and Asia. This "nuclear umbrella" protects the twenty-eight other members of NATO, Japan, South Korea, Australia, and arguably others. These nuclear security guarantees can be conceptualized as promises to play games of nuclear brinkmanship in the event of a crisis on behalf of noncontiguous and geographically distant allies against formidable nuclear-armed foes. The United States has a strong interest in protecting its allies and ensuring geopolitical stability in Europe and Asia. Nevertheless, in these contests, the balance of stakes generally favors US opponents. After all, Russia arguably has a greater interest in eastern Europe and China more of a stake in East Asia than does the United States. Since Washington starts from an endemic disadvantage in the balance of stakes, it seeks to make up for it with a favorable balance of military power. To credibly extend deterrence, in other words, the United States compensates for its stakes deficit with a capabilities surfeit.

This book addresses not only the benefits of a robust nuclear posture but also its costs. Critics of US nuclear strategy have argued that the pursuit of a robust nuclear arsenal is not only pointless but also risky, futile, dangerous, and costly. They have claimed that pursuing a lasting nuclear advantage is risky because imbalances in power can lead to first-strike incentives and an increased chance of nuclear war;[21] futile because adversaries will react quickly to close any gaps, resulting in unnecessary arms races;[22] dangerous because it will encourage other nations to develop nuclear weapons, undermining international nonproliferation efforts;[23] and financially costly, draining the national budget.[24] These criticisms, however, point to a contradiction similar to the one posited earlier. Presumably, Washington would not have pursued and maintained these enduring elements of its nuclear strategy for decades if the downsides were truly so severe.

The second part of the book, therefore, explores the alleged disadvantages of nuclear advantages. The book finds that there are, indeed, costs to the maintenance of a robust nuclear force, but that they are less steep than many claim. Turning first to strategic stability, it shows that theoretical logic and available empirical evidence suggest that nuclear superiority, not nuclear parity, contributes to more, not less, strategic stability. Next, to examine nuclear arms races, the book presents a new theoretical argument about the origins of "underkill." It explains why states are often unable or unwilling to match the nuclear capabilities of competitors and demonstrates that, empirically, nuclear arms races are uncommon and the United States has often achieved lasting nuclear advantages. This is followed by a study on the relationship between US nuclear weapons and nonproliferation. This study shows that there is not an observable link between a large US nuclear arsenal and the proliferation and nonproliferation policies of other states. Finally, an examination of the US nuclear budget explains that a robust nuclear force is indeed costly, but also affordable. If one believes, therefore, as then–US Secretary of Defense Ashton Carter argued in 2016, that nuclear weapons are the "bedrock of our security," and the "most important mission of the Department of Defense," then it is also a good value.[25]

This book attempts to explain the logic of American nuclear strategy, but this is not to suggest that the details of US nuclear strategy are unchanging or not subject to debate. To the contrary, features of US strategy have been altered over the years in response to new strategic environments and changing presidential administrations.[26] In addition, there have always been, and will likely continue to be, heated political and analytical fights about many aspects of US nuclear policy.[27] But, at the same time, there have been enduring elements of US nuclear posture, namely, the maintenance of nuclear force above and beyond a secure, second-strike capability, that existing scholarly theories simply cannot explain. This book attempts to articulate the underlying rationale for building and maintaining such a force.

Neither does this book provide an in-depth description of contemporary US nuclear policy. Readers interested in those matters can consult the congressionally mandated Nuclear Posture Review and the Nuclear Employment Strategy published by each US presidential administration.[28] Rather, this book gets at the deeper, strategic motivations for why US politicians, policymakers, operators, and warfighters have often shown an interest in maintaining a robust nuclear force and a favorable nuclear balance over potential adversaries.

While academics often engage in either/or debates, the argument of this book argues for a both/and understanding of nuclear dynamics. It maintains that nuclear superiority matters, but it also finds support for many traditional arguments in the field, including those advanced by Jervis and others.[29] I concur that a minimum nuclear force is likely sufficient to deter a deliberate enemy nuclear attack. Indeed, that is one of the central theoretical premises on which the argument of the book is based. After all, there are zero data points to suggest otherwise. If, however, one is interested in going beyond the question of deterring intentional nuclear attack to exploring other elements of nuclear diplomacy, then a broader understanding is needed. Nuclear weapons contribute to other national security objectives (or in the words of social scientists, dependent variables), including nuclear war outcomes, coercive bargaining, and deterrence of lower-level challenges, and to understand these issues, one must take into account the nuclear balance of power. Existing scholarship is not entirely incorrect, therefore. It is merely incomplete.

Similarly, this book also finds support for the idea that political stakes matter for crisis bargaining among nuclear-armed nations. Existing scholarship acknowledged that nuclear-armed states would often find themselves in high-stakes games of nuclear brinkmanship, but they argued that the nuclear balance of power was irrelevant to these contests.[30] Rather, they maintained that a state's resolve in these disputes depends on the issues at stake in the crisis. States fighting for national survival, for example, would be willing to run a greater risk and, therefore, be more likely to prevail, than states concerned with political influence in a distant geographic region. This book finds quite a bit of support for these arguments. But it also finds that the nuclear balance of power matters too.

Arguments that conventional military power shapes international crisis bargaining also find some support, but not to the exclusion of nuclear strength. To be sure, these factors are often correlated, but the book seizes on all available opportunities to tease them apart. The evidence suggests that both matter, but perhaps unsurprisingly, the nuclear balance of power tends to be more salient than the conventional balance in conflicts among nuclear-armed states.

Other alternative explanations for international crisis bargaining find less support. Recently scholars have argued that nuclear weapons are irrelevant due to a growing normative "nuclear taboo," or that their importance has been exaggerated as a result of "nuclear alarmism," but these arguments do not stand up in the face of the evidence.[31] The book demonstrates that nuclear weapons have featured prominently in great power competition from 1945 to the present.

Another more subtle variation of this argument holds that nuclear weapons matter for deterrence (threats to defend the status quo) but not compellence (threats aimed at changing the status quo). Nuclear compellence skeptics argue that nuclear weapons do not affect compellent threats because it is difficult to credibly threaten nuclear attack and because states cannot use nuclear weapons to take and occupy territory.[32] On these specific points they are correct, but they largely overlook other important mechanisms by which nuclear weapons influence international bargaining. As this book argues, leaders cannot credibly threaten to launch a suicidal nuclear war, but they can credibly threaten to risk one and the nuclear balance of power influences these contests in risk taking. Nuclear compellence skeptics consider the possibility of brinkmanship, but then they define it so narrowly as to render it virtually meaningless. Moreover, as we will see, the evidence presented in this book is much more supportive of the superiority-brinkmanship synthesis theory than of the nuclear compellence skeptics.

In a recent book, Vipin Narang analyzes the nuclear postures of regional nuclear powers.[33] This is groundbreaking work, but as Narang explicitly argues and as this book will show, his study of regional nuclear powers is often not relevant to understanding superpower nuclear postures or American nuclear strategy.

Recently, scholars have also debated whether democratic states enjoy an advantage in international crisis bargaining because they are better able to credibly signal their intent through the generation of "audience costs."[34] This book does not find much support for the idea that democratic states perform better than their autocratic counterparts in conflicts among nuclear powers. Future research can explore whether this is because nuclear crises operate according to a different logic, or perhaps because there is merit to the growing chorus of criticism against the democratic advantage hypothesis.[35]

Some might argue that the maintenance of a robust US nuclear force is driven by bureaucratic politics and the military services' parochial interests in garnering resources and prestige by being involved in the nuclear mission. These factors played some role in developing certain capabilities in the early days of the Cold War (such as the Navy's development of nuclear-armed submarines), but this explanation cannot account for why the United States has continued to sustain a robust nuclear force for decades. As we will see in chapter 7, the services have grown less enthusiastic about the nuclear mission over time, which they see as a diversion from their core organizational identities, and they have often been forced by civilian leadership to maintain and upgrade nuclear capabilities. Moreover, even proponents of bureaucratic politics explanations of arms races acknowledge that these factors only amplify and channel arming dynamics, but are generally insufficient on their own to produce a national decision to build up forces.[36]

In sum, the superiority-brinkmanship synthesis theory provides a better explanation for competition among nuclear powers than do rival theories.

This book contains several important implications for the academic study of nuclear deterrence theory and for policymakers responsible for formulating nuclear strategy. For decades, scholars have argued that advantages in the nuclear balance of power above and beyond a secure, second-strike capability do not matter. For example, in addition to the *Illogic of American Nuclear Strategy*, Jervis authored an article titled "Why Nuclear Superiority Does Not Matter."[37] David Alan Rosenberg examined the origins of what he termed America's unnecessary nuclear "overkill" capability.[38] As Glenn Snyder and Paul Diesing write in their classic study of nuclear deterrence, "There is the puzzling question of whether simple quantitative nuclear superiority does confer some bargaining advantage. . . . Pure logic gives a clear negative to this question."[39] They continue, "Perversely, the real world does not quite follow this logic. Many policy makers do seem to believe that simple 'superiority' somehow confers a crisis bargaining advantage. The belief may be explained in some cases as merely a lack of sophistication about nuclear strategic theory."[40] In other words, unable to make sense of empirical phenomena using their theories, scholars, such as Snyder and Diesing, did not discard their theories, but discounted the empirical evidence. This response is perhaps understandable, but the job of social scientists is to explain the world as it is, not to reject it as nonsensical.

For decades, however, a clear explanation for this behavior has not been forthcoming. Charles Glaser maintained that "the logical case" for the argument that nuclear superiority matters for international politics "is weak, proponents have done little to support their claims, and efforts to fill in the logical gaps in their arguments encounter overwhelming difficulties."[41] Barry Blechman and Robert Powell agree, writing, "If there is such a case, it has yet to be made."[42]

In contrast to previous scholarship, this book provides a novel theoretical explanation for why nuclear superiority matters even if both sides possess a secure, second-strike capability. In so doing, it helps to resolve what may be the longest-standing, intractable, and important puzzle in the scholarly study of nuclear strategy.

This book makes empirical as well as theoretical advances. Earlier generations of scholars were handicapped by a relative lack of data. As Jervis acknowledged at the time of his writing, "our knowledge of nuclear deterrence . . . is largely deductive. We have a number of plausible theories, but only very limited empirical evidence."[43] Over thirty years have passed, however, since he wrote these words, providing the current generation of scholars with decades of additional data and developments in social science methodology to apply to these long-standing questions. Recent years have seen an explosion of rigorous social science research on nuclear weapons issues.[44] Inference is improved with more data, so it is unsurprising that this book finds relationships and patterns among variables that were not yet evident when foundational studies were conducted decades ago.

This book also makes a methodological advance by modeling a technique useful for those interested in "bridging the gap" between scholarly international relations theory and foreign policymaking.[45] Scholars tend to design studies that examine the relationship between a single independent variable and a solitary dependent variable. But policymakers must wrestle with how a single independent variable (or in their conceptualization, a policy choice) might affect an entire range of dependent variables (i.e., national security interests). This book does not, therefore, stop after examining how nuclear posture relates to deterrence, but continues to consider how it affects other interests important to policymakers, including warfighting, stability, arms races, nuclear nonproliferation, and the national budget.

Perhaps most importantly, this book has implications for US nuclear policy. Indeed, it articulates a logic of American nuclear strategy. The book's central argument would suggest that, all else being equal, the United States (and other states in competitive security environments) should seek to maintain strategic superiority over any potential rival. But all else is rarely equal. Policymaking involves the setting of priorities and making difficult trade-offs among many desirable, but often conflicting, policy goals. Reasonable people, therefore, can and often do disagree about nuclear policy in particular and national security policy more broadly. The findings in this book cannot instruct policymakers about what their priorities should be, but good social science can more modestly inform them about what trade-offs they may face. Correctly understanding the effects of choices in strategic nuclear policy matters not simply for academic analysts of nuclear deterrence, therefore, but also for those who are charged with deterring nuclear conflict in the future.

Plan of the Book

This book is divided into two parts and nine chapters. The first part considers the advantages of nuclear superiority. The following chapter, chapter 1, presents the central argument of the book. It uses a game theoretic model and verbal argumentation to explain the superiority-brinkmanship synthesis theory. It demonstrates how a nuclear advantage increases a state's effective resolve and improves its bargaining leverage in international disputes. The chapter also develops alternative explanations for nuclear crisis bargaining that will be tested against the superiority-brinkmanship synthesis theory.

Chapter 2 analyzes nuclear war outcomes. It employs simple nuclear exchange calculations developed during the Cold War and finds that the nuclear balance of power meaningfully affects nuclear war outcomes. More specifically, it shows that a military nuclear advantage reduces the expected damage that a country would incur in the event of a nuclear war. This chapter serves two purposes. First, it demonstrates a central premise of the theoretical argument. Second, it provides the first empirical test of the argument against other, competing explanations of nuclear dynamics for a specific national security interest: nuclear war outcomes.

Chapters 3 to 5 constitute the empirical core of Part I. Chapter 3 employs quantitative evidence to examine the determinants of nuclear crisis outcomes.[46] The statistical analysis draws on an original dataset of nuclear crises and nuclear arsenal sizes from every nuclear power in the world from 1945 to 2001. It shows that nuclear superior states are more likely to achieve their basic goals in international crises.

In chapter 4, brief case studies of the Cuban Missile Crisis, the Sino-Soviet Border War, the 1973 Arab-Israeli War, and the Kargil Crisis employ pattern-matching and process-tracing methods to examine the casual logic of the argument. The analysis will show that in these cases leaders paid close attention to the nuclear balance of power, nuclear superior states were willing to run greater risks, and nuclear superior states were more likely to achieve their basic goals. While other factors, including conventional power and political stakes, played a roll, it is hard to dismiss the evidence that the nuclear balance of power also mattered. Alternative explanations, such as those that maintain that nuclear weapons are irrelevant or that they do not matter above and beyond a secure, second-strike capability, do not find support.

In chapter 5, I turn my attention to nuclear compellence and deterrence. Some scholars have argued that nuclear weapons matter for deterrence, but not compellence.[47] Employing the same dataset of militarized compellent threats that these scholars use to make their case, I show that, according to the data, a nuclear advantage has been a necessary condition for even attempting a compellent threat among nuclear-armed states. A nuclear-armed state has never issued a militarized compellent threat against a state with a larger nuclear arsenal. In other words, nuclear superiority deters states from issuing compellent threats.

Part II of the book turns to the possible negative consequences of nuclear superiority. Does the maintenance of a nuclear advantage over rivals cause strategic instability, arms races, nuclear proliferation, and national insolvency? Chapter 6 considers issues of strategic stability. It conducts a review of international relations theory, critiques strategic stability arguments, and refers to empirical evidence presented elsewhere in the book and in the broader international relations literature, to argue that nuclear superiority, is more, not less, stable than nuclear parity. It also argues that traditional arguments about strategic stability fail to differentiate between instability that may favor US interests and that which works to its disadvantage. In other words, a US nuclear military advantage, on balance, enhances US interests and global strategic stability.

Chapter 7 examines nuclear arms races. It develops a new theory of nuclear "underkill," reviews the quantitative literature on arms races, and conducts three brief case studies of the strategic relationships between the United States and its nuclear-armed rivals, to show that arms races are empirically rare and that Washington has consistently been able to maintain meaningful nuclear advantages over nuclear-armed rivals.

Does the maintenance of a robust nuclear posture cause nuclear proliferation? Chapter 8 considers this question. Drawing on the most prominent case of potential nuclear proliferation over the past decade, the Iranian nuclear crisis, and quantitative evidence on a dataset of US nuclear arsenal size from 1945 to 2010, it shows that there is no discernable evidence of a relationship between US nuclear posture and the proliferation and nonproliferation policies of other states.[48]

Chapter 9 considers the economic cost of a robust nuclear posture. It conducts a careful analysis of the US defense budget. It shows that the United States spends roughly $30 billion per year on nuclear weapons and delivery systems, which comes to about 5% of the US defense budget.[49] This is a significant number, but a modest amount relative to overall defense spending. Depending on the importance one places on the benefits of a robust nuclear force, therefore, a robust nuclear arsenal arguably comes at a good value.

The Conclusion reviews the argument and turns to the implications of the study's findings for theory and practice. The main thrust of the conclusion focuses on the implications of the argument for international relations theory. This analysis advances important scholarly debates on both the benefits and costs of a robust nuclear posture. The chapter finishes with an articulation of principles to guide policymakers as they refine US nuclear strategy to address emerging nuclear challenges around the globe.

PART ONE

THE ADVANTAGES
OF NUCLEAR ADVANTAGES

Toward a New Theory of Nuclear Deterrence

The Superiority-Brinkmanship Synthesis Theory

This chapter develops a new theory of nuclear deterrence, the *superiority-brinkmanship synthesis theory*. The theory brings together traditional arguments in the nuclear strategy literature about the advantages of nuclear superiority and combines them with nuclear brinkmanship theory to provide a novel theoretical explanation for why nuclear superiority provides states with geopolitical advantages. It argues that military nuclear advantages reduce a state's expected cost of nuclear war, increasing its effective resolve and enhancing its bargaining position. On the other hand, states in an inferior strategic position face a relatively higher cost of nuclear war, are less willing to run risks in a crisis, and are more likely to back down early in a dispute. This chapter serves, therefore, as the theoretical and conceptual core for the first half of the book.

The chapter is organized as follows: First, it defines the book's key concept: nuclear superiority. Second, it takes stock of the existing scholarship on nuclear deterrence and nuclear coercion. Third, superiority-brinkmanship synthesis theory is presented using a simple game theoretic model and verbal argumentation. The fourth section identifies observable implications of the synthesis and derives testable hypotheses that are explored later in the book. Fifth, it considers possible competing explanations for the drivers of deterrent and coercive success among nuclear powers. Sixth, and finally, the chapter concludes with a discussion of the research design for the empirical portion of the book.

The Elements of the Argument

Before detailing my theoretical argument about how the nuclear balance of power affects crisis bargaining, I define a core concept used throughout the study: nuclear superiority. To do so, I also elaborate on two key premises under-lying this concept. The first premise is that there are meaningful differences in states' expected costs of nuclear war, even at high levels of devastation. Second, I maintain that the nuclear balance of power greatly influences the expected cost of nuclear war, even when both sides possess secure, second-strike capabilities.

Nuclear Superiority

Nuclear superiority is defined as a military nuclear advantage over an opponent. It is operationalized according to a state's expected cost of nuclear war. A state possesses nuclear superiority if its expected cost of nuclear war is less than the expected cost of nuclear war for its adversary. Contrariwise, a state is in a posi-tion of nuclear inferiority if its expected cost of a nuclear exchange exceeds that of an adversary. According to this definition, a state can hold a military nuclear advantage even if the opponent possesses a secure, second-strike capability and even its expected costs of nuclear war are high, so long as the costs of nuclear war for an opponent are greater still.

Whether a state possesses nuclear superiority can be measured largely according to the nuclear balance of power. When a state possesses more nuclear warheads than its opponent, then, almost always, its expected costs of war will be lower than the expected costs of nuclear war for the opponent. There are a few qualifications to this rule, which are discussed throughout the book, but, as we see in what follows and in the next chapter, the nuclear balance of power is generally a reliable indicator of the relative expected cost of nuclear war. The remainder of this book thus uses the terms "nuclear superiority," "nuclear advan-tage," "military nuclear advantage," and "favorable nuclear balance of power" synonymously. It uses the term "robust nuclear posture" to describe a nuclear arsenal that is designed to limit a state's vulnerability to nuclear war and that is also generally larger and more sophisticated than what is required for a mere secure second-strike capability.

Variation in the Expected Costs of Nuclear War

I argue that there is meaningful variation in the expected cost of nuclear war, even at high levels of devastation. Nuclear strategists recognize that not all nuclear wars would be equally costly and that states vary in their vulnerability to nuclear war. To calculate the varying effects of nuclear war, analysts consider factors such as total number of deaths and casualties, economic destruction, expected length of time for society to recover from war, and all of these factors relative to an opponent.[1]

While even a single nuclear weapon detonated in the United States would be a tragedy of historic proportions, it is also the case that twenty nuclear detonations would be worse. And fifty would be worse still. And 1,780 nuclear strikes on the US homeland would make fifty look relatively appealing. (For those skeptical of this point and others made in this section, they will be substantiated in great detail in the next chapter). It would be unreasonable, especially for policymakers entrusted with protecting the security of its citizens, not to have a preference over these outcomes. Moreover, most people, when pushed to choose between bad and worse, would prefer an outcome in which a larger number of people, including possibly friends and family members, survive rather than perish.

As the Cold War nuclear strategist Herman Kahn argued, "Few people differentiate between having 10 million dead, 50 million dead, or 100 million dead. It all seems too horrible. However, it does not take much imagination to see that there is a difference."[2] For Kahn, nuclear war scenarios in which a country suffers 10 million deaths and requires 5 years to regain prewar levels of economic output versus one with 80 million deaths and 50 years of economic recuperation are "tragic, but distinguishable" outcomes.[3]

Some may grant that there are meaningful differences at relatively low levels of nuclear devastation, but speculate that one very quickly gets to a point where the death and destruction is so massive, that additional nuclear strikes would not make any difference other than to make the rubble bounce. In principle this is correct, but the scale of such a nuclear attack is much greater than many imagine. As John Mueller explained, "even 2,000 1-MT explosions with a destructive radius of 5-miles each would directly demolish less than 5-percent of the territory of the United States, for example . . . and kill less than 10% of the population."[4] Furthermore, a recent technical study found that to promptly kill 100% of Russia's population would require an enemy nuclear attack with approximately 140,000 nuclear warheads.[5] This is more than four times the number of warheads the United States possessed at the height of the Cold War.

For this reason, therefore, nuclear strategists and policymakers drew important distinctions between postwar outcomes often considered by scholars to be in the realm of mutually assured destruction (MAD). For example, in the late 1970s, then–Secretary of the Air Force Harold Brown argued, "even 25% casualties might not be enough for deterrence if U.S. casualties were disproportionately higher—if the Soviets thought they would be able to recover in some period of time while the U.S. would take three or four times as long, or would never recover, then the Soviets might not be deterred."[6] Similarly, defense analysts argued that even if the Soviet Union could destroy all major US cities in a nuclear attack, it might be prevented from killing US citizens living in small and medium-sized cities and in rural and outlying areas and that the United States had both a strategic incentive and a moral responsibility to protect these lives.[7]

Moreover, and importantly for this study, the height of the Cold War was unique, further bolstering the argument about meaningful differences in nuclear war outcomes. All other conceivable real-world nuclear exchanges would be far less devastating than Cold War scenarios for the countries involved. Most nuclear powers in most years, including Russia at present, stock far fewer nuclear weapons than Cold War heights. For example, at the time of writing, the best estimates are that America's nuclear-armed adversaries, Russia, China, and North Korea, possess approximately 1,780; 65; and 0 warheads, respectively, capable of reaching the continental United States.[8] Even if there was a time in the past when nuclear war among major powers meant Armageddon (which is at least doubtful), it is quite clear that we are not in that situation today.[9]

As Mueller correctly concludes, "although nuclear weapons are certainly exceptionally destructive, the common tendency to inflate their effects, sometimes to an absurd degree, can have undesirable intellectual and policy consequences."[10]

In sum, there are meaningful differences in nuclear war outcomes. This point is further elaborated and demonstrated in the next chapter. For now, I turn to the second premise underlying my theory: the nuclear balance of power is a central determinant of a state's expected cost of nuclear war.

The Nuclear Balance of Power and the Expected Costs of Nuclear War

The nuclear balance of power greatly affects a state's expected cost of nuclear war. When a state possesses more warheads that it can deliver to an opponent than the opponent can return to its territory, then, generally, its expected costs of war will be lower than its adversary's expected costs.

This is true for two simple reasons. First, in a complete nuclear exchange, a country that possesses more nuclear firepower will be able to inflict more damage in the event of nuclear war. It is estimated, for example, that China possesses 65 nuclear warheads capable of reaching the United States, while the United States maintains 2,072 deployed nuclear weapons that could be delivered to targets in China.[11] It is clear that while both sides would strongly prefer to avoid nuclear war, if a Sino-US dispute were to result in a nuclear exchange, China would suffer disproportionately.

Second, the nuclear balance of power affects the ability of a state to conduct "counterforce" nuclear targeting. As Charles Glaser elaborates in his study of US nuclear strategy, analysts in the "damage limitation school" maintain that US nuclear "superiority would reduce the cost to the United States in an all-out nuclear war."[12] Some states, including the United States, plan for counterforce nuclear targeting, that is, using nuclear weapons to destroy the nuclear weapons of an opponent, in an attempt to limit the damage that the opponent could impose in a nuclear attack.[13] Every enemy nuclear weapon that can be destroyed in a faraway missile silo or airbase before it can be used is a nuclear weapon that will not detonate on US territory. According to then–US Secretary of Defense Harold Brown, "we have always considered it important, in the event of war, to be able to attack the forces that could do damage to the United States and its allies."[14] Similarly, in President Obama's 2013 Nuclear Employment Guidance to the Department of Defense, he ordered "the United States to maintain significant counterforce capabilities against potential adversaries."[15] States with a nuclear advantage are expected to perform better in counterforce exchanges because they have more firepower with which to blunt the retaliatory capability of their opponents.[16]

To be sure, there are many other factors that influence a state's expected cost of nuclear war. The size of a state's territory and population affects its ability to absorb a nuclear attack. Some leaders or countries might be more willing to suffer the costs of nuclear war than others. Other scholars have shown that the ability to conduct counterforce strikes also depends on other characteristics of the force, including: the nuclear posture; intelligence, surveillance, and reconnaissance (ISR) capabilities; the accuracy of delivery vehicles; and warhead yields.[17] These and other elements contribute to the expected cost of nuclear war and, therefore, nuclear superiority as defined here. As such, these factors are considered whenever possible in this book, including when calculating the results of hypothetical nuclear exchanges in the next chapter.

Nevertheless, even when taking those factors into account, it is still the case that the quantitative nuclear balance between states is an important, if not the central, determinant of the expected cost of nuclear war. After all, the number of warheads in an arsenal imposes a hard ceiling on the amount of damage a state can inflict. Cutting-edge ISR capabilities and accurate delivery vehicles are of little use in a counterforce nuclear exchange, for example, if one does not possess sufficient warheads to hold a large portion of an adversary's nuclear forces at risk. Similarly, even large-yield weapons cannot compensate for numbers because greater numbers of warheads can physically cover more targets and much of the explosive power of large-yield weapons is wasted on most targets.

In sum, this section has conceptualized nuclear superiority as an advantage over an adversary in the expected cost of nuclear war. It has supported this conceptualization by arguing that there are meaningful differences in nuclear war outcomes and that this variation is determined in large part by the quantitative nuclear balance of power. Since these premises are so central to the book, I do not leave them to assumption, but subject them to rigorous empirical scrutiny in chapter 2.

Explaining Nuclear Conflict

Nuclear deterrence theorists have written about the logic of MAD.[18] When two states possess secure second-strike capabilities, both sides have the ability to launch a devastating nuclear response even after absorbing an enemy first strike. In this environment, neither state can physically defend itself against a nuclear attack and, therefore, must rely on deterrence to protect itself. Because the threat of nuclear exchange raises the cost of conflict, scholars have argued that nuclear weapons deter international war and may have contributed to an unprecedented period of great power strategic stability.[19]

The nuclear revolution, however, also raises significant theoretical and empirical problems. While nuclear weapons alter the logic of military conflict, they do not eliminate international competition. Nuclear-armed states still seek to coerce nuclear-armed adversaries.

They cannot, however, credibly threaten a nuclear exchange that would result in their own destruction. How then can states credibly threaten nuclear-armed adversaries? And what determines the outcomes of conflict in the nuclear era? Much of nuclear deterrence theory is a response to these questions.

Thomas Schelling proposed nuclear brinkmanship as an answer.[20] According to Schelling, states cannot credibly threaten a nuclear attack, but they can make "a threat that leaves something to chance."[21] If nuclear war is not entirely in the collective control of the participants, but could result from accident or inadvertent escalation, then states can threaten to take steps that increase the risk of nuclear war. States can credibly threaten to engage in a process—the nuclear crisis—that could spiral out of control and result in catastrophe.[22] As long as the benefit of winning the contested issue is potentially greater than each incremental increase in the risk of nuclear war, then threats to escalate nuclear crises are inherently credible.

In the nuclear era, therefore, states coerce adversaries by manipulating risk; political conflicts of interest become games of nuclear brinkmanship. States can escalate crisis situations, raising the risk of nuclear war in an effort to force a less-resolved opponent to submit. As the crisis progresses, the less resolved state will prefer to back down rather than risk nuclear exchange. The more resolved state, the state that is willing to run the greatest risk of nuclear war, prevails. In short, the nuclear revolution can be understood as a transformation of international politics from a competition in military capabilities to a "competition in risk taking."[23]

Brinkmanship theorists do not claim, however, that states eagerly bid up the risk of nuclear war.[24] Rather, they assume that leaders badly want to avoid nuclear war and face gut-wrenching decisions at each stage of a crisis. They can quit the crisis to ensure that they avoid nuclear war, but only at the cost of conceding an important geopolitical issue to their opponents.

Or, they can remain in the game a bit longer in an attempt to win, but only by increasing the risk that the crisis ends in a nuclear catastrophe.

Uncertainty plays an important role in brinkmanship theory.[25] If all states possessed complete information about their own resolve and the resolve of their opponents, nuclear crises would never occur. The less resolved state would simply concede the contested issue rather than enter a nuclear crisis that it has no prospect of winning. Brinkmanship theory assumes, therefore, that states possess incomplete information about their adversary's level of resolve; their adversary's beliefs about their resolve; their beliefs about their adversary's resolve; and/or, in some cases, perhaps even their own resolve. Nuclear crises are in part instruments, therefore, for revealing information about the balance of resolve.

According to brinkmanship theorists, the level of risk a state is willing to tolerate depends primarily on the state's political stakes in the conflict.[26] The higher the stakes, the more risk the state can credibly threaten to run. A state fighting over its national existence, for example, will be willing to accept a greater risk of nuclear war than a state fighting over a trade dispute or geopolitical influence in a distant region. The state that has the greater stake in the crisis, therefore, is more likely to ultimately prevail.

Brinkmanship theorists have not, however, explicitly incorporated the nuclear balance of power into their theoretical models.[27] Rather, they assume that both states possess secure, second-strike capabilities and that the cost of nuclear war is, therefore, equally devastating for both sides. Indeed, as Powell has recently written, "the balance of military power's irrelevance in standard accounts of brinkmanship is more a matter of assumption than deduction."[28] Since it is baked into their assumptions, brinkmanship theorists conclude that "nuclear superiority does not matter" in nuclear crises, and they theorize that the outcomes of nuclear crises are shaped solely by states' stakes in the crisis.[29]

Many policymakers believe that nuclear superiority provides states with a coercive advantage, but scholars have not articulated a clear logic by which nuclear superiority translates into improved crisis outcomes.[30] See, for example, the quotes on this point from Jervis, Glaser, and others in the Introduction.[31]

Moreover, until recently, neither set of theoretical claims had been subjected to systematic empirical investigation.[32] Previous scholarship had congregated around a few high-profile cases, but, with few exceptions, had not examined the entire empirical universe. Indeed, scholars advocating opposing positions often point to the exact same cases in support of their theoretical claims. In addition, the results of the more systematic inquiries had proven inconclusive. In what, until recently, was the widest-ranging qualitative examination of historical cases, Richard Betts analyzed explicit nuclear threats during the Cold War and concluded that neither the balance of resolve nor the balance of nuclear forces argument provides a satisfactory explanation, indicating that, perhaps, a synthesis was needed.[33]

Scholars have also studied related topics including the relationship between nuclear weapons possession and the timing, frequency, and severity of international conflict; the political utility of nuclear weapons; the dynamics and outcomes of interstate crises; "complex deterrence"; the effect of nuclear weapons possession on crisis outcomes; and conventional escalation and brinkmanship.[34] These scholars have not, however, focused on crises between nuclear-armed states, nor have they examined the relationship between nuclear superiority and crisis bargaining.

The Advantages of Nuclear Superiority

This section presents the superiority-brinkmanship synthesis theory.[35] It begins by considering a standard game theoretic model of nuclear brinkmanship, in which the balance of stakes underlying a crisis determines its outcome.[36] It then modifies the model to include nuclear superiority. By incorporating the nuclear balance into the model, it demonstrates that a nuclear advantage increases a state's level of resolve, improving its prospects for victory in nuclear crises.

Imagine two states, State A and State B, edging toward a nuclear crisis. The game begins with State A deciding whether to escalate the crisis or back down. If State A submits, then the game is over; State A loses and State B wins. If, on the other hand, State A escalates, then play shifts to State B. State B now faces the same two options: escalate or submit. If State B concedes, then State B loses and State A wins. If State B escalates, then the game continues.

States cannot escalate a dangerous nuclear crisis, however, without generating at least some risk of nuclear war. It is always possible that things will spin out of control, even if this is not the preferred outcome of either of the participants. At this stage in the game, therefore, an exogenous force (let us call it nature) imposes accidental nuclear war with some nonzero probability. If there is a nuclear war, then both states suffer the cost of nuclear disaster.

If there is no nuclear war, then the game continues. Play shifts back to State A, which must again decide whether to submit or escalate. If State A escalates in this round it can do so only by generating an even greater risk of nuclear catastrophe. Since we are deeper into the crisis, the risk of nuclear exchange has also increased. If there is no disaster, then play shifts back to State B, who must now create an even greater risk of nuclear war if it wishes to escalate. Play continues in this way until one state submits or until there is a nuclear war.

For each state, the game can end in one of three ways: the state can win, lose, or suffer a disaster. It is reasonably assumed that winning is preferable to losing, losing is preferable to nuclear disaster, and the status quo is preferable to either losing or disaster.

Since these are assumed to be rational states, they will continue to escalate the crisis as long as their expected payoff to doing so exceeds the expected payoff to submitting. The states' expected payoff to submitting is equal to the cost of losing the crisis. Since the state is choosing to back down immediately there is no uncertainty about the outcome.

The states' expected payoff to escalating is less certain because it includes some chance of winning the crisis but also some chance of suffering a nuclear exchange. The expected utility of escalating therefore, is the state's payoff to winning the crisis, weighted by the probability of avoiding disaster, plus the payoff of disaster weighted by the probability of suffering a disaster.

In equilibrium, states will escalate until they are indifferent between escalation and submission. This point, the point at which the payoff to escalating is equal to the payoff to submitting, is defined as a state's resolve. In other words, a state's resolve is the maximum risk of disaster that a state is willing to run in order to win the crisis.[37] A state's resolve is defined, therefore, as a function of: the payoff to winning, the payoff to submitting, and the payoff to disaster.

The more resolved state, which can be thought of as the state that is willing to tolerate the greatest risk of nuclear war, will win as long as the crisis does not end in disaster. The game is similar in form to an auction in which the winner is the player that bids the highest level of risk.[38]

Of course, a nuclear crisis would never occur if states possessed complete information about the balance of resolve. The less resolved state would prefer to submit immediately rather than run any risk of nuclear war to participate in a game that it stands to lose. To spark a crisis, therefore, states must be uncertain about the balance of resolve. Crises result when each state has reason to believe that it might be more resolved than its opponent. Uncertainty about an opponent's resolve could result from incomplete information about an opponent's payoff to winning, its payoff to submitting, or its payoff to disaster. The outcomes of brinkmanship games with incomplete information, therefore, are a function of a state's resolve, its beliefs about its opponent's resolve, and its opponent's beliefs about its resolve. More specifically, the more resolute a state is, the more resolute it is believed to be, and the less resolute it believes its adversary to be, the harder a state is willing to push a crisis.[39]

While less deterministic than in games with complete information, therefore, resolve still plays a critical role in games with incomplete information.[40] All else being equal, more resolved states are willing to push harder in a crisis and are more likely to win than their less resolved counterparts.

Brinkmanship theorists have drawn from this specification of resolve to derive hypotheses about the outcomes of nuclear crises. Brinkmanship theory demonstrates that the more resolved state will win so long as the crisis does not end in disaster.[41] And a state's resolve is a function of its payoff to winning the crisis and its payoff to losing the crisis. These values, the values that a state places on winning and on submitting in a nuclear crisis, are defined as a state's stakes in the crisis. According to Powell, "this specification of resolve formalizes the role played by the political stakes underlying the crisis. A state's resolve increases as its payoff to prevailing or cost to submitting go up."[42] Brinkmanship theorists have concluded, therefore, that states with a greater political stake in a crisis will be more likely to prevail.

Brinkmanship theorists have not, however, included the strategic nuclear balance in their formal theoretical models of nuclear crisis dynamics. Rather, existing models assume that the nuclear balance is not pertinent because both sides have secure second-strike capabilities and, therefore, the cost of a nuclear catastrophe is equivalent for all states.[43] These assumptions are made despite the fact—as was argued earlier in the chapter—that an imbalance in nuclear forces, even among states with second-strike capabilities, can make nuclear war more costly for some states than for others.

To build on existing models, therefore, I incorporate the nuclear balance into the payoff structure. To aid in this task, I draw on the two insights developed earlier in this chapter.[44] First, as discussed earlier, nuclear strategists recognize that not all nuclear wars would be equally devastating. Second, as was also discussed previously, nuclear strategists recognize that the nuclear balance of power influences the expected costs that a country would incur in the event of nuclear war.

To incorporate these insights into the nuclear brinkmanship model, let us assume State A enjoys a nuclear advantage over State B. The payoff to disaster for State A is the cost of absorbing a nuclear attack from State B. The payoff to disaster for State B, is the cost of absorbing a nuclear attack from State A. Since State B possesses a smaller arsenal than State A, in the event of a complete nuclear exchange, State A would absorb fewer nuclear strikes than State B, providing State A with a lower expected cost of disaster. In addition, nuclear superiority provides State A with a counterforce advantage, making it better able to limit the damage that State B could impose in the event of nuclear war. If the brinkmanship game were to end in disaster, therefore, State A could not prevent State B from launching an attack, but it would be better positioned to reduce the costs that State B could impose, again providing State A with a lower expected cost of nuclear disaster.

Of course, it is important to point out that the costs to disaster can still be large for both sides and a nuclear exchange is still the worst possible outcome, even for nuclear superior states. Nevertheless, by incorporating nuclear superiority into the model, we see that it is it is an unrealistic simplification to assume that all nuclear disasters are equally costly.

Returning to the above specification of resolve, we see that a state's resolve depends not just on its payoff to winning and to submitting but also on its expected cost of disaster. Therefore, if the expected cost of disaster is reduced for State A, and other values are held constant, then State A's resolve will increase. State A will be willing to run a greater risk of disaster and will be more likely to prevail in a crisis. Similarly, if the cost of disaster is increased for State B, then its resolve will decrease. It will be willing to hazard a smaller risk of disaster and will be less likely to prevail. Operating from within the framework of nuclear brinkmanship theory, we see that providing a state with nuclear superiority, much like increasing a state's political stake in the crisis, creates a theoretical expectation that a state's effective resolve will be increased.

This is not to argue that leaders in nuclear superior states believe that they can fight and win nuclear wars, nor is it to claim that they eagerly bid up the risk of nuclear war in a crisis. Rather, the intuition is more subtle. If the costs of catastrophe are lower for one state than another (even if the costs are high for both sides), then as leaders make the gut-wrenching decision about whether to submit or escalate, the submit option looks relatively more attractive to leaders in the nuclear inferior state at each stage of the crisis. In calculating the payoff to escalation, leaders in nuclear inferior countries factor the probability of nuclear war by a relatively higher cost of catastrophe. We should expect, therefore, that, on average, leaders in nuclear inferior states will be more likely to opt for submission.

On the other hand, as leaders in nuclear superior states make the same anguished calculations about whether to escalate the crisis or submit, they scale the probability of nuclear exchange against a relatively lower cost of nuclear disaster. Leaders in nuclear superior states still badly want to avoid a nuclear exchange, but because the costs of a nuclear exchange are relatively lower, we should expect that they will be willing, on average, to hazard a higher risk of disaster than their nuclear inferior opponents, making them more likely to ultimately win nuclear crises.

As stated in the introduction, the logic of the argument in simple terms is that in a game of chicken we might expect the smaller car to swerve first, even if a crash would be disastrous for both.[45]

In sum, a formal theoretical model of nuclear brinkmanship suggest that nuclear superior states would incur fewer costs in the event of a nuclear disaster, increasing their effective levels of resolve and improving their prospects of victory in a crisis.

Hypotheses

This logic suggests a number of hypotheses about the dynamics of competition among nuclear powers. The theoretical argument just outlined rests on the premise that there are meaningful differences in nuclear war outcomes and that the nuclear balance of power shapes state vulnerability to nuclear war. Rather than simply assume this proposition, I subject it to rigorous empirical examination in chapter 2. It, therefore, forms the first hypothesis of the book.

> Hypothesis 1: States with larger nuclear arsenals face a lower expected cost of nuclear war than their opponents.

Building on this initial proposition, the superiority-brinkmanship synthesis theory then argues that differences in nuclear war outcomes provide states with different incentives as they engage in high-stakes nuclear crises. Since superior states expect to suffer less damage, on average, in the event of nuclear war, then they should be willing to hazard a relatively greater risk of nuclear war. And, since nuclear crises are essentially competitions in risk taking, then we should expect nuclear superior states to be more likely to prevail in high-stakes crises.

> Hypothesis 2: Nuclear superior states will be more likely to achieve their goals in international crises.

To this point I have argued that nuclear superiority affects crisis outcomes, but does it also shape the initiation of conflict in the first place? James Fearon has argued that military capabilities affect crisis bargaining, but, since they are largely known to crisis participants beforehand, they should be taken into account before leaders select into crises.[46] Fearon hypothesizes, therefore, that we might not see a strong relationship between military power and the outcomes of conflicts that actually take place, but that rather the balance of power should exert its most important effects at the earlier selection stage. To the degree that this is correct, and applying this logic to the specific problem of nuclear competition, we might expect that the nuclear balance of power affects selection into crisis episodes and that nuclear superior states should be less likely to be challenged militarily.

> Hypothesis 3: Nuclear superior states will be less likely to be the targets of military threats.

In addition, the degree, and not simply the existence, of nuclear superiority may also shape crisis bargaining. The greater a state's level of nuclear advantage, the greater its payoff of disaster relative to an opponent. In addition, greater levels of nuclear superiority enhance a state's ability to conduct counterforce strikes, further increasing a state's absolute payoff of disaster. As a state achieves greater levels of nuclear advantage over an opponent, therefore, its relative payoff of disaster increases and its willingness to run risks in a crisis increases accordingly. All of these hypotheses, therefore, could be restated as continuous relationships. In other words, the greater the degree of nuclear advantage a state has over its adversary, the less its relative cost of nuclear war, the more likely it will be to achieve its goals in a serious crisis, and the less likely it will be subjected to a military challenge in the first place.

In sum, the superiority-brinkmanship theory presented here identifies three interrelated hypotheses that flow directly from the logic of the theory and that should be expected to influence empirical patterns of interactions among nuclear-armed states.

Alternative Explanations

There are other social science theories about the determinants of conflict among nuclear powers. This section presents several alternative explanations that are tested alongside the superiority-brinkmanship synthesis theory.

Second-Strike Theory

Perhaps the strongest challenge to the hypotheses elucidated previously is the prevailing view in the academy that a secure, second-strike capability (variants of which are known as an assured retaliation capability or an assured destruction capability) is sufficient for deterrence.[47] According to this logic, in order to deter a rational adversary, a state needs the ability to absorb an opponent's nuclear first strike and retain enough surviving warheads to retaliate with a devastating nuclear counterstrike. Once a state has achieved such a secure, second-strike capability, its opponent cannot physically defend itself from a nuclear attack even if it strikes first. A state with a second-strike capability, therefore, can ensure that a nuclear war will be unacceptably costly for its opponent.

Although these scholars recognize that policymakers have pursued military nuclear advantages, they argue that this is illogical behavior motivated by a failure to understand the effect of the "nuclear revolution" on international politics.[48] They therefore dismiss attempts to "conventionalize" nuclear competition and argue that military nuclear advantages do not matter.[49] These scholars recognize that nuclear-armed states may find themselves in serious crises, but they argue that these competitions are determined by the balance of stakes, not the balance of nuclear forces.

There are debates within this school about "how much is enough" for deterrence.[50] Scholars argue whether deterrence can be achieved with a minimum nuclear posture (such as a few nuclear warheads) or whether it requires a secure, second-strike capability.[51] Others draw distinctions between "assured retaliation" and "assured destruction."[52] For the purposes of this research, however, these scholars are best grouped together because they agree much more with one other than with the superiority-brinkmanship synthesis theory. They concur that (1) there is a certain finite amount of nuclear capability sufficient for deterrence, (2) additional nuclear capabilities above and beyond this threshold do not meaningfully affect nuclear competition, and (3) the nuclear balance of power between states does not matter once this threshold has been reached. These are all claims that the superiority-brinkmanship synthesis theory rejects. Acknowledging, therefore, the different camps within this school, I subsequently refer to this group of ideas as the *second-strike theory*.

This school of thought makes a very different set of predictions concerning the three hypotheses explicated previously. The second-strike school would maintain that (1) there are not meaningful differences in nuclear war outcomes between states with second-strike capabilities; (2) a second-strike capability is necessary for deterrence, but a more robust nuclear posture or a military nuclear advantage does not contribute to bargaining power or deterrence; and (3) outcomes of high-stakes crises are determined not by the nuclear balance of power but by the balance of political stakes.

The logic of this set of arguments is admirably clear, but there is reason to be skeptical of these claims. First, as discussed already, and as is demonstrated in the next chapter, it is simply unrealistic to make strong claims about the nuclear balance of power not affecting nuclear war outcomes. Scholars in the second-strike school might argue that their arguments only apply to situations of MAD and grant that there can be meaningful differences in nuclear war outcomes among states that lack a secure, second-strike capability. If this is the case, however, then the scholarly community should be much clearer that this set of arguments is intended to apply only to a narrow subset of nuclear dyads, such as the United States and the Soviet Union at the height of the Cold War, and does not provide a broader logic of nuclear competition.

Moreover, as this book shows, these arguments do not stand up to scrutiny even in situations of MAD. Mutually assured destruction does not mean mutually assured, complete and utter annihilation. If it did, then proponents of this school would be on firmer ground. But, even in MAD, much would survive even the most horrific nuclear exchanges. Former US defense secretary Robert McNamara famously defined "assured destruction" as the ability to destroy 25% of a state's population and 50% of its industrial production.[53] These are terrifyingly large numbers to be sure, but they also mean that the other half of the state's industry and 75% of its population would not be held at risk. To stubbornly maintain that nuclear capabilities above and beyond this level do not matter, therefore, proponents of this school find themselves in the unenviable position of needing to explain why the other half of a state's industrial capacity and three-quarters of its population are not worth protecting. Moreover, they would need to explain either why policymakers are indifferent to the survival of three-quarters of their own citizens' lives or why these issues have no bearing on international politics. As we see throughout the book, these arguments are untenable.

Second, scholars in this camp began with a sound logical idea that applies to a very specific outcome, but it has been extended to empirical domains where the logic no longer holds. The second-strike school is correct that any rational leader should be incredibly unlikely to intentionally initiate a major war against a state with a secure, second-strike capability. But what if states are interested in things other than deterring major wars? States are also concerned with limiting damage to themselves and their allies in the event that, god forbid, a nuclear war breaks out. States are also interested in achieving their goals in high-stakes nuclear crises. States would also like to deter lower-level militarized threats and coercion against themselves and their allies. The second-strike school offers little help in explaining these other important outcomes. Second-strike theory is valuable to a point, but it is a relatively narrow theory to describe a narrow outcome among a narrow set of cases. Unlike superiority-brinkmanship synthesis theory, it does not offer a broader and generalizable explanation of nuclear politics.

While there are reasons to be skeptical of the prevailing academic wisdom, therefore, these hypotheses are further evaluated against the empirical evidence in the remaining chapters of this book.

Nuclear Irrelevance Theory

Others have argued that nuclear weapons are irrelevant to nuclear coercion or even to international politics all together. John Mueller has made the latter, stronger claim.[54] He maintains that the post-1945 international system contained many sources of stability and that it was not nuclear weapons, therefore, that deterred conflict among the great powers. Moreover, he argues that nuclear weapons have not been employed since 1945 and that it is difficult to imagine ways in which they could have conceivably been used. As he colorfully puts it, "for more than 60 years now all they've done is gather dust."[55] He concludes, therefore, that nuclear weapons have not had a major impact on international politics and if they had never been invented, world history would look much the same.

Like much of Mueller's scholarship, this claim is provocative and counterintuitive, but there are competing theoretical and empirical grounds on which to believe it is incorrect. After all, nearly all other scholars of nuclear weapons disagree. Whether it be the second-strike school, "proliferation optimists," theorists of the nuclear revolution, brinkmanship theorists, or others, existing approaches concur that nuclear weapons have fundamentally shaped conflict among nuclear-armed states (most just doubt that nuclear superiority matters).

A similar, but more modest, claim comes from Nina Tannenwald, who makes the case for the "nuclear taboo."[56] She argues that there is a strong normative prohibition against the use of nuclear weapons. She maintains that the norm first appeared in the 1960s and has developed, gradually gaining strength through fits and starts, since that time. Due to this taboo, Tannenwald claims that the use of nuclear weapons has become "unthinkable" and time and again US officials did not consider using nuclear weapons, even in situations in which nuclear weapons use could have advanced US interests.

Tannenwald makes a strong case that many US leaders evince a moral inhibition against the use of nuclear weapons, but the theory is less compelling in other ways. She does not demonstrate that this inhibition is truly taboo-like in its strength. After all, unlike nuclear-armed states with nuclear arsenals and employment strategies, most humans do not actively develop and maintain tools and contingency plans to engage in other taboo behaviors, such as cannibalism. Moreover, any American inhibitions on nuclear use do not appear to extend beyond its leadership. Recent scholarship shows that the American public is quite willing to support nuclear strikes on an enemy if it means saving American lives.[57] Moreover, Tannenwald focuses only on the United States and does not convincingly show that the taboo extends to other countries. If other states are willing to threaten or use nuclear weapons, then the United States must take that reality into account in its own national security strategy. Further, like many other scholars of nuclear issues, she zeroes in on a narrow outcome, decisions on intentional nuclear use, and, thus, overlooks much of the action in nuclear politics. Her theory does not tell us much, if anything, about nuclear war outcomes, or about deterrence and coercion episodes between nuclear-armed states. Moreover, the argument that leaders are loathe to intentionally launch a nuclear war is consistent with the central argument of this book. The superiority-brinkmanship synthesis theory also maintains, albeit for different reasons, that leaders are unable to credibly threaten nuclear war and it is for this reason that they must settle for threatening to risk one.

Still, it is possible to derive a broad, testable hypothesis from Tannenwald's writings that apply to the questions addressed in this book. If she is correct, we might expect that the nuclear balance of power mattered in the early days of the nuclear era, but its effect has been gradually diminished over the past few decades as the normative taboo against nuclear use has strengthened over time.

Another more modest nuclear irrelevance claim holds that nuclear weapons matter for deterrence (defined as a military threat designed to defend the international status quo), but not for compellence (a military threat aimed at changing the international status quo). Nuclear compellence skeptics have recently argued that nuclear weapons are not useful for compellence because it is difficult to credibly threaten their use and because they cannot be used to take and hold territory.[58] Conducting a statistical analysis on a new dataset of militarized compellent threats (MCTs) from 1918 to 2000, they find that there is no relationship between the possession of nuclear weapons and militarized compellent success.

This argument appeals to Schelling's canonical distinction between deterrence and compellence, but, on closer examination, we can see that these are in fact radically different theoretical propositions.[59] It is one thing to argue, as Schelling did, that compellence is more difficult than deterrence. It is quite another to claim, à la nuclear compellence skeptics, that nuclear weapons do not influence compellence at all. After all, it is possible that compellence is less likely to succeed than deterrence, but that nuclear weapons influence both. This interpretation is more consistent with Schelling's conceptualization, as his work focused precisely on how nuclear weapons irrevocably altered international coercion. One could grant, therefore, that compellence is harder than deterrence, but still argue that attempting to compel a nuclear-armed adversary from a position of nuclear inferiority is even harder still. If this is the case, then, contrary to the claims of nuclear coercion skeptics, the nuclear balance of power still matters for compellence.

Moreover, nuclear compellence skeptics risk placing excessive theoretical weight on an overly fine distinction between deterrence and compellence. It is close to inarguable that forcing an adversary to do something is harder than forcing it not to do something, at least in theory. As prominent critics point out, however, the distinction between deterrence and compellence is often a semantic one impossible to distinguish in practice.[60] Let us take the Cuban Missile Crisis, the most high-profile nuclear crisis in history, as an example. Was this a case of deterrence from Washington's perspective because the United States attempted to defend the pre-crisis status quo by deterring the Soviet Union from completing its installation of nuclear-armed missiles in Cuba? Or is it a case of compellence because Washington was striving to force Moscow to remove missiles it had already shipped to the island? There are reasonable arguments to be made either way. As Frank Gavin writes, "More fundamentally, as the 1958–1962 period makes clear, defining the status quo—and coding who is the 'compeller' and who is the deterrer—is often in the eye of the beholder."[61] If it is difficult to distinguish in practice between deterrence and compellence, even in the most important cases, then this poses problems for theories that attempt to draw radically different expectations based on those distinctions. It is hard to fathom that the underlying determinants of international power politics are fundamentally altered according to arguable semantic definitions of when and where one marks the status quo. If nuclear weapons matter at all, then it is likely that they affect both deterrence and compellence. If not, then perhaps they matter for neither.

Finally, nuclear compellence skeptics' claims that nuclear weapons are not useful for compellence because it is difficult to credibly threaten their use and because they cannot be used to take and hold territory are too facile. No one has ever maintained that they are good for occupying territory. Rather, the claim is that they are the ultimate means of holding an enemy state at risk, regardless of whether the enemy can be defeated on the battlefield. Moreover, for over a half century, leading scholars have argued that nuclear weapons matter even while fully acknowledging that it is difficult to credibly threaten their use. Indeed, nuclear deterrence theory begins with the credibility problem; it does not end there. Robert Powell, for example, has even labeled nuclear deterrence theory "the search for credibility."[62] For decades, scholars and strategists have devised ways to increase the credibility of nuclear threats. As Schelling argued, in the nuclear era, states cannot credibly threaten to intentionally start a suicidal nuclear war, but they can make a "threat that leaves something to chance."[63] In other words, they play games of nuclear brinkmanship.

Nuclear compellence skeptics consider the possibility of brinkmanship, but they define it so narrowly as to render it virtually meaningless. They argue that leaders often seek to avoid brinkmanship because they like to maintain control and do not want to risk the possibility of accidents in a crisis. This is true, but there are competing pressures at play. Leaders are also loathe to cave to an enemy in a high-stakes geopolitical standoff. They also prefer to avoid waging deliberate war against a nuclear-armed rival. Brinkmanship is the only other game in town. So, they play, reluctantly.

Moreover, contrary to claims of nuclear compellence skeptics, brinkmanship does not necessarily mean voluntarily ceding control of one's nuclear forces. Rather, leaders can try to cling to the illusion of control as much as they like, but when they enter an escalating crisis with another nuclear-armed state, the shadow of nuclear warfare and the risks of unintended escalation hang over the conflict, whether leaders like it or not.

Finally, and related, nuclear compellence skeptics charge that brinkmanship is hard because leaders often misinterpret signals that opponents try to send. It is certainly the case that signals are frequently misinterpreted in international politics, but the message that pressing a dangerous conflict against a nuclear-armed rival could result in nuclear catastrophe is not that difficult to understand. Indeed, as we see in the case studies of nuclear crises in chapter 4, leaders in all four cases understood full well the dangers they faced.

In sum, there are many theoretical reasons to doubt claims that nuclear weapons are irrelevant to international politics broadly, or to compellence specifically. Nevertheless, these ideas are subjected to empirical tests in the chapters to come.

Regional Nuclear Posture Theory

Vipin Narang has studied the nuclear postures of regional powers.[64] Unlike the superpowers, he argues, regional powers are unable to develop robust nuclear postures as defined here and are therefore forced to make choices among three more limited, alternative postures: catalytic, assured retaliation, and asymmetric escalation. According to his definitions, catalytic posture is similar to minimum deterrence as described previously. Assured retaliation is largely synonymous with a secure, second-strike posture. And asymmetric escalation is a posture aimed at using nuclear weapons early in a conflict in order to deter, and if necessary defeat, an opponent's conventional attack. The majority of his study is devoted to explaining how states select among this menu of postures, but he also considers how these postures affect the initiation of military conflict. He finds that only asymmetric escalation deters conventional conflict. In other words, in order to deter lower-level conventional conflicts, states must choose a posture specifically designed to deter lower-level conventional conflict.

Narang's is a fine book, but it is of limited utility to the present study.[65] First, Narang explicitly excludes the superpowers, whereas this study is focused squarely on one of the major superpowers (in addition to developing a broader logic of nuclear competition). Second, the present study explains the logic of what is defined in the introduction as a "robust" nuclear posture, whereas, in choosing not to study the superpowers, Narang necessarily eliminates this type of posture from his book altogether. Third, unlike this study, Narang focuses on states' nuclear postures in isolation, without considering the arguably more important and contentious issue of the nuclear balance of power between states. Fourth, Narang devotes much attention to the causes of posture development and, to a lesser degree, how posture affects conventional conflict, but does not consider the full range of outcomes examined in this study.

Nevertheless, if Narang is correct, we might expect that regional powers with asymmetric escalation postures would enjoy more bargaining leverage and would, therefore, perform better in competitions among nuclear powers. This idea is considered in the empirical chapters to follow.

Conventional Military Power Theory

Conventional military power may influence coercion among nuclear-armed states. Nuclear weapons have not been used in conflict since 1945, whereas the employment of conventional force is a (perhaps depressingly) routine feature of international politics. Some may argue, therefore, that conventional military power is more usable and, therefore, should be more likely than nuclear weapons to affect deterrence and coercion, even among nuclear-armed states.

There is also strong reason to believe, however, that nuclear weapons shape international conflict, even if they are never employed on the battlefield. Paul Nitze, a senior defense official in several US administrations from the 1950s to the 1970s, likened international politics to a game of chess:

> The atomic queens may never be brought into play; they may never actually take one of the opponent's pieces. But the position of the atomic queens may still have a decisive bearing on which side can safely advance a limited-war bishop or even a cold-war pawn. The advance of a cold-war pawn may even disclose a check of the opponent's king by a well-positioned atomic queen.[66]

States must, therefore, take into account the fact that nuclear weapons exist and could be used when making decisions that could lead to the use of force. Brinkmanship theory also assumes that there is some possibility that even small-scale militarized disputes could eventually escalate to full-scale nuclear exchange. Indeed, the vast majority of scholars believe that nuclear weapons matter. As reviewed above, there are vigorous debates about how much is enough and whether they matter for compellence, but nearly all who study this issue (except perhaps Mueller) believe that nuclear weapons have greatly affected politics among nations.

This is likely a debate that is best conceived of, therefore, as both/and rather than either/or. In all likelihood, nuclear weapons and conventional military power matter when it comes to conflict among nuclear-armed states, although it would not be surprising if nuclear forces, still the most formidable weapons on Earth, take on greater salience in conflicts among nuclear powers. Still, the idea that conventional military power affects competitions among nuclear states is explored in the empirical component of the book.

Democratic Advantage Theory

A final alternative explanation holds that domestic political institutions shape the nature of international crisis bargaining. James Fearon has argued that democracies enjoy an advantage in international coercion because they can better signal resolve through the generation of domestic political "audience costs."[67] In democracies, when a leader makes a highly visible international threat and then backs down, he or she will be held accountable by domestic political audiences, such as legislatures, political opponents, or the general public. This could result in the leader's reduced political support and even ouster from office. In order to avoid these "audience costs," therefore, democratic leaders should be reluctant to issue clear threats unless they are willing to follow through on them. Moreover, and importantly, foreign leaders are likely to take seriously threats issued by democratic leaders. They understand that democratic leaders incur a potential cost from bluffing, so they interpret democratic threats as credible signals of intent.

On the other hand, leaders of autocratic states can issue international threats with very little concern for political costs because their domestic audiences are not able to hold them accountable. They can more easily bluff, and foreign leaders are less likely to interpret their threats as costly signals. The upshot of this theory, therefore, is that democracies enjoy a coercive advantage in international crisis bargaining.

Another version of this argument holds that there is also variation in the ability of different types of autocratic regimes, such as between personalistic dictatorships and single-party states, to generate audience costs and this also affects crisis bargaining.[68]

Moreover, and potentially more challenging for the superiority-brinkmanship synthesis theory, Fearon argues not only that domestic institutions matter for crisis bargaining but also that the balance of stakes and the balance of military power do not. He asserts that leaders know full well the interests at stake and the military balance of power before selecting into crises. Therefore, the influence of stakes and power should be exerted at this earlier selection stage of the crisis. If leaders still decide to enter a crisis, therefore, then stakes and military power should no longer matter because their effects have already been fully taken into account. This brings him to his argument that intracrisis bargaining dynamics, such as the generation of "audience costs," are the primary determinant of crisis outcomes.

On reflection, however, this argument poses less of a challenge to the superiority-brinkmanship synthesis theory than it may initially appear. Indeed, the theories are dealing to some degree with separate issues and are, at least in part, mutually reinforcing. First, the audience cost hypothesis does not make any claims about nuclear war outcomes. It does not have any bearing, therefore, on Hypothesis 1. In addition, the audience cost argument further bolsters Hypothesis 3. Fearon explicitly argues that the balance of power should influence leaders as they consider the initiation of conflict. This is supportive of the idea that the nuclear balance of power affects deterrence.

The stronger tension is with Hypothesis 2. If leaders fully account for the balance of power before selecting into crises, then nuclear superiority should not shape the outcome of high-stakes nuclear crises.

There are theoretical reasons, however, to be skeptical of this aspect of Fearon's theory. Schelling, Jervis, Powell, Glaser, and others have all argued that the balance of stakes is central to nuclear crisis bargaining, but Fearon claims that the effect of both stakes and military power should be neutralized by the time a crisis emerges.[69] If Fearon is correct, then much of academic nuclear deterrence theory, not just the argument in this book, is incorrect. This is possible, of course, but it is worth noting there are serious academic heavyweights on both sides of this debate.

Moreover, as Jonathan Kirshner has argued, the idea that military power and resolve are fully accounted for by leaders prior to selecting into crises, presupposes that leaders possess superhuman capabilities to assess the balances of power and resolve and to foresee the future.[70] After all, he argues, even with reams of statistics, we cannot predict with certainty the outcome of tomorrow's New York Yankees game. One team may be favored, but there is still significant room for chance. Similarly, leaders cannot perfectly assess the balance of stakes and power and foresee how precisely they will affect international crisis bargaining. The upshot is that military power (and the nuclear balance of power) could affect both the selection into and the outcome of international crises.

Furthermore, to a large degree, this is an empirical, not a theoretical, question. If Fearon's theory is correct, then we should expect the entire effect of nuclear superiority to be attenuated in the selection stage before the time at which states reach a peak crisis. The bias in any empirical study on this question, therefore, should be against finding any evidence of a relationship between the nuclear balance of power and crisis outcomes. If, on the other hand, we still find evidence of a relationship in the crisis outcome stage, even after affects have been partially attenuated in the selection stage, then this will provide particularly strong support for Hypothesis 2.

More fundamentally, there is cause to doubt audience cost theory itself. Scholars have gradually chipped away at the theoretical foundations of the audience cost argument in recent years. They have pointed out that the theory rests on a series of questionable assumptions about the nature of international politics.[71] Do domestic publics really play close attention to foreign affairs? Do they truly care whether there is a gap between their leaders' words and deeds? If so, do leaders face meaningful audience costs when they back down from previous commitments? Do foreign leaders genuinely assess an enemy's credibility on this basis? If one cannot answer all of these questions in the affirmative, then the premises of audience cost theory, and the theory itself, is weakened.

Finally, audience cost theory finds only mixed support in the empirical record. Several scholars have failed to find evidence of audience cost mechanisms at play in high-profile crises involving threats from democratic states.[72] Much of the evidence for audience cost theory, therefore, rests on quantitative analyses, but a recent study shows that after one accounts for superpower alliances, the findings of a statistical relationship between democratic political regime type and international dispute reciprocation vanishes.[73] This suggests that democracies may excel in crisis bargaining not due to audience costs but, at least in part, because they are backed by a democratic superpower, the United States.

Still, the idea that democracies (and perhaps certain types of autocracies) enjoy a coercive advantage in international politics has been among the most influential arguments in international relations theory over the past two decades and it is, therefore, considered in the empirical tests in the following chapters.

Research Design

To adjudicate among these theories, this book employs a multimethod research design that includes quantitative and qualitative methodologies and foreign policy analysis. Many political science books attempt to explain a single dependent variable, but this book focuses on how a single independent variable, nuclear posture, affects several, separate but related, dependent variables: nuclear war outcomes, nuclear crisis outcomes, deterrence and compellence, stability, arms races, nuclear proliferation, and the defense budget. As such, each dependent variable requires its own research design, and the implementation of each study is explained in further detail in its respective chapter. Throughout, however, I follow best practices for social science research, and the remainder of this section discusses the principles that guide the design of this study.

To avoid the pitfalls of relying exclusively on a single research method, I employ a multimethod approach.[74] The large-N analysis allows me to look for relationships among variables in large pools of data. The statistical analysis draws on an original dataset of nuclear arsenal size to analyze the relationship between nuclear capabilities and: nuclear crisis outcomes (chapter 3); the initiation of MCTs (chapter 5); and nuclear proliferation and nonproliferation (chapter 8). In some chapters, I also draw on the statistical findings of other scholars when adjudicating the support for and against various arguments.

Although many nuclear weapons–related issues are relatively rare, there is sufficient data for statistical analysis and, indeed, in recent years there has been an explosion of quantitative research on nuclear issues published in the field's best journals.[75] While some question the value of studying nuclear weapons with numbers, there is a growing consensus that quantitative analysis, in combination with other methods, greatly contributes to our understanding of nuclear proliferation.[76]

In addition to the quantitative analysis, qualitative studies permit pattern matching and process tracing of the theoretical argument in specific case studies.[77] To choose the case studies, I employ a number of decision rules. As recommend by King, Keohane, and Verba, I select cases with variation on the key independent and dependent variables.[78] I also employ most and least-likely case design, often with strong countervailing conditions, to provide a range of hard tests for the argument. I also ensure gradations on measurements of my theory's independent variable, to test how the magnitude of nuclear imbalances affects the dependent variables.[79] Where possible, I select influential cases that have received past attention from social science researchers.[80] If the theory cannot account for what are thought to be the most important cases, then some might question its utility even if it holds up well in other less prominent cases. Due to greater data availability and because this study seeks to explain American nuclear strategy, there is a particular, but not exclusive, focus on cases involving the United States. At the same time, data from other cases are brought to bear to demonstrate that the basic logic of nuclear competition extends more broadly.

Finally, for some of the chapters, traditional social science research methods are insufficient and I instead rely on tools developed for foreign policy analysis. For example, it is impossible to use observational data to analyze something that has never happened. For the study of the expected cost of nuclear war in chapter 2, I use nuclear exchange calculations developed during the Cold War to examine the expected costs of hypothetical nuclear exchanges. And I employ budgetary analysis in chapter 9 to discuss the costs of nuclear modernization on the defense budget.

We return to the details of the research design in future chapters. At this point, however, we put the methodological discussion on hold. The next chapter turns to an examination of the most horrific, but perhaps most important, dependent variable considered in this book: nuclear war outcomes.

2

Nuclear War Outcomes

Many scholars working on nuclear strategy refrain from writing, talking, or even thinking about nuclear war.[1] Rather, they focus on the requirements for successful nuclear deterrence in isolation without taking the next step and asking what happens if deterrence fails. This is understandable; as the Cold War strategist Herman Kahn argued, few people are comfortable "thinking about the unthinkable."[2] But doing so is necessary if one truly hopes to understand nuclear strategy. After all, in order to effectively practice deterrence, one must have an understanding of what it is one is attempting to deter. As Clausewitz argued, "war is a continuation of politics by other means," and there is a clear logical connection between the prospect of nuclear war and the politics of nuclear deterrence and coercion.[3] Any serious analysis of nuclear strategy must, therefore, begin by looking straight into the abyss of nuclear catastrophe. Few do. But, that is the purpose of this chapter.

In particular, this chapter explores the idea that the nuclear balance of power matters for nuclear war outcomes. It tests this proposition by analyzing simulated nuclear exchanges between the United States and its nuclear-armed rivals: Russia, China, and North Korea. Drawing on both historical and contemporary data on the nuclear postures and strategies of these states, it shows that a state's expected cost of nuclear war depends heavily on the nuclear balance of power. The results provide strong support for the superiority-brinkmanship synthesis theory. On the other hand, the major alternative explanation for nuclear war outcomes, the idea that the nuclear balance of power does not matter for nuclear war outcomes among states with secure, second-strike capabilities, does not find support.

The rest of the chapter continues in three parts. First, it describes the research design for assessing nuclear war outcomes. Second, it turns to the results of the nuclear exchange simulations. Finally, it reviews the findings, discusses their implications, and offers concluding remarks.

Assessing Nuclear War Outcomes

To evaluate the effect of the nuclear balance of power on nuclear war outcomes, this chapter performs nuclear exchange calculations between the United States and its potential nuclear adversaries in the world today.

Research Design

To perform these tests, I begin by ensuring variation on the key independent variable: the nuclear balance of power. The nuclear balance of power between the United States and its rivals is affected by both America's nuclear forces and the nuclear forces of its potential adversaries. First, I examine changes to nuclear war outcomes after varying adversary nuclear posture. Fortunately, there is natural variation on this variable in the world today. At the time this study was conducted, in 2015, America's potential nuclear adversaries, Russia, China, and North Korea, were believed to possess 1,780; 65; and 0 warheads, respectively, capable of reaching the continental United States.[4] I therefore examine whether the expected costs of nuclear war for the United States vary in hypothetical nuclear exchanges with these countries. To increase variation on the independent variable and to examine the effects of changes to the nuclear posture of a single nuclear adversary over time, I conduct an additional test. I consider a hypothetical nuclear exchange between the United States and China in 2006, when it was estimated that China possessed only 20 nuclear warheads capable of reaching the continental United States.[5]

Beyond Russia, China, and North Korea, there exist other nuclear-armed states, but they are not included in this analysis because they are not plausible US adversaries. Britain and France are formal US treaty allies. Israel is an extremely close security partner. India and Pakistan are neither formal allies nor sworn enemies and the United States cooperates with both on a range of security issues. It is nearly impossible at the present moment to imagine a direct military conflict between Washington and either New Delhi or Islamabad.

Next, I consider variations to the independent variable through alterations in US nuclear posture. In recent years, prominent advocates have recommended that the United States make "deep cuts" to the size of its nuclear arsenal.[6] They urged Washington to cut its forces from the approximately 2,000 nuclear warheads it possesses today down to 450. I therefore consider nuclear exchanges involving the United States using both its current posture and this hypothetical, reduced posture.

For all tests, I model exchanges by drawing on the best available information about each of the nuclear powers' nuclear posture and strategy. I also consider each of the above exchanges under conditions of both an enemy first strike and an enemy second strike. This allows me to ensure the robustness of the findings to assumptions about the sequencing of the hypothetical nuclear exchanges. It also provides a test of one of the underlying assumptions of the superiority-brinkmanship synthesis theory: robust nuclear postures enable states to meaningfully limit damage to themselves in the event of a nuclear war.

By examining a single nuclear target, the United States, I focus on the primary subject of this study. In addition, this choice allows me to hold constant the characteristics of the nuclear target, including population and territorial size. By allowing only the nuclear balance of power to vary, I can better isolate its effects on the expected cost of nuclear war.

If the logic of the superiority-brinkmanship synthesis theory is correct, we should predict that the expected damage to the US homeland in the event of nuclear war will depend on the nuclear balance of power between the United States and its adversaries. The expected cost of nuclear war to the United States should increase along with either increases in the size of adversaries' nuclear arsenals or decreases in the size of the US nuclear arsenal.

The secure, second-strike hypothesis would expect a different result. It would predict that once a US adversary possesses a secure, second-strike capability, the consequences of nuclear war will be so catastrophic as to defy attempts to draw meaningful distinctions. Moreover, another, stronger variant of this argument would go further and maintain that any nuclear war, even if the adversary lacks an assured retaliatory capability, would be so cataclysmic as to make damage comparisons meaningless.

Measuring the Expected Cost of Nuclear War

To measure the expected cost of nuclear war, I employ three primary measures.[7] First, in each nuclear exchange, I count the expected number of enemy warheads that will detonate on or above US soil. Second, I gauge the estimated number of US metropolitan areas struck in the attack. Third, and finally, I assess the expected number of human casualties in each exchange. The larger the number of expected nuclear detonations on US soil, the more US cities hit, and the more people who are killed and injured, the more damaging the attack.

Counting the number of expected nuclear detonations and number of cities struck is a straightforward exercise, but measuring accurately the expected number of deaths and injuries in a nuclear war is notoriously difficult.[8] To provide a rough estimate of the number of expected deaths and injuries, I count the populations of the cities hit in each nuclear exchange. This measure is imperfect, but it provides a reasonable proxy measure for assessing the rough number of people affected by a nuclear attack.[9]

This measure may overestimate the true number of casualties in some ways and underestimate it in others, but there is no reason to believe that it is systematically biased in either direction. On one hand, it does not account for the possibility that: the nuclear fallout cloud might drift and kill people in nearby cities; radiation may contaminate food and water supplies sickening people in other areas; the electromagnetic pulse (EMP) may cause damage to critical infrastructure (such as air traffic control systems), leading to casualties; the fallout cloud may block the sun's rays leading to "nuclear autumn," that is, a temporary decrease in temperature, a fall in agricultural production, and disruptions to food supply. (The prospect of a broader "nuclear winter" has been ruled out by leading scientists and is discussed in further detail later).[10]

On the other hand, this method overcounts in some ways because a nuclear attack on a heavily populated area will not kill 100% of the population. Many will promptly perish due to the blast wave and heat of the explosion. Others will eventually succumb to injuries sustained in the explosion, from radiation sickness, or due to the combination. Still others may survive, but their lives will be irrevocably altered. They may be injured by the blast or they may suffer lingering effects of radiation sickness. Even if they are not physically injured, however, they could suffer emotional and psychological trauma as their city will suffer economic devastation; parts of their hometown may be uninhabitable for years to come; and they will have lost friends, family, and colleagues.

By measuring the population sizes of the cities struck, therefore, I am measuring nearly all of the casualties as traditionally defined (deaths and injuries) as well people directly affected by the attack. Moreover, since the same measure is applied to all scenarios, and our primary theoretical interest is comparing nuclear exchange outcomes across scenarios, any shortcomings of the measure will be manifest in each scenario. Most importantly, there is no reason to believe that the measure systematically biases for or against the hypothesis under examination. Data on the populations of major metropolitan areas in the United States is drawn from the US Census Bureau.[11]

In addition to these three measures, the expected damage of nuclear war is also assessed using a visualization tool. For each hypothetical nuclear exchange, the number, location, and blast of each strike are plotted on a map of the continental United States. In addition to the numbers, therefore, this tool provides a more intuitive means of eyeballing the variation, if any, of nuclear devastation across scenarios. For all strikes, the approximate size of the nuclear weapons' physical effects are modeled with the aid of Alex Wallerstein's Nukemap program.[12]

This study does not directly consider the economic cost of the attack or the damage to a nation's nuclear retaliatory capabilities when assessing the expected damage of nuclear war.[13] Unfortunately, there is not reliable, disaggregated data available on the GDP of all the metropolitan areas that are subject to attack in the following scenarios. Since much of the US economic base is located in cities, however, the count of number of cities struck provides at least an indirect means of measuring and comparing the relative economic costs of nuclear war scenarios. This chapter considers damage to nuclear forces to the degree that it is relevant to counterforce exchange scenarios, but it does not consider lost nuclear forces as a cost of nuclear war in and of itself. Ultimately, US officials are concerned primarily with protecting the US population and nuclear forces are but a means to that end. For other nations, this calculation may very well be different, but this is a book on US nuclear strategy.

Neither does this analysis consider the expected cost of nuclear war to allies. Of course, the United States has a strong interest in protecting its allies in Asia and Europe, but their inclusion would greatly complicate the analysis without altering the central strategic equation. A state can most credibly threaten nuclear war in the event of an attack on its homeland. So, it is the homeland vulnerability that is most relevant to brinkmanship theory and, ultimately, to how well the United States can credibly extend deterrence to its allies.

What about Nuclear Winter and Human Extinction?

At this point, some may object to the above attempt to measure gradations of nuclear war by claiming that the effects of any nuclear war would be unimaginable and could potentially even result in "nuclear winter" and complete human extinction. The possibility of nuclear winter, however, has long been dismissed by leading scientists.[14]

In the early 1980s, the scientist and public intellectual Carl Sagan and colleagues popularized the idea of "nuclear winter."[15] He and other experts argued that the heat from a nuclear explosion would set ablaze wooden structures and other flammable material in cities, sending large quantities of smoke into the Earth's atmosphere, thus blocking out the sun's rays. This would have the effect of reducing the Earth's temperature and wiping out global agricultural production. Crude climate models at the time estimated that the effect could be so large as to result in mass starvation and possibly even human extinction. The arguments had a profound effect on elites and the general public on both sides of the Iron Curtain. Then–Soviet Premier Mikael Gorbachev later admitted that fear of nuclear winter was a factor motivating him to end the Cold War.[16]

Subsequent research employing more sophisticated climate modeling has demonstrated, however, that early fears about nuclear winter resulting in human extinction were overblown.[17] Even scientists who initially proposed the idea, including the physicist Richard P. Turco (the person who coined the phrase "nuclear winter") disavowed these arguments just a few years later. Climate scientists working in this area today sometimes refer instead to the possibility of "nuclear autumn." The smoke from a large-scale nuclear exchange could indeed obstruct sunlight and reduce agricultural production, but the effects would be milder than Sagan and others warned in the early 1980s.

Evidence against nuclear winter comes not only from better climate models but also from data obtained from analysis of other events that emitted large quantities of smoke into the Earth's atmosphere, such as the firebombing of Dresden and Tokyo during World War II, Saddam Hussein's ignition of 600 oil wells in Iraq during the first Gulf War, and the volcanic eruptions at Krakatoa and Tambora.[18] Tambora, for example, was a 33-gigaton explosion, equivalent to the simultaneous detonation of 2.5 million Hiroshima-size bombs. These events all spewed large amounts of soot into the Earth's atmosphere, but only Tambora resulted in a noticeable decrease in the Earth's temperature, and the effects were not catastrophic. (Indeed, it is said that Mary Shelly was inspired to write *Frankenstein* during an unusually gloomy European summer in 1816 that, unbeknownst to her, was the result of the Tambora volcano in faraway Indonesia).[19]

Depending on the size, timing, and location of a nuclear attack, agricultural production could be affected and this could result in disruptions to food supplies in vulnerable populations around the world. As such, "nuclear autumn" is included as a possible source of casualties in the above discussion. Most importantly for our purpose in this section, however, nuclear war, at least with nuclear forces heretofore accumulated, would not mean nuclear winter, human extinction, or the end of the world.

Enemy Capabilities and Strategy

To accurately assess the expected damage of a nuclear exchange with each of the United States' nuclear-armed adversaries, I must begin with information about the nuclear capabilities and strategies of Russia, China, and North Korea. In addition, to accurately model an enemy second strike after a US first strike, I need to outline US counterforce capabilities and strategy. That is the function of this section.

Russia

As of 2015, Russia possessed an estimated 1,780 strategic, deployed nuclear warheads capable of reaching the continental United States.[20] This includes 1,050 warheads delivered by 311 silo-based and mobile ICBMs. Russia also has six Delta IV submarines, equipped with 16 SLBMs, each of which carries up to four warheads. In addition, the first three of Russia's new Borey-class subsurface ballistic nuclear submarines (SSBNs) have been loaded or have initiated sea trials. Each is armed with 16 new Bulova SLBMs that carry up to six warheads apiece. Finally, Russia has approximately 60 deployed nuclear bombers, which can deliver nuclear-armed air-launched cruise missiles.

In the event of a large-scale nuclear war, it is believed that Russia would pursue a combination counterforce and countervalue targeting strategy, with a priority going to the counterforce mission.[21] Once military targets have been adequately covered, it is believed that Russia would use any remaining capabilities in a countervalue attack to maximize the damage to the United States.

China

As of 2015, Beijing possessed an estimated 45 nuclear-armed intercontinental ballistic missiles (ICBMs), carrying approximately 65 warheads capable of reaching the continental United States.[22] This includes 25 DF-31A and 20 DF-5A missiles. Some of China's DF-5As are believed to have been equipped with MIRV (multiple independently targetable reentry vehicles) warheads in recent years and may be capable of carrying up to three warheads per missile. China has been working on a sea leg of its nuclear force for several decades, but, to date, it has not yet begun deterrence patrols. China's People's Liberation Army (PLA) Air Force does not have a role in the nuclear mission. Before the DF-31A was deployed in the mid-2000s, China only possessed 20 DF-5As capable of reaching the continental United States. In what follows we consider nuclear exchanges both with China's current and its past nuclear arsenals.

China is believed to possess a pure, countervalue targeting strategy.[23] In the event of a large-scale nuclear war, it is believed that it would aim its nuclear warheads at America's largest metropolitan areas with the intent of inflicting maximum levels of destruction.

North Korea

As of 2015, the best available evidence indicates that North Korea does not yet have the ability to deliver a nuclear warhead to the continental United States, but, if current trends continue, it could have such a capability in the near future.[24] North Korea is believed to possess enough nuclear material for up to twenty-one nuclear warheads, and it continues to test longer-range ballistic missiles, including an SLBM.[25] Questions remain about whether North Korea can miniaturize a nuclear weapon to fit on the nosecone of a ballistic missile. And it has yet to demonstrate an intercontinental capability or a successful reentry vehicle.[26]

Some US military officials have stated that they believe North Korea has the ability to deliver nuclear weapons to US territory, but this is almost certainly a planning assumption made out of abundance of caution, not an assessment of current capabilities.[27]

The United States

As of 2015, the United States possessed 2,072 nuclear warheads on ballistic missiles and bomber bases. This force consists of: 440 ICBMs; 1,152 warheads on SLBMs; 200 nuclear air-launched cruise missiles (ALCMs); and 280 nuclear gravity bombs.[28] The United States adheres to a pure counterforce targeting strategy. As President Obama's Report to Congress on his Nuclear Employment Guidance to the Department of Defense states:

> The new guidance requires the United States to maintain significant counterforce capabilities against potential adversaries. The new guidance does not rely on a "counter-value" or "minimum deterrence" strategy. The new guidance makes clear that all plans must also be consistent with the fundamental principles of the Law of Armed Conflict. Accordingly, plans will, for example, apply the principles of distinction and proportionality and seek to minimize collateral damage to civilian populations and civilian objects. The United States will not intentionally target civilian populations or civilian objects.[29]

To be sure, even a pure counterforce strategy would require destroying military targets in heavily populated areas and would result in significant collateral damage. The purpose of US nuclear strategy, however, is not to destroy cities, but to destroy an enemy's war-making capability.

Nuclear Targeting and Warhead Allocation

To increase the probability that a target is destroyed, states often plan to allocate multiple warheads to important targets. When conducting a nuclear strike, a nuclear warhead could fail at many points: the delivery vehicle may be destroyed by an enemy preemptive attack; the delivery vehicle may fail to properly launch; the delivery vehicle may be intercepted by enemy defenses; the delivery vehicle or warhead may be the victim of fratricide from other nearby nuclear detonations; the delivery vehicle may miss its intended target; the warhead may fail to detonate; or the warhead may detonate but fail to destroy the target.[30] To ensure that important targets are destroyed, therefore, nuclear planners can allocate more than one warhead to each target.[31] As a rule of thumb, outside analysts often assume that two or three warheads will be allocated to each target.[32] For the below analysis, I assume that states allocate three warheads to the most important counterforce targets, two warheads to subsidiary counterforce targets, and, depending on warhead availability, one or two warheads to countervalue targets.[33]

Simulation Analysis and Results

First Strike Analysis

To begin the analysis, I consider a hypothetical nuclear first strike on the continental United States from Russia, China, and North Korea. This analysis shows, in support of Hypothesis 1, that the expected damage to the United States depends on the nuclear balance between the United States and its opponents. The larger the nuclear arsenal of the opponent, the more devastating the nuclear war for the United States.

As stated earlier, I model a Russian combined counterforce and countervalue attack, with a priority in a nuclear first strike going to blunting America's nuclear retaliatory capability. Moscow must target, therefore, America's 440 ICBM silos at Malstrom Air Force Base in Montana; Minot Air Force Base in North Dakota; and Warren Air Force Base which spans the borders of Wyoming, Colorado, and Nebraska.[34] Russia must also target the United States' two strategic nuclear submarine bases at Bangor, Washington, and King's Bay, Georgia.[35] In addition, Moscow would target US strategic air bases: Minot, Barksdale Air Force Base in Louisiana, and Whiteman Air Force Base in Missouri.[36] I assume that Russia allocates three warheads to each of these critical targets. A second set of less critical counterforce targets receives two warheads per target. This includes about 70 other military bases in the United States with a potential role in the nuclear mission, including Offutt Air Base in Omaha, Nebraska, the home of US Strategic Command.[37] In addition, Russia would need to target roughly ten important command and control targets in Washington, DC, and elsewhere. Finally, the remaining 262 warheads are aimed, two apiece, at the United States' most populous 131 cities in order to destroy US industrial capability and inflict massive destruction.[38]

To simplify the analysis and to provide the hardest possible test for my theory, I assume that states employ every warhead in their arsenal in a nuclear attack. In other words, they do not preserve warheads to deter future attacks or to address other enemies. This assumption is certainly debatable and may even be somewhat unrealistic, but it is made because it biases against the central argument of this book. If I had assumed that states hold back portions of their arsenal, then critics could have charged that I was intentionally attempting to limit the expected damage of nuclear war in order to demonstrate meaningful differences in war outcomes even in situations of MAD. The idea that states would expend their entire nuclear arsenals in the event of a major nuclear war is at least possible and, importantly, it sets up a difficult test for my theory.

Next, to simulate a Chinese attack on the United States, and consistent with Chinese strategy and capabilities as described previously, I assume China targets one nuclear missile against each of the United States' forty-five largest cities.[39] China's MIRV missiles can release multiple warheads. The distances that these separate warheads on the same missile can travel from one another is a closely guarded secret, but it is known that they must be allocated to relatively nearby targets.[40] I therefore model the effect of each MIRV missile releasing its entire payload against a single city.

The test using China's 2015 nuclear arsenal, however, is only the first step. Next, I simulate a full-scale Chinese countervalue attack on the continental United States, circa 2006. At that point in time, China possessed twenty DF-5A ICBMs capable of reaching the US homeland. I assume that Beijing targets Washington, DC (which, at #22, comes in just outside the top twenty US population centers) and the United States' nineteen largest cities.[41]

Finally, I simulate a North Korean nuclear attack against the United States. As stated previously, as of 2015, Pyongyang lacked the ability to deliver nuclear warheads to the continental United States.

First-Strike Results

The results of these simulations are presented in Table 2.1 and visualized in Figures 2.1, 2.2, 2.3, and 2.4. As a reminder, the superiority-brinkmanship synthesis theory would predict meaningful differences in nuclear war outcomes depending on the nuclear capability of the US adversary. The alternative, second-strike theory, would expect that we do not find meaningful differences, at least among states with second-strike capabilities. This would include Russia and China.

Turning first to a full-scale Russian nuclear attack against the United States, we can see in Table 2.1 and Figure 2.1 that such a nuclear war would devastate the country. The United States could expect approximately 1,780 nuclear detonations on US soil. The 131 most populous areas would suffer nuclear disasters, including cities ranging from New York City; to Salt Lake City, Utah; to Huntsville, Alabama; and to Tallahassee, Florida. Just below this threshold, the cities barely spared a direct nuclear attack would include Chattanooga, Tennessee; Jackson, Mississippi; and Peoria, Illinois. The casualty figures would run upward of 70 million people.

Table 2.1 **Nuclear Exchange Simulation Results, Expected Damage to the United States under Various Scenarios**

US Nuclear Posture	Attack Sequence	Adversary	Number of Nuclear Detonations	Number of Cities Destroyed	Number of Casualties
Current	Adversary First Strike	Russia	1,780	131	69,656,847
		China, 2015	65	45	47,640,704
		China, 2006	20	20	33,937,790
		North Korea	0	0	0
	Adversary Second Strike	Russia	66	12	27,661,159
		China, 2015	5	5	7,942,986
		China, 2006	0	0	0
		North Korea	0	0	0
After Deep Reductions	Adversary First Strike	Russia	1,780	791	125,185,545
	Adversary Second Strike	Russia	469	211	81,801,754

A Chinese nuclear attack would also be horrific, but less devastating than a Russian strike. Turning back to Table 2.1 and to Figure 2.2, we can see that a Chinese nuclear attack would result in 65 nuclear detonations on US soil. America's 45 largest cities from New York City to Oakland, California, would be devastated. And nearly 50 million casualties would result. While a Chinese nuclear attack would be cataclysmic, it must also be noted that, compared to a Russian attack, much more of the country would survive. Major US metropolitan areas outside the top 45 would not be directly targeted. This list of cities spared in a Chinese, but not a Russian, first strike would include Minneapolis and St. Paul, Minnesota; Cleveland and Cincinnati, Ohio; New Orleans, Louisiana; Tampa, Florida; Honolulu, Hawaii; St. Louis, Missouri; Pittsburgh, Pennsylvania; Madison, Wisconsin, and many others. This does not even begin to list the many suburbs, exurbs, and small towns across the country that would also avoid a direct nuclear attack. All told, an estimated 20 million additional human lives would survive a Chinese nuclear attack, but would be held at risk in a Russian nuclear attack.

Figure 2.1 Nuclear exchange simulation results, Russia first strike on the United States.

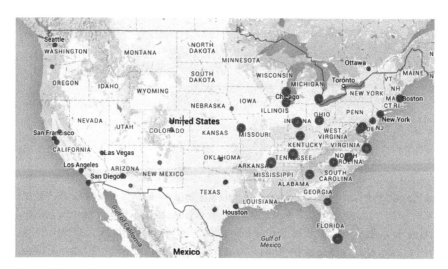

Figure 2.2 Nuclear exchange simulation results, China first strike on the United States, 2015.

We next model a Chinese nuclear strike on the United States in 2006, when China possessed only twenty nuclear missiles capable of reaching the US home-land. The results are available in Table 2.1 and Figure 2.3. We again see that such a nuclear strike would no doubt be devastating. Twenty nuclear detonations would inflict grave harm on twenty of America's most important cities and result in an estimated 34 million casualties.

We also see, however, that much of the country would survive the attack. Following the same targeting rules, and adjusting only the size of China's nuclear

Figure 2.3 Nuclear exchange simulation results, China first-strike on the United States, 2006.

Figure 2.4 Nuclear exchange simulation results, North Korea first-strike on the United States.

forces, we can see that a Chinese attack in 2006 would have been much less costly than a Chinese nuclear attack today. As Chinese nuclear capabilities have grown, the amount of destruction it can inflict on the United States has also increased. Unlike an attack at present, a 2006 Chinese nuclear attack would have spared many major US cities, including Boston, Seattle, Denver, Nashville, Baltimore, Louisville, Portland, Milwaukee, Las Vegas, and many others. Accordingly, China, at present, can hold approximately 16 million more American lives at risk than it could just one decade ago.

Finally, we examine North Korea. These results are presented in Table 2.1 and Figure 2.4. As we can see a North Korea nuclear attack against the United States is not thought to be possible at the time of the study. It would result in an estimated zero nuclear detonations, zero cities destroyed, and zero casualties. It would, therefore, be less costly than a Russian or Chinese nuclear attack against the United States. This is despite the fact that North Korea may already possess a minimum nuclear deterrent according to some definitions.

This analysis provides strong support for a central hypothesis of this book: the expected damage of a nuclear war depends heavily on the nuclear balance of power between states. Holding the target state constant, we see that decreasing the attacker state's nuclear forces results in a corresponding decrease in the expected damage to the United States. Russia possesses more warheads than China and, accordingly, it can inflict more damage on the United States in the event of a nuclear war. Similarly, China has a more nuclear capable force than North Korea and can also, therefore, threaten more destruction to the US homeland. In addition, comparing China's nuclear forces in 2006 and 2015, we see the same relationship holds when varying the same attacker state's capabilities over time. The larger China's nuclear arsenal, the greater the expected damage to the US homeland, holding all else constant.

On the other hand, the second-strike hypothesis does not find support. The nuclear balance of power matters for nuclear war outcomes. Extreme arguments about minimal or existential deterrence are easily dismissed. North Korea today possesses some minimal nuclear deterrent capability, but a nuclear war with North Korea would cause very little if any damage to the US homeland, while a nuclear exchange with Russia or China would unleash massive devastation. Yet, even arguments that set a higher bar for assured retaliation do not find support. At present, there is little doubt that Russia and China both possess secure, second-strike capabilities.[42] For those in the second-strike school, this is the threshold beyond which additional nuclear capabilities do not matter. But we saw that additional nuclear capabilities above and beyond this point are in fact quite consequential. The expected costs of a nuclear war with Russia are much greater than the expected costs of nuclear exchange with China. To argue otherwise, one would have to maintain that the destruction of 86 US cities, including Honolulu, New Orleans, and Pittsburgh, does not matter. One would also have to argue that the loss of 20 million American lives is inconsequential. Such a position is untenable.

After all, since 9/11, US officials have gone to great lengths to prevent even a single US city from being destroyed in a nuclear terror attack. If New Orleans, for example, were to be destroyed in a nuclear attack today, it would be considered the worst attack on American soil in US history. If US officials knew of an imminent attack on the Big Easy, they would go to great lengths to prevent it and, if they failed to do so, they would face intense political accrimination. It defies common sense, therefore, to maintain that America's leaders would be indifferent to the loss of New Orleans *and* 85 other cities in a much larger nuclear catastrophe.

To the common question of why we should be concerned about increases in Russian or Chinese nuclear arsenal size given that they already possess a large nuclear force, therefore, the answer is simple: dozens of US cities and millions of American lives are potentially at stake.

Second Strike Analysis

Next, we simulate a nuclear exchange between the United States and its adversaries that begins with a US counterforce strike. This section again demonstrates that the nuclear balance of power between Washington and its rivals greatly affects the expected costs of nuclear war. Indeed, this effect is even more noticeable when the United States is able to conduct the initial nuclear strike. In addition, therefore, this section demonstrates the value of a robust nuclear posture; the damage the United States would suffer in the event of nuclear war is much less if it possesses a strategy and posture that permits it to conduct a damage-limiting first strike that blunts its adversary's nuclear capability.

We begin with an analysis of a US–Russia nuclear exchange. A US counterforce nuclear strike on Russia would seek to destroy Russia's ICBM silos and strategic air and sea bases. The United States would target Russia's 140 ICBM silos. These are known, fixed targets and are, therefore, vulnerable to US attack. Moscow possesses another 171 land-based mobile missiles, based in shelters in 40 garrisons.[43] The garrisons are also fixed targets and, therefore, vulnerable to a first strike. When the missiles are on patrol, conducing exercises, or if they are alerted and dispersed from garrison in the event of a crisis, they cover a large patrol territory and are difficult to target. Normally, however, the missiles are in garrison. Patrols are generally conducted one regiment (consisting of nine launchers) at a time.[44] Moreover, Austin Long and Brendan Green argue that the United States has a number of tools at its disposal to track and target mobile missiles. They are still extremely difficult targets when on the move, but not completely invulnerable.[45]

Next, Russia possesses nine nuclear submarines stationed at two major submarine bases, the Northern Fleet is headquartered at Yagelnaya Bay on the Kola Peninsula and the Pacific Fleet is based at Rybachiy.[46] The bases are fixed and relatively easy targets. It is not possible for Russia to have all nine boats at sea. Generally, at least one boat per fleet is in dry dock and another is undergoing longer-term maintenance, which leaves five boats.[47] In normal times, Russia does not have any of its submarines on deterrence patrol. Rather, it has adopted a "dock-alert" system in which it keeps its submarines in port at all times, making them vulnerable to a first strike.[48] In the event of an escalating crisis with the United States, however, these forces could be dispersed from their bases. Tracking and targeting submarines on patrol at sea can be a difficult task. Like mobile missiles, submarines are designed to be a survivable leg. As Long and Green point out, however, US antisubmarine warfare capabilities are quite sophisticated and Washington had some success in hunting Russian nuclear submarines during the Cold War.[49] Like mobile missiles, therefore, these are difficult targets, but not completely invulnerable.

As mentioned previously, Russia possesses roughly sixty deployed strategic bombers.[50] Nearly all of these bombers are based at Russia's two strategic bomber bases at Engels and Ukrainka. Others may be found at the Ryazan training base, the Kazan production plant, or the Zhukovsky design plant. Finally, another half dozen or so might be on training flights or temporarily at one of Russia's fifty-four other air bases. Russia's fixed air bases are vulnerable targets. Any Russian bombers in the air and out of range of the blast and other effects at the time of a US attack would likely survive.

Finally, I assume that the United States would target roughly 150 other command and control and early warning sites, nuclear weapons production and storage facilities, and conventional bases.[51]

To conduct a counterforce strike on Russia, the United States, as of 2015, possessed 2,072 nuclear warheads on ballistic missiles and bomber bases. This force consists of: 440 ICBMs; 1,152 warheads on SLBMs; 200 nuclear ALCMs; and 280 nuclear gravity bombs.[52] Not all of these forces, however, would be available for a first strike. In normal conditions, 95% of the ICBM force is ready to launch.[53] The United States generally has 8–10 of its 14 nuclear submarines at sea at any one time.[54] None of the bomber force is on alert for nuclear operations, but a large portion of the force could be alerted quickly if necessary.[55]

To assign weapons to targets and estimate the likely effects, I draw heavily on Lieber and Press's analysis, which is the most detailed, open-source estimate of a US nuclear first strike in the recent academic literature.[56] (As we see later, however, I differ with Lieber and Press on one important assumption, which leads to an important difference in the final analysis). By assigning stealthy and fast-arriving nuclear forces (such as stealth bombers and ALCMs) to Russia's early warning and command and control systems, Washington could blind Moscow and greatly complicate Russia's ability to launch on warning, or quickly retaliate with a large portion of its strategic nuclear force.[57] Second, Washington can assign other fast-arriving weapons (like SLBMs and ICBMs) to the Russian forces capable of responding most quickly (such as ICBMs, submarine bases, and mobile missile garrisons) to increase the effectiveness of the first strike and save slower-arriving weapons (such as bombers) for follow-on strikes and for targets incapable of retaliating directly, such as nuclear weapons storage and production areas. Finally, by assigning multiple warheads to each aim point, Washington can greatly increase the probability that it kills the intended target. As previously, therefore, I allocate three warheads to Russia's strategic offensive nuclear capabilities and two warheads each to other counterforce targets.

Employing similar targeting principals and assuming that Russia does not have any mobile forces on patrol or on alert, Lieber and Press maintain that a splendid first strike in which the United States completely destroys Russia's retaliatory nuclear force is achievable.[58] They are correct that Russia's fixed targets, such as ballistic missile silos and bases, would be destroyed with high probability in a US nuclear first strike. Their assumption that Russia's mobile legs can be fully neutralized, however, is quite optimistic and has been questioned by several analysts.[59] I relax this assumption, therefore, and assume that one regiment of Topol-M mobile ICBMs and one Sineva SSBN survive the initial US strike. This surviving force includes nine 800-kiloton warheads from the Topol-M unit and 64 MIRVd 100-kiloton warheads on 16 launchers in the SSBN.

Since a US first strike has already taken place, much of America's nuclear forces do not remain to be targeted in a Russian reprisal. Rather than aim warheads at empty ballistic missile silos, therefore, I assume that Russia uses its remaining nuclear forces to attack America's strategic submarine bases, airbases, and command and control nodes. It then employs the remaining 30 warheads, two apiece, for a countervalue strike against the 15 largest cities in the continental United States from New York to Columbus, Ohio.

Since this scenario begins with a US counterforce attack and a damage limitation goal in mind, I assume Washington is prepared to intercept incoming missiles with its homeland ballistic missile defense system. At the time of the study, the United States deployed 30 interceptors in Fort Greely, Alaska, and Vandenberg, California.[60] Open-source data indicates that, in the heat of conflict, the interceptors may have approximately a 25% success rate.[61] Employing this figure, I assume that the United States is able to destroy 7 incoming warheads, but the remaining 66 penetrate and reach their intended target.

China presents a more manageable set of nuclear targets. Because China does not employ bombers for the nuclear mission and its sea-based leg is not yet conducting deterrence patrols, an attacker need only focus on China's ICBM missile force. As discussed previously, this includes 20 silo-based DF-5s and 25 mobile DF-31As, divided into three brigades.[62] Washington would also want to destroy an estimated 75 command and control, early warning, missile training and testing facilities, and nuclear weapons production and storage sites, including the plutonium production plants at Jiuquan and Guangyuan, and the uranium gaseous diffusion plant at Lanzhou, and the Lop Nur nuclear test site.[63]

To conduct the attack, the United States possesses over 2,000 nuclear warheads spread across its strategic triad. Employing the same targeting principles as above, I allocate three warheads to each of China's fixed ballistic missile silos. I also target each of the 75 related, command and control, missile, and nuclear facilities with two warheads apiece.

This leaves approximately 1,700 US warheads to potentially be used to target China's 25 mobile missiles. China's ICBMs are divided into three brigades.[64] Each base consists of a central launch control facility, multiple garrisons, rail transfer points, and launch pads. It is possible to identify the launch control facilities and garrisons, using commercial satellite imagery.[65] These facilities are hardened, but, like any fixed target, it is possible to destroy them with an accurate ground-burst detonation and a warhead of sufficient yield. The United States could also target any launch pads it is able to identify. Washington also has, as discussed above, a number of methods at its disposal for tracking and targeting mobile missiles.[66] Further complicating China's ability to absorb a strike and conduct a retaliatory strike is that the missiles, even those on patrol, are not believed to be uploaded with nuclear warheads in normal circumstances. Moreover, it is believed that they are not stored in garrison but rather in several central depots. This means that in the event of a crisis, the warheads would have to be transferred to garrison and then uploaded onto missiles, which would then be sent on deterrence patrol, further complicating China's ability to retaliate with these forces.

Given these realities, it is possible that a US counterforce strike on China's nuclear forces at present could succeed in disarming China's entire ICBM force. As one of China's leading nuclear analysts, Li Bin, writes, "Even with such conservative assumptions, it would appear that the United States has the capability to destroy all twenty DF-31-like mobile missiles if their locations at the start of the war were known."[67] If the United States can succeed in a disarming first strike against China, then it can completely limit damage to itself in the event of nuclear war.

In an abundance of caution and assuring any bias works against the central hypothesis under investigation, let us assume that one-third of the ballistic missile force (seven missiles) survives the initial US counterforce strike and is employed in a countervalue reprisal against the United States. As above, the US homeland ballistic missile defense system will attempt to intercept these missiles and will enjoy a 25% success rate. Since the DF-31A is not thought to be able to range the entirety of the United States, the five remaining missiles are targeted against cities on the West Coast.[68]

As we saw earlier, North Korea lacks the ability to deliver nuclear weapons to the United States. This situation does not change in a US first-strike scenario. A North Korean nuclear second strike on the US homeland, therefore, looks exactly like a North Korea first strike.

Second-Strike Results

What is the expected damage to the US homeland in a nuclear exchange with Russia, China, and North Korea, when the United States is able to strike the first blow? The results are displayed in Table 2.1 and in Figures 2.5, 2.6, and 2.7. Beginning with a Russian second strike, we can see that the United States would lose its strategic air and naval bases, and a dozen of its largest cities would be devastated. It would suffer upward of 28 million casualties.

Once again, even after a US first strike, a Chinese nuclear reprisal on the United States would be catastrophic, but less devastating than Russian retaliation. As we can see, a Chinese nuclear second strike, in this scenario, would destroy parts of Los Angeles, San Diego, San Jose, San Francisco, and Seattle and kill approximately 8 million people. But the rest of the country would escape direct nuclear attack. And, in 2006, before China expanded its nuclear forces, the United States likely enjoyed a splendid first-strike capability against China (not shown).

As seen earlier, North Korea's fledgling nuclear posture prohibits it from inflicting any measureable damage to the US homeland.

These findings provide strong support for the superiority-brinkmanship synthesis theory. Once again, we find that the nuclear balance of power matters for nuclear war outcomes. Even in a second-strike scenario, Washington's expected damage in a nuclear war depends on the nuclear capabilities of its adversary. The larger an adversary's nuclear force, the more devastation it can inflict on the United States. As in the first-strike scenario, a second strike from Russia would be most damaging, followed by China, and then North Korea.

Figure 2.5 Nuclear exchange simulation results, Russia second strike on the United States.

Figure 2.6 Nuclear exchange simulation results, China second strike on the
United States.

Figure 2.7 Nuclear exchange simulation results, North Korea second strike on the
United States.

Moreover, this set of tests provides additional support for the central argument of this book by demonstrating concretely that a robust nuclear posture
reduces the expected damage of nuclear war. Holding adversary capabilities
constant, the costs of nuclear war to the US homeland will be much less if the
United States is able to initiate the exchange with a counterforce strike. In a
Russian first strike, as we saw above, the United States is expected to lose 131
cities and 70 million people. If, however, the United States is able to strike the
first blow, America's expected losses drop to 12 cities and 28 million casualties.

The corresponding numbers for Chinese nuclear attacks are 45 cities and 48 million casualties in a first strike and 5 cities and roughly 8 million casualties in a second strike. Whether simulating a nuclear exchange with Russia or China, the outcome is less devastating if the United States is able to strike first, demonstrating the importance of US nuclear counterforce capabilities and strategy.

Once again, the secure, second-strike hypothesis does not find support. Even though Russia and China are both widely thought to possess secure, second-strike capabilities, their ability to hold the US homeland at risk in a retaliatory strike varies greatly. Not all second-strike capabilities are created equal. To conclude otherwise, one would have to maintain that it does not matter whether 7 major US cities are destroyed or whether up to 20 million Americans live or die.

Moreover, the assured retaliation school dismisses the importance of counterforce targeting. But the difference between a Russian first strike and a Russian second strike on the US homeland is 119 US cities and over 40 million US casualties. The equivalent difference in numbers for Chinese first and second strikes are 40 cities and 43 million lives. If one believes that the potential nuclear destruction of tens of cities and tens of millions of US citizens is germane to international politics, then the second-strike theory does not find support.

US Deep Reductions Analysis

To this point, we have held US nuclear forces constant while varying the capabilities of the adversary. The next step will be to hold constant adversary forces, while varying US nuclear posture. Many national security analysts advocate that the United States make deep reductions to the size of its nuclear arsenal.[69] They argue that such cuts would not harm US security because Washington would still maintain a formidable nuclear arsenal and a secure, second-strike capability. This section tests this argument. It analyzes both a Russian nuclear first and second strike in a situation in which Washington has reduced the size of its nuclear arsenal. In both scenarios, it finds that deep reductions to the US nuclear force greatly increase the expected cost of nuclear war for the United States.

To design a reduced US nuclear force, I follow the recommendations of the Global Zero US Nuclear Policy Commission Report, chaired by retired general and former commander of US Strategic Command, James Cartwright.[70] The report calls for the United States to eliminate its ICBM force and reduce the nuclear arsenal to 450 strategic, deployed warheads, with 360 warheads on SLBMs and 90 B-61 gravity bombs on B-2 bombers.[71] The report argues that if Russia is unwilling to make similar reductions, the changes to US posture could be "implemented unilaterally."[72] To isolate the effects of changes to US posture,

I therefore hold adversary forces constant and assume that Russian forces remain as they were in 2015.

To model a Russian first strike, I follow the targeting guidelines outlined earlier. The major change in this scenario is that the number of counterforce targets Russia needs to cover will be greatly reduced because Washington has eliminated 440 ballistic missile silos. For a successful counterforce mission, therefore, Russia can badly degrade, but not completely eliminate, the US nuclear deterrent by targeting two strategic submarine bases and three strategic air bases. Were Russia to conduct such an attack, Washington would be left with only nuclear submarines on patrol and bombers in the air or temporarily stationed at other bases. Most importantly, Russia would no longer need to allocate a large portion of its warheads to targeting hardened ballistic missile silos. With 440 aim points eliminated, at three warheads per aim point, 1,320 Russian nuclear warheads would be liberated to hit other targets or to be held in reserve. Indeed, one of the greatest benefits of the ICBM force is to serve as a "warhead sink" that will absorb a large portion of an adversary's nuclear arsenal in the event of nuclear war.[73]

With fewer counterforce targets to cover and following the Russian targeting guidelines outlined above, I assume that Russia uses the spare 1,320 warheads for countervalue strikes against American cities to inflict massive devastation. At two warheads per city, this allows Russia to cover an additional 660 cities and towns above and beyond the 131 cities targeted above.

Next, we turn to a US nuclear counterforce strike on Russia after deep US reductions The major difference from the earlier test is that Washington now has fewer warheads with which to conduct its initial counterforce strike. It is not possible for the United States to cover the full range of counterforce targets in Russia with a high probability of success. Indeed, some US strategists have argued that if the United States were to drop below 1,000 warheads, then the United States could no longer maintain a serious counterforce strategy and would instead need to switch to a pure countervalue targeting strategy.[74]

If we assume that the United States follows such advice and switches to a countervalue strategy, then it would not be able to blunt any of Russia's strategic nuclear forces. In such a scenario, there would little difference between a Russian second strike with a deeply reduced US nuclear force and the Russian first strike displayed in Figure 2.1.

To isolate the effects of a change to arsenal size and to avoid introducing other sources of variation, let us assume that Washington sticks with its counterforce strategy even with a greatly reduced arsenal. This could be done in order to maintain the Law of War principles of distinction and proportionality in its nuclear targeting practices. In this case, US planners would have to make difficult decisions about whether to select fewer aim points, or whether to assign fewer warheads to each aim point and, therefore, accept a lower probability that each target is killed.

I assume that planners would want to destroy the most important fixed targets with a high degree of certainty. I, therefore, assign the 450 warheads as follows: 3 warheads each to 140 Russian ICBM silos, 2 strategic naval bases, and 2 strategic airbases; and 2 warheads each to the 9 most important command and control and early warning sites. This means that the United States is unable to target the mobile missile force, the minor airfields, and a large number of command and control and nuclear weapons production and storage facilities.

In this scenario, more of Russia's nuclear arsenal survives, including Russia's entire mobile ICBM force. This includes 333 warheads on 171 missiles. Since the United States cannot target all of Russia's minor airbases, the half dozen or so Russian strategic bombers on training flights or temporarily at other bases survive. Each is armed with between 6 and 16 ALCMs. As in the previous Russia second-strike scenario, I assume that one nuclear submarine flushes to sea, armed with its 64 MIRVd 100-kiloton warheads. In sum, I estimate that 469 Russian strategic warheads would remain after a US first strike conducted with a reduced US arsenal.

Employing the same targeting plans as above for a Russian second-strike and calculating the same success rate for US homeland ballistic missile defenses, Russia would be able to carry out a counterforce strike on remaining US strategic assets and retain enough warheads to allocate two apiece in a counter value mission against the United States' largest 211 cities.

US Deep Reductions Results

What are the effects of a reduced US nuclear posture for the expected damage to the US homeland in the event of nuclear war? The results are presented in Table 2.1 and Figures 2.8 and 2.9. As we can see, in a Russian first strike on a United States with a reduced nuclear posture, America's 791 largest urban areas, every city with a population of at least 50,000 inhabitants, would be destroyed. The list of targeted cities would include Niagara Falls, New York; Caldwell City, Idaho; and Joplin, Missouri. The number of casualties would exceed 125 million people.

This is the most devastating scenario considered in the chapter. Shifting the nuclear balance of power by reducing the US nuclear force and holding Russian forces and targeting strategy constant, shifts the expected cost of a Russian nuclear first strike on the United States from 131 to 791 urban areas destroyed and from 70 million to over 125 million US casualties. With fewer US nuclear forces to hold at risk, Moscow is freed up to allocate a greater number of its nuclear forces to countervalue targets, increasing the expected damage to the United States.

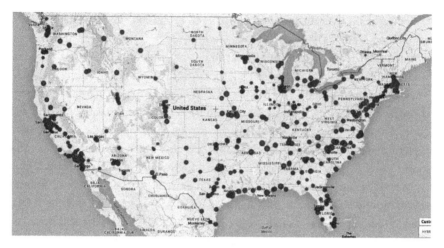

Figure 2.8 Nuclear exchange simulation results, Russia first strike on the United States after US deep reductions.

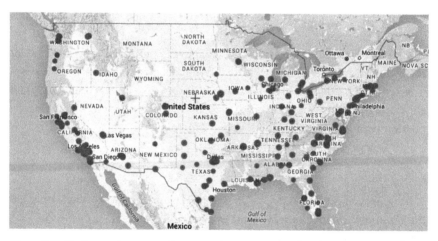

Figure 2.9 Nuclear exchange simulation results, Russia second strike on the United States after US deep reductions.

We see a similar pattern with regard to a Russian second strike on the US homeland. By reducing the size of the US nuclear arsenal, the United States has fewer warheads with which to conduct a counterforce strike, allowing more Russian warheads to survive and, ultimately, be used to counterattack the United States. In this scenario, visualized in Figure 2.9, the rest of America's strategic capabilities would be destroyed along with its 211 largest urban areas. Casualties from such a strike would number approximately 82 million people. The cost of unilaterally cutting the size of the US nuclear arsenal, therefore, would be to increase the number of Russian warheads that can reach the United States, following a US first strike, from 66 to 469. The expected damage to the United States would increase from 12 to 211 destroyed urban areas and from 28 to 82 million US casualties.

These results again provide strong support for the central argument of this book. Tilting the nuclear balance of power away from the United States, by reducing the size of the US nuclear arsenal in this case, drastically increases the expected cost of nuclear war to the United States.

Once again, this analysis does not provide support for the second-strike hypothesis. By shifting from a position of rough parity with Russia into a position of clear inferiority, the United States makes itself more vulnerable to a nuclear exchange, even as it retains a secure second-strike capability. Regardless of whether Russia strikes first or second, the expected damage to the US homeland greatly increases if the United States reduces the size of its nuclear arsenal. In order to defend the second-strike hypothesis, one would have to stubbornly maintain that whether hundreds of US cities are destroyed and tens of millions of American live or die is immaterial.

Conclusion

This chapter analyzed the effect of the nuclear balance of power on nuclear war outcomes. It found that the nuclear balance of power between the United States and its adversaries affected the expected damage that the US homeland would suffer in the event of a nuclear war. Increases in adversary nuclear forces and decreases in US nuclear forces, both changes that tilt the nuclear balance of power away from Washington, were shown to directly increase the expected cost of nuclear war for the United States. This relationship was demonstrated in a number of nuclear exchange simulations that considered variations in adversary nuclear posture, US nuclear posture, and attack sequencing. Moreover, variations in nuclear war outcomes were far from trivial across scenarios. Rather, the differences were counted in dozens of cities destroyed and millions of lives lost. The results of this chapter, therefore, provide strong support for the central argument of this book. The nuclear balance of power matters for nuclear war outcomes.

The alternative explanation, which holds that variations in the nuclear balance of power do not matter, especially when both sides possess a secure, second-strike capability, did not find support. Each and every test found significant differences in the expected cost of nuclear war that hinged directly on the nuclear balance of power between the United States and its adversaries. At present, both Russia and China are thought to possess an assured retaliatory capability, but in test after test, the expected costs of nuclear war involving Russia's larger nuclear forces proved more devastating. Moreover, in direct contrast to the claims of second-strike theory, US nuclear arsenal size and counterforce targeting also greatly affected the expected cost of nuclear war.

Reframing the discussion from one of dependent variables to US national security interests, this chapter demonstrates an important reason why the United States sustains a robust nuclear posture. If, heaven forbid, a nuclear war were to occur, US nuclear superiority can save millions of American lives. To those who ask why the United States cannot afford to make deep cuts to its large nuclear arsenal, there are many answers, but one is quite simple: for every nuclear weapon cut, many American lives could be lost. These are lives that could have been saved if the United States had simply retained a more robust nuclear force. To those who question why we worry when adversaries build up their nuclear forces or cheat on arms control agreements, the answer is the same.

At this point, readers may grant that the nuclear balance of power matters for nuclear war, but they may be skeptical that it affects nuclear deterrence or other aspects of geopolitics. After all, they might claim, since these nuclear war scenarios are all so terrible, politicians might not make distinctions between horrific nuclear nightmares and those that are even worse. For this reason, politicians will do all they can to avoid any nuclear war and none of these scenarios will ever come to pass. This chapter, they may charge, was an interesting intellectual exercise, but these nuclear calculations have little influence on the day-to-day events that we actually witness.

This objection is plausible, but the counterargument may be even more compelling. In setting nuclear deterrence policy and especially when confronted with high-stakes nuclear crises, leaders are forced to come face-to-face with nuclear disaster. It would, therefore, seem intuitive that the actions taken during nuclear crises are tightly linked with nuclear war outcomes that lie just over the brink. And the factors that matter for the latter should also influence the former.

This is not a debate, however, that can be definitively settled in the theoretical realm. To some degree, what we have is a series of empirical questions about how variation in state vulnerability to nuclear war affects nuclear politics. Perhaps the most obvious place to look for a relationship, therefore, is just one step back from the brink of nuclear catastrophe. Does the nuclear balance of power affect nuclear crisis outcomes? It is to this issue that we turn in the next chapter.

The Correlates of Nuclear
Crisis Outcomes

Does the nuclear balance of power matter for nuclear coercion? The previous chapter showed that the nuclear balance of power affects the expected cost of nuclear war, but does a military nuclear advantage also translate into a bargaining advantage? To answer these questions, this chapter conducts a large-N statistical analysis, examining empirical evidence from high-stakes crises between nuclear-armed states. If the superiority-brinkmanship synthesis theory is correct, we should expect that nuclear superior states will be more likely than inferior states to achieve their basic goals in international crises. If not, we should expect to find that the nuclear balance of power has no bearing on crisis outcomes and that, rather, bargaining dynamics are driven exclusively by other factors, such as second-strike capabilities and political stakes.

Drawing on a quantitative analysis of a data set of fifty-two nuclear crisis dyads that includes information on nuclear arsenal size and delivery vehicles, I examine the impact of nuclear superiority on nuclear crisis outcomes.[1] I find a powerful relationship between nuclear superiority and victory in nuclear crises. Specifically, nuclear superior states are over ten times more likely than nuclear inferior states to achieve their basic goals in international crises. These findings hold even after controlling for second-strike capabilities, political stakes, conventional military capabilities, and selection into nuclear crises. In addition, the results are robust to the exclusion of each individual crisis and even to the exclusion of each individual country, alleviating concerns that the intermediate population size might render the results sensitive to coding or modeling decisions.

In sum, this chapter provides strong empirical support for the central argument of this book. Nuclear superiority matters not just for nuclear war outcomes but also in international crises between nuclear-armed adversaries. The remainder of the chapter continues in three parts. First, it details the data set employed in the quantitative analysis. Next, it turns to an analysis of the results of the statistical study. Finally, it concludes with a summary of the key findings and their implications for the hypotheses explored in this book.

Nuclear Crisis Data

To examine the outcomes of nuclear crises, I constructed an original nuclear crisis data set, drawing from the list of international crises prepared by the International Crisis Behavior Project (ICB). The data set contains information on the outcomes of nuclear crises, nuclear arsenal size, and the balance of political stakes from 1945 to 2001.[2] According to the ICB, a crisis is an interstate dispute that threatens at least one state's values, has a heightened probability of military escalation, and has a finite time frame for resolution.[3] A nuclear crisis is defined as a crisis in which both states in the crisis possess nuclear weapons.[4] As stated previously, a nuclear crisis can occur whether or not nuclear weapons are used, are explicitly threatened, or are the disputed issue in the crisis. I do not include crises in which only one actor in the conflict possesses nuclear weapons because this study focuses on the outcomes of crises between nuclear-armed states.[5] The unit of analysis is the dyad crisis, following past research on international crises.[6] This is the appropriate unit of analysis because a number of central variables in the analysis, such as the balance of political stakes and nuclear superiority, can only be measured at the dyadic level. I use directed dyads because the dependent variable, nuclear crisis outcomes, varies for each state in the crisis dyad.[7] I follow a standard practice of pairing states together in a crisis dyad only if one state "perceives that the other state has directed a threatening or hostile action against it."[8] Using these coding rules, I identify fifty-two nuclear crisis dyads involved in twenty unique nuclear crises from 1945 to 2001.[9] Examples of the nuclear crises contained in this data set include: the Cuban Missile Crisis between the United States and the Soviet Union in 1962, the Sino-Soviet Border War of 1969, and the Kargil Crisis between India and Pakistan in 1999. A list of all the nuclear crises contained in the data set is available in Table 3.1.

The nuclear crises listed in Table 3.1 exhibit varying degrees of escalation, but all are properly included in a study of nuclear crisis outcomes. Some crises, such as the Cuban Missile Crisis, escalated to a high level, while others ended relatively quickly. It would be unwise, however, to select crises for study based on their level of escalation, such as excluding crises that did not reach significantly high levels of violence. After all, each of the cases included in the study meets ICB's definition of an international crisis as described earlier. Moreover, as explained in chapter 1, scholars have long maintained that nuclear weapons are an ever-present factor lurking in the background of political conflicts

Table 3.1 **Nuclear Crises, 1945–2001**

Crisis Name	Year	Nuclear-Armed Participants
Korean War	1950	Soviet Union, United States
Suez Crisis	1956	Great Britain, Soviet Union,* United States*
Berlin Deadline	1958	Great Britain, Soviet Union, United States
Berlin Wall	1961	France, Great Britain, Soviet Union,* United States
Cuban Missile Crisis	1962	Soviet Union, United States*
Congo Crisis	1964	Soviet Union, United States*
Six-Day War	1967	Israel,* Soviet Union, United States*
Sino-Soviet Border War	1969	China, Soviet Union*
War of Attrition	1970	Israel, Soviet Union
Cienfuegos Submarine Base	1970	Soviet Union, United States*
Yom Kippur War	1973	Israel, Soviet Union, United States*
War in Angola	1975	Soviet Union,* United States
Afghanistan Invasion	1979	Soviet Union,* United States
Able Archer Exercise	1983	Soviet Union, United States
Nicaragua, MIG-21S	1984	Soviet Union, United States
Kashmir	1990	India, Pakistan
Taiwan Strait Crisis	1995	China, United States*
India/Pakistan Nuclear Tests	1998	India, Pakistan
Kargil Crisis	1999	India,* Pakistan
India Parliament Attack	2001	India,* Pakistan

Note: A state's victory in a crisis is denoted by an asterisk. Not all crises have victors, and some crises have multiple victors. For a list of when countries acquired nuclear weapons, see Kroenig and Gartzke, "A Strategic Approach to Nuclear Proliferation."

between nuclear-armed states. They can shape bargaining dynamics whether or not states actually engage in direct armed-conflict or explicitly threaten nuclear use. In addition, the nuclear brinkmanship framework examined here explicitly requires nuclear crises to exhibit varying levels of escalation. In some crises, states will be willing to push hard in order to achieve their goals, but in others they will look down the game tree, assess that they will be unlikely to prevail, and immediately decide to submit. In sum, crises between nuclear powers, regardless of their level of escalation, occur within a nuclear brinkmanship framework and provide an appropriate test of the hypotheses advanced earlier.

The binary dependent variable is *Outcome*. It measures whether a country achieves victory in a nuclear crisis. The variable is drawn from an ICB variable that measures whether the outcome of a crisis for each actor is victory, compromise, stalemate, or defeat. Following past research on crisis outcomes, I dichotomize this variable to code whether or not a state achieves victory in a crisis.[10] A victory is defined as a crisis in which an actor achieves its "basic goals."[11] A loss is recorded if the crisis ends in compromise, stalemate, or outright defeat.[12] For example, the United States is coded as winning the Cuban Missile Crisis because it achieved its basic goal of forcing the Soviet Union to withdrawal its missiles from Cuba. The Soviet Union is coded as losing the Cuban Missile Crisis because it was unable to achieve its basic goal of maintaining its missiles in Cuba.[13] Multiple states achieve their basic goals in some crises, while many other crises do not produce a clear victor. A victory is recorded in eighteen of the fifty-two nuclear crisis dyads. Information on the winners of nuclear crises is also available in Table 3.1.[14]

I construct independent variables to test the hypotheses explicated previously. *Superiority* measures whether a state enjoys nuclear superiority over its opponent in a crisis. To begin the construction of this variable, I gathered detailed information on the size of nuclear arsenals in each nuclear weapon state in every year from 1945 to 2001. An online data appendix provides information on the coding rules and sources used to calculate nuclear arsenal sizes.[15] The size of nuclear arsenals ranges from a low of zero (France from 1960 to 1963) to a high of 40,723 (the Soviet Union in 1986).[16] Using this information, I code a binary variable to indicate whether a country had more nuclear weapons than its opponent in each crisis.

To examine whether states enjoyed greater levels of nuclear superiority over their opponents, I created *Nuclear ratio. Nuclear ratio* is calculated as the number of nuclear weapons possessed by State A divided by the total number of nuclear weapons in the arsenals of State A and State B combined. The theoretical and empirical range of the variable is from 0 to 1.

These are admittedly basic measures, but as explained in Chapter One and demonstrated in Chapter Two, simple warhead counts provide a fairly accurate assessment of the nuclear balance of power and the expected costs of nuclear war. Moreover, they go beyond the existing quantitative literature on nuclear weapons, which codes nuclear possession as a dichotomous variable, "1" if a country possesses nuclear weapons and "0" if it does not.[17] In addition, a more detailed quantitative measure of the nuclear balance of power does not exist for every nuclear power in every year from 1945 to the present and it is hard to imagine what form such a measure might take. Finally, even more detailed qualitative assessments of the nuclear balance of power almost always produce the same results as a simple warhead count. Russia enjoys a clear superiority over China, Britain, France, and Israel. The United States possesses a military nuclear advantage over China and North Korea. China enjoys superiority over India and so on. Indeed, the only cases for which a simple warhead count may or may not accurately reflect the nuclear balance of power are the United States and the Soviet Union after 1978 when Moscow possessed more warheads, but Washington arguably had a qualitative advantage, and India and Pakistan in recent years when the nuclear balance was simply unclear. The robustness of the quantitative results will be tested to the exclusion of these two sets cases. In addition, more fine-grained qualitative assessments will be offered in the case studies. For the purposes of this chapter, however, a simple warhead count provides a more than suitable measure of the nuclear balance of power.

I also created a number of variables to test the alternative hypotheses presented in chapter 1. To examine the second-strike hypothesis, I include *2nd strike*, a dichotomous variable that gauges whether a state possesses submarine-launched ballistic missiles (SLBMs) or mobile missiles or maintains nuclear-armed aircraft on continuous airborne alert.[18] These types of forces are especially likely to survive an opponent's first strike and virtually guarantee their possessors with an assured second-strike capability.[19] The online data appendix provides information on the coding rules and sources used to calculate whether a country possesses a second-strike capability.[20]

All of these various measures of nuclear capabilities also allow me to test the nuclear irrelevance hypothesis. If nuclear weapons do not matter for nuclear coercion, then we should not expect any of these variables to be correlated with improved crisis outcomes.

The second-strike hypothesis also maintains that political stakes, not the nuclear balance of power, determines crisis outcomes. To account for the effects of political stakes, I include a number of control variables. We may expect that states will have a greater stake in a crisis that occurs nearer to their homeland than one that takes place in a distant geographic region.[21] Scholars argue, for example, that future nuclear confrontations between the United States and regional adversaries will necessarily disadvantage Washington because geographical proximity will tip the balance of stakes in the regional adversary's favor.[22] Indeed, analysts often use the language of geography, such as core versus peripheral interests, to describe a state's stake in a crisis. *Proximity* is a binary variable, which measures whether the geographic location of the crisis is closer to State A than it is to State B.[23] For example, in the Cuban Missile Crisis, the United States is coded "1" and the Soviet Union is coded "0" because Cuba is closer to the United States than to Russia. For nuclear crises between countries that share a common border, such as the nuclear crises between India and

Pakistan, this variable is scored "0" because geographical factors did not clearly favor either side.[24]

I also include an alternate measure of political stakes, which gauges the relative gravity of the crisis for the involved actors. *Gravity* draws on ICB data that codes the gravity of a crisis for each actor from 0 (economic threat) to 6 (a threat to national existence).[25] A state is coded as "1" if a crisis is more severe for itself than it is for its opponent.[26] For example, the Yom Kippur War of 1973 is coded as a 5 for Israel (threat of grave damage), and 4 for the Soviet Union (threat to influence). In this case, the balance of stakes favored Israel; Israel was coded "1" and the Soviet Union "0."[27]

To test the regional nuclear powers hypothesis, I included a dichotomous variable that assesses whether a country possesses an "asymmetric escalation" posture. Narang does not explicitly argue that these postures shape crisis outcomes, but he does maintain that they contribute to deterrence.[28] It is not much of a logical leap, therefore, for one to hypothesize that they might also aid in coercion.

Consistent with the conventional military power hypothesis, we may expect states that enjoy conventional military superiority over opponents to be more likely to prevail in nuclear crises. On the other hand, conventional military superiority might not be particularly relevant in a crisis among nuclear powers. To control for this factor, I generate *Capabilities*. I employ a power ratio variable that assesses the capabilities of State A divided by the total combined capabilities of both State A and State B.[29] Capability is a composite index containing information on total population, urban population, energy consumption, iron and steel production, military manpower, and military expenditures.[30]

As noted in chapter 1, other scholars have argued that democracies are more likely to win crises because they select into crises they are more likely to win and because domestic audience costs enable them to make more credible commitments.[31] To assess the effect of domestic regime type on the outcomes of nuclear crises, I include *Regime*. I use Polity scores, which range from −10 (most autocratic) to + 10 (most democratic), from the Polity IV data set.[32]

I also include a number of additional control variables.[33] We may expect that states with larger populations are better able to absorb a nuclear attack and, therefore, may push harder in a crisis.[34] If one US city were completely destroyed in a nuclear attack, for example, much of the country would remain intact. One nuclear explosion in a small country such as Israel, however, could very well threaten the state's existence. *Population* measures the size of a state's total population, drawing on data from version 3.02 of the Correlates of War data set and extracted using EUGene.[35]

Crises that exhibit high levels of violence may be more likely to produce a clear winner. To control for the use of force in a crisis, I include *Violence*. The

4-point ordinal variable is drawn from the ICB data and measures the level of violence in a crisis and ranges from 1 (no violence) to 4 (full-scale war).

Finally, we may expect countries that exist in competitive security environments to be less likely to win nuclear crises, as each crisis may be the manifestation of an underlying and intractable dispute.[36] To control for a state's security environment, I generate *Security*. Following Beardsley and Asal, I calculate the average number of crises that a state experiences each year.[37]

Empirical Analysis

I begin by analyzing cross-tabulations of nuclear superiority and nuclear crisis outcomes. The results, presented in Table 3.2, demonstrate that states are unlikely to achieve victory in nuclear crises. States have achieved a clear victory in only 35% of nuclear crises. In the other 65% of cases, nuclear crisis participants lost; they were unable to achieve their basic goals and instead experienced compromise, stalemate, or defeat.

The table also shows, however, that the possession of nuclear superiority greatly improves a state's chances of victory in nuclear crises. States that enjoy nuclear superiority over their opponent have won 54% of the nuclear crises in which they have been involved, compared to only 15% for countries in a position of nuclear inferiority, and 35% for all crises participants. In fact, 14 of 18, or 78%, of all nuclear crisis winners possessed nuclear superiority over their opponents. A chi-square test demonstrates that the probability of observing this difference between nuclear superior and nuclear inferior states, if nuclear superiority has no bearing on crisis outcomes, is 0.004. This test permits me to reject the null hypothesis that there is no relationship between nuclear superiority and nuclear crisis outcomes. In sum, cross-tabulations demonstrate that states with larger nuclear arsenals are more likely to win nuclear crises.

Table 3.2 **Cross-Tabulations of Nuclear Crisis Outcomes, 1945–2001**

		Outcome		
		Win	*Loss*	*Total*
Superiority	Yes	14 (54%)	12 (46%)	26 (100%)
	No	4 (15%)	22 (85%)	26 (100%)
	Total	18 (35%)	34 (65%)	52 (100%)
	$X^2 = 8.497$ ($p = 0.004$)			

While the nuclear crisis participant is the most appropriate unit of analysis for this study, one could focus on the crisis itself to examine how many crises were won by the country in the crisis with the most nuclear weapons. This exercise produces similar results. Of the twenty nuclear crises, 55% included a winner with the most weapons in the crisis, only 10% had a winner that did not possess the most warheads, and 35% did not produce a clear winner (not shown in the tables).[38]

Next, I turn to the results of the regression analysis. I employ probit models to test claims about the correlates of nuclear crisis outcomes.[39] Robust standard errors are adjusted for clustering by crisis dyad to correct for interdependence of observations.[40] Table 3.3 presents the results. I first explore the hypothesis that states that enjoy nuclear superiority over their opponents are more likely to achieve victory in nuclear crises. Turning to the statistical results, we see that *Superiority* is statistically significant and positively correlated with victory in nuclear crises when considered alone (Model 1), when nested within a fully specified model (Model 2), and when included in a trimmed model (Model 3). The analysis reveals a strong empirical link between nuclear superiority and victory in nuclear crises.

Using *Clarify*, I assess the substantive effect of shifting from nuclear inferiority to nuclear superiority on the expected probability of victory in nuclear crises after controlling for other confounding factors.[41] The expected probability of victory in a nuclear crisis for a country in a position of nuclear inferiority is 6%.[42] A country that enjoys nuclear superiority, by contrast, enjoys an expected probability of victory of 64%.[43] Therefore, a move from a position of nuclear inferiority to a position of nuclear superiority, holding all other values constant, is associated with a 58% increase in the expected probability of victory in a nuclear crisis.[44] Or, in other words, nuclear superior states are more than ten times more likely to achieve their basic goals in a nuclear crisis than similar nuclear inferior states. Nuclear superiority has a substantively important effect on the outcomes of nuclear crises.

The examination of nuclear superiority and nuclear crisis outcomes is only the first step, however. Next, I present a more fine-grained test of the hypothesis by examining whether increasing levels of nuclear superiority are associated with improved outcomes in nuclear crises.

The results support the claim that greater levels of nuclear superiority are positively associated with victory in nuclear crises. *Nuclear ratio* is positive and statistically significant when tested alone (Model 4), when nested in a fully specified model (Model 5), and when included in a trimmed model (Model 6). In substantive terms, a shift from the least to the most favorable nuclear balance is associated with an 88% increase in the probability of victory.[45] This dramatic effect is obvious in Figure 3.1, which plots the conditional effects of

Table 3.3 **Nuclear Superiority and Nuclear Crisis Outcomes, 1945–2001**

Variables	Model 1	Model 2	Model 3	Model 4	Model 5	Model 6
Superiority	1.117**	2.005**	1.877***			
	(0.413)	(0.676)	(0.459)			
Nuclear ratio				1.294*	4.252***	2.479***
				(0.509)	(1.306)	(0.622)
Proximity		1.666***	1.196***		2.323***	1.283***
		(0.409)	(0.238)		(0.551)	(0.284)
Gravity		−0.760			−0.952	
		(0.755)			(0.875)	
Regime		0.032			0.036	
		(0.038)			(0.033)	
Capabilities		0.451			−1.602	
		(1.667)			(1.713)	
2nd strike		2.296*	0.566		2.328	
		(1.096)	(0.501)		(1.315)	
Population		−9.54e−07			2.52e−07	
		(1.44e−06)			(1.59e−06)	
Violence		0.299**	0.239*		0.333**	0.205*
		(0.104)	(0.097)		(0.119)	(0.087)
Security		−7.320			−7.611	
		(5.911)			(6.719)	
Constant	−1.020***	−3.159***	−3.025***	−1.091***	−3.883***	−2.786***
	(0.277)	(0.844)	(0.898)	(0.313)	(1.030)	(0.561)
N	52	52	52	52	52	52
Wald chi^2	7.32	303.70	40.28	6.47	797.25	22.88
Log pseudolikelihood	−29.107	−22.663	−24.818	−30.240	−22.572	−26.456
Pseudo R^2	0.1322	0.324	0.260	0.098	0.327	0.211

Note: Robust standard errors adjusted for clustering by crisis dyad in parentheses. *significant at 5%, **significant at 1%, ***significant at 0.1%. All tests are two-tailed.

the nuclear balance on the expected probability that a state will win a nuclear crisis. At the extreme left of the figure, we see that countries that possess few of the aggregate number of nuclear weapons within a crisis dyad have less than a 5% chance of winning a nuclear crisis. As we move to the right of the figure, however, we see that an increase in the proportion of nuclear weapons that a

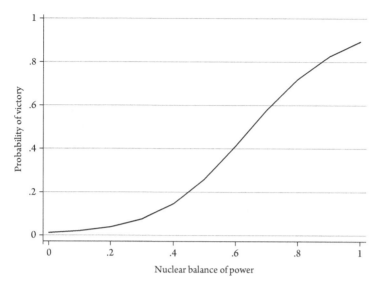

Figure 3.1 Conditional effect of the degree of nuclear superiority on the probability of victory in nuclear crises, 1945–2001. Note: Estimates obtained from Model 5. Level of nuclear superiority is from lowest (0) to highest (1).

state possesses within a crisis dyad results in a corresponding increase in the probability of victory. Indeed, as we arrive at the extreme right of the figure, we see that the probability of victory increases to over 85% for states that possess nearly all of the nuclear weapons within a crisis dyad. In other words, states with the most favorable nuclear balances are over 17 times more likely than states with the least favorable nuclear balances to achieve their goals in international crises.

Next, I turn to the competing hypotheses. There is some evidence that a secure, second-strike capability may provide an advantage in a nuclear crisis, even after taking into account the nuclear balance between states. The sign on the coefficient of *2nd Strike* is positive and statistically significant in Model 2, but does not reach statistical significance in the other models. Also consistent with the second-strike hypothesis, I find some support for the idea that political stakes shape crisis outcomes. *Proximity* is positive and statistically significant in every model in which it is included. Consistent with expectation of the previous brinkmanship literature, states are more likely to win nuclear crises that take place nearer to their own territory. On the other hand, *Gravity* does not reach statistical significance in any model.

The nuclear irrelevance hypothesis does not find any support. Contrary to the claims of these scholars, several measures of nuclear capability are correlated with nuclear crisis outcomes. As an additional test, to examine whether the emergence of a worldwide "nuclear taboo" in the early

1960s made it more difficult to threaten nuclear use, I reran the tests on a sample of nuclear crises that took place after 1960.[46] The evidence shows that, contrary to the nuclear taboo argument, the nuclear balance of power is correlated with crisis outcomes even in recent years.

Asymmetric escalation postures do not appear to aid states once they enter a crisis. Indeed, the variable was dropped from the models because, despite four appearances in nuclear crises, no state with an asymmetric escalation posture has ever emerged victorious.

Contrary to the conventional military power hypothesis, *Capabilities* is not statistically significant in any of the models in which it is included. Interestingly, however, in the tests on all crises, including nonnuclear states and not just nuclear powers, both *Capabilities* and the various nuclear-related measures reach statistical significance. This suggests that conventional military power matters for crisis outcomes broadly, but is not a significant factor in crises among nuclear powers.

I find no support for the idea that democratic states outperform their autocratic rivals in nuclear crises. *Regime* does not reach statistical significance in any of the models in which it is included. While past studies show that democracies are more likely to win international crises, the evidence presented here suggests that regime type does not matter in crises among nuclear powers.

Next, I briefly comment on the control variables.[47] *Violence* is statistically significant, and the sign on the coefficient is positive in every model in which it appears. As expected, the more violent the crisis, the more likely it will be to produce a clear winner.[48] Finally, the other control variables are not statistically significant. Population size and the severity of a state's security environment do not appear to shape the outcomes of nuclear crises.

US–USSR Nuclear Crises, 1949–1989

Next, to analyze the effect of changes in the nuclear balance on nuclear crisis outcomes within a single dyad over time, I analyze the outcomes of the thirteen nuclear crises that transpired between the United States and the Soviet Union during the Cold War.

Figure 3.2 depicts the size of the US nuclear advantage relative to the Soviet Union, measured in numbers of nuclear warheads over the course of the Cold War period. The figure reveals the shifts in the nuclear balance between the two countries over time. We can see that the United States enjoyed nuclear superiority over the Soviet Union at the beginning of the Cold War. The size of this advantage increased until 1964, when Washington possessed 25,530 more nuclear weapons than Moscow. Beginning in the mid-1960s, however, the Soviet Union began cutting into the United States' margin of strategic superiority. By 1978,

Figure 3.2 US-USSR nuclear balance and crisis outcomes, 1949–1989. Note: The y-axis depicts the US nuclear advantage relative to the Soviet Union measured in numbers of nuclear warheads.

the Soviet Union had surpassed the United States in terms of total number of nuclear warheads and maintained this advantage until the end of the Cold War.

The figure also displays the Cold War nuclear crises between the superpowers and their outcomes. We can see that the United States was more likely to win nuclear crises when it possessed nuclear superiority over the Soviet Union. While Washington enjoyed a nuclear advantage over Moscow, it achieved its basic goals in six out of ten, or 60%, of the nuclear crises in which it was involved. This is much higher than the 35% winning percentage experienced by the average nuclear crisis participant.

Moreover, the figure also shows that Washington's success in nuclear crises improved as its level of nuclear superiority over the Soviet Union increased. We can see that when Washington had at least ten thousand more nuclear warheads than Moscow, it won five out of six, or 83%, of the crises in which it was involved. Furthermore, the single crisis that the United States lost when it possessed a large margin of strategic superiority, the Berlin Wall Crisis of 1961, is a conflict that some historians consider to have been a victory for the United States.[49] Arguably, therefore, the United States won 100% of nuclear crises when it enjoyed a high level of nuclear superiority over the Soviet Union. In contrast, the United States' winning percentage was much lower from a position of nuclear inferiority. When the United States possessed fewer warheads than the Soviet Union, it won zero out of three, or 0%, of the nuclear crises in which it was involved. (More detail on some of these cases is presented in the next chapter).

In sum, this section presented evidence to suggest that the positive relationship between a nuclear advantage and nuclear crisis outcomes is also evident within a single dyad over time. The United States fared much better in its nuclear crises when it enjoyed a nuclear advantage over the Soviet Union.

Robustness Tests

This section presents the results of a number of robustness tests to examine whether the observed relationship between nuclear superiority and nuclear crisis outcomes is the result of a selection effect, the results are sensitive to modeling decisions due to the intermediate number of nuclear crises, or the findings are dependent on the character of the nuclear balance between the states.[50]

I first examine whether the results are being driven by a selection effect. It is possible that states that enjoy nuclear superiority are more likely to win nuclear crises because nuclear superior states are more likely to initiate crises they expect to win. It is also possible that leaders account for readily observable factors, such as military power, when deciding to initiate a crisis, which could have the effect of neutralizing superiority's effect on crisis outcomes.[51] To test for possible selection effects, I conducted three separate tests. First, I controlled for which state in the dyad initiated the crisis. If nuclear superior states are more likely to win crises because they select into crises they expect to win, we should find that the targets of nuclear crises are less likely to win nuclear crises and that *Superiority* is no longer statistically significant after controlling for crisis initiation. Second, I employed a Heckman probit model to examine the determinants of nuclear crises outcomes conditional on selection into nuclear crises.[52] I began by estimating a first-stage model of the onset of nuclear crises. The universe of cases is all dyads in which both states possess nuclear arms from 1945 to 2001. I then estimated a second-stage regression model of nuclear crises outcomes, conditional on selection into nuclear crises. Third, as recommended by some critics of the Heckman model, I incorporated all of the observable factors that may influence selection into a single equation that models the outcome of interest only.[53] In each of these tests, *Nuclear ratio* was positive and statistically significant even after accounting for selection into nuclear crises.[54] In addition, among the control variables, *Proximity, 2nd strike,* and *Violence* also found some support. In sum, a variety of tests demonstrate that the relationship between nuclear superiority and nuclear crisis outcomes is not the result of a selection effect.

Next, the intermediate number of nuclear crises raises the possibility that the results may be sensitive to coding and modeling decisions. To assess the sensitivity of the findings, I conducted a number of additional tests. First, to examine whether the inclusion or coding of any individual crisis was driving the results, I sequentially removed each crisis from the data set and reestimated the statistical models. Second, to assess whether the results were contingent on the behavior of any particular country, I removed each country in turn from the first position within the directed dyad and reran the analysis.[55] Third, one might argue that crisis participants in a defense pact with a more powerful state should not be included in the data set as separate observations. To address this concern, I removed all of the observations containing Britain and France from the data set and repeated the above statistical tests. Fourth, as indicated above, I removed the close calls for quantitative measures of superiority (dyads containing the United States and the Soviet Union after 1978, and India and Pakistan) and reran the tests. In all sets of tests, the core results were unaltered. *Superiority* and *Nuclear ratio* remained statistically significant and positive in every model. In sum, the core results are not sensitive to the removal of particular crises, or even entire countries from the data set.

In addition, one may wonder whether the findings of this analysis extend to dyads between nuclear states and nonnuclear opponents. Superiority-brinkmanship synthesis theory is a theory about behavior between nuclear-armed states, so a case universe including nonnuclear states is not an appropriate environment in which to test hypotheses derived from brinkmanship theory. Nevertheless, if nuclear superiority provides a strategic advantage against other nuclear-armed states, then it is reasonable to expect that it might have a similar effect against nonnuclear states. To test this idea, I compiled data on 709 international crisis dyads from 1945 to 2001. Repeating the above tests, I again found support for the idea that nuclear superiority improves a state's performance in a crisis. *Superiority* and *Nuclear ratio* were positive and statistically significant in every model. Nuclear superiority provides countries with a strategic advantage not only against other nuclear-armed states but also against nonnuclear weapon states.

Finally, I assess whether the findings presented earlier hold only below a certain threshold of nuclear arsenal size and sophistication. It is possible that nuclear superiority may help states win nuclear crises when one or more of the countries involved possess small or unsophisticated arsenals that could be vulnerable to an opponent's first strike. Nuclear superiority may provide less of an advantage, however, once both states possess a secure second-strike capability. To examine this possibility, I conducted a series of tests in which I examined the relationship between nuclear superiority and nuclear crisis outcomes in subsamples of data in which both states in the dyad undoubtedly possessed a secure second-strike capability. In each successive test, I raised the threshold of nuclear capabilities required to be included in the sample. Analyzing these subsamples of data, I find that nuclear superiority is correlated with nuclear crisis outcomes even among states with large and sophisticated nuclear arsenals. In sum, there is no evidence to suggest that the observed relationship between nuclear superiority and nuclear crisis outcomes holds only beneath a certain threshold of nuclear arsenal size and sophistication.

Conclusion

This chapter examined the outcomes of nuclear crises. I found that in order to explain the patterns of victory in crises involving nuclear-armed states, one must look to the nuclear balance between states. States that enjoy nuclear superiority over their opponents are over ten times more likely to prevail in nuclear crises. This finding holds, even after controlling for the conventional military balance of power and for selection into nuclear crises. The results were also robust to the exclusion of each individual crisis and each individual nuclear weapon state.

These findings provide strong support for the superiority-brinkmanship synthesis theory. According to the theory, crises are competitions in risk taking, but nuclear superior states are willing to run greater risks than their nuclear inferior opponents. Nuclear superiority increases the length of time that a state can remain in a nuclear crisis before the costs of escalation outweigh the costs of submission. A nuclear advantage thus allows states to push harder in a crisis, making them more likely to ultimately prevail. In contrast to previous debates that pitted the balance of resolve against nuclear superiority, I demonstrate that the two factors come together to form a coherent strategic logic. Nuclear superiority aids states in games of nuclear brinkmanship by increasing their levels of effective resolve.

In support of the second-strike school, this chapter found that the possession of secure, second strike capabilities improve a state's performance in nuclear crises. This chapter also provided some support for the idea that political stakes shape crisis outcomes. States are more likely to win crises that occur nearer to their own territory. This finding is consistent with previous brinkmanship literature, which maintains that political stakes are an important determinant of victory in nuclear crises. In contrast to the previous literature and the second-strike school, however, this chapter also demonstrated that stakes alone do not determine crisis outcomes. Instead, a state's resolve to press a nuclear crisis is a function of both political stakes and the balance of nuclear forces. In both theory and evidence, therefore, we see that the second-strike school gets part of the story right, but stops short of a complete explanation.

Other arguments for coercive success fare less well. The nuclear irrelevance school does not find any support in these tests. The results show that nuclear weapons are relevant to nuclear crisis outcomes. Asymmetric nuclear postures may contribute to deterrence for regional powers, but the tests in this chapter showed that they are not correlated with the achievement of political goals in nuclear crises. Conventional military power was correlated with crises outcomes in the test that examined all states, including nonnuclear states, but it did not reach statistical significance in tests on the subset of nuclear powers. This suggests that in crises among nuclear powers, the nuclear, not the conventional, balance of power is most salient. Neither was the argument that democratic states enjoy a coercive advantage supported in the data. This finding may represent an additional blow to the democratic advantage school, or it may simply suggest that crises among nuclear powers operate according to their own distinct logic.

In sum, this chapter demonstrates strong support for the central argument of this book. But how do these patterns from large samples of data play out in specific cases? Are the mechanisms of superiority-brinkmanship synthesis theory evident in the historical record? Do leaders truly pay close attention to the nuclear balance of power? Are leaders in nuclear superior states more willing to run nuclear risks, as the theory would predict? It is to these questions that we turn in the next chapter.

4

The Mechanisms of Nuclear
Crisis Outcomes

Has nuclear superiority mattered in historical cases of showdowns between nuclear powers? Did the nuclear superior state enjoy a coercive bargaining advantage? These are the questions this chapter addresses. It examines the effect of nuclear superiority on crisis outcomes in a series of short case studies of the most important nuclear crises of the nuclear era: the Cuban Missile Crisis, the Sino-Soviet Border War, the 1973 Arab-Israeli Crisis, and the Kargil Crisis.

The analysis once again provides strong support for the central argument of the book. It illustrates the effect of the nuclear balance of power in specific cases and demonstrates that the causal mechanisms predicted by the theory are in fact in operation. In these cases, we see that leaders paid close attention to the nuclear balance of power, nuclear superior states were willing to run greater risks, and nuclear superior states were more likely to achieve their basic goals. Alternative explanations, such as those that maintain that nuclear weapons are irrelevant, or that they do not matter above and beyond a secure, second-strike capability, do not find support.

The rest of the chapter proceeds in three parts. First, it explains the research design and case selection criteria. Next, it presents the case studies. Finally, it offers a brief conclusion.

Research Design and Case Selection

This section briefly explains the research design and case selection criteria employed in this chapter. Following the advice of King, Keohane, and Verba, I select cases with variation on the key independent and dependent variables.[1] Each case pits adversarial states with varying nuclear capabilities against one another, ensuring variation on the independent variable. There is also variation on the dependent variable, because some crisis participants achieve their basic political goals and others do not.

I also take full advantage of most and least-likely case study designs. To some degree, these are all least likely, or hard, cases. Scholars have maintained that hard cases are those with strong "countervailing conditions" based on prior theory and research.[2] The dominant second-strike theory posits that nuclear balances of power do not matter once both states possess an assured retaliatory capability and, in all of the below cases, the weaker state at least arguably possesses a nuclear retaliatory capability. Previous theory would predict, therefore, that we should not see any evidence that the nuclear balance of power matters. Evidence that the nuclear balance of power matters even in these least likely cases, therefore, would provide especially strong support for my theory.

A most and least likely case design approach would also exploit variation in gradations of the independent variable from the proposed theory. More likely cases for my theory would be those with stark imbalances of nuclear power and less likely cases would be those in which states' nuclear capabilities are more evenly matched. This study includes two examples of the former (Cuban Missile Crisis, Sino-Soviet Border War) and two of the latter (1973 Arab-Israeli War, Kargil Crisis). The superiority-brinkmanship synthesis theory would strongly predict victory for the superior state in the first set of cases, but only weakly predict victory in the second set. Desirable crisis outcomes for the superior state in any of the cases provides evidence for the theory, but the support is especially strong if superior states prevail even in the least likely cases.

I focus on cases in which there were fairly high levels of escalation. This serves two purposes. First, these are the cases with data; nonevents do not provide material for analysis. This does not lead to concerns about "selecting on the dependent variable" because the dependent variable of this chapter is crisis outcomes, not crisis escalation, and because I have already analyzed the entire universe of empirical cases in the previous chapter.[3] Second, methodologists often recommend selecting "crucial" cases.[4] It would be problematic if the argument of this book could not account for the most salient cases that have received the most attention from previous scholars and policymakers, such as the Cuban Missile Crisis.

In each case, I conduct a pattern-matching exercise to assess the correspondence between the independent and dependent variables.[5] In other words, I assess whether the nuclear superior state achieved its basic goals in the crisis. In the terminology of James Mahoney, I am looking for independent variable causal process observations (CPOs). James Mahoney states that an independent variable CPO "provides information about the presence of an independent variable (or about the presence of a particular range of values on an independent variable)."[6] He argues, "these observations are essential for testing theories in many domains of scientific research where the key issue is whether a cause occurred in the manner and/or at the time posited by the theory."[7] In each of the following cases, I begin by assessing which state possessed an advantage in the nuclear balance of power. Next, I consider which state or states achieved their basic political goals.

To study these variables, I begin with the definitions, concepts, and measures of nuclear superiority and crisis outcome provided in the previous chapter. For the measurement of each, however, I go beyond these measures to make full use of the qualitative evidence available in the historic record. For example, when gauging nuclear superiority, I begin with aggregate quantitative assessments, but then proceed to also examine a state's ability to promptly deliver nuclear weapons to the territory of its opponent in the heat of the crisis by considering additional factors such as the readiness of deployed forces and the types and ranges of strategic and tactical warheads and their associated delivery vehicles. To measure crisis outcome, I consider additional contextual information and the arguments for and against plausible alternative codings. In all cases, however, the more fine-grained assessments of these variables serve to provide additional confidence in the quantitative codings from chapter 3.

Evidence that states with a military nuclear advantage achieved their crisis goals provides support for the superiority-brinkmanship synthesis theory. Information about superior states failing to reach their objectives counts as evidence against.

Next, and most importantly, this chapter also examines the causal mechanisms and traces the process between the nuclear balance of power and crisis outcomes.[8] In the words of Mahoney, this chapter is looking for mechanism CPOs, which "provides information about whether an intervening event posited by a theory is present. . . . The leverage they provide derives from the ability of individual observations to confirm or challenge a researcher's prior expectations about what should occur."[9] In the cases, I search for two principal mechanism CPOs. First, I examine whether the nuclear balance of power appears to have influenced the state's willingness to escalate the crisis. If the superiority-brinkmanship synthesis theory is correct, we should expect that nuclear superior states will be more willing to run risks of nuclear war than their inferior opponents. We might expect that they will make explicit nuclear threats, place nuclear weapons on high alert, and/or escalate the crisis through the posturing or use of conventional forces. On the other hand, we might expect that nuclear inferior states will be less likely to engage in these behaviors.

Second, I look for evidence from both sides of "superiority talk."[10] Did policymakers pay close attention to the nuclear balance of power? Did they talk about it? Did they personally believe that the superior state possessed a bargaining advantage? Did they make private or public statements to this effect? Did they explicitly invoke the nuclear balance of power as a reason for crisis escalation or restraint? Evidence of superiority talk in the empirical record will provide additional support for the central argument of this book.

Each section also briefly considers evidence for and against the major alternative explanations, including: second-strike theory, nuclear irrelevance theory, regional nuclear posture theory, conventional military power theory, and the democratic advantage theory.

Case Studies

This section will present a series of short case studies on nuclear crises: the Cuban Missile Crisis, the Sino-Soviet Border War, the 1973 Arab-Israeli Crisis, and the Kargil Crisis.

The Cuban Missile Crisis

The Cuban Missile Crisis may be the most studied international crisis in history, and the facts of the case are well known to most readers.[11] In 1962, the Soviet Union began deploying medium- and intermediate-range nuclear-capable missiles in Cuba. Once fully deployed, these missiles would have been capable of holding at risk much of the continental United States. When President Kennedy received intelligence on the deployments in October 1962, he confronted the Soviet Union's premier Nikita Khrushchev and demanded the missiles be removed, sparking a 13-day standoff. After considering more aggressive options, including air strikes on the missile sites and an invasion, Kennedy decided to enforce a naval blockade around the island to prevent the Soviet Union from completing additional missile transfers. The Kennedy administration fully understood that escalating the crisis could lead to a broader war in Europe and even a full-scale nuclear exchange. After the crisis, Kennedy estimated that the risk of nuclear war had been "somewhere between one out of three and even."[12] In the end, however, the Soviet Union removed the missiles from Cuba in exchange for a public US pledge not to invade the island, bringing the crisis to a close. Years later it was revealed that in addition to the publicly revealed trade, Washington had also privately pledged to withdraw its own medium-range Jupiter missiles from Turkey.

The Nuclear Balance of Power

The nuclear balance of power in the Cuban Missile Crisis favored the United States. Moscow possessed a secure, second-strike capability, but, in the event of a nuclear war, the expected costs to Russia were higher than the expected costs to the United States. In 1962, the United States possessed an arsenal of 25,540 nuclear warheads, while Russia maintained 3,346.[13] The balance of forces was as lopsided in the realm of deployed strategic forces. At the peak of the crisis, the United States had over 3,500 generated nuclear weapons, 1,479 bombers, 1,003 refueling tankers, and 182 missiles (including ICBMs and SLBMs) ready for employment.[14] In contrast, the Soviet Union possessed approximately 300 to 500 deployed strategic warheads, 42 ICBMs capable of reaching the United States, zero SLBMs, and 150 long-range bombers.

US theater nuclear forces in Europe also contributed to the US strike capability against the USSR's homeland. The United States possessed over 4,000 nuclear weapons in Europe, including approximately 500 that could have reached Soviet territory.[15] This provided the United States an additional ability to threaten damage to Russia. While the Soviet Union possessed about 500 medium- and intermediate-range forces capable of threatening US allies and bases in Europe, they could not reach the continental United States.

Indeed, the placement of missiles in Cuba was an attempt to begin to rectify this significant strategic imbalance. Of the thirty-six MRBMs sent to Cuba, it is now believed that approximately six to eight were ready for launch by the time of the crisis.[16] The Soviet Union also deployed other tactical nuclear weapons to Cuba to be used in the event of an invasion or to hold at risk the US military base at Guantanamo Bay, but these forces were not capable of reaching the continental United States.

Leaders on both sides were well aware of the imbalance in strategic forces. Soviet General Anatoly Gribkov stated that Khrushchev and his military advisers estimated that, in the Crisis, the United States possessed a roughly 17:1 strategic nuclear advantage.[17] One year before the Cuban Missile Crisis, in September 1961, Kennedy received a briefing from General Lyman L. Lemnitzer, the chairman of the US Joint Chiefs of Staff, on the likely effects of a nuclear exchange with the Soviet Union.[18] The briefing showed that the Soviet Union possessed a secure, second-strike capability and in the event of nuclear war, it would have been able to destroy major cities on the US East Coast. It also showed however, that the United States had a large nuclear advantage.[19] As Scott Sagan concludes, "By any quantitative or qualitative measure of nuclear power . . . the United States possessed massive superiority."[20]

Crisis Outcome

Consistent with superiority-brinkmanship synthesis theory, the United States, the nuclear superior state, achieved its goals in the Cuban Missile Crisis. The Soviet Union, the nuclear inferior state, did not. The Cuban Missile Crisis was primarily a dispute over the issue of the placement of Soviet intermediate and medium-range missiles in Cuba. Moscow desired to maintain the missiles in Cuba. Washington demanded they be removed. The crisis was resolved in the United States' favor when the missiles were withdrawn. This is the standard historical interpretation of the Crisis and also the coding provided by the ICB dataset and existing scholarly studies on nuclear weapons and compellence.[21]

Some revisionist scholarship has suggested that the Soviet Union may have actually won the Cuban Missile Crisis because it wrung from the episode a US pledge not to invade Cuba. In addition, Moscow achieved the subsequent withdrawal of US Jupiter missiles from Turkey.[22] At minimum, therefore, revisionist scholars might argue that the crisis was a draw because both sides won some concessions.

This alternative coding, however, is difficult to sustain. The crisis was first and foremost about the status of Soviet missiles in Cuba, not about other issues, and this central conflict of interest was resolved in Washington's favor. As colleagues and I have written elsewhere:

> We would not conclude that the Denver Broncos "won" Super Bowl XLVIII—a game they lost badly to the Seattle Seahawks—because their appearance in the game increased Broncos merchandise sales. The Broncos undoubtedly benefited in many ways from their Super Bowl appearance, but this hardly means that they won the game. Similarly, even if the Soviets got something out of the Cuban missile crisis, they failed to obtain their main objective—namely, keeping the missiles in Cuba. Our respective codings of this case reflect the most direct interpretation of the crisis' outcome.[23]

This is also the way the participants themselves interpreted the outcome. Khrushchev himself saw the episode as a Soviet defeat. He reportedly told his colleagues in the Politburo that they had to defuse "the danger of war and nuclear catastrophe, with the possibility of destroying the human race. To save the world, we must retreat."[24] As then–US Secretary of State Dean Rusk famously put it, "We're eyeball to eyeball, and the other fellow just blinked."[25]

In sum, consistent with standard interpretations, the Cuban Missile Crisis is best coded as a US victory.

Risk Taking

Throughout the Cuban Missile Crisis, the United States demonstrated a greater willingness than the Soviet Union to escalate the conflict at both the conventional and nuclear levels and to run the inherent risks of nuclear war those actions entailed.

At the conventional level, the United States imposed a naval blockade of Cuba and raised the risk of conflict by stopping and boarding ships bound for the island. The Soviet Union also engaged in conventional military action. Most notably, Moscow shot down a US U2 surveillance plane overflying the island. In the end, however, it was the Soviet Union that literally swerved its conventional forces in the game of chicken, turning around its convoy of missile-carrying ships in the face of the American naval blockade.

We see a similar US willingness to run risks in the nuclear domain. Although less well known than the conventional military posturing, the United States also took concrete escalatory steps in the nuclear domain. During the Cuban Missile Crisis, the U.S. Strategic Air Command (SAC) went on Defense Condition (DEFCON) II, the second-highest state of readiness for nuclear war, for the first time in history. America's ICBMs and one-third of its strategic bomber force were placed on alert. As explained by David Burchinal, a US Air Force general involved in the Crisis, "we got everything we had in the strategic forces . . . counted down and ready and aimed and we made damn sure they saw it."[26]

This is not to say that the United States eagerly took risks or recklessly bid up the risk of war. Rather, throughout the crisis, US officials feared escalation and took steps to prevent escalatory spirals. But at the same time, US officials rattled the nuclear sabre in a bid to achieve their geopolitical goals. As Trachtenberg writes:

> the specter of nuclear war was deliberately manipulated to support American objectives in the crisis. . . . McNamara's assumption was that nuclear preparations would serve to deter Soviet responses in general; that is, the implied nuclear threat was not directed simply at the possibility that the U.S.S.R. might consider using its nuclear forces . . . the risk of nuclear war did play a role. Indeed, this risk was overtly and deliberately exploited. But this was a deadly game, played reluctantly.[27]

By comparison, the Soviet Union, the nuclear inferior state in the crisis, was much less willing to run a risk of nuclear war. Moscow did take some actions in the nuclear domain. Both the United States and the Soviet Union conducted a series of atmospheric nuclear tests at the height of the crisis.[28] In recent years, more evidence has come to light that makes apparent that both sides were preparing for theater nuclear use in the event of an invasion of Cuba. The Soviet Union planned to use tactical nuclear weapons on invading US forces and against the US military base at Guantanamo Bay. And at least one Soviet commander on the ground at the time has claimed that, in the event of a US invasion of Cuba, he would have employed intermediate-range missiles against the US homeland, even though he did not have authority from Moscow to do so.[29] Similarly, the

United States loaded two aircraft carriers stationed off the coast of Jamaica with forty nuclear gravity bombs for delivery by tactical aircraft.[30]

In sharp contrast to the United States, however, the Soviet Union did not go on strategic nuclear alert during the Cuban Missile Crisis. As Washington prepared for strategic nuclear war, Moscow did not alert a single nuclear-capable bomber or ICBM. Although not widely understood in the West, the Cuban Missile Crisis was the closest the world has ever come to a nuclear war largely because the United States, not the Soviet Union, stepped out on the brink.

As General Burchinal describes it, "we had a gun to [Khrushchev's] head and he didn't move a muscle."[31] Richard Betts writes that the Soviet nonalert was "remarkable" and "equivalent to a threatened dog rolling over belly up."[32] As Trachtenberg concludes, Soviet "strategic 'inferiority' appears to have had a profound effect on their behavior in the crisis."[33]

Superiority Talk

Consistent with the central argument of this book, the details of the Cuban Missile Crisis demonstrate that leaders paid close attention to the nuclear balance of power, they invoked the nuclear balance of power in their debates, and they explicitly linked the nuclear balance of power to policy recommendations about crisis escalation. For example, during the Crisis, General Maxwell Taylor, who by then had replaced Lemnitzer as chairman of the Joint Chiefs of Staff, wrote in a memo to Secretary of Defense Robert McNamara, "we have the strategic advantage in our general war capabilities . . . this is no time to run scared."[34] Similarly, Secretary of State Dean Rusk said to the members of the EXCOMM, including President Kennedy, "One thing Mr. Khrushchev may have in mind is that . . . he knows that we have a substantial nuclear superiority . . . he also knows that we don't really live under fear of his nuclear weapons to the extent . . . that he has to live under ours."[35] An Air Force general and head of SAC, Curtis LeMay repeatedly invoked US superiority as a reason for taking more aggressive action, including an invasion of the island and, if necessary, general nuclear war.[36] Even in advocating for a restrained approach, Secretary of Defense Robert McNamara took into account the nuclear balance of power, arguing "if we had to fight a war with the Soviet Union, we'd have fewer casualties today than if we had to do it later. But it's not clear that we have to fight them. So for God's sake, let's try to avoid it."[37] According to C. Douglas Dillon, a cabinet adviser to President Kennedy during the Crisis, the answer is straightforward: "Our nuclear preponderance was essential. That's what made the Russians back off."[38] The above statements are as close to "smoking gun" evidence as one can reasonably expect to find in qualitative, social science research.[39]

There is less available information about the decision-making process of Soviet officials during the Cuban Missile Crisis, but the available evidence suggests that Soviet leaders were cognizant of their nuclear inferiority and that this may have encouraged them to submit. For example, following the crisis, Vasili Kuznetzov, the USSR's first deputy minister of foreign affairs, said, referring to the balance of nuclear power, which was shifting in Moscow's favor, "You Americans will never be able to do this to us again."[40] And, according to Fidel Castro, Khrushchev told him that it was Soviet nuclear inferiority that forced them to back down in the Cuban Missile Crisis.[41]

Indeed, the very occurrence of the crisis provides evidence that the nuclear balance of power mattered. As explained above, Moscow already possessed an assured retaliation capability, but it placed missiles in Cuba in order to decrease its margin of nuclear inferiority vis-à-vis the United States. This is evidence that its leaders were cognizant of, and concerned about, its nuclear inferior position. Explaining his decision later, Khrushchev wrote, "Our missiles would have equalized what the West likes to call 'the balance of power.' "[42]

Complicating this easy assessment, however, are several statements on the American side explicitly disavowing the importance of nuclear superiority. Dean Rusk, who, as we saw above, emphasized the nuclear balance of power in the midst of the crisis, staked out the contrary position years later, claiming, "the simple fact is that nuclear power does not translate into useable political influence."[43] Moreover, several veterans of the Crisis, including Rusk, writing decades later, argued that the outcome of the Crisis demonstrates "not the significance but the insignificance of nuclear superiority."[44]

The ambiguity in the historical record may be best exemplified by one anonymous US official involved in the Crisis who, when asked whether America's nuclear advantage had anything to do with the outcome, replied, "hell no."[45] When asked if he would have been just as comfortable, therefore, navigating the Cuban Missile Crisis from a position of nuclear inferiority, he also replied, "hell no."[46]

Despite the presence of some ambiguity, the evidence of "superiority talk" on balance favors the superiority-brinkmanship synthesis theory. First, even statements of denial demonstrate that, at a minimum, nuclear superiority was an issue on participants' minds worthy of recognition and discussion. The more damning evidence for the thesis would have been if the topic of nuclear superiority had never even been broached.

Moreover, utterances made in the midst of the crisis, or shortly thereafter, likely provide better insight into how leaders were actually thinking at the time decisions were being made. But nearly all of the available statements denying the importance of the nuclear balance came well after the crisis had been resolved, sometimes decades later. And nearly all of the statements referencing the nuclear balance of power during the Crisis suggest that speakers believed that it was significant. Furthermore, the statements from Cuban Missile Crisis veterans denying the importance of nuclear superiority years later can also be questioned because these statements were motivated at least in part by partisan politics and an effort to shape contemporary debates.[47] These former Democratic administration officials employed this argument in 1982 as part of a broader effort to criticize Republican President Ronald Regean's plans for a defense build up.

Summary

In sum, the Cuban Missile Crisis provides support for the superiority-brinkmanship synthesis theory. Policymakers in the nuclear superior state, the United States, were cognizant of their nuclear advantage, referred to their nuclear advantage in the heat of the crisis, and pointed to the advantage as a reason for a forward-leaning US approach. The United States was more willing to escalate at the conventional, and even more clearly, at the nuclear level. And, in the end, the United States achieved its basic goal of forcing Soviet missiles out of Cuba.

On the other side of the crisis, there is some evidence (although the record is less clear) that Soviet officials were cognizant of their nuclear inferiority and they believed this handicapped them during the crisis. The Soviet Union was less willing to escalate at the conventional and nuclear level. And, in the end, Moscow failed to achieve its primary goal of maintaining nuclear missiles in Cuba.

Other scholars have reached a similar conclusion. According to Richard Betts, when examining the outcome of the Cuban Missile Crisis, "It is hard to avoid the conclusion that the imbalance of nuclear power—US superiority—was an influence."[48]

Alternative Explanations

We next turn to an analysis of alternative explanations for the Cuban Missile Crisis. Some of these theories find support, while others do not. None, however, provides a more compelling explanation for the Crisis than the superiority-brinkmanship synthesis theory.

Second-Strike Theory

The second-strike theory provides a partial explanation for the facts of the case, but on several key points it is not supported by the historical record. Consistent with the theory, both the United States and Russia possessed a secure, second-strike capability and both sides feared the devastating consequences of nuclear war. Both sides were deterred from launching an intentional nuclear first strike and, instead, attempted to coerce each other by playing a game of brinkmanship.

Consistent with the theory, the side with arguably the greater stake in Cuba, the United States, ultimately prevailed. After all, Cuba is only 90 miles off the US coast, whereas for the Soviet Union the crisis was about projecting influence into a distant geographic region.

Other aspects of the crisis, however, cannot be adequately explained using second-strike theory. First, and fundamentally, if the nuclear balance of power does not matter, as second-strike theory maintains, then the crisis should have never occurred. The Soviet Union already possessed a secure, second-strike capability. Moscow should have had no reason to place missiles in Cuba, and Washington should not have been concerned if they did. Instead, Khrushchev placed nuclear weapons in Cuba with the specific intention of offsetting Russia's nuclear inferiority. Moreover, Washington objected to missiles' placement in Cuba for precisely this reason. US assessments at the time, including from the CIA and the US Joint Chiefs of Staff, concluded that the deployments marked a meaningful shift in the nuclear balance of power.[49] To be sure, there were other factors at play. Kennedy was worried about broader US credibility if he capitulated in this high-profile showdown, and Khrushchev wanted to visibly increase the Soviet commitment to Cuba to deter a US attack. Still, Khrushchev could have deployed other forces to Cuba to serve as a sign of Moscow's commitment. Instead, he chose nuclear missiles that greatly increased the Soviet Union's ability to hold the US homeland at risk. And Kennedy acquiesced to the maintenance of other Soviet capabilities on Cuba, but it was the nuclear forces in range of the US homeland that were not permitted to stand. Consistent with the superiority-brinkmanship synthesis theory, therefore, but not second-strike theory, the shift in the nuclear balance of power that these missiles represented mattered to both sides.

Second, unlike the evidence in support of the central role for the nuclear balance of power, the evidence that the balance of stakes was a decisive factor is weak. While the balance of nuclear power was clear, the balance of stakes was not. Moreover, there is no record of the participants explicitly invoking an advantage or disadvantage in the balance of stakes or citing it as a reason to either press or restrain action during the Crisis. Indeed, as Francis Gavin has argued, "looking at available archival sources, it is clear that both the Soviet Union and the United Sates saw the stakes as being higher for themselves."[50]

Third, and most importantly, the assured retaliation argument cannot account for all of the "superiority talk" we saw in this case. Second-strike theory would not expect policymakers on both sides to pay close attention to, talk about, or act on the basis of the nuclear balance of power. But they did. Why? Second-strike theorists can only argue, as they have in the past, that this is because policymakers are mistaken and that they, the theorists, understand nuclear strategy better than power-holders they are studying. This may work as a rhetorical defense of an entrenched position, but it does not pass muster as social science.

Nuclear Irrelevance Theory

Nuclear irrelevance arguments do not find support in this case. If nuclear weapons are irrelevant, or if there is an ironclad taboo against their use, then a major crisis over nuclear missiles should not have occurred, policymakers would not have discussed the nuclear balance of power or feared the possibility of nuclear war, and they would not have placed nuclear weapons on alert, or otherwise attempted to engage in nuclear coercion.

The more modest irrelevance argument about how nuclear weapons matter for deterrence, but not compellence, also fails to find support. Nuclear skeptics acknowledge that the Cuban Missile Crisis is generally considered evidence in favor of nuclear superiority, but they still reject the notion that nuclear weapons were a major contributing factor to the outcome.[51] Given the above evidence, however, it is impossible to sustain the argument that nuclear weapons were irrelevant. As Trachtenberg concludes in his study on the role of nuclear weapons in the Cuban Missile Crisis, "It is clear . . . that the risk of nuclear war did play a role."[52]

Regional Nuclear Posture Theory

Both participants in this crisis were superpowers. A theory about regional nuclear postures, therefore, is not relevant to this case.

Conventional Military Power Theory

The conventional balance of power argument finds some support in this case, but it alone does not provide a satisfactory explanation. The United States enjoyed a clear conventional military advantage in the Western Caribbean. This allowed the United States to deploy a naval blockade and placed the onus for further escalation on the Soviet Union.

But other facts of the case are inconsistent with an explanation that relies on conventional power to the exclusion of nuclear forces. First, the Cuban Missile Crisis was intimately linked with the related US-Soviet conflict over the status of Berlin.[53] Kennedy and his advisers feared that if the United States moved on Cuba, Khrushchev would simply retaliate in Berlin, a place where the Soviet Union enjoyed a conventional military advantage.[54] Viewed in this broader context, therefore, it is not clear that the conventional balance favored Washington. Khrushchev could have easily neutralized the US advantages in conventional power and stakes in Cuba by moving on Berlin. But he did not. Why?

The conventional balance argument cannot provide an easy explanation for why Khrushchev backed down in Cuba while also refraining from escalating asymmetrically against Berlin, but the superiority-brinkmanship synthesis theory can. Indeed, US officials explicitly attempted to use US nuclear superiority to achieve general deterrence beyond Cuba. McNamara, for example, pointed out on October 16 that American military action in Cuba would probably lead to a Soviet military response "some place in the world."[55] The United States, he argued, should recognize that possibility "by trying to deter it, which means we probably should alert SAC, probably put on an airborne alert, perhaps take other alert measures."

Most importantly, however, unlike the superiority-brinkmanship synthesis theory, the conventional military power hypothesis simply cannot account for all of the evidence reviewed previously that demonstrates the clear importance of nuclear weapons in this crisis.

In the end, the case seems to provide support for the idea that both nuclear and conventional military power mattered in the Cuban Missile Crisis, but nuclear power played a more central role. Even Bernard Brodie, often a skeptic of the political utility of nuclear weapons, argued that it was a "a mischievous interpretation" of the Cuban Missile Crisis "to hold that its outcome was determined mostly by our conventional superiority."[56]

Democratic Advantage Theory

At a superficial level, the democratic advantage argument finds some support in this case. A democratic state, the United States, and an autocratic state, the Soviet Union, engaged in a diplomatic showdown and, in the end, the democratic state prevailed. On closer inspection, however, and as other scholars have shown, one cannot find evidence for the mechanisms postulated by audience cost theory in the Cuban Missile Crisis.[57]

Political Settlement

Although it is not one of the major alternative theoretical accounts for crisis outcomes, I also consider another interpretation that is commonly evoked when explaining the Cuban Missile Crisis: political settlement. This interpretation holds that it was only through shrewd bargaining that nuclear conflict was averted.[58] More than a triumph of military threats, this account holds, the Cuban Missile Crisis was a victory for diplomacy. Washington traded Jupiter missiles in Turkey and a pledge not to invade Cuba in exchange for Moscow's removals of its missiles in Cuba. Neither side got all of what it wanted, but the political compromise was preferable to a continued risk of nuclear war.

This account is a mostly fair description of the crisis and may serve as a satisfactory interpretation among historians, but it is not a social scientific explanation. The Cuban Missile Crisis (like all international crises) was indeed political in nature. As Clausewitz argued, "war is a continuation of politics by other means."[59] Short of one side utterly defeating an opponent and forcibly imposing its will, all crises, and nearly all wars, eventually result in a political settlement. The Cuban Missile Crisis was no different. The key question is not whether there was a political settlement but, rather, what drove the settlement? Why did one side achieve its basic goal while the other did not? Did the nuclear balance of power have an effect and how significant was this effect? The political settlement explanation is not incorrect, but it is largely beside the point.

The Sino-Soviet Border War, 1969

In 1969, China and the Soviet Union were involved in a border dispute that nearly resulted in nuclear war.[60] The dispute began on March 2, 1969, when Chinese troops ambushed Soviet forces on the disputed Zhenbao Island in the Ussuri River, which served as a natural border between the two nuclear powers. The border had been in dispute for more than a century and negotiations over the issue collapsed earlier in the decade, prompting Moscow to take a tougher line with Beijing. Morevoer, China was also fearful of the Soviet Union in the wake of the Sino-Soviet split, the Soviet invasion of Czechoslovakia in 1968, and the recent announcement of the Brezhnev doctrine, which declared a Soviet right to interfere in other Communist nations for the purpose of strengthening international Communism. The Chinese raid was meant to demonstrate strength and deter any possible Soviet aggression.[61] The idea of striking a first blow as a means of deterring conflict may seem counter-intuitive to Western readers, but it is consistent with a long tradition in Chinese strategic thought, including Mao Zedong's concept of an "active defense."[62]

In this instance, however, the raid served to inflame rather than dampen conflict. The Soviet Union retaliated on March 15, and border skirmishes continued throughout the summer of 1969. In an effort to resolve the dispute, the Soviet Union demanded that China engage in negotiations over the border issue, but Beijing refused. To force China to the table, Moscow continually increased the pressure throughout the summer and fall, including by issuing a series of escalating nuclear threats. China initially dismissed the threats as bluster, but eventually became convinced that a Soviet nuclear attack might be imminent. On October 20, 1969, the crisis was resolved as Mao submitted to Brezhnev's demands and agreed to negotiations.

The Nuclear Balance of Power

The Soviet Union enjoyed a clear nuclear superiority over China in the crisis. The Soviet Union possessed 10,671 warheads compared to an estimated 50 in China.[63] The imbalance was just as stark when measured in terms of delivery vehicles. By the late 1960s, Moscow had developed a robust triad of missiles, bombers, and submarines and was aiming for strategic parity with its superpower rival, the United States. It possessed approximately 440 ICBMs, 700 MRBMs and IRBMs, 100 SLBMs, 300 SLCMs, and 900 heavy and medium bombers capable of reaching China.[64] China, on the other hand, had tested its first nuclear weapon only 5 years before and was still developing a fledgling nuclear force. Beijing possessed approximately 10 MRBMs and a handful of strategic bombers capable of reaching Russia.[65]

Crisis Outcome

In the Sino-Soviet Border War, China failed in its bid to deter Soviet aggression and instead inadvertently provoked one of the most dangerous crises of the Cold War.[66] It may have demonstrated, that, unlike other weaker Commnist bloc states, it would not grant supremacy to Moscow without a fight. But, in this case, it was a losing fight as Beijing succumbed unwillingly to Moscow's demands for talks. The Soviet Union achieved its basic goal of compelling China to the negotiating table to discuss the Zhenbao Island issue.[67]

Other scholars have written that the outcome of the Crisis is inconclusive because the Soviet Union did not dictate terms in the talks that followed, but this argument does not do justice to the historical case.[68] The crisis was not over the precise provisions of subsequent agreements, but whether to have talks at all. And, in this objective, Moscow succeeded.

As Henry Kissinger writes of the Border War in his memoirs, "in the war of nerves, China had backed down."[69] According to a Top Secret CIA assessment at the time, "for the Chinese, the issue is simple: prevention of possible war. Mounting Soviet military and diplomatic pressure, including hints of Russian nuclear attack, has had the desired effect of bringing Peking to the table."[70]

Risk Taking

Throughout the crisis, the Soviet Union was more willing to engage in risk-taking behavior, responding with conventional force along the border, issuing a series of escalating nuclear threats, and turning the crisis into an explicit game of nuclear brinkmanship. China responded with limited conventional counter-threats of its own, but, in the end, backed down in the face of what was perceived to be the credible threat of Soviet nuclear attack.

Moscow's first response to the Chinese raid was to escalate the conflict conventionally along the border. That summer, beginning on June 1, China accused the Soviets of initiating 429 border incidents, not just at Zhenbao Island but also along the full length of the Sino-Soviet border. On August 13, for example, the Soviet Union struck Chinese forces near the China-Kazakh border with tanks and helicopters, killing 38 soldiers.[71]

Moscow's nuclear saber rattling also began that same month when it deployed bomber units nearer to China's borders in Mongolia and Siberia and exercised bombing runs on mock Chinese nuclear facilities.[72] These exercises were paired with a strategic communications campaign in which Soviet news stories were broadcast into China in Mandarin warning of an imminent nuclear attack. In August, the Soviet Union made an ostentatious personnel move, appointing Vladimir Tolubko, the former deputy commander of the strategic rocket forces (the Soviet military service in control of Russia's nuclear weapons), as the new head of the Far Eastern Military District, with responsibility for defense against China.[73] The significance of this move was not lost on the Chinese, who complained about it and other instances of Soviet nuclear coercion to foreign interlocutors. For example, according to a CIA assessment, "the Chinese ambassador in Paris complained on September 19 that the Russians were now 'threatening China with nuclear war' and have moved their best rocket expert to the border as commander of the armed forces in the area."[74]

Initially, China discounted the nuclear threats, but this started to change when the Soviet Union began consultations to feel out the likely response of foreign governments in the event of a Soviet nuclear attack on China's nuclear program. For example, on August 18, Boris Davydov, second secretary of the Soviet Embassy in Washington, asked the US diplomat William Stearman "point blank what the US would do if the Soviet Union attacked and destroyed China's nuclear installations."[75] When his American interlocutor expressed concern about escalation, Davydov assured him that China would be deterred from retaliating due to Moscow's superior nuclear capability. The United States immediately transmitted the out briefing of these meetings to Chinese diplomats. In addition, on August 27, 1969, CIA Director Richard Helms briefed the press about Soviet inquiries to foreign governments about a preemptive nuclear strike on China.[76] Contemporaneously, Beijing was receiving similar messages from other foreign governments, including Australia, Finland, and Italy.[77]

Adding further to the credibility of the threats, Victor Louis, a Soviet citizen and journalist known by US and Chinese intelligence to have close government ties, wrote in the *London Evening News* on September 16 that there "was not a shadow of a doubt that Russian nuclear installations stand aimed at Chinese nuclear facilities."[78] He elaborated that Moscow had "a variety of rockets to choose from" if it chose to conduct such an attack.[79]

It was around this time that China began to take the threats seriously. On September 11, 1969, Mao met with Soviet Prime Minister Alexei Kosygin and pressed him on Soviet nuclear intentions.[80] Throughout September, China engaged in crash preparations for war, including attempts to relocate some of China's nuclear assets to Tibet.[81] On October 1, 1969, Chinese National Day, Mao, fearing a Soviet preemptive strike, shut down Chinese airports and placed the military on high alert.[82]

Believing that in the absence of talks, a nuclear strike may be imminent, Mao finally agreed to a series of negotiations.[83] Even after Mao gave in to Soviet demands, the fear of a nuclear strike lingered. He assessed that the initial Soviet delegation to Beijing might have even been a cover for a Trojan-horse-style nuclear attack.[84] On October 20, 1969, as the Soviet diplomats arrived, Mao ordered the Chinese leadership to disperse throughout the country to ensure continuity of government in the event of a decapitating strike. The day before, on October 19, Chinese Defense Minister Lin placed China's nuclear weapons on alert for the first time in China's history.[85]

China did not simply roll over, however, in the face of Russian nuclear threats. Rather, it resisted Brezhnev's demands for negotiations throughout the spring and summer. Over the course of the crisis, it habitually responded to Soviet nuclear threats with reminders of China's signficiant conventional forces at the Ussuri River and the possibility of a large-scale conventional reprisal. Moreover, China also readied nuclear forces, conducting its first underground and thermo-nuclear tests in September and, as mentioned previously, placing nuclear weapons on alert in October.

Still, these moves do not reveal a Beijing that was prepared for escalation dominance over Moscow. Soviet officials responded to China's conventional threats with plans to obliterate any invading Chinese forces with tactical nuclear weapons.[86] Moreover, China's late-stage nuclear tests and alerts were most likely not escalatory signals, but rather, last-ditch efforts to test the readiness of an infant nuclear force in the face of what appeared to be an impending superpower nuclear attack.[87]

Both sides, therefore, engaged in behavior that risked escalation to the nuclear level, but throughout the crisis, it was the Soviet Union taking the initiative and China that was forced to respond. Moscow pushed the crisis, while Beijing maneuvered in an attempt not to be pushed around. And, in the end, Mao acquiesced under the pressure of the Soviet nuclear threats.

Superiority Talk

Throughout the crisis, officials paid attention to the nuclear balance of power, they understood that the Soviet Union enjoyed nuclear superiority, and they believed that this was a source of Soviet strategic advantage. For example, *Krasnaya Zvezda*, the official newspaper of the Soviet Ministry of Defense, wrote on March 8, 1969, "The formidable weapons entrusted to [the Strategic Rocket Forces] by the motherland for the defense of the Far East are in strong, reliable hands. Let any provocateurs always remember this."[88] On March 15, 1969, a Soviet radio broadcast into China in Mandarin detailed the Soviet nuclear advantage over China proclaiming:

The whole world knows that the main striking force of the Soviet Armed Forces is its rocket units. The destruction range of these rockets is practically unlimited. They are capable of carrying nuclear warheads many times stronger than all the explosives used in past wars put together. . . . Now let us take a look at what Mao Tse-Tung can summon to counter the Soviet Armed Forces in case he decides to carry out a military adventure against us. Does he have at his disposal rockets capable of carrying nuclear warheads? As we know, the Chinese Armed Forces have no such weapon. What about aircraft? The Chinese Air Force has only a limited number of fighters and they are very much outmoded. They are the type of planes which the Soviet Air Force discarded several years ago. . . . Thus if Mao Tse-Tung and his group were to meet the Soviet Union in a contest of strength, they would certainly end up in utter defeat.[89]

These assessments were evident not only in public communications but also in private diplomatic correspondence. As discussed already, Davydov predicted to his American interlocutor that China would be deterred from responding, even to a Soviet nuclear attack, due to Russia's overwhelming nuclear superiority.

China also appeared to acknowledge, at least tacitly, the existence of a Soviet nuclear advantage. When faced with nuclear threats, it did not counter with nuclear threats of its own. Instead, it repeatedly responded with reminders of China's conventional forces in the border region and the possibility of a massive Chinese conventional retaliation. For example, in a July 1969 report, the Chinese military explained to the Chinese Communist Party leadership that China's best response to a Soviet nuclear attack would be a prolonged ground war. In one threat directed at Moscow, the Chinese leadership announced that any country that dared to strike China would be "drowned in a people's war" fought by "hundreds of millions of Chinese and the Chinese People's Liberation Army."[90]

Chinese officials also made several direct statements admitting that Soviet nuclear superiority enhanced Moscow's leverage during the crisis. In the negotiations that concluded the crisis, for example, "Beijing claimed on more than one occasion that its bargaining position was disadvantaged because 'above the negotiating table hangs the Soviet atomic bomb.'"[91]

Summary

In sum, this case provides strong support for the superiority-brinkmanship synthesis theory. The actors involved were aware of the nuclear imbalance in favor of the Soviet Union and believed that this nuclear superiority provided Moscow with bargaining leverage. The nuclear superior side was willing to escalate the crisis, issuing a series of nuclear threats to pressure its inferior opponent. The nuclear inferior Chinese took these threats seriously and did not match Soviet escalation with nuclear counterthreats of their own. The crisis was resolved when the superior state, the Soviet Union, achieved its goal of compelling a reluctant China to the negotiating table. As defense analyst Michael Gerson concludes his study of the episode, "this case stands out as a rare case of successful nuclear compellence: the Soviets used nuclear threats to effectively compel China to the negotiating table."[92]

Alternative Explanations

Alternative explanations for this case fare less well. Second-strike theory and conventional military power theory find some support, but not to the exclusion of the factors highlighted by superiority-brinkmanship synthesis theory. On the other hand, the evidence is not at all supportive of nuclear irrelevance theory. Regional nuclear posture theory and audience cost theory are not applicable to this case.

Second-Strike Theory

Second-strike theory receives some support in this case. Consistent with the idea of a nuclear revolution, both nuclear powers feared the prospect of a major conflict and neither was willing to intentionally initiate a large-scale war. Both sides were, however, willing to run some risk of conflict and to manipulate the risk of war, demonstrating the traditional brinkmanship theory logic. And, in the end, one side backed down before the crisis escalated.

Other aspects of this case cannot, however, be explained by second-strike theory. The theory would expect that the crisis outcome would be determined by the balance of stakes, not the balance of military power, yet it is not at all clear that the balance of stakes favored one side or the other. After all, the dispute involved a shared border and, therefore, the territorial integrity of both states. Moreover, the facts of the case do not reveal a significant focus on the balance of stakes or on how an imbalance of stakes may have favored the ultimate victor of the crisis. The stakes were clearly high for both sides. Indeed, a limitation of second-strike theory is that it is somewhat indeterminate for the most important crises, crises in which the stakes are high for all sides.

Also, as in the Cuban Missile Crisis, the theory cannot account for the recurring role of the nuclear balance of power in the crisis. The theory maintains that the nuclear balance of power does not matter, but, as we saw earlier, there is substantial evidence that the nuclear balance of power did matter in this case. Once again, scholars wedded to this camp might argue that policymakers were irrational to pay attention to the nuclear balance of power. They might claim that the scholars know better than their subjects. If our goal is to understand the case as it actually transpired, however, this line of argumentation does not help.

Nuclear Irrelevance Theory

Nuclear irrelevance theory, once again, fails to find empirical backing. Actors in this crisis were attuned to the nuclear balance of power and they issued and were ultimately swayed by explicit nuclear threats. These facts are inconsistent with arguments about the irrelevance of nuclear weapons or claims about a strong taboo against nuclear use. More sophisticated arguments about the irrelevance of nuclear compellence also fail to find support in this case. The Soviet Union leveraged its nuclear superiority through a series of explicit nuclear threats to compel China to the negotiating table. As mentioned above, other analysts have studied this case and concluded that it is a clear instance of successful nuclear coercion.[93]

Regional Nuclear Posture Theory

Once again, this theory is not applicable to this case. The victor of this crisis, the Soviet Union, was a superpower and is, therefore, not included in taxonomies of regional powers' nuclear postures.

Conventional Military Power Theory

Conventional forces played a role in this crisis, but not to the exclusion of the nuclear balance of power. As discussed earlier, China sought to offset the Soviet's nuclear advantage with threats to employ China's substantial conventional forces at the border. There is evidence the Soviet Union took these threats seriously. A Russian defector to the United States, Arkady Shevchenko, for example, stated that the Soviet Politburo was "terrified" of a large-scale Chinese invasion.[94]

Still, the conventional balance alone did not drive the crisis. The Soviet military was not terribly bothered by the Chinese conventional threats. As explained above, they believed they could simply annihilate an invading Chinese force through the employment of tactical nuclear weapons, including nuclear mines planted on the border.[95] More importantly, it was the Soviet nuclear, not Chinese conventional, threats that were the most prominent feature of the crisis as events unfolded. And, in the final outcome, it was the nuclear superior state, not the state relying primarily on conventional threats, that achieved its basic goals. Once again, it appears that both nuclear and conventional power mattered, but, in this crisis among nuclear-armed states, nuclear forces were more salient.

Democratic Advantage Theory

This case is beyond the scope of the democratic advantage theory. Both crisis participants were communist autocracies, so predictions that democracies enjoy a crisis bargaining advantage cannot be tested in this case. Since these states also shared a similar communist autocratic regime type, theories of "autocratic audience costs" also do not provide much analytical leverage.[96]

The 1973 Arab-Israeli Conflict

According to the US Department of State's Office of the Historian, the 1973 Arab-Israeli War "brought the United States closer to a nuclear confrontation with the Soviet Union than at any point since the Cuban missile crisis."[97] The war began on October 6, 1973, when Egypt and Syria launched a combined attack against Israel's forces in the Sinai Peninsula and the Golan Heights. After 2 weeks of fighting, the momentum turned against the Arab militaries. On October 22 and 23, 1973, the United States and the Soviet Union ushered two separate resolutions through the United Nations Security Council, calling for an immediate ceasefire, to be followed by peace negotiations. In spite of the UN resolutions, Israel continued to advance its position in the Sinai Peninsula and was on the verge of completely encircling the Egyptian Third Army.

Fearing for the fate of its Egyptian allies, Soviet Premier Brezhnev sent a message to US President Nixon on October 24 proposing that the United States and the Soviet Union deploy forces to the region to enforce the ceasefire. If Washington was unwilling to participate, Brezhnev continued, then Moscow would be forced to consider a unilateral intervention. On the same day, the Soviet Union began preparing forces, including 7 airborne divisions and 40,000 combat troops, for a military deployment to the region.

On October 25, 1973, the United States made a series of nuclear threats and placed its nuclear forces on alert in a bid to deter Moscow's intervention in the conflict. The crisis ended later that day. The Soviet Union stood down its forces and dropped demands for a large peacekeeping force. Israel ceased its military activities. Talks between Egypt and Israel began in late October and led to the Sinai Disengagement agreement of January 1974.

The Nuclear Balance of Power

In 1973, the United States enjoyed a nuclear advantage over the Soviet Union. The United States possessed 27,835 nuclear warheads compared to 15,878 on the Soviet side.[98] The overall picture was similar when considering deployed warheads and delivery vehicles. As of mid-1973, the United States deployed 6,784 strategic warheads on 1,054 ICBMs (including MIRV ICBMs), 656 SLBMs, and

496 long-range bombers. In contrast, the Soviet Union possessed only 2,220 deployed, strategic warheads on 1,550 ICBMs, 550 SLBMs, and 140 long-range bombers.[99] Washington also likely enjoyed a qualitative edge in the accuracy and reliability of its delivery vehicles.[100]

Others have argued that this nuclear balance should be characterized as one of rough nuclear parity, because both sides possessed large arsenals and a clear nuclear retaliatory capability.[101] The central argument of this book, however, maintains that nuclear advantages matter for international security even at high force levels and even when both sides possess a secure, second-strike capability. While the Soviet Union had certainly closed the gap on its Cold War rival by 1973, the nuclear balance of power still favored the United States. Nevertheless, given the massive number of nuclear weapons on both sides and the more even nuclear balance of power, this could be considered a less likely or hard case for the theory. We might expect, therefore, a more moderate effect of strategic superiority on the crisis outcome and dynamics.

Crisis Outcome

In the 1973 nuclear alert, the United States achieved its major goal of deterring Soviet intervention in the Middle East. Washington also succeeded in persuading Israel to promptly implement the ceasefire with Egypt and come to the negotiating table. Some may assume that the United States' overriding concern was the ceasefire, but, as Henry Kissinger explained to Chinese Ambassador Huang Chen at the height of the crisis on October 25, "we have one principal objective, to keep the Soviet military presence out of the Middle East and to reduce the Soviet influence as much as possible."[102] In his study of the crisis, Richard Betts concurs, writing, "Kissinger wanted the alert to show American toughness and to freeze the Soviets out of the resolution of the crisis. In this latter goal, he succeeded in spades."[103]

The record for the Soviet Union is somewhat more mixed. Moscow also achieved its goal of a rapid ceasefire and negotiations. Brezhnev, in a zero-sum competition with the United States, however, also hoped to use the crisis to enhance Moscow's influence in the Middle East.[104] He was interested in either a joint or unilateral military intervention to ensure a continued Soviet role in the region and to maintain a tight relationship with its Arab allies. In this task, Moscow failed. Indeed, although well beyond the immediate crisis outcome, the direct Israeli-Egyptian negotiations, which were launched in the midst of the crisis, would result several years later in a far-reaching peace agreement that further weakened Russian influence and elevated the United States as the centerpiece of the regional security order. As Betts writes, "within a short time, [Egyptian President Anwar] Sadat's policy shifted to cooperation with the United States and the Soviets were ejected from their role in Egypt."[105] So, while the immediate resolution was at least somewhat to Moscow's satisfaction, it failed in its broader strategic objectives. Indeed, the ICB dataset codes the crisis as a victory for the United States and a compromise for the Soviet Union.[106]

Risk Taking

Both the United States and the Soviet Union ran risks in the crisis, but the United States reached for higher rungs on the escalation ladder. Frustrated at Israel's initial refusal to obey the UN resolution, Brezhnev threatened unilateral military intervention and prepared his conventional forces for deployment to the region.

But Washington matched the Soviet threats and raised them. In the early morning hours of October 25, 1973, the United States placed its military forces on DEFCON-3, visibly increasing the readiness of its conventional and nuclear forces to their highest level since the 1962 Cuban Missile Crisis. At 5:40 am, deliberately timed to arrive after the Soviets received intelligence of the Untied States' increased nuclear alert status, US Deputy National Security Adviser Brent Scowcroft had a message delivered to Soviet Ambassador Dobrynin stating that the United States was opposed to the deployment of US or Soviet forces and that it viewed the threat of unilateral Soviet intervention "as a matter of gravest concern, involving incalculable consequences."[107] At noon, US Secretary of State and National Security Adviser Henry Kissinger gave a public press conference, which warned of the dangers of nuclear confrontation between the United States and the Soviet Union. He reminded the world that "we possess, each of us, nuclear arsenals capable of annihilating humanity" and that Soviet actions did not "justify the unparalleled catastrophe that a nuclear war would represent."[108]

By taking these steps, Washington issued clear public and private threats and, going beyond Moscow, engaged in overt nuclear brinkmanship. Kissinger explicitly referred to the risk of nuclear war in his public threats. In addition, the United States cocked the hammer on its nuclear forces by flushing nuclear submarines to sea, repositioning nuclear-capable B-52 bombers, and readying the ICBM force. In the end, the Soviet Union did not deploy conventional forces or go on nuclear alert. It did not cross US redlines. And it did not achieve its full-range of goals in the crisis.

Superiority Talk

There is some evidence that US officials believed that the nuclear balance of power enabled them to credibly raise the risk of nuclear war. Later in the decade, Kissinger said that he would not be able to repeat the nuclear alert due to the shift in the balance of nuclear power.[109] This interpretation was supported by an National Security Council staffer who claimed that, in the midst of the crisis, Kissinger declared, "this is the last time we will ever be able to get away with this."[110]

There is also some, albeit scant, evidence that the Soviet Union took the nuclear threats seriously. According to Barry Blechman and Douglas Hart in the interview of US officials involved in the crisis, Soviet officials never protested in private communications that Washington had overreacted or misinterpreted Soviet intentions to intervene. Rather, these officials claimed that Brezhnev "understood the seriousness of the American signals sent by the nuclear threat."[111]

Summary

This case once again provides support for the superiority-brinkmanship synthesis theory. The nuclear superior state, the United States, was willing to run a risk of nuclear war, and it achieved its basic goals in the crisis. The most prominent US policymaker in the crisis appears to have believed that America's bargaining position was bolstered by its nuclear advantage. On the other hand, the nuclear inferior state, the Soviet Union, was unwilling to run a risk of nuclear war and, in the end, it failed to achieve all of its crisis objectives.

Alternative Explanations

Once again, the alternative explanations perform less well in explaining this crisis. Some of the other theories can account for aspects of the crisis, but not to the exclusion of the factors identified by the superiority-brinkmanship synthesis theory. Others are inconsistent with the facts of the case altogether.

Second-Strike Theory

Second-strike theory finds some support in this case. Consistent with the theory, the United States and the Soviet Union existed in a state of MAD and neither side contemplated a deliberate attack on the other. Rather, they sought to exert coercive pressure by escalating an ongoing crisis.

Second-strike theory does not shed much light, however, on the crisis outcome. The theory would predict that the state with the greater stake would be more willing to run risks and, therefore, more likely to prevail. The stakes in the crisis, however, were of comparable gravity for both sides. Both Moscow and Washington wanted an end to hostilities, and both wanted to maintain their influence in the region. Unlike the superiority-brinkmanship synthesis theory, second-strike theory cannot offer a plausible account for why the United States was more willing to run a risk of nuclear war, or why it achieved a greater share of its crisis objectives.

Moreover, second-strike theory cannot account for the evidence that the nuclear balance of power seemed to matter. The United States enjoyed nuclear superiority and was willing and able to issue nuclear threats to achieve its goals. Henry Kissinger, perhaps the most influential statesmen in modern American history, appears to have believed that US nuclear superiority bolstered these nuclear threats. For superiority-brinkmanship synthesis theory, these facts are to be expected and easily explained. For second-strike theory, they are inexplicable.

Nuclear Irrelevance Theory

Nuclear irrelevance theory once again fails to find evidentiary support in this case. Contrary to the idea that nuclear weapons are irrelevant, or that there is a strong normative taboo against threatening their use, the United States raised the specter of nuclear war in a bid to achieve its objectives. Moreover, the Soviet Union noticed the threats, which may have influenced their decision-making.

Some may question whether the threats were superfluous and doubt that Moscow had any real intention of intervening. There is substantial evidence, however, that Moscow would have followed through on its threat to intervene had it not been for the US nuclear alert. Soviet force mobilizations were well under way before the nuclear threats were issued. The alert of 7 airborne divisions and 40,000 combat troops indicated much more than a mere bluff. One Soviet warplane deployed to the region went so far as to touch down in Egypt, only to turn around and return to the Soviet Union in the wake of the US threats. Senior US officials involved in the crisis were convinced that, absent a US response, a Soviet intervention was imminent.[112] As one participant put it, "they had the capability, they had the motive, and the assets (i.e., transport aircraft) had disappeared from our screens."[113] In addition, as also noted above, some US officials involved in the crisis maintain that the responses of their Russian interlocutors essentially acknowledged the influence of American nuclear threats on Soviet behavior.[114] Nuclear skeptics have recently written that this case shows that nuclear threats are often misinterpreted in crisis because Brezhnev reportedly said, "Nixon is too nervous—let's cool him down." [115] But this quote shows a leader in an inferior position looking for an off ramp toward de-escalation. It is, therefore, also fully in line with the expectations of superiority-brinkmanship synthesis theory.

As Blechman and Hart write, even if none of the officials believed nuclear war was imminent, "it does not detract from the role played by the risk of nuclear war in resolving the crisis, nor the perception by at least some American decision-makers that emphasizing these dangers could help to achieve the U.S. objective."[116] These are not facts supportive of the idea that nuclear weapons are irrelevant.

Regional Nuclear Posture Theory

Once again, this theory is not helpful for understanding this case. The crisis participants were superpowers and neither, therefore, possessed a regional power nuclear posture.

Conventional Military Power Theory

Arguments about conventional military power are indeterminate in this case. Given the lack of significant numbers of US or Soviet forces on the ground in the region and the ongoing mobilizations on both sides, it is unclear who enjoyed a usable conventional advantage in the theater. US officials involved in the crisis later stated that the crisis was evolving so quickly that neither side had the time to accurately plan or assess what form a conventional conflict might take.[117] Unlike the United States, however, the Soviet Union did ready a large number of conventional forces for possible intervention. If anything, therefore, Moscow likely enjoyed the conventional advantage. Regardless of whether one considers this a case of Russian advantage or rough parity, however, this theory cannot explain why the United States achieved a larger portion of its desired end state. Moreover, the crisis was resolved in the immediate wake of both a nuclear show of force and a verbal nuclear threat, making it difficult to argue that the threat of conventional force alone resolved the conflict. Conventional military power theory is simply not much help in understanding the outcome of this crisis.

Democratic Advantage Theory

Democratic advantage theory finds at least some superficial correspondence with the facts of this case. The democratic state, the United States, issued public threats and ultimately achieved its basic goals in a crisis with the autocratic Soviet Union. Contrary to the predictions of the theory, however, two of the most important elements of the US threats, the nuclear alert and Scowcroft's private message, were highly visible to Moscow, but not the US domestic audience. Moreover, there is little indication that Moscow was particularly focused on US internal debates or that Moscow viewed the US threats as credible due to domestic political audience costs. Perhaps future research will show that Brezhnev was swayed by the credibility of US threats due to audience costs, but proponents of audience cost theory have not yet marshaled any evidence to this effect and this study found no such evidence.

The Kargil Crisis

Finally, we turn our attention to a more recent crisis and one that does not involve the superpowers. The Kargil Crisis was a conflict between nuclear-armed India and Pakistan that occurred from May to July 1999.[118] Because the crisis is more recent than the others, there have been fewer in-depth studies of the case, resulting in less material for analysis. Yet, the available information suggests that the facts of the case are largely consistent with the superiority-brinkmanship synthesis theory.

The conflagration was rooted in the historic tensions over control of the disputed Kashmir region. In February 1999, Pakistan inserted paramilitary forces across the Line of Control (LOC), which serves as the de facto border between the two countries, and took up positions in abandoned Indian control posts in the Kargil sector of Kashmir. Pakistan's goal was to cut off India's supply route from Kashmir to Ladakh with the hope that this would force India to withdraw forces from the Siachen Glacier in Kashmir and negotiate a broader settlement to the Kashmir dispute. The infiltration was discovered in May, when, in response to a tip from local shepherds, an Indian scouting unit went to investigate and was captured and tortured to death by Pakistani forces. On May 26, India responded with a major military operation to expel Pakistan's paramilitary forces from the Indian side of the LOC. India mobilized 200,000 troops and bombarded Pakistani positions with artillery and air power. Although India sustained heavy losses, including having several fighter planes shot down, its forces slowly began reclaiming positions from Pakistan's paramilitary forces.

In addition, both made thinly veiled nuclear threats. India placed its nuclear forces on alert, and, although Pakistan officially denies it, some experts believe Pakistan also readied its nuclear forces.

On July 2, 1999, Pakistan's prime minister, Nawaz Sharif, flew to Washington to meet with US President Bill Clinton in the hope that the United States would intervene and force a ceasefire, locking in Pakistan's territorial gains. Instead, Clinton demanded that Pakistan withdraw all forces from the Indian side of the LOC.

Facing a worsening military position and international diplomatic opposition, on July 4, 1999, Sharif agreed to the troop withdrawal and formally recognized the legitimacy of the LOC. Although sporadic fighting continued for several weeks, the crisis drew to a close by the end of July.

The Nuclear Balance of Power

In 1999, India likely maintained a nuclear advantage over Pakistan. It is difficult to know the precise nuclear balance of power, as both states are secretive about their nuclear forces and neither maintains actively deployed nuclear warheads. Rather, warheads and delivery vehicles are thought to be de-mated and stored separately and are only assembled in the event of a crisis. Due to these factors, outside analysts attempt to estimate the size of India and Pakistan's nuclear arsenals based on their fissile material production capability and their means of nuclear delivery. India enjoyed a temporal lead in constructing a nuclear force, conducting its first nuclear test (a so-called peaceful nuclear explosion [PNE]) in 1974. India and

Pakistan both became declared nuclear powers with a string of nuclear tests in May of 1998, but since the mid-2000s, Pakistan has arguably placed greater priority on its nuclear forces as a means of offsetting India's conventional military superiority. Due to these factors, most analysts assess that India's head start gave it a nuclear advantage initially, but that, over time, Pakistan has closed the gap and in recent years may have even attained superiority over India.[119] David Albright, from the Institute of Science and International Security estimated that, in 1999, at the time of the Kargil Crisis, India had produced enough nuclear material for 65 nuclear warheads and Pakistan possessed sufficient material for 39.[120]

Moreover, Pakistan was also more vulnerable to a nuclear exchange, which is also relevant when assessing a state's expected cost of nuclear war and, therefore, the nuclear balance of power. To this point, this chapter has considered large, continental-size powers with some capacity to absorb a nuclear attack. India also fits this description. It occupies a subcontinent and in 1999 possessed a population of over 1 billion people dispersed throughout its territory. But Pakistan is a comparatively small state, with only 135 million people at the time of the crisis, and suffers from a notorious lack of strategic depth. The shorter-range delivery vehicles available to both states in 1999 enabled India to better hold at risk a larger portion of Pakistani territory than vice versa. Further, Pakistan's concentrated population makes it vulnerable to countervalue targeting. Over 10% of its population is located in just two cities, Karachi and Lahore. Indian officials have remarked that they can hold most of Pakistan at risk by targeting only seven aim points.[121] If one were to conduct a detailed nuclear exchange calculation, such as those presented in chapter 2, one would see that these factors increase Pakistan's vulnerability to strategic nuclear attack. In sum, when considering all of these factors, it is highly likely that India enjoyed nuclear superiority over Pakistan at Kargil.

To be sure, however, given the small arsenal sizes and significant uncertainty in the strategic balance of power, this is the hardest case for the theory. We may expect, therefore, only a modest effect of the relatively even nuclear balance of power on the crisis outcome. Even in this difficult case, however, we find some evidence for the theory.

Crisis Outcome

India achieved its basic goals at Kargil, and Pakistan did not. India succeeded in its objectives of forcing a Pakistani troop withdrawal, reclaiming territory on the Indian side of the LOC, and receiving a political commitment from Pakistan to recognize the sanctity of the LOC and prohibit future border incursions. In contrast, Pakistan failed in its attempts to control military outposts on the Indian side of the LOC; sever India's supply lines to Kashmir, and force a favorable settlement to the Kashmir dispute.

Some may object to this coding by pointing out that the Kargil settlement did not put a definitive end to Pakistani cross-border raids into India, but this sets too high a standard for what is required in order for a crisis to be determined a success. Crises rarely result in the permanent resolution of underlying geopolitical disputes. Rather, one must focus on the tangible goals sought in the crisis and assess whether or not those were achieved.[122] By this standard, India achieved its goals and Pakistan failed. Consistent with this perspective, the ICB also codes this case as a victory for India and a defeat for Pakistan.[123]

Risk Taking

Both India and Pakistan showed a willingness to run risks in the crisis, but, in the end, it was Pakistan that actively sought diplomatic off ramps and ultimately withdrew its forces to de-escalate the crisis.

India initially escalated the crisis by mounting a major military operation against Pakistani forces in Kashmir. To be sure, India carefully calibrated its operations. It did not advance beyond the LOC into Pakistani-controlled Kashmir and it refrained from mobilizing for an invasion of Pakistan's vulnerable Punjab. At the same time, it did conduct a major combined arms operation against Pakistani forces in its bid to retake Kargil.

India also supported its conventional actions with nuclear threats. India moved to "readiness state 3" and prepared nuclear warheads for mounting on delivery vehicles.[124] Verbal nuclear threats were also issued through the Indian media. The *Times of India*, for example, ran an editorial arguing that Pakistan would not dare continue the fight against a nuclear India because while "Pakistan's generals may not mind sacrificing a few hundred of their soldiers and Afghan mercenaries to Indian air strikes . . . they are not going to expose their own cities to needless risk."[125]

Pakistan also ran serious risks in the crisis, but, in the end, it backed down. Contrary to the expectations of the theory of this book, Pakistan initiated the crisis with its cross-border raid. In fact, many scholars have examined the role that Pakistan's fledgling nuclear arsenal may have played in emboldening Pakistan's initial action.[126] Moreover, when India retaliated, Pakistan initially fought back and downed several Indian aircraft that had crossed the LOC. In addition, Pakistan also attempted to signal the risks of nuclear escalation. Pakistan's Foreign Secretary Shamshad Ahmad issued a thinly veiled nuclear threat in a newspaper interview at the height of the crisis, warning that Pakistan "would not hesitate to use any weapon in our arsenal to defend our territorial integrity."[127] It is uncertain whether Pakistan also prepared its nuclear forces for use. US policymakers indicate that it did, but informed Pakistanis deny these claims.[128] It is clear, however, that Pakistan was unwilling to provide military reinforcements to the irregular troops in Kashmir on the Indian side of the LOC, behavior very different from similar crises in 1948 and 1965. Moreover, in the end, it eventually agreed to withdraw its forces from across the LOC.

Superiority Talk

There is substantial evidence that officials on both sides were cognizant of the danger of nuclear escalation. There is also some, albeit much more limited, evidence that the strategic balance of power was on the minds of top officials in the crisis. Most prominently, when discussing why Pakistan ultimately backed down at Kargil, then–Indian Defense Minister George Fernandez replied that the reason was simple: in the event of a nuclear exchange, "we might have lost part of our population, but Pakistan may have been completely wiped out."[129] India's then-National Security Adviser Brajesh Mishra concurred with this assessment, arguing, "Pakistan can be finished by a few bombs... anyone with a small degree of sanity would know that [nuclear war] would have disastrous consequences for Pakistan."[130]

To be sure, no policymaker statement recorded years after events transpired should be taken at face value, but Fernandez and Mishra did not have anything to gain by appealing to Indian strategic superiority. Fernandez's most direct personal involvement was with the victorious conventional campaign in Kargil, and his own legacy would have been better burnished with claims about the importance of India's conventional forces and military strategy. Moreover, these statements cannot be interpreted as an attempt to justify Indian nuclear strategy, as New Delhi's official doctrine does not tout strategic superiority but, rather, promotes a minimum deterrent force and "a no-first use" policy.[131]

Summary

In sum, the facts of the Kargil Crisis are at least consistent with the expectations of the superiority-brinkmanship synthesis theory. The superior state, India, was willing to escalate in ways that Pakistan did not expect, some of its policymakers were cognizant of the nuclear balance of power and claimed that this provided them with a geopolitical advantage, and, in the end, New Delhi achieved its goal of expelling Pakistani forces from Kashmir.

Alternative Explanations

With the exception of nuclear irrelevance theory, many of the alternative explanations can provide at least a partial explanation of the Kargil case. None of them, however, is obviously superior to the account provided by the superiority-brinkmanship synthesis theory.

Second-Strike Theory

Whether these states possessed a secure, second-strike capability at the time of the Kargil Crisis is open to debate and depends on the threshold one chooses. According to standard definitions, these states lacked an assured retaliatory capability. Neither state possessed a large and dispersed nuclear force, nuclear-armed submarines, or deployed mobile missiles at the time of the crisis. If the states lacked a second-strike capability, then the theory does not offer firm predictions. It might suspect, consistent with prenuclear models of warfare, that the state with aggregate military advantages should prevail.

If one sets a lower threshold for the nuclear capabilities required for assured retaliation, then second-strike theory arguably finds some support. India and Pakistan both possessed nuclear weapons, and both states evinced clear caution for fear of nuclear escalation. At the same time, both states manipulated the risk of escalation, including verbal threats and military mobilizations.

Second-strike theory still struggles, however, to explain the outcome. Why did India win and Pakistan capitulate? One could argue that the balance of stakes favored India because it was defending the status quo while Pakistan was attempting to revise it, but this only reopens the semantic issues raised earlier about when and where one marks the status quo. Was India engaged in deterrence because it was defending the preexisting LOC, or was it conducting a compellence campaign because it was attempt to force entrenched Pakistani paramilitary forces to retreat? Both interpretations are reasonable, thus calling into question any explanation relying exclusively on the balance of political stakes.

Moreover, unlike the central argument of this book, second-strike theory cannot account for why some officials, including India's minister of defense, appeared to believe the nuclear balance of power mattered. We can either charge that India's top defense official is misguided about the drivers of the conflict he personally oversaw, or, more convincingly, conclude that second-strike theory excludes an important variable: military nuclear advantages.

Nuclear Irrelevance Theory

The nuclear irrelevance theory clearly fails in this case. Nuclear weapons were central to the conflict. Both sides were attentive to the possibility of nuclear escalation, may have readied nuclear weapons for use, and issued overt nuclear threats. The United States intervened and helped mediate a resolution to the crisis at least in part because it wanted to forestall a nuclear exchange in South Asia.[132] Some Indian officials believed their country's strategic advantage helped push back Pakistan from the brink. All of these facts are inconsistent with the key tenets of nuclear irrelevance theory. The Indian and Pakistani nuclear threats and alerts are contrary to the idea that there is a taboo against nuclear use. And the fact that India compelled Pakistan to withdraw its forces in the heat of a crisis between nuclear powers is in tension with the nuclear compellence skepticism variant of the theory.

Regional Nuclear Posture Theory

Regional nuclear posture theory is operative for the first time because this case deals specifically with regional nuclear powers. The theory is designed to explain the initiation of conflict and it succeeds in this regard, but it is less helpful when it comes to understanding the conflict's outcome. Regional posture theory maintains that "asymmetric escalation" postures enhance deterrence. Consistent with the predictions of the theory, India's "assured retaliation" posture was insufficient to deter Pakistan's cross-border raid and Pakistan's "asymmetric escalation" posture induced caution in India and forestalled a major, conventional conflict.[133] Yet, despite having the less aggressive regional nuclear posture, it was New Delhi that achieved its basic crisis goals. Superiority-brinkmanship synthesis theory can help explain this outcome; regional nuclear posture theory cannot.

Conventional Military Power Theory

The outcome of this conflict is also consistent with the predictions of conventional military power theory. The conventional superior state, India, achieved its basic political goals and Pakistan, the weaker conventional state, did not. Yet, other aspects of the case demonstrate that it was not conventional power alone that mattered.

Both states held back force that could have potentially been brought to bear and, as we saw previously, they held back in no small measure because they were wary of nuclear escalation. It is possible that both states looked ahead to the likely outcome of the conventional conflict and Pakistan decided that it could not win. Yet, the prominent role of nuclear weapons highlighted above and the US intervention (also driven in part by fears of nuclear escalation) were salient factors pushing the crisis toward an early resolution. The military balance likely played a role, but not to the exclusion of the nuclear dimension of the conflict.

Democratic Advantage Theory

The outcome of Kargil is superficially consistent with the democratic advantage argument, but the mechanisms of the case are not. India, an unquestionable democracy, achieved its basic goals in the crisis. Pakistan, a nondemocracy in 1999 according to standard measures, did not.[134] Contrary to the predictions of democratic advantage theory, however, India did not make concrete public threats with the goal of generating audience costs. Moreover, there is no evidence that Pakistan's leaders paid close attention to the domestic debate in India or backed down due to the mechanisms identified by audience cost theory. It is possible that future scholarship will turn up evidence to support this case, but such support was not found in this study and has not yet been produced by the theory's advocates in this or other prominent cases.

Conclusion

This chapter analyzed the mechanisms of the superiority-brinkmanship synthesis theory in four case studies: the Cuban Missile Crisis; the Sino-Soviet Border War; the 1973 Arab-Israeli conflict; and the Kargil Crisis. In all four cases, the theory found support. Leaders paid attention to the nuclear balance of power and believed that nuclear superiority enhanced their bargaining leverage, nuclear superior states were more willing to escalate dangerous crises, and nuclear superior states achieved their basic goals. Contrariwise, leaders in inferior states, in at least some cases, felt hampered by their strategic disadvantage. Moreover, inferior states were more likely to de-escalate crises and ultimately failed to achieve their basic goals. In sum, superiority-brinkmanship theory finds strong support in both large-N quantitative analysis and in qualitative case studies of the most important crises of the nuclear era.

Some alternative arguments also found some support but, on balance, performed less well than superiority-brinkmanship synthesis theory. Others were completely inconsistent with the available evidence. Elements of second-strike theory were often supported, but, at the same time, it nearly always struggled to explain crisis outcomes and was unable to account for recurring policymaker interest in the nuclear balance of power. Regional nuclear posture theory was not often applicable to the superpower crises explored in this chapter, but it did offer important insights into Kargil, the one crisis to which it was best suited. Conventional military power shaped many of these crises, but not to the exclusion of, and indeed mostly in a subordinate role to, the nuclear balance of power. Democracies often achieved their goals in these crises, but there is no evidence for the "audience costs" mechanisms postulated by democratic advantage theory. Finally, nuclear irrelevance theory proved itself irrelevant. In all four of these crises, nuclear weapons played a prominent role.

To this point, the book has demonstrated that nuclear superiority matters for nuclear war and crisis outcomes. But does the nuclear balance of power affect the deterrence of conflict in the first place? To address these questions, the next chapter turns to issues of deterrence and compellence. Or, more precisely as we will see, it explores the deterrence of compellence.

5

Nuclear Deterrence
and Compellence

One branch of nuclear irrelevance theory grants that nuclear weapons matter for deterrence (threats designed to defend the status quo), but claims that they do not for compellence (threats aimed at revising the status quo).[1] These scholars have criticized scholarship on nuclear crisis outcomes, such as that conducted in the previous two chapters, because they charge that by looking at all nuclear crises, this research design conflates crises dealing with deterrent and compellent threats, threats which they claim operate according to distinct logics. If the superiority-brinkmanship synthesis theory is correct, however, we should expect the nuclear balance of power to matter not only for deterrent but also for compellent threats. So, which position is correct? Does nuclear superiority matter for compellence?

To help resolve this debate and to provide a further test of the superiority-brinkmanship synthesis theory, therefore, this chapter examines whether nuclear superiority matters for compellent threats. Drawing on the Militarized Compellent Threat (MCT) data set, the same data set used by nuclear irrelevance theorists, I find that the nuclear balance of power is central to patterns of international coercion.[2] Indeed, the evidence is clear and compelling in simple descriptive statistics. Since 1945, nuclear-armed states have issued forty-nine compellent threats against nuclear inferior states and zero compellent threats against nuclear superior states. For nuclear-armed powers, therefore, in this sample of data, nuclear superiority has been a necessary condition for even attempting compellence. Compellence may be more difficult than deterrence, as Schelling and others have maintained, but this chapter demonstrates that engaging in nuclear compellence from a position of inferiority is even harder still.[3] In short, nuclear superiority deters compellence.

This chapter proceeds in five sections. First, it discusses the difficulty of studying deterrence and further explains the purpose and research design of this chapter. Second, it reviews and critiques the scholarship of the nuclear irrelevance theorists on compellence. Third, it presents data used to analyze the relationship between the nuclear balance of power and militarized compellent threats. Fourth, it conducts the data analysis and discusses the results. Fifth, and finally, it concludes with the implications of the analysis for the central argument of this book.

The Challenges of Studying Deterrence

The primary purpose of nuclear weapons is not to win nuclear wars or crises, but to deter conflict, especially nuclear attack by other nuclear-armed states. An analysis of deterrence, therefore, is central to any study of the role of nuclear weapons in US nuclear strategy or in international politics. At first blush, one might conclude that nuclear weapons have ably served this deterrence function without fail. No nuclear-armed state has ever suffered a nuclear attack or been the victim of major conventional military aggression. The United States, for example, has possessed a robust nuclear force for decades, and in that time it has been able to deter attacks against itself and its allies.

There is, however, a classic problem in the study of deterrence. If an attack does not occur, is it because deterrence worked, or is it because the adversary never had any intention of attacking?[4] Answering this question definitively is difficult because there is no variation on the dependent variable; in other words, no state has ever conducted a nuclear attack on another nuclear-armed state.

One method scholars have used to get around this issue, therefore, is to look at lower levels of conflict where there are meaningful patterns of variation.[5] While nuclear-armed states have not been subjected to major attack, they have been victims of threats, challenges, and military disputes. If nuclear deterrence works, then we might expect that nuclear powers (or in our case, nuclear superior powers) will be less likely, on average, to be targeted by these lower-level threats.

Understanding the origins of these smaller-scale disputes also teaches us something about the deterrence of full-scale nuclear war. After all, it is incredibly unlikely that nuclear war will occur as a bolt-out-of-the blue strike. It is hard to fathom that any world leader will wake up one day, look herself in the mirror, and say, "today is a good day for nuclear war." Rather, it is much more likely that any nuclear exchange would first begin as a much lower-level military challenge, escalate into a crisis, and then, only as a last step, to nuclear exchange. By understanding why states escalate or back down in crises (chapters 3 and 4) and why they issue military threats in the first place (the purpose of this chapter) we are also coming closer to explaining the deterrence of nuclear war itself. This chapter pursues this objective, therefore, by examining the conditions under which states issue MCTs.

Explaining Nuclear Weapons
and International Coercion

Nuclear compellence skeptics do not believe that nuclear weapons are potent coercive instruments.[6] They argue that nuclear weapons are ineffective tools of compellence because nuclear weapons are not useful for taking or holding territory and, due to their immense destructive power, it is difficult for policy-makers to credibly threaten their use. Consistent with this perspective, in a test of 210 compellent threat episodes from 1918 to 2001, they find that nuclear-armed states are no more likely to achieve compellent success than nonnuclear states.

There are several problems, however, with this analysis. First, it relies heavily on the problematic distinction between deterrence and compellence. As was argued in chapter 1, some scholars question whether this is anything more than a seman-tic difference.[7] Moreover, even if one grants the distinction in theory, it becomes quite murky in practice. How does one define the status quo? Where does one draw the line in real-world crises? And which threats are defending the status quo and which are revising it? And why are these definitional issues so central to the role of nuclear weapons in international politics? After all, if nuclear weapons matter in international politics, it is not obvious why their influence depends on questionable decisions made by outside analysts about where to mark the status quo. But, nuclear compellence skeptics do just this, dividing all of post–World War I history into episodes of military threats designed to revise the status quo and everything else.

Second, as this book argues, there is good reason to believe that military nuclear advantages matter, but nuclear compellence skeptics focus narrowly on whether the challenger possesses nuclear weapons. They do not, therefore, care-fully account for the nuclear balance of power between challenger and target and how nuclear superiority might affect coercive outcomes.[8]

Third, they exclusively study the outcome of compellent threats that take place and not on the antecedent causes of the initiation of compellent threats. Their studies do not allow them, therefore, to explore the idea that nuclear superior states are more likely to achieve compellent success because they are more willing to try. Nor do they study whether nuclear superior states are more or less likely to be threatened themselves. This methodological choice is important. After all, states do not issue threats randomly. The conditions that cause states to issue threats in the first place might also affect the prob-ability of coercive success. As Fearon argues, military power is an important factor in international politics, but because the balance of power is known to leaders before entering into conflict, we might not see a relationship between power and the outcomes of confrontations that actually take place.[9] Instead, we should expect the effects of military advantages to be expressed most clearly at the earlier, selection stage. This potential selection problem is most problematic for scholars, such as nuclear compellence skeptics, who maintain that military power, in this case nuclear weaponry, does not affect patterns of international coercion. By focusing only on the outcome of the threats that take place, they risk overlooking military power's most important effects at earlier stages.

In an attempt to account for this selection problem, these scholars report a robustness test using a Heckman selection model, but a "post-1945" dummy variable does not serve as an adequate exclusion restriction as the authors claim. The "post-1945" variable does predict having nuclear weapons, but the instrument is poor because pre-1945 and post-1945 cases are not directly comparable. At best, this approach captures the effect of nuclear weapons that is due to the instrument, that is, due to the fact that nuclear weapons were invented, but not due to the most important reason for variation, namely that some states have them and others do not. Moreover, scholars increasingly argue that the Heckman cure is worse than the disease and advise improved approaches, such as including all the variables that could affect the selection and outcome stages into a single equation that models the outcome of interest only.[10] Alternatively, instead of a reliance on complicated regression models in general, Achen recommends "careful graphical and cross-tabular analysis" in order to "justify statistical specifications [and] show that they really fit the data."[11]

This brings us to the fourth problem with nuclear compellence skeptics' analysis. They present the end results of complicated regression analysis, but they do not take steps recommended by Achen and other methodologists to present simple descriptive statistics, such as cross-tabulations. As a result, it is difficult for readers to discern what is really going on under the hood in their study.

In sum, previous research has not provided a complete picture of how the nuclear balance of power affects international coercion. This chapter, therefore, advances the research agenda on nuclear weapons and compellence in three ways. First, it focuses on the effect of the nuclear balance of power, not simply nuclear possession. Second, it considers the initiation, as well as the outcome, of militarized compellent threats. Third, and finally, it presents simple descriptive statistics to present a more accurate and fine-grained picture of the data. To ensure comparability with previous scholarship, it relies on an analysis of preexisting data of nuclear compellent threats used by the nuclear irrelevance theorists. It is to this data that we now turn.

Empirical Analysis

To test the hypotheses about the nuclear balance of power and compellent threats, I draw on the Militarized Compellent Threat (MCT) data set, the same data set employed by nuclear compellence skeptics.[12] The dataset contains 210 observations of interstate compellent threats, occurring between 1918 and 2001. In each coded episode, a challenger issued a compellent demand against a target state and threatened to use force if the target refused to comply. Since the argument of this book deals with nuclear weapons, I focus on the nuclear era from 1945 to 2001, which leaves us with 118 compellent threat episodes.[13] To examine how the nuclear balance of power affects the initiation and outcome of compellent threats, I embed the MCT data in a larger data set that includes information on all directed dyads in the international system from 1945 to 2001 extracted using EUGene.[14] All variables are from Sechser and Fuhrmann unless otherwise noted.[15]

The Data

This study examines two dependent variables. To gauge the determinants of compellent threat initiation, I create *Threat initiation*, a dichotomous variable coded "1" if the challenger issued a MCT in a given dyad-year and "0" otherwise. The second dependent variable is the success of the compellent threat. A threat is successful when a target state voluntarily complies with all compellent demands without the challenger having to resort to the use of military force. *Success* is a dichotomous variable coded "1" if the episode was resolved successfully and "0" otherwise.

The key independent variable is *Nuclear superiority*. As in chapter 3, I code this dichotomous variable "1" if the challenger possesses more nuclear warheads than its opponent in a given year and "0" otherwise.

Analysis

In a separate article, colleagues and I conduct multivariate regression analysis on this data and find that nuclear inferior states are less likely to initiate MCTs and less likely to achieve compellent success.[16] This chapter presents some simple descriptive statistics and cross-tabular analysis that clearly and powerfully reveal the same basic finding. I first explore the idea that nuclear superior states will be more likely to issue compellent threats. Turning to Table 5.1, I find overwhelming support for this hypothesis. Since 1945, nuclear-armed states have issued forty-nine militarized compellent threats, and all

Table 5.1 **The Nuclear Balance and Militarized Compellent Threats, 1945–2001**

Nuclear Status	Success	Failure	Attempts
Nuclear-Armed Superior Challenger	10	39	49
Nuclear-Armed Inferior Challenger	0	0	0
Nonnuclear Challenger	16	53	69

forty-nine of these threats were against inferior countries. Seven threats were against nuclear-armed states with fewer nuclear weapons and forty-two were against states that lacked nuclear weapons altogether, but zero were directed at nuclear states with larger nuclear arsenals. This finding is stunning. It suggests the nuclear balance of power is determinative when it comes to patterns of international coercion. Since 1945, nuclear-armed states have issued zero threats against nuclear superior countries. In other words, for nuclear-armed states, nuclear superiority has been a necessary condition for the issuance of a compellent threat.

Moreover, nuclear superior states have succeeded in compelling adversaries in ten out of these forty-nine attempts, for a success rate of approximately 20%. Seven of the forty-two threats against nonnuclear states were successful and three of the seven threats against nuclear-armed but inferior states worked. This overall success rate of roughly 20% is similar to the average success rate in nuclear crisis outcomes seen in chapter 3. Furthermore, the absolute number of successes is much greater than the absolute number of compellent successes for nuclear inferior states, which, like their number of attempts, is zero. As the hockey great Wayne Gretzky once said, "you miss 100% of the shots you don't take."

Some may question the validity of this data and wonder whether it is really the case that nuclear states have never attempted to threaten superior states. I too have questions about this data set. Has North Korea, for example, never issued a compellent threat against the vastly superior United States? According to this data set, it has not. This coding could be due to the specific way the data set's creators define a compellent threat, the time period under analysis, or a simple mistake in the coding. Regardless of the reason, this data set is the best possible arena in which to test the superiority-brinkmanship synthesis theory and nuclear compellence. For even when using a data set that was originally used to demonstrate that nuclear weapons do not matter for compellence, I find that nuclear superiority is, in fact, all important for compellence.

This finding provides strong support for the superiority brinkmanship synthesis theory. Nuclear superiority is highly relevant to patterns of international coercion. Military nuclear advantages deter compellence.

Alternative Explanations

I now turn to consider alternative explanations. I begin with nuclear compellence skeptics because these scholars used this exact same data set in support of their conclusion that nuclear weapons do not matter for nuclear compellence. Readers may be wondering, therefore, how they came to their conclusion. The answer is simple. First, they included many cases of nonnuclear states threatening other nonnuclear states. Second, they compared the success rates of nuclear-armed challengers to the success rate of nonnuclear challengers, conditional on a threat being issued. As we can see in Table 5.1, nonnuclear states issued 69 threats and were successful 16 times. This success rate, 16 out of 69, or 23%, is not statistically different from the success rate of nuclear superior states: 10 out of 49, or roughly 20%. They conclude, therefore, that nuclear weapons do not matter for compellence.

This finding, however, is incomplete at best. First, it overlooks the importance of the nuclear balance of power. As shown above, every threat issued by a nuclear-armed state was issued by a nuclear superior state. Nuclear inferior states have never issued a threat. Again, this strongly suggests that the nuclear balance of power and, therefore, nuclear weapons matter for compellence.

Second, it does not compare the frequency with which nuclear superior states issued threats against the same frequency for nonnuclear states. Nuclear superior states issued threats 49 times in 47,074 interactions with other states, or roughly one threat for every one thousand opportunities. In addition, they achieved compellent success in ten of these cases or roughly one successful compellent threat in every 4,700 possible opportunities. In contrast, nonnuclear states issued 69 threats in 1,073,681 interactions, or once in every 15,500 opportunities. They were successful 16 times, or one in every 67,000 opportunities. The chi-squared statistic indicates that the probability of observing these differences if nuclear superiority has no effect on the issuance of a compellent threat is less than 0.001. Contrary to the claims of nuclear compellence skeptics, this analysis provides evidence of a link between the nuclear balance of power and the initiation of militarized compellent threats.

Lebron James is one of the best basketball players of his generation. Kay Felder is a role player on Lebron's team, the Cleveland Cavaliers. If, in a game, Lebron made 15 out of 30 shots from the floor and scored 30 points, this would be considered a commanding performance. If, in the same game, Felder came off the bench, took two shots and made one, few would take much notice. One of these athletes was clearly much more successful than the other. No one would maintain that these performances were the same because both athletes shot 50% from the field. Yet, this is exactly the case that compellence skeptics present with their statistical analysis.

To be sure, part of this difference might be explained by capacity as many nonnuclear states simply lack the ability to credibly employ force against many other states. Still, this fact is consistent with the central argument of this book that robust nuclear capabilities enhance a state's ability to engage in international coercive diplomacy. Moreover, such an explanation cannot account for the drastic difference in success rates between nuclear superior and nuclear-armed but inferior dyads as the vast majority of the states in a position of nuclear inferiority (including the Soviet Union vis-à-vis the United States during the first half of the Cold War, China against the Soviet Union/Russia, and Pakistan against India) possess a clear ability to use force against their nuclear superior opponents.

In sum, nuclear superior states are much more likely than nonnuclear states to achieve compellent success because they are much more likely to try. Examining success outcome conditional on a threat taking place, as nuclear compellence skeptics have done, obscures this reality. These strong findings are also inconsistent with the arguments of broader nuclear skepticism theory or the idea that there is a strong taboo against nuclear use. If it is certain that nuclear weapons will not be used, then it is hard to provide another explanation for why nuclear superior states enjoy an unblemished record in nuclear coercive bargaining.

I now turn to evaluate other, alternative explanations. Second-strike theory finds some support. Three out of the seven threats made by nuclear superior states against other nuclear-armed states were against states that possessed secure, second-strike capabilities as defined and measured in chapter 3. So, threats against states with a second-strike capability are rare, but their rate of successful deterrence is not unblemished and, therefore, falls short of the record shown by nuclear superior states.

Regional nuclear posture theory does not provide much data for meaningful analysis. Asymmetric escalation postures are extremely rare. According to Narang, the only states to have ever adopted asymmetric escalation postures are France since 1960 and Pakistan after 1998.[17] When this rare event is layered against another rare event, compellent threats, there is very little opportunity for researchers to observe states with these postures participating in compellent threat episodes. According to the MCT data, a nuclear-armed France issued three compellent threats against Serbia in the 1990s and was successful once. And Pakistan was the target of a failed threat by India in 2001. Perhaps this suggests that it is difficult to coerce states with asymmetric escalation postures, but, in the end, there is just not enough data here to begin to draw even tentative conclusions.

There is a tight correlation between nuclear superiority and conventional superiority, and readers may wonder whether the findings of this chapter are driven largely by conventional military power. It would stand to reason that both matter at least to some degree. Turning to the data, however, we find that

conventionally superior, but nuclear inferior states have been subjected to compellent threats by nuclear-armed states twenty-three times, whereas nuclear
superior and conventionally inferior states have never been so targeted. This
suggests that nuclear superiority is a much more reliable indicator of compellent threats than conventional superiority. Moreover, although the result defies
easy explanation, in their regression analysis, nuclear compellence skeptics actually find that conventional military power is negatively correlated with coercive
success.[18]

The relationship between democracy and compellent success has also been
explored elsewhere, and scholars have found that there is not a statistically significant relationship between these variables.[19]

Finally, one might object that there may be a lurking variable, call it an aggressive strategic culture, which causes some states to both build large arsenals and
coerce neighbors. According to this conceptualization, it is not superiority, but
an underlying propensity for aggression driving these results. But this interpretation is inconsistent with the obvious fact that almost all nuclear-armed states
are inferior in relation to some states, but superior vis-à-vis others. For example, during much of the Cold War, Moscow possessed superiority over Beijing,
but not Washington. If superiority-brinkmanship synthesis theory is correct,
we should expect that nuclear states will be more willing to issue threats against
inferior opponents. Table 5.2 rearranges the same basic information from

Table 5.2 **List of Compellent Threats by Nuclear-Armed States, 1945–2001**

Country	Threats against Nuclear Superior States	Threats against Nuclear Inferior States
United States	0	17
Soviet Union	0	7
Great Britain	0	9
France	0	3
China	0	3
Israel	0	3
South Africa	0	6
India	0	1
Pakistan	0	0
Total	**0**	**49**

Table 5.1 to reveal that this theoretical expectation is met without exception. Empirically, we see that nearly all nuclear-armed states have issued compellent threats at some point, but the very same states prove to be more or less aggressive depending on the arsenal size of the adversary. They issue threats against inferior, but not superior, opponents. This more detailed analysis provides further support for the hypothesis that nuclear superiority has a powerful effect on patterns of MCTs.

Conclusion

This chapter found that nuclear superiority matters for deterrence and compellence. States in a position of nuclear superiority are more likely to issue compellent threats and to achieve compellent success. Or, looked at from the other direction, nuclear superior states are less likely to be targeted by military threats; nuclear superiority deters compellence. Indeed, among nuclear armed-states since 1945, nuclear superiority has been a necessary condition for issuing compellent threats. These results provide strong support for the central argument of this book.

At the same time, these findings call into question the major alternative theory about nuclear weapons and compellence: nuclear irrelevance theory. The data show that military nuclear advantages matter for international coercion. Compellence is difficult, but compelling from a position of nuclear inferiority is even harder still.

Second-strike theory finds some support in this chapter. Regional nuclear posture theory does not provide enough data for meaningful analysis. And the evidence does not support the idea that conventional military power or democracy increase the chances of successful compellence.

To this point, the book has presented clear evidence that nuclear superiority provides its possessor with important benefits in international politics. It limits damage in the event of a nuclear war and provides it with a coercive advantage in international crisis diplomacy. But certainly such a potent tool cannot be an unmitigated good. In addition to these benefits, does not nuclear superiority carry significant costs as well? Part II of this book picks up this challenge.

PART TWO

THE DISADVANTAGES
OF NUCLEAR ADVANTAGES?

6

Strategic Stability

This, the second part of the book, examines the possible negative consequences of a robust nuclear posture. It shows that the most commonly cited costs of nuclear superiority (strategic instability, arms races, nuclear proliferation, and runaway defense budgets) are either exaggerated or nonexistent. When the full range of costs and benefits are taken into account, therefore, we see that there is good reason to maintain military nuclear advantages. There is, indeed, a logic to American nuclear strategy.

We begin in this chapter with a discussion of strategic stability. Many nuclear deterrence theorists and policy advocates have argued for decades that nuclear superiority has a glaring downside: it increases the risk of nuclear war.[1] They argue that the nuclear balance of power is most stable when both states possesses a secure, second-strike capability and rough nuclear parity. In this condition, they argue, neither state has an incentive to intentionally launch a nuclear war. The acquisition of a military nuclear advantage, however, is "destabilizing" and may give both states new incentives to contemplate nuclear first use. Clearly, the benefits of nuclear superiority demonstrated to this point might pale in comparison to the increased risk of suffering a devastating nuclear exchange. This raises a key question: does nuclear superiority undermine strategic stability?

This chapter examines the question in detail and finds that this conventional wisdom is incorrect. It argues that nuclear superiority likely contributes to greater levels of strategic stability. Moreover, it maintains that traditional arguments about strategic stability fail to differentiate between good instability, that which might favor US interests, and bad instability, which works to the disadvantage of Washington and its allies. When this distinction is taken into account, we see that US superiority enhances positive instability and dampens negative instability. In short, strategic stability should be listed among the benefits, not the possible costs, of an American nuclear advantage.

The rest of the chapter continues in four parts. First, it reviews the conventional wisdom about strategic stability that exists in some policy advocacy circles. Second, it turns to international relations scholarship on the causes of war to examine the existing state of knowledge about imbalances in military power and war. Third, it conducts an examination of the logic of traditional strategic stability arguments in the nuclear-specific context. Fourth, it examines the existing empirical evidence on the nuclear balance of power and escalatory risks. Finally, the chapter concludes with a review of the findings and their implications for the central argument of this book.

Strategic Stability: The Conventional Wisdom

Stability may be the most overused and poorly defined concept in the policy community. In the foreword to a recent volume on strategic stability, for example, Thomas Schelling begins by writing, "My first question on approaching this volume was, 'What is strategic stability?' "[2] Stability clearly has a positive valence and instability a negative one, so given the choice in the abstract, most people would instinctively choose stability. For this reason, policy advocates often justify proposals by arguing that their preferred course of action would contribute to stability and their opponent's policies would be "destabilizing."[3] As the Schelling quote demonstrates, however, what precisely is meant by stability and how various policy proposals contribute to it, is not always entirely clear. Stability has been variably used to mean peace, a lack of tension in bilateral relations, the absence of an arms race, the absence of pressures to escalate a crisis, and just about everything desirable other than baseball and apple pie.

Fortunately for our purposes, some have been more careful in defining their terms, and we will base our analysis on these more concrete concepts. In international relations scholarship, stability generally means the absence of war among the great powers.[4] Stabilizing factors, therefore, are those that reduce the probability of great power war. Similarly, in the nuclear policy realm, the clearest definition of strategic stability is a situation in which nuclear-armed states lack incentives to intentionally launch a nuclear first strike against a nuclear-armed rival.[5] Policies that reduce nuclear first-strike incentives, therefore, are considered to be stabilizing, and those that increase the risk of nuclear war are destabilizing. (Arms race stability, another possible definition of strategic stability, is considered in the next chapter).

The origins of the term "strategic stability," like much else in this field, can be traced to the first generation of American nuclear strategists. Months after the bomb was dropped, defense intellectuals like Bernard Brodie realized that nuclear weapons, due to their massive destructive capabilities, had the potential to deter great power war.[6] They also believed that the development of nuclear forces in both the United States and the Soviet Union could lead to a broader international stability due to this symmetrical balance of terror between the superpowers.

Shortly, thereafter, however, the RAND analyst Alfred Wohlstetter pointed out that this balance of terror may be more "delicate" than many believed.[7] In what began as a bomber basing study for the US Department of Defense, Wohlstetter began to worry that the US bomber force may be vulnerable to a Soviet nuclear first strike. If Moscow thought that it could get away with a successful nuclear first strike against the United States' primary means of delivery, then it might be tempted to do so. Wohlstetter's study prompted a panic among US defense officials and analysts, who feared that the Soviet Union might be in a position to launch a nuclear surprise attack on America's strategic forces. To avoid this fate, Washington's immediate response was to alter its mobilization plans to ensure that its strategic bomber force could be alerted quickly in a crisis. If nuclear-armed aircraft could get off the ground before the initiation of any hostilities, then the Soviet Union would not be able to destroy them on runways and in hangars at a small number of air bases in Europe and the United States. Moreover, if Moscow had no hope of destroying them, the logic continued, then it would have no reason to attack in the first place.

In subsequent years, the United States took additional steps to ensure a survivable nuclear force, including deploying nuclear weapons on ICBMs in hardened silos and in submarines at sea. Indeed, these steps to ensure the survivability of the force bequeathed to us the nuclear triad that forms the backbone of US nuclear posture to this day.

Given this experience, it was not a large logical leap for some US analysts to assume that Moscow might have similar fears.[8] If America ever developed a first-strike capability against the Soviet Union, then Moscow might panic and respond in ways potentially contrary to American interests. For example, it too might decide to launch its nuclear forces in the early stages of a crisis before they could be destroyed in an American nuclear attack. Many US analysts came to the conclusion, therefore, that there may actually be benefits for the United States to ensure that the Soviet Union also maintained an assured retaliatory capability. So long as Moscow felt secure that its nuclear weapons could not be destroyed, then it would have no reason to launch them. In short, according to this line of thought, the goal was to avoid "delicate," or unstable, balances of power. In other words, strategic stability could only be achieved through mutual vulnerability to nuclear war.

It bears noting that this logic is 180 degrees away from how defense planners tend to think about security competition in the conventional military realm. Generally, it is believed that one protects oneself by increasing military power and reducing vulnerabilities to an opponent's forces. To ensure one's safety in a nuclear world, on the other hand, strategic stability theorists maintain the opposite: that states are most secure when they are vulnerable to the nuclear forces of an opponent. States are less safe when they possess a nuclear first-strike capability, according to this line of argument, because their inferior opponent might paradoxically have more of an incentive to launch a nuclear attack. The most stable nuclear balance of power would be one in which both states possesses survivable arsenals of roughly equal size. The most stabilizing nuclear posture would include countervalue forces and targeting policies capable of doing great damage to an enemy's society, but incapable of holding its nuclear forces at risk. Any US strategies or capabilities that might provide the United States with a nuclear advantage, according to this logic, are to be resisted because they might be "destabilizing." Continuing the paradoxical nature of this set of arguments, nuclear forces and strategies intended to intentionally slaughter the other side's civilian populations are stabilizing and, therefore, good. Whereas forces and strategies that target only an opponent's military forces are destabilizing and, therefore, abhorrent.

Over the years, the idea that military nuclear advantages might increase the risk of war has come to be applied not only to a perfect first-strike capability, but to any development that might improve one's counterforce capabilities or limit one's vulnerability to nuclear war. Quantitative nuclear warhead advantages, MIRV warheads, accurate or prompt delivery systems, counterforce doctrines and policies, missile defenses, civil defenses, conventional prompt global strike, and hypersonic glide vehicles have all been opposed for this reason.[9] In short, many of the very elements of a robust nuclear posture that the United States has long maintained and pursued are thought to be "destabilizing" according to strategic stability theorists.

These criticisms continue to the present day. For example, in 2010, Michael Gerson argued that the United States should adopt a nuclear "no first use" policy because if adversaries fear a US nuclear first strike, then they might have an incentive to go first, undermining strategic stability.[10] In 2016, Charles Glaser and Steve Fetter argued that the United States should abandon a counterforce strategy for China, because "U.S. damage-limitation capabilities and efforts to preserve and enhance them are likely to create pressures that increase . . . the overall probability of nuclear war between the United States and China."[11] In 2017, Caitlin Talmadge argued that Chinese fears of US counterforce strikes could lead to Chinese nuclear escalation.[12] And The New York Times reported in August 2017 that President Trump's plans to modernize the US nuclear arsenal could be "destabilizing."[13] These arguments have always been controversial. Indeed, perhaps the central divide in debates over US strategic policy is often over the question of whether the desired end state is superiority or mutual vulnerability. On the side of vulnerability, one often finds Democrats, the US Department of State, arms control advocacy groups, and a majority of international relations scholars (who, it bears noting, also tend to be on the left side of the political spectrum). On the side of superiority, one generally finds Republicans, the US Department of Defense, the national laboratories in the Department of Energy, the defense industry, and right-leaning think-tank experts.

Yet, despite these debates, the United States has tended to develop and maintain a robust nuclear force in the face of unrelenting criticism from opponents. We see these fights playing out again today as Washington continues to improve its missile defense capabilities, test hypersonic weapons, and modernize its nuclear arsenal in spite of outside pressures to stop.[14]

This then returns us to the central question of the book: is US nuclear strategy illogical? Is Washington increasing the risk of nuclear war in a quixotic quest for illusory strategic advantages? Or is it rather notions of strategic stability themselves that are unsound?

International Relations Theory, Causes of War, and Nuclear Strategic Stability

This section explores the concept of strategic stability through the prism of international relations theory. It shows that, contrary to the claims of strategic stability theorists, state-of-the-art international relations research would suggest that nuclear superiority is stabilizing and it is in fact nuclear parity that is destabilizing.

When considering a specific problem, a good international relations scholar will often ask: what is this a case of? When trying to understand the ongoing insurgencies in Iraq and Afghanistan in the mid-2000s, for example, many smart analysts recognized these as cases of the broader phenomenon of interethnic civil war and turned to the academic literature on this subject for guidance.[15] This section makes a similar move. Arguments about military nuclear advantages and nuclear strategic stability are essentially arguments about how the military balance of power affects the likelihood of war. What then does the international relations scholarship tell us about this subject?

International relations scholars have long debated the effects of balances of power or preponderances of power for international stability. Traditional realist arguments have maintained that the balance of power is a near law-like phenomenon in international politics. As Jean-Jacques Rousseau wrote, "It maintains itself without effort, in such a manner that if it sinks on one side, it reestablishes itself very soon on the other."[16] Taking the balance of power as a given, structural realists have theorized about whether different distributions of power balances are more or less stable. Kenneth Waltz, for example, theorized that multipolar worlds, with several great powers, are less stable than bipolar worlds, made up of only two major powers.[17]

Other international relations scholars, however, did not take the balance of power for granted. They theorized that preponderances of power are possible and may be more stabilizing than power balances. In 1973, for example, Geoffrey Blainey famously argued that the fundamental cause of war was, in fact, disagreements about the balance of power.[18] He argued that in order for two states to choose to go to war, leaders on both sides must believe that they have at least some shot of winning. And he argued that both sides were likely to believe they had a shot of winning when they were close to evenly matched. On the other hand, according to Blainey, a clear preponderance of power is the surest guarantor of peace.

James Fearon has further developed this line of thinking in what has become the dominant theoretical paradigm for understanding international conflict in contemporary international relations theory: the bargaining model of war.[19] Fearon conceives of war, and much of international politics, as a bargaining problem. Two states have a significant disagreement over some issue (whether it be territory, policy, or something else), but fighting a war over the dispute is suboptimal, because wars are costly and states would be destroying some of what they are fighting over. It would be much better to simply come to a negotiated settlement and avoid the costs of conflict. War, therefore, according to Fearon, should be understood as a breakdown in bargaining. He argues that among rational states there are three causes of bargaining failure: private information and incentives to misrepresent that information, issue indivisibility, and problems of credible commitment.

The first cause, private information and incentives to misrepresent, is most relevant to the question of strategic stability. Fearon maintains that if the balance of military power and the balance of resolve were perfectly known, then war would never occur. States would assess the likely outcome of conflict based on which side was stronger and which side cared more about the issue at stake. Then they would cut an appropriate deal that reflected the bargaining power of the two sides as determined by the underlying balances of power and resolve. Rather than fight a costly war in what was bound to be a losing effort, the weaker state would simply concede the contested issue. It would be better off with this bargain than it would be to fight and lose a war only to arrive at a similar outcome. According to this perspective, therefore, in a world with perfect information and rational states, war would never occur. The problem is that states do not have perfect information about the power and resolve of their adversaries, and this can lead to bargaining failure. As Blainey argued decades before, wars result from disagreements about which side will win.

Even the imperfect information problem could be resolved in theory, according to Fearon, because states could simply reveal information about their power and resolve in order to clear up any misperceptions. The problem with this solution, however, is that both sides have an incentive to misrepresent their power and resolve. In order to get the best possible bargain short of war, states have an incentive to portray themselves as more powerful and more willing to fight over the contested issues than they actually are. How many times have leaders promised that "all options are on the table" when they really had no intention of ever using force? This prevents states from accurately revealing true information about their power and resolve and obstructs peaceful resolutions to conflicts. Since all states have an incentive to say they are willing and able to fight if necessary to get their way, their opponents have no way of knowing who is sincere and who is bluffing. So, if a state assumes wrongly that its opponent is bluffing, then bargaining can break down and war can occur even among "rational" states. In sum, according to Fearon, private information about the balance of power and the balance of resolve and incentives to misrepresent that information are a cause of war.

When are states most likely to make mistakes about the balance of power (our focus in this chapter)? Holding other factors constant, war is most likely when there is military parity. When there is a rough balance of power, the outcome of conflict is less certain and bargaining failure more likely. When, on the other hand, there is a clear preponderance of power, the outcome of conflict can be predicted with greater confidence. The more lopsided the balance of power, the less likely states are to misperceive it, and the more likely they will be to reach a bargain short of military conflict.

This theoretical logic has also been supported in recent empirical research. Scholars have consistently shown a tight correlation between rough parity in the balance of power and the frequency of militarized interstate disputes. Contrariwise, imbalances of power are associated with peace.[20] As Douglas Gibler writes in a recent issue of the *American Political Science Review*, "study after study finds that equally-capable states experience higher rates of conflict."[21]

Bringing this discussion back to the question of strategic stability, therefore, contemporary international relations theory suggests that a lopsided nuclear superiority should enhance strategic stability and nuclear parity should be destabilizing. Would China's leaders be more likely to believe that they could prevail in a nuclear conflict with Washington if Beijing possessed 2,000 nuclear weapons capable of reaching the United States, rather than the 65 or so it possesses today? Intuition would suggest that they would, but this is diametrically opposed to the arguments of strategic stability theorists. This suggests either that traditional arguments about strategic stability are mistaken, or that nuclear conflict operates according to its own special logic. It has been argued, for example, the high cost of nuclear war convinces leaders facing a nuclear-armed opponent that they have no shot of winning at an acceptable cost, thus eliminating uncertainty about the balance of power. This is plausible, but it is not the case made by strategic stability theorists. Rather, strategic stability theorists argue the exact opposite. They claim that nuclear-armed states may intentionally choose to start nuclear wars with nuclear-armed states when there is an imbalance of nuclear power. As we will see in the next section, this argument does not hold up under interrogation, even in a nuclear specific context.

Why Strategic Instability Is Not a Cost of US Nuclear Superiority

This section will reevaluate the traditional notions of nuclear strategic stability and show that the logic of these arguments is quite weak and rests on many questionable assumptions. Moreover, a more careful consideration suggests that, if anything, US nuclear superiority enhances instability that works in Washington's favor and diminishes problematic instability. In sum, therefore, strategic instability is not a cost of US strategic superiority.

In theory, there are two possible pathways by which US nuclear superiority could increase the risk of nuclear war: either a nuclear superior United States may strike first, or a nuclear inferior US adversary may have an incentive to initially pull the nuclear trigger. We explore each of these possibilities in turn.

A Nuclear Superior United States Strikes First

Strategic stability theorists argue that a US first-strike advantage is destabilizing, but this section shows that, in fact, a US first-strike advantage is just that: an advantage.

Typically, strategic stability theorists argue that a US nuclear advantage is destabilizing because it could entice an enemy to strike first. I will cover this argument later in the chapter. Logically, however, the first reason that nuclear superiority might increase the risk of nuclear war is that the side with nuclear superiority (in this case the United States) might initiate a nuclear war because its leaders assess that they could initiate a "splendid" first strike.[22] In other words, they may believe that they could conduct a nuclear attack that would succeed in disarming an adversary, allowing them to fight and win a nuclear war while avoiding retaliation altogether, or suffering only acceptable levels of damage in return.

The strategic stability paradigm assumes that first-strike advantages are destabilizing regardless of which side possesses it, but from Washington's point of view, there is a clear difference between a US ability to conduct a first strike and an adversary's ability to conduct a first strike on the United States. Namely, the latter is much more threatening.

It is obvious that a US nuclear posture that renders the United States vulnerable to an enemy first strike would be dangerous for the United States. That position of extreme weakness could invite an enemy nuclear attack on the United States and its allies, or render them vulnerable to nuclear coercion. Fortunately, as the first state to develop nuclear weapons, the United States has never faced this situation, and, if it did, it would be motivated to take whatever steps necessary to expand and strengthen its nuclear forces in order to deter potential enemy nuclear attacks. On this point, therefore, strategic stability theorists and I agree: an extreme imbalance of power (in favor of US enemies) is problematic (for the United States).

Let us then consider the possibility of a US first strike. The United States currently possesses a splendid first-strike advantage against roughly 190 states. This list includes all of the nonnuclear weapon states in the international system and the three nuclear-armed states (Israel, Pakistan, and India) whose nuclear delivery systems currently prevent them from launching a nuclear attack against the US homeland. (Of course, it is nearly impossible to imagine the United States conducting a nuclear attack on any of these countries, but it does have the capability.) At present, the United States can conduct, or threaten to conduct, a nuclear attack against these countries without worrying about the possibility of nuclear retaliation against US territory. As we saw in the first part of the book, this nuclear superiority provides a significant source of strategic advantage. Would the United States be more secure if it possessed a more "stable" nuclear deterrence relationship with North Korea, Venezuela, Iran, or other states? Would the United States be better off if Iran had a reliable means of holding US cities hostage with nuclear threats? It is hard to answer this question in the affirmative. The United States would be worse off in such a scenario. The United States would have less leverage over these states and be vulnerable to nuclear coercion and even nuclear attack. For decades, therefore, there has been a bipartisan consensus that the United States must work to stop the spread of nuclear weapons to additional states.

Some scholars, known as proliferation optimists, challenge these views, but as I have argued at length elsewhere, they work from an unsophisticated understanding of deterrence theory and their arguments contain internal, logical contradictions.[23] Moreover, their arguments have never found favor in the corridors of power.[24]

To be sure, US superiority may tempt Washington to use nuclear weapons first, undermining stability as defined in this chapter. Indeed, the United States was the only country to use nuclear weapons in wartime, against a nonnuclear

Japan in World War II. For this reason, a US first strike advantage likely does increase the risk of US nuclear use, but this is not a problem for the United States. After all, the United States won a world war with the help of its nuclear superiority over Japan. Instability due to the possibility of US first use is, therefore, instability that is desirable from Washington's perspective. It is good instability. It certainly is not a reason for Washington to refrain from pursuing military nuclear advantages.

The same is true when considering America's relations with established nuclear powers, such as Russia and China. With a large margin of superiority over these rivals, Washington might be tempted to launch a splendid first strike. This would certainly be "destabilizing" in the sense that it would increase the risk of nuclear war, but, again, this is a nuclear war of the United States' choosing. The purpose of US national security policymaking is often, and should be, to provide the president with a range of options. While any US president should be extremely cautious about employing nuclear weapons, there are conceivable scenarios in which a US president might want the ability to conduct a nuclear first strike. Indeed, the 2010 US Nuclear Posture Review explicitly states that the United States reserves the right to use nuclear weapons against nuclear weapon states and against nonnuclear weapon states in noncompliance with their nonproliferation obligations.[25] In the event that these states engage in major conventional aggression, or a chemical or biological weapons attack against the United States or its allies, for example, a US president might decide to use nuclear weapons first. Moreover, even if the president never chooses to conduct a nuclear first strike, the ability to credibly do so is necessary in order to deter adversaries and reassure allies. Although the United States does not possess a splendid first strike capability over Russia and China, such a capability would very much be in the US national interest.

A possible objection may be that a US nuclear attack on a nuclear power would be dangerous because it might not fully succeed in disarming its opponent. Since Russia and China have delivery vehicles capable of reaching the United States, any US nuclear first strike that failed to destroy every single Russian or Chinese warhead could result in nuclear retaliation against the US homeland.

This is an important consideration and the primary reason why any US president would be extremely hesitant to conduct a nuclear first strike against a nuclear-armed country. Indeed, it is nearly impossible to imagine a US president launching a nuclear first strike on Russia or China. But, if in an extreme scenario, a US president still chose to launch a nuclear attack knowing full well the likely consequences, this would be a deliberate choice because he or she believes the attack is in America's interests and that the alternatives are even worse. Furthermore, and as demonstrated throughout this book, the ability to credibly do so, even if the option is never employed, enhances Washington's bargaining leverage in scenarios short of war.

The fear of possible retaliation following a US nuclear first strike, therefore, is not a good reason why the United States should not maintain a nuclear advantage over rivals. Indeed, the principal fear in this scenario is that a disarming strike might not work. The concern, therefore, is one of insufficient US superiority, not too much.

In sum, a nuclear balance of power that provides the United States with a first-strike capability may very well be destabilizing, but it is instability in America's favor and, therefore, not a good reason why Washington should not pursue the capability.

A Nuclear Inferior Adversary Strikes First

The second, and more common, argument as to why nuclear superiority might be destabilizing is because the state in the position of nuclear inferiority (in this case, America's adversaries) may feel "use 'em or lose 'em" (UELE) pressures, but this argument also withers under interrogation.[26]

According to strategic stability theorists, a US nuclear advantage increases the danger of nuclear war because the inferior opponent may fear that its nuclear arsenal is vulnerable to a first strike. Rather, than wait for the adversary (in this case the United States) to move first and wipe out, or seriously blunt, its strategic forces, the argument goes, the inferior state may decide to intentionally launch a nuclear war early in a crisis in order to avoid suffering a disarming first strike. This is the logic most often invoked by strategic stability theorists when they claim that US nuclear advantages are destabilizing. This is also the precise problem identified and inspired by Wohlstetter's basing studies.

Use 'em or lose 'em enjoys a certain superficial plausibility, but, upon closer inspection, there are two fundamental reasons why the logic simply does not hold up. First, it ignores the fact that the superior state retains a healthy ability to retaliate. So, even if the inferior state is worried about having its nuclear weapons eliminated in a first strike, the decision to launch its nuclear weapons first as a coping mechanism would be a decision to intentionally launch a nuclear war against a state with at least a secure, second-strike capability. This means that even if the inferior state launches its nuclear weapons first, it will be virtually guaranteed to suffer devastating nuclear retaliation. Moreover, given that it is in a situation of extreme inferiority (so extreme that it might even be vulnerable to a preemptive nuclear strike), this would mean intentionally launching a devastating nuclear war that will likely turn out much worse for itself then for its opponent. It would simply be irrational for a state to intentionally launch a nuclear war against a state with an assured retaliatory capability.

Let us consider a concrete example. The United States maintains nuclear superiority over China, as we have seen in previous chapters. Strategic stability theorists want us to believe that if the United States takes additional steps to further enhance its superiority, then China would face even greater temptations to launch a nuclear first strike against the US homeland in the event of a serious crisis. In other words, strategic stability theorists hold that China would be so worried about losing a devastating nuclear war against United States that it would intentionally choose to start a devastating nuclear war against the United States. The argument does not make sense.

But academic deterrence theorists and other critics of American nuclear strategy try to have it both ways. They attempt to argue that a second-strike capability is sufficient to deter any nuclear-armed state from launching a nuclear attack. Therefore, they advocate that the United States need not build a nuclear force that goes beyond this requirement because a second-strike capability is more than enough. But, then they warn that if Washington strengthens its nuclear forces too much, other countries will be tempted to launch a nuclear attack against a United States armed with a second-strike capability. So, which is it? Does a second-strike capability reliably deter intentional nuclear attack, or not? If not, then they cannot maintain that a second-strike capability is more than enough for deterrence. If so, they cannot claim that a second-strike capability-plus will provoke a nuclear attack.

Some readers may retort that my argument also attempts to have it both ways too, but they would be mistaken. As the attentive reader will recall, this book has consistently argued that a second-strike capability *is* sufficient to deter an intentional nuclear attack and that nuclear superiority contributes to a state's national security goals in other ways: limiting the damage of nuclear war, deterring lower-level disputes, and enhancing bargaining leverage in high-stakes crises. In sum, the argument of this book is internally consistent, but the claims of strategic stability theorists contain a logical contradiction.

Furthermore, UELE arguments are unpersuasive for a second reason. These arguments overlook the fact that the inferior state has a more attractive option at each stage of the crisis: backing down and living to fight another day. A state in a position of inferiority involved in a high-stakes crisis always has a choice between three options: (1) intentionally launching a nuclear first strike in a devastating nuclear war that it will almost certainly lose; (2) playing brinkmanship, escalating the crisis, and raising the risk of nuclear war in a contest that it is also likely to lose; or (3) simply de-escalating the crisis and avoiding any further danger. Faced with this menu, option 1 is by far the least attractive, but this is precisely the option we must believe leaders will purposely choose in order for the UELE logic to hold. This is untenable. Indeed, much of nuclear deterrence theory and strategy as it has developed over the past 70 years is based on the premise that option 1 is simply unacceptable. Contrary to the claims of strategic stability theorists, therefore, UELE does not pose a problem to strategic stability.

To be sure, if a nuclear war were preordained to occur with 100% certainty, then an inferior state might have good reason to go first, but the risk of nuclear war is never certain. Indeed, the risk of nuclear war is in the control of both states. To avoid any risk of nuclear conflict, all they must do is capitulate. While an unattractive option, it is more desirable than intentionally launching a devastating nuclear war that it is bound to lose. Indeed, even the highly stylized game theoretic model in chapter 1, which relies on a spontaneous risk of nuclear war, assumes that states can avoid any further risk of catastrophe by submitting at any stage of the crisis.

There are five possible counterarguments to these claims, but none of them are persuasive. First, one could argue that the above case against strategic stability theory rests on states making rational calculations, but the leadership of future US adversaries might not be fully rational. Kim Jong Un in North Korea, for example, may be irrational or extremely risk acceptant and may be willing to run great risks of, or even to intentionally fight, a nuclear war. This is possible. But, if this is the case, then, we should not expect strategic stability through mutual vulnerability and nuclear parity to discourage him from starting a nuclear war either. Surely, the subtleties of strategic stability theory would be lost on a lunatic. Moreover, even madmen and excessive risk takers have some understanding of power. If anything, a future reckless leader should be even more willing to launch a catastrophic nuclear war from a position of parity (i.e., a situation of so-called strategic stability), than from a position of inferiority.

Second, one might counter that states will refrain from UELE in most circumstances, but in truly dire straits, when their backs are against the wall and they have nothing left to lose, then we cannot rule out the possibility of inferior states lashing out with nuclear strikes. For example, they might claim, a state on the verge of being overrun in a conventional invasion might use nuclear weapons rather than lose everything.[27] Some analysts believe that Russia or North Korea, for example, may conduct limited nuclear "de-escalation" strikes rather than lose a conventional war against the United States.[28] This is a compelling argument, but note that this is not an argument about UELE, or about the nuclear balance of power. Rather, this is an argument about the dangers of putting an opponent's back against the wall in international politics. This is a cardinal rule of diplomacy, but it is not a reason to avoid military nuclear advantages. Indeed, if anything (and as above), a country in a dire position would likely be even more tempted to gamble for resurrection through nuclear use from a position of parity, rather than from a position of severe inferiority. Once again, the idea that US nuclear superiority somehow increases the risk of nuclear war against the United States does not add up.

Third, and related, my colleagues have argued that it is possible that a US adversary might pursue a limited nuclear war strategy with a vulnerable nuclear force. Rather than lose the opportunity to "escalate to de-escalate," therefore, the state may conduct a limited nuclear strike early in a crisis to shock the United States into suing for peace, before the United States succeeds in wiping out its nuclear forces. This would be a true UELE situation, they maintain, because the enemy is incentivized to escalate early precisely in order avoid losing the option. This argument, however, solves one logical contradiction only to create another. Theories of limited nuclear war do not maintain that limited nuclear strikes are decisive in and of themselves. Rather, they have coercive power because they signal the threat of more devastation to come. It is one of the highest rungs on brinkmanship's escalation ladder. If a state is vulnerable to a first strike, however, then it cannot credibly threaten that there is more devastation to come. The United States would have little incentive to sue for peace in response to a limited strike from such a state. It could simply retaliate (with the full moral and legal authority that would follow victimization in a nuclear attack) and disarm the enemy's remaining nuclear forces. Again, this state would be better off simply backing down than inviting the disarming nuclear strike it was trying to ward off. If, on the other hand, the state has a survivable force, then it would not have needed to escalate early for fear of UELE in the first place.

The only possible exception to this logic would be for a state with a vulnerable force, following a limited nuclear war strategy, that believes that Washington's stake in the crisis is so insignificant, that the United States would prefer to back down after suffering a limited strike, rather than follow through with a disarming retaliatory strike of its own. This would be one rational pathway to nuclear escalation due to UELE, but it is a bit of a stretch. A number of unusual conditions must be necessary to make this scenario possible. It is certainly not the broad class of instability problems often portrayed by strategic stability theorists. Moreover, it is a problem that can be addressed. In these cases, Washington can simply take additional steps to demonstrate its stake in these scenarios and to disabuse adversaries of the notion that Washington would simply buckle after a limited nuclear attack from a state with a vulnerable nuclear force.

Fourth, one Washington DC-based colleague has argued that the theory of this book itself provides a reason for superiority to undermine stability. He argued that a state in an inferior position may conduct a massive counterforce nuclear strike on the United States in order to vault itself into the superior position and then use its newfound superiority to deter US retaliation. This is certainly an interesting idea. But it would again require us to believe that the state would intentionally launch a massive nuclear war against a state with a second-strike capability. This is a notion that is contrary to every major theory of nuclear deterrence, including strategic stability theory itself. In addition, this argument would have to maintain that this hard-to-fathom scenario would be more likely if the United States enjoys superiority. But, if anything, an enemy attempt to conduct a nuclear first strike and then "deter our deterrent" should be more attractive to an enemy in a position of parity than one in an inferior position.[29]

Fifth, and finally, some might object that UELE does not cause leaders to intentionally launch nuclear war, but rather, in a bid to ensure the survivability of their arsenals, they might be forced to take steps to ensure, should the need arise, that they can use them before they are wiped out. They might be tempted, therefore, to adopt launch on warning nuclear postures, put their nuclear forces on hair-trigger alerts in a crisis, or delegate nuclear launch authority to low-level commanders. While these steps might be logical to ensure the survivability of the force, they also might make it harder for national leadership to control exactly when and how nuclear weapons are used and, therefore, increase the risk of accidental or inadvertent nuclear exchange. In other words, this line of argument essentially holds that inferior states will be more willing to run risks of nuclear war in serious crises.

Note, however, that this logic runs exactly counter to the expectation of the superiority-brinkmanship synthesis theory. The central argument of this book maintains that inferior states will be much more cautious in games of brinkmanship. Theoretically, the argument of this book demonstrates that there is good reason why inferior states should be less willing to run nuclear risks—because they will suffer disproportionality should things escalate. Which perspective is correct? To some degree, this is a debate that cannot be definitively settled in the empirical realm. We therefore finish this chapter with a consideration of the empirical record.

Strategic Stability: The Evidence

If the UELE argument from strategic stability theory is correct, then we should expect that nuclear inferior states will intentionally launch nuclear wars against states with superior nuclear arsenals. We should also expect that inferior states will engage in risky behavior in high-stakes crises to ensure that their nuclear weapons can be launched before they are destroyed. If, on the other hand, the argument of this book is correct, then we should expect that nuclear inferior states should never intentionally launch nuclear wars and they should be hesitant to run risks of nuclear war against nuclear superior adversaries.

Turning back to the empirical record reviewed in the first half of the book, we see that nuclear inferior states have frequently backed down in high-stakes crises with nuclear superior opponents. Nuclear inferior states have placed forces on alert in crises and have otherwise run risks of nuclear war, but they have been less, not more, likely to do so than their superior opponents. Nuclear inferior states have never issued a compellent threat against a nuclear superior opponent.

And nuclear inferior states have never intentionally launched a nuclear war against a superior opponent due to UELE fears or for any other reason.

It is certainly possible that some future leader may intentionally launch nuclear weapons in order to avoid the risk that they will be destroyed in a nuclear attack. But logic and over 70 years of evidence give us strong reason to be skeptical that this is a likely outcome.

Conclusion

This chapter examined the effect of the nuclear balance of power on strategic stability. Specifically, it examined past arguments about how US nuclear superiority might undermine strategic stability and increase the risk of nuclear war. By reviewing international relations theories on the causes of war, examining the specific logic of strategic stability theory, and considering the available evidence, this chapter did not find any support for the idea that imbalances in nuclear power cause dangerous strategic instability. In fact, if anything, theory and evidence suggested that a preponderance of power reduces the risk of war. Moreover, this chapter showed that US nuclear superiority increases instability that works in Washington's favor and dampens problematic instability.

As it relates to US nuclear strategy, therefore, this chapter suggests that nuclear strategic stability is not a downside to the maintenance of a robust nuclear posture. These findings, therefore, provide further support for the logic of American nuclear strategy.

Surely, however, there is no such thing as a free lunch. Certainly, some readers may be thinking, there must be some disadvantage to a preponderant American nuclear force. Perhaps a large nuclear force instigates arms races with other nuclear powers? Turn the page to find out.

7

Arms Races

This chapter considers the effects of a robust nuclear posture on nuclear arms races. To this point, we have shown that US nuclear superiority provides several strategic benefits and does not undermine strategic stability. Critics have argued however, that attaining enduring military nuclear advantages is difficult if not impossible because it will likely provoke rival states to respond in kind with their own military arms build-up, offsetting any initial US advantages.[1] Moreover, in making the attempt, the United States might provoke a costly and unnecessary arms race, ultimately leaving itself in an even worse position than where it began.

This chapter evaluates these claims. Drawing on existing international relations scholarship and an empirical examination of US strategic arms competitions with its nuclear-armed rivals, it argues that, contrary to the above arguments, unnecessary arms races are not generally a significant cost to the maintenance of a robust nuclear force. In order for arguments about US superiority provoking undesirable arms races to be correct, four premises must be true: first, US nuclear-armed rivals must be willing and able to match US capabilities; second, adversary nuclear posture decisions must be driven to a significant degree by US nuclear posture and not by other factors; third, any arms races that do occur must have been avoidable at an acceptable cost; and, fourth, the United States must fail in bids to achieve meaningful and enduring military advantages over its rivals. (Questions about the financial cost of nuclear weapons are deferred to chapter 9).

This chapter shows that these four premises rarely hold. First, it advances new theoretical propositions on "nuclear underkill" to delineate the theoretical reasons why US adversaries are often unwilling or unable to respond to US nuclear advantages. Second, it shows that enemy military buildups often occur irrespective of US nuclear force posture decisions. Third, it explains that competing in and winning arms races is sometimes a necessary, if undesirable, part of international politics. Finally, turning to the empirical record, the chapter shows that arms races are rare and that the United States has consistently been able to achieve meaningful and enduring strategic advantages over its nuclear-armed rivals.

In sum, nuclear arms races are not generally a significant downside of US nuclear strategy. Before we turn to these arguments, however, the chapter begins with a review of arguments about why some believe a robust US nuclear posture might provoke arms races.

Why a Robust Nuclear Posture Might Provoke Arms Races

Many international relations theorists and policy analysts have criticized US nuclear strategy, arguing that a robust nuclear force will result in unnecessary and costly arms races.[2] They maintain that efforts to gain enduring military advantages over other capable states are at best costly and pointless and, at worst, self-defeating and dangerous.

The canonical "spiral model" theory of arms racing provides the intellectual underpinnings for many of these arguments.[3] The theory begins from the assumption that security is scarce in an anarchic international system. The system is rife with uncertainty about other states' intentions and, in this environment, security-seeking states are constantly faced with a "security dilemma."[4] They can choose to increase their military power as a means of enhancing their security. But, by expanding its arms, a state may simply provoke its newly insecure adversary into matching or exceeding that buildup. The advantage sought will have proven ephemeral, while the action-reaction sequence will leave both states with high defense burdens and strained political relations. The dilemma states face then is between remaining vulnerable in an anarchic international system or attempting to enhance their security in a way that ultimately may leave them even less secure. In this "spiral model" of world politics, arms buildups often prove foolish in the end. Instead, scholars in this camp recommend that states avoid arms races through arms control or to otherwise signal benign intentions in an effort to reduce mutual mistrust.[5]

Throughout the nuclear era, theorists opposed US attempts to achieve superiority for precisely these reasons. For example, during the Cold War, Charles Glaser argued, "U.S. superiority . . . would generate an intense arms race. . . . in virtually all cases MAD is preferable to a world in which the United States had strategic superiority."[6] And over a quarter century later, in 2016, Glaser and Steve Fetter argued that the United States "should forgo [a damage limitation] capability [over China] because the prospects for preserving [such a] capability are poor . . . and the escalatory and political costs would be relatively large."[7]

These criticisms have not been limited to the ivory tower. Many analysts, commentators, and policymakers have opposed US nuclear strategy throughout the years, with their current target being contemporary US nuclear modernization plans. In 2016, the *New York Times* warned that the pursuit of "a new generation of . . . nuclear weapons . . . threaten(s) to revive a Cold War-era arms race and unsettle the balance of destructive force among nations."[8] The most vociferous critics see arms racing as the inevitable conclusion of US modernization, arguing that it will "force unwelcome actions by others."[9] Former Secretary of Defense William Perry agreed, saying in a July 2015 speech criticizing the Obama administration's nuclear modernization plans, "We're now at the precipice, maybe I should say the brink, of a new nuclear arms race. This arms race will be at least as expensive as the arms race we had during the Cold War, which is a lot of money."[10] Even President Obama, whose administration decided to proceed with nuclear modernization, acknowledged these concerns, saying, "We do have to guard against, in the interim, ramping up new and more deadly and more effective systems that end up leading to a whole new escalation of the arms race."[11]

These arguments deserve to be taken seriously. After all, it would be unwise to sink resources into the pursuit of military nuclear advantages only to find oneself in a less secure position in the end. But are critics correct to expect arms racing to be the likely response to a robust US nuclear posture?

The Origins of Underkill

This section demonstrates that enemy nuclear arms buildups often do not occur at all, even in the face of a robust US nuclear force. The potential adversary may simply not be motivated or able to compete. Critics of US nuclear forces have railed against American nuclear "overkill," but international relations scholars have devoted scant attention to the more common, and perhaps more puzzling, phenomenon: nuclear underkill.[12] This section delineates the reasons why nuclear-armed states cede military nuclear advantages to their rivals.

Resource Constraints

States may desire to arms race but simply lack the capacity to do so. During the Cold War, for example, France explicitly decided against building a superpower arsenal because it lacked the means. Instead, in the words of the father of France's Cold War nuclear doctrine, Colonel Pierre Gallois, France pursued a "nuclear strategy of the means."[13] As explained by France's then-president, Charles de Gaulle, "we do not have the ambition to make a force as powerful as those of the Americans or the Soviets, but a force proportionate to our means, our ends, our size."[14] As the French statesman Raymond Barre described, "it was the less costly option ... France, a medium-sized nation with limited resources, cannot pretend seeking parity with the two great nuclear powers. The only way which is opened to us is that of the current strategy."[15] Similarly, at present, it is conceivable that North Korea, or other states, might harbor a desire to match America's nuclear forces warhead-for-warhead, but, given size and resource constraints, such a course of action is simply not possible.

Organizational Capacity

States may harbor a desire to match an adversary's capabilities but simply lack the organizational capacity to build, or maintain effective command and control over, the weapon system, dissuading them from pursuing it. Taylor Fravel and Evan Medeiros have argued that China's decision to maintain no more than a "lean and effective" deterrent, for example, may have been due to these and other factors.[16] China's leaders did not fully trust military commanders to maintain positive control over a diverse arsenal of hundreds or thousands of deployed nuclear weapons, and strategists were not given the freedom to engage in doctrinal development. Instead, therefore, they maintained a relatively small arsenal with warheads concentrated in nondeployed status in central storage facilities. China has begun to field nuclear weapons on mobile missiles in recent years, but this organizational factor constrained China's nuclear modernization for over a half century. Similar considerations are limiting Beijing's ability to conduct deterrent patrols with nuclear-armed submarines today.[17]

Timeline of Weapons Development

Even if a state decides to match an adversary's capability, the timeline for the development of new weapons systems often takes a decade or longer, providing substantial windows of superiority for the first mover. For example, the United States first developed stealth technology for its B-2 Spirit bomber in the waning days of the Cold War. Potential US adversaries were prompted to seek their own stealth technology, but doing so has not been quick or easy. In 2011, China tested its first stealth fighter, but at the time of writing it still had not achieved operational deployments. Many defense analysts believe the American stealth advantage may soon be eroded.[18] Nevertheless, the development of stealth technology helped provide the United States with a significant air power advantage that has endured for over three decades and counting. Perhaps one could argue that this was a waste because China might eventually close the stealth advantage. The more reasonable view would seem to be that three decades of air superiority was quite valuable and worth the effort. In sum, even if arms expansions eventually instigate an adversary response, they can still result in a lasting period of meaningful superiority.

Bureaucratic Resistance

Even if a state's leaders would like to match an enemy's capabilities, it might face internal resistance from bureaucratic interests that prefer to forego or shed those capabilities. Past theories of arms races have obsessed over how bureaucratic interests can fuel arms races, but they have largely overlooked how they can dampen them as well.[19] For example, the US Navy was for decades uncomfortable with its tactical nuclear mission, which it believed detracted from the Navy's core focus on power projection and naval airpower. Naval officers also chafed at the onerous procedures required to keep nuclear weapons safe and secure. When President George H. W. Bush and Michael Gorbachev pledged to the 1991 Presidential Nuclear Initiatives (PNIs), the US Navy eagerly shed its tactical nuclear capabilities.[20] The process began with nuclear sea mines and torpedoes and was completed in 2010, when the Navy retired its last nuclear-capable tactical system, the TLAM-N. In the meantime, the Russian Navy retained and even enhanced its tactical naval nuclear capabilities.[21] To be sure, these outcomes largely reflect the preferences of the national leaderships in the two countries, but the divergent responses might not have been as stark were it not for the fact that Washington was pushing on a wide open bureaucratic door. Indeed, at present, with the return of a Russian nuclear threat, some analysts are calling for a return of a nuclear SLCM, but the US Navy is once again putting up opposition.[22] Contrary to the standard bureaucratic politics models of arms racing, the Navy does not want to resurrect the capability. Similarly, there are many today in the US Air Force who would be happy to eliminate ICBMs because they do not fit comfortably inside an organizational culture that celebrates manned aircraft and the pilots who fly them. Bureaucratic interests and organizational culture are often an obstacle to arms racing.

Strategic Choices

States have different strategic preferences and they may, therefore, choose to respond to US arms buildups in ways that are not threatening to the United States. In this way, the United States can retain or enhance a robust posture without provoking an arms race that renders itself more vulnerable than when it began. For example, in the early stages of the Cold War, the United States maintained a large strategic bombing advantage over the Soviet Union. Moscow could have responded by increasing its own strategic bombing capability, increasing the vulnerability of the US homeland to nuclear attack. Instead, Russia invested in a nationwide system of air defenses to better protect itself from US strategic bombers.[23] Given its historical experience as the victim of several invasions from the West, the Russians placed a high priority on homeland defense.[24] The United States would have been more concerned about a Russian strategic bomber expansion, but Moscow's own strategic preferences put them on a course that provided the United States with the gift of a lasting offensive advantage.

Strategic Culture

In addition, states may have a strategic culture that disinclines them toward arms races generally or with respect to nuclear or other specific weapons systems. The best example may be China's decades-long commitment to a "lean and effective" deterrent. As explained already, one explanation for China's maintenance of a relatively small nuclear arsenal points to organizational challenges that prevented the maintenance of effective command and control of a robust arsenal. The other commonly proffered rationale, however, is rooted in Chinese strategic culture.[25] According to this interpretation, Mao Zedong, and later Deng Xiaoping, believed that a small arsenal was sufficient for deterrence and China did not need, therefore, to construct a nuclear arsenal on the superpowers' model. These charismatic leaders left a strong mark on Chinese strategic culture that remains to this day. While the Chinese may believe their arsenal to be sufficient, the end result is that both Washington and Moscow have been able to maintain an enduring nuclear superiority over Beijing.

Nuclear Multipolarity

States may also choose to build an underkill capability as a result of the complications of global, nuclear multipolarity. If states design their nuclear force postures around the challenges and opportunities presented by one specific adversary, then it might give away possible advantages to others. In the 1987 Intermediate-Range Nuclear Forces (INF) Treaty, Washington and Moscow agreed to dismantle these capabilities in a bilateral arms control agreement, allowing China and nearly every other nuclear-armed power an advantage in this area. As Russian President Putin lamented in a meeting with US officials in 2007, "it will be difficult for us to keep within the framework of the treaty in a situation where other countries do develop such weapons systems, and among those are countries in our near vicinity."[26] It was precisely these concerns that have prompted Russia to cheat on its INF commitments, testing an intermediate-range GLCM in 2014.[27] Still, the United States stands firmly by its treaty commitments, ceding an advantage in this space to its rivals.

Nuclear Alliances

States underinvest in their nuclear forces because they rely on the nuclear capabilities of nuclear-armed allies. France and the United Kingdom likely built smaller nuclear arsenals than they might have otherwise because they were able to rely on America's nuclear forces. As Albert Wohlstetter argued about British and French nuclear capabilities, "The burden of deterring general war, as distinct from limited wars, is still likely to be on the United States and, therefore, so far as our allies are concerned, on the alliance."[28]

Other Origins of Underkill

There are other factors that cause states to underinvest in their strategic capabilities. This section did not pretend to provide an exhaustive catalog but rather, more modestly, to advance several theoretical propositions about why action-reaction arms races might not occur. There are myriad obstacles that prevent states from quickly and automatically matching an adversary's strategic posture.

Where Are All the Arms Races? An Empirical Investigation

For our next step in considering a theory of underkill, we turn to the empirical record. Are arms races a common feature of international politics as predicted by the spiral model? Or, more consistent with the theory of underkill, are they relatively rare? There is a large body of international relations scholarship devoted to the quantitative analysis of the causes and consequences of arms races.[29] Within this literature, the most widely applicable definition of an arms race is a situation in which two rivals each increase their defense spending or military personnel by at least 8% per year for 3 or more years consecutively.[30] By this broad definition, there have been 554 unique instances of arms races since 1816.[31] With a baseline of over 1 million dyad-years, arms races occur in a small percentage (less than 1/10 of one percent) of possible interactions. These statistics demonstrate that arms races are a recurring feature of international politics. At the same time, they also show that they are less common than the spiral model of arms races might lead us to believe.

Moreover, *nuclear* arms races are even rarer still. In fact, according to this scholarship, there have been zero arms races between nuclear-armed states. Not even the competition between the two superpowers during the Cold War qualifies as an arms race according to these studies.[32] One can certainly question the coding rules employed. Perhaps this is not a reliable measure if it does not capture what many consider to be the preeminent arms race of the 20th century. On the other hand, this finding should at least give us pause and challenge us to rethink our prior assumptions. Was the Cold War truly an example of an intense nuclear arms race? Leading political scientists in this area, applying consistent standards and decision rules accepted by other scholars, have found no evidence that it was.

Moreover, even if two states rapidly expand their forces, it does not follow that the states have necessarily entered an arms race. Rather, one or both states might be building for other reasons.

The Enemy Is Building for Other Reasons

The spiral model maintains that US opponents build nuclear weapons in an action-reaction cycle of responses to US procurement decisions, but this argument does not take into account the possibility that states also expand their strategic arsenals for many other reasons. Evidence of enemy nuclear expansion or modernization is not necessarily evidence that the United States has provoked an arms spiral. On the contrary, in many cases, US enemies engage in arms build-ups regardless of what the United States does.

Indeed, international relations scholarship has posited a number of drivers of state nuclear arms expansions other than action-reaction arms racing. Some scholars argue that military organizational cultures intrinsically favor offensive doctrines and this encourages the construction of large military forces, which are necessary to sustain offensive strategies.[33] Others assert that scientists working on issues of national security cause nuclear weapons enhancements through the dispassionate pursuit of technical breakthroughs, such as intercontinental ballistic missiles with multiple warheads or nuclear cruise missiles.[34] Still others point to defense industries' interest in constantly upgrading weapons to support commercial growth, occasionally matched by policymakers' and politicians' needs to acquire what are arguably unnecessary weapons to support their defense industrial base or local economies. In short, these scholars argue that what appears to be an arms race for the latest capabilities is actually the result of largely domestic considerations.[35] Scholars argue that external threats are often cited to justify these programs, but that international developments are not the central drivers.[36]

Most of these studies focus on the determinants of US nuclear expansion during the Cold War, but the basic theoretical arguments equally apply to other states, including US rivals. In their previously classified study on the Cold War arms competition, for example, Ernest May, John Steinbruner, and Thomas Wolfe concluded that they could not find evidence of an action-reaction arms race.[37] The authors concluded that military expansion in the Soviet Union was driven by a mix of internal and external factors, but that there was scant evidence that procurement decisions on one side or the other were the result of direct interactions with the opponent's procurement plans.

US Secretary of Defense Harold Brown agreed that US nuclear weapons were not the primary cause of Moscow's nuclear expansion. When asked about American actions contributing to the Soviet nuclear modernization in congressional testimony, Secretary Brown famously, and pithily, replied, "when we build, they build. When we stop, they build."[38]

In recent years, Brown's aphorism can be taken even further to "when we cut, they build." President Obama vowed to rid the world of nuclear weapons and worked to reduce the size of the US nuclear arsenal in the hope that other nations would follow America's lead. If the spiral model of arms races is correct and enemy nuclear postures are a response to American arms buildups, then we should have expected other states to also downsize their arsenals, or at least maintain current levels, as the United States reduced. Instead, Russia, China, India, Pakistan, and North Korea all went in the other direction, expanding and modernizing their arsenals. As Brad Roberts, a deputy assistant secretary of defense for nuclear and missile defense policy in the Obama administration, explains, the United States was "apparently alone among the states with nuclear weapons to believe that it has more nuclear weapons than it needs."[39] This provides additional evidence against the spiral model of arms races and support for the idea that US enemies build for reasons that have little to do with US behavior.

Due to their head start, Russia and China are completing nuclear modernization cycles while Washington continues to debate whether and how to modernize its own forces. Critics charge that US plans risk provoking a new arms race, but it is hard to see how that is possible, given that adversary nuclear modernization programs are already well underway. A more accurate description would be that there is an arms race taking place, and the United States is sitting it out. As then–Secretary of Defense Ashton Carter argued in 2016, US nuclear modernization programs are "not intended to stimulate competition from anyone else, we know they aren't having that effect because the evidence is to the contrary."[40]

In sum, to the degree that nuclear expansion and modernization programs in US rivals are driven by considerations other than US nuclear capabilities, then arms races are not a direct cost of a robust US nuclear posture.

The Deterrence Model

If an adversary state is able and willing to match US nuclear capabilities and it designs its forces to match or beat Washington, then an arms race may very well occur. But it does not follow that the arms race is a cost of a robust US nuclear posture. Rather, it may be a benefit. Indeed, competing in and winning arms races is sometimes a necessary, if undesirable, part of international politics.

Then–US President Elect Donald Trump generated controversy in December 2016, when he responded to critics who feared that his proposed policies risked starting an arms race with Russia and China by saying, "Let it be an arms race ... we will outmatch them at every pass and outlast them all."[41] His response only further outraged his critics, but Trump had a point.

The canonical spiral model is only one theory of arms competitions. In the alternative "deterrence model," prevailing in an arms race is necessary in order to deter an aggressive rival.[42] According to this model, strategic competitions, including arms races, are not the result of mutual suspicions and arms spirals, but are rather caused by fundamental conflicts of interests between states, such as contested territorial claims or ideological disagreements. Faced with a revisionist, or so-called greedy, adversary, states must arm themselves to deter the threat from their expansionist rival. Failing to do so would give the greedy adversary a free pass and risk sacrificing vital interests in the face of enemy expansion. If the enemy is seeking to challenge one's interests and is building up its military forces to do so, then one must arm in order to defend oneself. Moreover, in addition to augmenting deterrence, the devotion of scarce resources to military expenditures can serve as a costly signal of resolve to stand firm on the issues in dispute.[43] In this way, arms races can "substitute" for war by helping to eliminate uncertainty over power and resolve. If one is facing an aggressive adversary building up capabilities to threaten one's interests, then, as Trump defiantly and correctly responded, "let it be an arms race."

According to international relations theories of arms racing, therefore, there is a prior question to answer before predicting whether a robust US nuclear posture will provoke an unwanted arms race, namely: does Washington find itself in the spiral or deterrence model? In other words, one must ask whether America's nuclear-armed adversaries are "security seeking" or "greedy." If US adversaries are merely "security seeking," then critics of a robust US nuclear force are correct and a dangerous and unnecessary arms spiral might very well result from US modernization or other force enhancements. If on the other hand, US adversaries are "greedy," then an arms race may very well occur, but this is not a reason for the United States to opt out. Quite the contrary, if US adversaries are greedy, then the United States must enter into an arms race if it hopes to protect its interests. Competing in and winning the arms race in this environment is necessary to deter aggressive challengers. In other words, contrary to popular discourse, arms racing is not necessarily a problem. Sometimes, it is the best policy.

During the Cold War, for example, the Soviet Union would almost certainly have posed a greater threat to US global interests had it not been for America's containment policy and the effort to meet attempts at Soviet expansion with the threat of sufficient military force.[44] And, as we discuss in more detail in what follows, there is reason to believe that America's nuclear-armed adversaries today are also "greedy" states that must be deterred. As Brad Roberts writes, "each of these regimes [Russia, China, and North Korea] is inherently revisionist in character. Putin's slogan 'new rules or no rules' illustrates this point."[45] If this is the case, then US nuclear modernization and perhaps even participation in a future nuclear arms race may be a necessary and desirable step to defend America's interests.

Can the United States Achieve Meaningful Strategic Advantages?

The final section turns to the empirical record to discover whether the United States has been able to achieve superiority over nuclear-armed rivals. If critics of US nuclear posture are correct, then we should expect any US advantages to be ephemeral as adversaries respond quickly to negate any advantages. If, on the other hand, the argument of this chapter is correct, then we should expect that Washington has been able to avoid unnecessary arms races and to maintain meaningful strategic advantages.

To conduct this test, this section simply analyzes the history of US strategic competitions with its nuclear-armed rivals: China, North Korea, and Russia. It shows that, with regard to China and North Korea, the United States has avoided a major strategic arms competition and has always maintained a clear strategic advantage. The case of Russia is more complicated. For many, it is the paragon of an action-reaction spiral. Still, this chapter provides evidence that Moscow's military enhancements were often driven by factors other than America's nuclear posture; the Soviet Union and Putin's Russia were greedy states and arms build-ups were necessary to deter them; and, finally, Washington has been able to achieve meaningful military advantages even in its interactions with Russia. Taken together, this section undermines the case for the spiral model and provides significant support for the logic of American nuclear strategy: the United States can maintain enduring nuclear superiority without sparking unnecessary arms races.

China

In strong support of the argument of this chapter, the United States and China have never engaged in an intense nuclear arms race and Washington has possessed an enduring strategic nuclear advantage over Beijing for more than 70 years. The United States claimed superiority when it became the first country to build nuclear weapons in 1945 and, as we saw in chapter 2, Washington still retains a large nuclear advantage over China to this day. As of 2015, the United

States possessed approximately 2,000 nuclear warheads capable of reaching China's homeland, whereas China only had roughly 65 nuclear warheads able to range the continental United States. As discussed earlier, there may be several reasons for America's continued strategic advantage over China. Strategic culture may have contented China with a minimum deterrent. In addition, organizational constraints may have prevented Beijing from fielding a more diverse and robust nuclear force.

At present, China is expanding and modernizing its forces, and this is likely at least in part a response to US strategic force enhancements.[46] By increasing the size of its arsenal and moving to mobile systems, Beijing can be assured of maintaining an assured retaliatory capability even as the United States deploys homeland ballistic missile defenses and researches hypersonic glide vehicles.

At the same time, however, there is no indication that China's changes to its strategic forces are meant to close the strategic capabilities gap between itself and the United States. In my many meetings with Chinese officials and experts in Beijing and Washington each year, my interlocutors continually deny any interest in matching America's nuclear forces. Despite persistent worries from senior US officials, it does not appear that China has made a decision to "sprint to parity" with the United States.[47] It is certainly possible, of course, that China could choose to arms race in the future. Given America's head start, however, it would take China a significant amount of time to cut into America's large margin of nuclear superiority.

In sum, contrary to arms spiral arguments, the United States has maintained a meaningful nuclear superiority over China for over 70 years and will likely continue to foster these advantages well into the future. Costly and unnecessary nuclear arms races are not a cost of a robust US nuclear posture in this case.

North Korea

The United States and North Korea have not engaged in a nuclear arms race. Rather, the United States has maintained a substantial nuclear superiority over North Korea from 1945 to the time of writing. North Korea entered the nuclear club in October 2006, and since that time has been working to expand its fledgling arsenal. As discussed in chapter 2, North Korea may have enough nuclear material for up to 21 nuclear warheads. It possesses short- and intermediate-range delivery systems and is developing intercontinental systems. At the time of this study, it is not believed to have mastered the ability to fit nuclear warheads on the nosecone of a ballistic missile and the necessary reentry vehicle technology. Given current trajectories, it is likely that North Korea will eventually acquire the ability to reach the continental United States with nuclear weapons.

In support of the spiral model, North Korea may be a "security-seeking" state. Many analysts believe that Kim's nuclear program is motivated primarily by concerns of regime survival.[48] Other analysts believe, however, that North Korea's nuclear program may be aimed with giving Pyongyang the ability to invade South Korea to reunify the peninsula under its control while deterring US intervention. If the latter interpretation is correct, then the United States should stand ready to arms race with North Korea, if necessary, to protect itself and its allies.

Fortunately, there is little reason to believe that US efforts to maintain strategic advantages over Pyongyang will prove difficult for the United States. Furthermore, it is likely that this advantage will continue indefinitely despite Pyongyang's best efforts. Given Washington's large margin of superiority and Pyongyang's small size and poor economic conditions, it is nearly impossible to imagine that it will ever be able to reach strategic parity with the United States.

In sum, the United States can and will continue to possess a meaningful nuclear superiority over North Korea. Costly and unnecessary nuclear arms races are not a cost of a robust US nuclear posture in this case.

Russia

The Russian case is the most challenging to the central argument of this chapter. For some, Russia–US relations are the prototypical example of the spiral model.[49] Indeed, many academic theories of arms racing were inspired by the Cold War nuclear arms race. According to this interpretation, both the United States and the Soviet Union were security-seeking states. In a foolish search for absolute security, they spent astronomically on nuclear arsenals, and, in the end, they were both more vulnerable than where they started, with tens of thousands of nuclear warheads pointed at each other. As Paul Warnke famously argued, the two superpowers were like "apes on a treadmill."[50]

Upon closer examination, however, there is reason to doubt the central tenets of the spiral model interpretation. First, Moscow's arms expansions were driven by a mix of factors, and it is not at all clear that it was responding to Washington in a dysfunctional action-reaction cycle. The Soviet Union was intent on developing a robust nuclear force regardless of US actions. (Recall Secretary Brown's quote, cited previously.) The history behind the development of the thermonuclear weapon provides an example of this dynamic. Analysts in the United States argued for years that the US test of a thermonuclear weapon had provoked Moscow to respond, but we now know that the Soviet Union was committed to developing the "super" either way and did not require additional motivation from the United States.[51] Moreover, newly declassified evidence released since the end of the Cold War provides further support for this interpretation. As referenced earlier, May, Steinbruner, and Wolfe conclude that they were unable to find evidence of an action-reaction spiral in Moscow's procurement decisions.

The idea that Moscow's nuclear posture decisions are not heavily influenced by those made in Washington receives further support when looking at Russia's current nuclear posture. Russia maintains nuclear capabilities, including tactical naval nuclear weapons, such as torpedoes, mines, and depth charges, which the United States has long since shed. Furthermore, Putin continues to expand Russia's nuclear capabilities into new areas with no prompting from the West, developing, for example, an undersea nuclear-armed drone, and testing an intermediate-range GLCM. As Secretary Carter explained in the quote cited earlier, the evidence does not support the idea that America's nuclear posture is prompting an arms buildup in Russia.

Second, even if there was a Cold War nuclear arms race (which the above discussion at least calls into question) it was likely necessary to defend the United States' core interests. If this is the case, then it cannot be considered a regrettable cost of a robust US nuclear posture, but one of its most persuasive justifications. As George Kennan explained in the famous long telegram, Communist Russia counted on the continued spread of workers' revolutions in order to sustain its legitimacy.[52] Kennan argued that if Russian expansion could be contained, the system would collapse from within due to the system's internal contradictions. This containment strategy formed the basis of the US approach to the Soviet Union for 50 years and ultimately proved successful. By the 1980s, the United States was winning the arms race, and this, combined with the Soviet Union's internal governance and economic problems, eventually convinced Mikhail Gorbachev and other Soviet leaders to unilaterally opt out of the competition.[53] Similarly today, analysts debate whether Putin's aggressive actions and nuclear threats are a defensive response to NATO expansion in eastern Europe, or a new round of aggression motivated by imperial ambition.[54] There is considerable evidence to support the latter view. Putin has argued that the collapse of the Soviet Union is the "greatest geopolitical catastrophe of the 20th century" and that he is intent on resurrecting a "greater Russia" in eastern Europe.[55] Recall also, Putin's above motto of "new rules or no rules." A new arms competition may be in the making, therefore, but if so, it may be the type of arms race in which the United States must compete and win in order to protect itself and its allies.

Finally, and providing the strongest support for the argument of this book, despite Moscow's massive nuclear capabilities, the United States has consistently been able to achieve meaningful nuclear advantages. From 1945 until the mid-1970s, the United States possessed a clear strategic superiority over the Soviet Union. By the middle of that decade, the Soviets had achieved quantitative parity, which was locked in through a series of arms control agreements, but the United States continued to look for a qualitative edge, developing more sophisticated warheads and delivery systems.

Furthermore, even though Washington does not currently enjoy a quantitative nuclear advantage over Russia, it has been able to maintain significant damage limitation capabilities against it. As we saw in chapter 2, if the United States had not fostered these capabilities, it would be much more vulnerable to a hypothetical nuclear exchange with Russia, across a full range of scenarios, than it is today. Far from futile, therefore, America's robust nuclear posture provides it with meaningful damage limitation against Russia, which Moscow has not been able to negate.

While not as clear-cut as the China and North Korea cases, therefore, the Russia case still provides evidence supportive of the central argument of this chapter. Russia expanded its military capabilities for reasons that were only partly to do with the United States. Deterring Russian aggression during the Cold War and at present with sufficient military force was likely vital to defending American national interests. And, finally, the pursuit of a robust nuclear posture has provided the United States with meaningful damage limitation capabilities, rendering it less vulnerable to nuclear war with Russia and enhancing nuclear deterrence.

Conclusion

This chapter examined the relationship between nuclear posture and nuclear arms races. In case studies of US strategic relations with Russia, China, and North Korea, it found that action-reaction arms races as described in the "spiral model" are uncommon and that the United States has been able to consistently achieve and maintain enduring military nuclear advantages over rivals. To account for these findings, the chapter advanced several propositions, grounded in existing international relations theory, about the determinants of nuclear "underkill." It argued that financial, temporal, bureaucratic, cultural, and other factors can prevent a country from actively participating in arms races with the United States. Moreover, it also argued that adversary nuclear expansions are often driven by their own internal logics and are often not a response to the United States. Finally, it maintained, consistent with the "deterrence model," that occasionally, participating in, and winning, nuclear arms races is a necessary, if unfortunate, part of international political competition.

In broader terms, this chapter provided further support for the logic of American strategy. Contrary to persistent claims to the contrary, the United States can maintain enduring strategic advantages over rivals without provoking expensive and unnecessary arms races. Arms competitions may occasionally occur, so this potential cost cannot be dismissed out of hand. But, they are not so common or problematic as to invalidate Washington's desire to pursue meaningful and enduring strategic advantages.

So, we are still left searching, therefore, for the purported costs of American nuclear superiority. If a robust US nuclear posture does not provoke its nuclear-rivals into arms races, perhaps it encourages nonnuclear states to consider pursuing their own nuclear weapons option?

8

Nuclear Nonproliferation

Will the pursuit of military nuclear advantages merely encourage other countries to build nuclear weapons, undermining America's nonproliferation goals?[1] Many policy advocates focusing on nuclear proliferation believe that a robust US nuclear arsenal is an important determinant of proliferation decisions in other states and that the United States can dissuade nuclear proliferation elsewhere by reducing the size of its own nuclear arsenal. As Deepti Choubey explained in 2008, "A renewed debate on the desirability and feasibility of nuclear disarmament has emerged among US policy makers and influential people on both sides of the political aisle. The notion that preventing the spread of nuclear weapons is much harder without also reducing their number seems to be motivating much of this interest."[2] According to this view, there is a link between the US nuclear arsenal and the spread of nuclear weapons to other countries and, in order to prevent nuclear proliferation, therefore, Washington must first make changes to its own nuclear arsenal.

But is this view correct? The idea has the backing of many adherents, but it has not been subjected to systematic empirical scrutiny. Moreover, there is a well-developed academic literature on the causes of nuclear proliferation, and, with one exception, this research has not directly identified America's nuclear arsenal as a possible cause of nuclear proliferation.[3]

This chapter challenges the notion that US nuclear posture has a significant bearing on the proliferation and nonproliferation behavior of other states. Contrary to the received wisdom in some policy advocacy circles, this chapter maintains that state decisions on nuclear nonproliferation issues are driven by a range of other security, economic, and political factors and, once these considerations are taken into account, there is little if any remaining variance to be explained by the US nuclear posture or Washington's commitment to nuclear disarmament.

To test these claims, this chapter employs a multimethod approach, drawing on both qualitative and quantitative analysis. First, in a brief case study of the world's most prominent contemporary nuclear nonproliferation challenge, the Iranian nuclear program, the chapter shows that US nuclear posture did not appear to be a driver of the major developments in Iran's nuclear program or the international community's response to it. Next, using a data set on US nuclear arsenal size from 1945 to 2011, the chapter examines the relationship between one important measure of a robust US nuclear posture, the size of the US nuclear arsenal, and a variety of nuclear nonproliferation outcomes. Consistent with the central argument of the chapter, it finds that there are a wide variety of security, economic, and political factors that correlate with the spread of nuclear weapons and with other states' nuclear nonproliferation policies. It finds no evidence, however, of a relationship between the size of the US arsenal and: the exploration, pursuit, or acquisition of nuclear weapons by other countries; the provision of sensitive nuclear assistance to nonnuclear weapon states; and voting on nonproliferation issues in the United Nations Security Council (UNSC). These findings are robust to alternate conceptualizations and measurements of US nuclear weapons and in various historical time periods including the Cold War and the eras following the Treaty on the Nonproliferation of Nuclear Weapons (NPT).

The findings of this chapter, therefore, provide further support for the central argument of this book. Contrary to the critics of US nuclear posture, the United States can pursue and maintain a robust nuclear posture without undermining its nonproliferation objectives.

The rest of the chapter continues in three parts. First, it reviews theoretical arguments for and against the idea of a link between US nuclear weapons and nuclear proliferation elsewhere. Second, it presents qualitative and quantitative empirical evidence. Finally, it concludes with implications of the analysis for our understanding of the causes of nuclear proliferation and for American nuclear strategy.

Why US Nuclear Weapons Might Affect Nuclear Proliferation

The NPT is an international institution that enshrines into international law a formal link between arms control and nonproliferation.[4] One of the grand bargains of the NPT is the promise by nonnuclear weapon states not to acquire nuclear weapons in exchange for the nuclear weapon states' pledge in Article VI "to pursue negotiations in good faith on effective measures relating to cessation of the nuclear arms race and nuclear disarmament."[5] According to a view held in some circles, therefore, if the United States is not seen to be making progress toward Article VI, then the NPT will be weakened and other countries will be more likely to defect on their end of the bargain and build nuclear weapons. Contrarily, if Washington is seen as pursuing disarmament, which can be done most visibly by cutting America's large stockpile of nuclear weapons, then the NPT will be strengthened and other countries will be less likely to build nuclear weapons.

Proponents of this view also believe that US nuclear weapons policy can affect not only state decisions to proliferate, but also state decisions on nuclear nonproliferation policy toward other proliferators. Choubey laments:

> [Too many analysts focus] narrowly on what influence the United States [nuclear posture] directly has on the decision making of a government considering proliferation. It fails to include a key to successful nonproliferation strategy, which is the behavior of other nations to shape the context in which states embarking on proliferation deal with pressures to desist and, moreover, on the willingness of other states to join in enforcement.[6]

In other words, it is difficult for the United States to build international support for nuclear nonproliferation efforts, such as putting pressure on Iran to place curbs on its nuclear program, when the United States itself maintains a large arsenal or is not otherwise seen as making progress toward Article VI. If the United States, the most powerful state in the international system, maintains a large nuclear arsenal to provide for its own security, other countries might be less able or willing to articulate what could be perceived as a hypocritical idea that nuclear proliferation is an illegitimate option for other states. Such views are supported by anecdotal evidence from US diplomats who report that foreign governments' unwillingness to support international nonproliferation measures are the result of the United States' unwillingness to make further progress on its Article VI commitments.[7]

The established view, therefore, rests on a clear logic, but there are at least two reasons to doubt its posited relationship between US policy and other state's decisions. First, the linkage hypothesis is supported by theory and anecdote, but not by systematic empirical analysis. In a recent study, Jeffrey Knopf theorizes a set of plausible arguments for and against the link between disarmament and nonproliferation, but he does not subject the question to empirical tests.[8] Rather, he writes that in conducting his research he aims "to facilitate future empirical testing of the linkage premise."[9] His study concludes, "To say anything more definitive requires additional empirical research. . . . more fine-grained analyses are needed."[10]

Other scholars agree that there is a need for systematic empirical study of the relationship between US nuclear weapons and nuclear proliferation. As Christopher Chyba writes, "there has been too little empirical work dedicated to understanding what role U.S. nuclear weapons policy actually plays in . . . states' nonproliferation decisions."[11] In sum, scholars have identified a need for empirical studies on the link between US nuclear weapons and nuclear proliferation, but the academy has not filled this lacuna.

Second, there is a large body of academic research on the causes of nuclear proliferation and nonproliferation policy and this scholarship has not identified US nuclear policy specifically as an important factor.[12] Indeed, when taking into account what is already known about nuclear proliferation and nonproliferation policy, there is reason to doubt the existence of a US nuclear weapons–nuclear proliferation link. It is to this issue that we turn in the next section.

Questioning the Link between US Nuclear Weapons and Nuclear Proliferation

This section develops an argument about the determinants of nuclear proliferation and nuclear nonproliferation policy. It argues that when deciding whether to initiate a nuclear weapons program and when formulating policy toward potential nuclear proliferation in another state, statesmen must consider a variety of security, economic, and political factors and that these variables will ultimately shape the state's response. After this panoply of factors is taken into account, there is little reason to believe that US nuclear posture, if considered at all, will have a significant impact on the ultimate outcome.

We begin with an examination of why states build nuclear weapons. Existing studies on why countries explore, pursue, and acquire nuclear weapons have examined the role played by security threats, domestic politics, and international norms; levels of economic development; the receipt of sensitive nuclear assistance; civilian nuclear cooperation agreements; economic development strategies; proliferation rings; state institutions; and the psychology of individual leaders.[13] Despite decades of research and numerous identified causes, however, academic studies have not specifically proposed the size of the US nuclear arsenal as an important determinant of nuclear proliferation.

To examine why this might be the case, let us imagine a leader of a potential proliferant state, State A, deciding whether to begin a nuclear weapons program. What are the factors that this leader might consider? Given scholarly knowledge about nuclear proliferation, we might expect that the leader would ask whether the possession of nuclear weapons would bring major benefits in the form of enhanced security, domestic political standing, or international prestige. The leader might also consider whether his or her state has the technical capability to produce nuclear weapons. If not, the leader might explore whether other more advanced nuclear states might be willing to assist with sensitive nuclear technology transfers. Next, the leader might ask whether and what kind of international resistance the state might face on its path to the bomb. If his or her nuclear pursuit is uncovered, will other countries apply diplomatic pressure in an attempt to force an abandonment of the program? Will they levy international sanctions? If so, could the national economy withstand the sanctions? Will other states use covert means or take overt military action to stop the program? And, finally, would the benefit of acquiring nuclear weapons outweigh these other costs?

When considering this wide range of pressing matters, it is hard to imagine that leaders would stop to assess US nuclear policy or the size of the US nuclear arsenal. Further, even if they did, it seems unlikely that these factors would be among the most important considerations. Would a leader be more likely to build nuclear weapons if the United States possessed the roughly 2,000 weapons it had at the time of writing, than if Washington possessed only 1,000 nuclear warheads, as President Obama proposed in the summer of 2013? One would be hard pressed to answer this question in the affirmative.

To be sure, states might consider the size of the US nuclear arsenal to the degree that they expect nuclear war with the United States, but for the vast majority of states in the international system, threat perceptions are much more likely to be determined by the capabilities of regional rivals.[14] Moreover, even states directly threatened by the United States are more likely to confront, and therefore fear, America's conventional, as opposed to its nuclear, capabilities.[15] In addition, for nonnuclear weapon states, the fact that the United States possesses nuclear weapons at all might be threatening regardless of the precise size of the US arsenal.

Furthermore, there are other states for which a large US nuclear arsenal might conceivably be a source of reassurance. In a series of multilateral and bilateral treaties, including the North Atlantic Treaty Organization (NATO) charter, Washington commits itself to come to the defense of its allies in the event of armed attack. If allied states question the credibility of the US security guarantee, they could be tempted to pursue independent nuclear capabilities. The maintenance of a large US nuclear arsenal might reassure America's security partners and, therefore, prevent proliferation. Yet, there is also reason to doubt that nuclear arsenal size affects extended deterrence, as existing empirical studies point to the importance of conventional military capabilities and the strength of the patron's commitment to protégé security, not patron arsenal size.[16]

In sum, according to this theoretical perspective, we might expect US nuclear posture to be peripheral, if not irrelevant, to states' proliferation decisions.

Let us next move on to consider the determinants of states' nonproliferation policies. There is a smaller, but growing literature on this subject, explaining why states vary in the degree to which they are willing to help or hinder nuclear programs in other states, such as whether they provide sensitive nuclear assistance to a proliferator or whether they consider military action to stop the spread of nuclear weapons.[17] A state's nonproliferation stance toward proliferators has been attributed to the political relationship between the state and the proliferator, a state's ability to project conventional military power over the proliferator, the existence of common enemies with the proliferator, and history of past conflict with the proliferator.[18] As with the causes of nuclear proliferation, however, scholars have not proposed the size of the US nuclear arsenal as a determinant of nuclear nonproliferation policy.

Let us again return to a hypothetical leader, this time of State B, determining how to respond to State A's advancing nuclear program. The leader must first decide whether she supports or opposes State A's bid to join the nuclear club and, then, subsequently ask what steps she should take to achieve her objectives. To arrive at a decision, the leader may ask how nuclear proliferation in this case affects her state's security. She might then consider how nuclear proliferation might affect the security of other states. If State A's proliferation constrains State B's enemies, for example, State B might even find nuclear weapons in State A at least somewhat desirable.[19] If, as is more likely, State B decides to try to stop State A's program, she must then decide what, if any, measures to take. Could State B's policies have a significant effect on State A's nuclear development? If not, can State B simply free ride on the efforts of others? Should State B implement sanctions? How much could curtailing trade and investment with the proliferator hurt State B's own economy? Could State B take covert or military action against State A's program or provide diplomatic support to other more powerful states to do so? Does the potential security benefit of reducing the probability that State A acquires nuclear weapons outweigh the costs of doing so? Would getting tough with State A hurt State B's diplomatic relations with State A? Would not getting tough with State A hurt State B's relationship with other states, including great powers attempting to curtail the global spread of nuclear weapons?

As in the above discussion, once these factors are taken into account, it is hard to imagine that State B's leaders would stop to consider the size of the US nuclear arsenal. Again, it strains credulity to argue that State B would be more likely to adopt a tougher nonproliferation policy State A if the United States possessed fewer nuclear weapons than it does today.

In sum, according to this alternate theoretical perspective, when one considers the panoply of factors that shape states' proliferation and nonproliferation policies, it is unlikely that the details of US nuclear posture would be the decisive, or even a relevant, determinant of the ultimate outcome. If this perspective is correct, we should expect to see no relationship between US nuclear weapons and proliferation outcomes.

This is a debate that cannot be entirely settled in the theoretical realm, however, and the remainder of the chapter will subject these competing claims to empirical tests.

Empirical Analysis

Several types of empirical analysis prove useful to examine the relationship between US nuclear posture and nuclear proliferation. First, I conduct a brief qualitative analysis on the most prominent case of nuclear proliferation and nonproliferation over the past decade: the Iranian nuclear crisis. While a single case cannot provide a definitive test, it can provide a plausibility probe into the questions under investigation. If US nuclear arsenal size did not play a clear role in this case, there is at least some reason to doubt its impact in other less salient cases. Next, to provide a more comprehensive examination, I employ systematic quantitative analysis on the determinants of nuclear proliferation and nuclear nonproliferation policy, which will form the core of the empirical analysis.

The Iranian Nuclear Crisis

This section presents a brief qualitative analysis of the international crisis surrounding Iran's nuclear program. It modestly seeks to identify the key analytic questions, briefly sketch the major events in the development of the Iranian nuclear crisis, and weigh evidence for the various theoretical approaches highlighted previously, by drawing on: existing scholarship, major news outlets, analyses in policy journals and think-tank reports, and author interviews.[20] It shows that existing accounts of the crisis point to a variety of pressing security, economic, and political factors that drove the major developments in the crisis and that America's nuclear weapons are not featured among these foremost factors.

The Iranian nuclear crisis presents several clear questions, including: Why has Iran pursued an advanced nuclear capability? Why has Tehran, at times, agreed to place limits on this program? And, why was the international community, at first reluctant to confront Iran, willing to ratchet up pressure over time?

If the linkage arguments are correct, then we should expect to see US nuclear weapons policy exerting a noticeable effect on these outcomes. This hypothesis will be supported to the degree that Iranian nuclear advances and the international community's reluctance to get involved were a reaction to America's robust nuclear arsenal. Similarly, this idea will also be supported by evidence indicating that increasing international pressure and Tehran's willingness to accept limits on the program came in response to US nuclear reductions. If, on the other hand, the central argument of this chapter is correct, then we will find that Iran's nuclear program and the international response to it are driven largely by other factors.

Iran's nuclear program was initially an effort to build nuclear weapons in response to Saddam Hussein's use of chemical weapons in the Iran-Iraq War in the 1980s.[21] The program continued as a means to develop at least a latent nuclear weapons capability in order to deter outside aggression from other external threats, including Israel and the United States, and possibly to help Iran to achieve its stated goals of becoming a predominant power in the region. Over the years, however, Iran has been willing to place limits on this program in response to outside pressure. In October 2003, Iran agreed to suspend its enrichment program as it pursued a diplomatic agreement with the so-called EU-3 group of European powers and, in part, because it feared that, after the US invasion of Iraq, it might become the next target of American military action. Throughout this period, the United States worked to bring Iran's case to the UNSC, but other powers were reluctant to support this effort, mostly because of their economic interests in the country. As Iran increased its provocations, however, including by tearing off the International Atomic Energy Agency (IAEA) seals on its centrifuges and resuming enrichment activities in July 2004 and electing the firebrand president Mahmoud Ahmadinejad in August 2005, the international community prepared to take action. The first of six UNSC resolutions against Iran was passed on December 23, 2006. As Iran's program advanced and the Iranians stonewalled in international negotiations, the international pressure mounted. Fearing that the only alternative to tough diplomacy to stop Iran's program might be military conflict, many countries were willing to support ever-tougher economic penalties. Most notably, in the spring of 2012, the EU passed an oil embargo and Iran was expelled from the SWIFT (Society for Worldwide Interbank Financial Telecommunication) international banking system. Other major importers of Iranian oil, including China, India, and South Korea, also agreed to reduce purchases from Iran. The sanctions had a significant effect, sending Iran's economy into recession and leading, in August 2013, to the election of President Hassan Rouhani, a relative moderate, with a mandate to seek relief from international pressure. Under Rouhani's leadership, Tehran once again agreed to limits in the November 2013 interim nuclear deal, known as the Joint Plan of Action (JPOA) in exchange for modest lifting of sanctions. These negotiations eventually led to a more comprehensive accord, the Joint Comprehensive Plan of Action (JCPOA).

In sum, the evidence suggests that Iran's nuclear program has been motivated by several factors, including a desire to deter direct security threats and to advance Iran's standing in the Middle East. Still, Tehran has been willing to place limits on the program in response to international pressure. Several drivers have shaped the international community's response. It was at first reluctant to put pressure on Iran, due to economic interests, but it was willing to ratchet up sanctions in response to the growing threat posed by Iran's advancing nuclear program and in order to stave off more destabilizing options.

The Iran case provides less support for the alternative explanation that nonproliferation is affected by US nuclear posture. At a superficial level, there is some correspondence between US arms control measures, including President

Obama's Prague speech promising a "world without nuclear weapons" in 2009 and the signing of the New START Arms Control Treaty with Russia in 2010, and the subsequent increase in EU sanctions. But the strength of this apparent relationship is called into question by the fact that international sanctions against Iran began much earlier, in 2006, under an American administration widely viewed as skeptical of disarmament. Moreover, the pressure on Iran continued to mount even as the Obama administration arms control agenda visibly lost momentum after New START. Finally, despite voluminous reporting on this issue, existing mainstream accounts rarely, if ever, mention US nuclear weapons as a salient driver of developments in the Iranian nuclear crisis.

As Nitin Chadda, former director for Iran affairs at the National Security Council in the Executive Office of the US President from 2011 to 2015, explains, "our success in building an international coalition against Iran was primarily the result of our sustained commitment to a meaningful diplomatic process, which included a realistic and clearly articulated end state vis-a-vis Iran's nuclear program. We had also been greatly aided by the provocative nuclear behavior of the Iranians." When asked about the role of US nuclear weapons policy, he said, "the President's clear commitment to disarmament has been a helpful framing principle in multilateral settings, but, as it relates to Iran policy, while serving as an intellectual basis for the policy approach to Iran, it was secondary to these other more specific features that helped to sustain the international coalition."[22]

In sum, this brief analysis of the Iranian nuclear crisis provides little reason to believe that there is a link between US nuclear posture and the proliferation and nonproliferation behavior of other states. Nevertheless, a single case cannot be determinative and may be open to multiple interpretations. For this reason, we next turn to the quantitative analysis.

Quantitative Analysis

This section first examines the determinants of state decisions to explore, pursue, and acquire nuclear weapons. Next, to study the effect of US nuclear weapons on other states' nonproliferation policies, it analyzes the correlates of state decisions to provide sensitive nuclear assistance to nonnuclear weapon states and voting patterns on nuclear proliferation issues in the UNSC.

Nuclear Proliferation

This section analyzes the relationship between US nuclear weapons and the exploration, pursuit, and acquisition of nuclear weapons. The universe of analysis is the country-year and includes all nonnuclear weapon states in the international system from 1945 to 2000, the final year for which data on many of the control variables are available.[23] The dependent variables measure whether countries *Explore, Pursue,* or *Acquire* nuclear weapons, respectively. These variables are drawn from a study by Singh and Way,[24] which analyzes the correlates of nuclear proliferation.[25]

The key independent variable is *US Arsenal.* It measures the size of the US nuclear arsenal in number of warheads in every year from 1945 to 2010.[26] I count all nuclear warheads in the US arsenal, including tactical and strategic nuclear weapons.[27] The variable ranges from a low of six in 1945 to a high of 31,255 in 1967. Information on the size of the US nuclear arsenal from 1945 to 2010 is displayed in Figure 8.1.

US nuclear arsenal is the best possible starting point for this empirical research agenda for at least two reasons. First, many claims about US nuclear weapons posing an obstacle to nonproliferation focus on the size of the US arsenal and recommend nuclear reductions as the appropriate solution.[28] Second, arsenal size is a concept that is easily amenable to measurement and, thus, large-N quantitative analysis. Some may argue that the size of the US nuclear arsenal is not an ideal gauge of the theoretical concept, but, in practice, there is not a better one. For that reason, a full assessment of the linkage hypothesis should start with US nuclear arsenal size, but it also requires studying possible alternative measures of the independent variable. Some alternatives are examined in the robustness test section of this chapter.

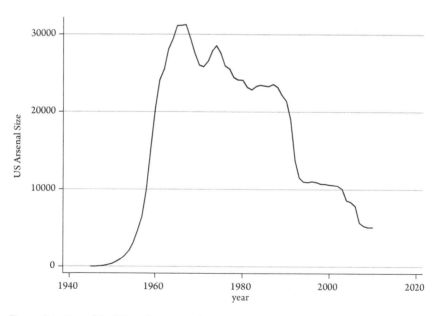

Figure 8.1 Size of the US nuclear arsenal, 1945–2010.

I control for other factors thought to influence the probability that a country engages in proliferation-related behavior, including levels of economic development, gauged by both *GDP per capita* and *Industrial capacity*; the intensity of a state's security environment, measured by whether a country is engaged in a *Rivalry* and whether it has a *Security guarantee* from a nuclear-armed state; domestic political *Regime type; Openness* to the international economy; and *Liberalization*, or movements toward greater levels of economic openness. I also include a measure to assess the *Year* of the observation to account for the possibility that states may have been more likely to consider the nuclear option at the beginning of the nuclear era.[29] More detailed information on the definition and measurement of these variables can be found in Singh and Way.[30] In the models assessing nuclear acquisition, I also control for whether the country has ever received *Sensitive nuclear assistance* from a more advanced nuclear state.[31]

I employ Cox proportional hazard models and cluster robust standard errors by country. The results are presented in Table 8.1.

As we can see in Table 8.1, there is no relationship between the size of the US arsenal and the probability that countries explore (model 1), pursue (model 2), or acquire (model 3) nuclear weapons.[32] *US arsenal* is not statistically significant in any of the models. There is no support for the idea that the size of the US arsenal is correlated with the probability that other countries proliferate.

Consistent with the argument of this chapter and previous research, however, we can see that there are several security, economic, and political variables that are correlated with nuclear proliferation behavior. Countries with a security rival are more likely to engage in all three levels of proliferation. Similarly, countries above a certain level of industrial capacity are more likely to explore and pursue the bomb. The receipt of sensitive nuclear assistance increases the probability that a country acquires nuclear weapons. *Year* is negative and statistically significant in models 1 and 2, demonstrating that, consistent with expectation, states were more likely to begin nuclear activity early in the nuclear era. There is some evidence to support the idea that liberalization affects proliferation. The sign on the coefficient for *Liberalization* is positive and statistically significant in model 2.

The analysis of US nuclear weapons on the proliferation behavior of all states, however, is only the first step. It is possible that US nuclear weapons affect proliferation behavior differently in different categories of states, negating each other's effects in the aggregate data. Next, therefore, I explore the possibility that the relationship between US arsenal size and nuclear proliferation depends on whether the potential proliferant is a US ally. To begin, I include *US arsenal × US guarantee*, a term that interacts *US arsenal* with a dichotomous variable that gauges whether the country has a security guarantee from the United States, *US guarantee*. I also include both lower-order terms.[33] Next, I split the sample and

Table 8.1 **Hazard Models of Nuclear Proliferation, All States, 1945–2000**

Independent Variable	1 (Explore)	2 (Pursue)	3 (Acquire)
US arsenal	−0.060 (0.042)	−0.020 (0.049)	−0.075 (0.063)
Security guarantee	−0.899 (0.615)	−0.917 (0.652)	
Sensitive nuclear assistance			1.683* (0.753)
GDP	3.24e–03 (0.055)	−0.019 (0.051)	
Industrial capacity	2.245*** (0.544)	2.201** (0.750)	37.234 (67.682)
Rivalry	1.435*** (0.426)	2.197** (0.758)	2.476* (1.075)
Regime type	−0.007 (0.031)	0.016 (0.031)	
Openness	−0.013 (0.012)	−0.022 (0.014)	
Liberalization	−0.042 (0.025)	0.054* (0.026)	
Year	−0.087** (0.031)	−0.097*** (0.028)	−0.166 (0.098)
Log likelihood	−69.513	−47.226	−25.018
Number of countries	157	157	187
Total observations	5,317	5,665	7,239

Statistically significant parameter estimators are denoted by * ($p < 0.05$), ** <($p < 0.01$), *** ($p < 0.001$). Coefficients are estimates for Cox proportional hazard models; robust standard errors, adjusted for clustering by country, are in parentheses. GDP = gross domestic product. Model 3 presented trimmed to take into account available degrees of freedom. Full models also reveal a statistically insignificant relationship between *US arsenal* and *Acquire*.

analyze the relationship between the size of the US nuclear arsenal and proliferation behavior in samples of US allies and US nonallies separately.[34] In both sets of tests, I find that there is no relationship between the size of the US arsenal and the proliferation behavior of either allies or nonallies. There is no support for the idea that US allies are less likely, or US nonallies more likely, to explore, pursue, or acquire nuclear weapons, the larger the size of the US nuclear arsenal. Once again, I find support for the idea that other security, economic, and political variables are correlated with the spread of nuclear weapons.

Nuclear Nonproliferation Policy

Next, I turn to nuclear nonproliferation policy. To begin, I explore the determinants of sensitive nuclear technology transfers. Providing sensitive nuclear assistance is the most direct way in which a country can aid another country's pursuit of a nuclear weapons capability. If the size of the US nuclear arsenal complicates US efforts to get cooperation on nuclear nonproliferation, we may expect to find a positive relationship between the size of the US nuclear arsenal and the probability that other countries provide sensitive nuclear assistance. If, on the other hand, state decisions to provide sensitive nuclear assistance are driven by other factors, we should expect to find no relationship between these variables.

Granted, the provision of sensitive nuclear assistance is not an ideal measure of state support for the nuclear nonproliferation regime, but, unfortunately, an ideal measure does not exist. For this reason, this chapter performs a number of tests on a range of dependent variables in an attempt to test the above hypotheses. At a minimum, sensitive nuclear assistance is certainly among the useful indicators as the transfer of sensitive nuclear materials and technology to non-nuclear states is clearly in tension with the spirit of the nonproliferation regime. While even strongly held norms are sometimes violated, if the conventional wisdom is correct, it would still be reasonable to expect to find variation in levels of violations over time to correspond with variation in US nuclear posture.

To conduct these tests, I repeat the analysis from my book, *Exporting the Bomb*, on the correlates of sensitive nuclear assistance after including *US arsenal*.[35] The data set contains yearly information for all capable nuclear suppliers and potential nuclear recipient dyads in the international system from 1951 to 2000. Capable nuclear suppliers include nuclear weapon states, like the United States, and states that possess sensitive nuclear technology, but that have not produced nuclear weapons, such as Japan. The unit of analysis is the directed-dyad year.[36]

The dichotomous dependent variable is *Sensitive nuclear assistance*. It measures whether a capable supplier state provided sensitive nuclear assistance to a potential nuclear recipient in a given year. Detailed information on the definition and measurement of this variable can be found in Kroenig.[37]

The key independent variable is *US arsenal*. I also control for the other factors demonstrated to affect patterns of sensitive nuclear assistance including: the *Relative power* between supplier and recipient; the presence of a common *Enemy* between the supplier and recipient; whether the supplier is in a defense pact with a superpower (*Superpower pact*); the economic circumstances of the supplier, measured by *GDP per capita*, levels of *Economic growth, Openness* to the international economy, and *Trade dependence* with the potential recipient; domestic political *Regime type*; whether the supplier is a member of the *NPT* or Nuclear Suppliers Group (*NSG*); *Distance* and *Distance squared* between supplier and recipient; the security environment of the recipient (*Disputes*); the *GDP per capita* and economic *Openness* of the recipient; and whether the recipient is a member of the NPT.[38]

I employ logistic regression to test claims about the correlates of sensitive nuclear assistance. Robust standard errors are adjusted for clustering by dyad. The results are presented in Table 8.2.

Table 8.2 reveals that there is no relationship between the size of the US nuclear arsenal and the probability that other countries provide sensitive nuclear assistance. *US arsenal* is not statistically significant in a full (model 1) or trimmed (model 2) model. There is no support for the idea that the smaller the size of the US arsenal, the less likely other countries are to engage in sensitive nuclear transfers.

Consistent with the argument of this chapter and previous studies,[39] I find that strategic factors, namely the relative power between supplier and recipient, the presence of a common enemy, and the dependence of the supplier on a superpower patron are correlated with sensitive nuclear assistance. I also find that *Trade dependence, NSG, Distance, Distance squared*, and *Openness (recipient)* are statistically significant correlates of *Sensitive nuclear assistance*.

Table 8.2 **Correlates of Sensitive Nuclear Assistance, 1951–2000**

Independent Variable	1	2
US arsenal	−0.013	2.54e−03
	(0.034)	(0.022)
Relative power	−27.053*	−34.102***
	(11.808)	(9.890)
Common enemy	1.746***	2.098***
	(0.507)	(0.579)
Superpower pact	−1.307**	−1.575**
	(0.425)	(0.561)
GDP per capita	0.027	
	(0.094)	
Economic growth	4.063	
	(2.800)	

Table 8.2 **Continued**

Independent Variable	1	2
Openness	−0.002 (0.009)	
Trade dependence	31.024** (10.910)	32.999** (12.014)
Regime type	−0.049 (0.043)	
NPT	−1.178 (0.789)	
NSG	2.385* (0.995)	1.556* (0.717)
Distance	21.475** (8.377)	19.282* (8.384)
Distance squared	−1.364** (0.524)	−1.220* (0.529)
Disputes (recipient)	0.144 (0.150)	
Superpower pact (recipient)	0.513 (0.849)	
GDP per capita (recipient)	0.021 (0.020)	
Liberalization (recipient)	0.008 (0.022)	
Openness (recipient)	−0.014** (0.005)	−0.011* (0.005)
NPT (recipient	−0.039 (0.652)	
Constant	−87.764** (33.722)	−79.661* (33.206)
N	81,952	81,952

Statistically significant parameter estimators are denoted by * ($p < 0.05$), ** ($p < 0.01$), *** ($p < 0.001$). The dependent variable is sensitive nuclear assistance coded from 0 (no assistance) to 1 (assistance). Robust standard errors are in parentheses and are adjusted for clustering by dyad. The model is estimated after including spline corrections for temporal dependence (Beck, Katz, and Tucker, 1998).

As the final test of the link between US nuclear weapons and other states' nonproliferation policies, I analyze the relationship between the size of the US nuclear arsenal and state voting behavior on nonproliferation issues in the UNSC. When states are found to be in noncompliance with their NPT obligations by the IAEA Board of Governors (BOG), their case is referred to the UNSC for consideration. UNSC members can enforce violations of the NPT by, for example, passing UNSC resolutions to impose sanctions on NPT violators. Other nuclear proliferation issues can also be taken up by the UNSC independent of a BOG recommendation. If the maintenance of a large nuclear arsenal complicates US efforts to get international cooperation on international nuclear nonproliferation efforts, then we should expect to find a negative relationship between the size of the US arsenal and whether countries vote "yes" on UNSC resolutions related to nuclear nonproliferation.

To conduct the analysis, I construct a new data set on votes in the UNSC on nuclear proliferation issues from 1945 to 2011. The data set contains information on 375 votes by 75 countries in 25 separate UNSC resolutions. Data on UNSC votes are drawn from the United Nations' official website, and a list of the resolutions is available in the Data Appendix.[40] The unit of analysis is the country-vote.

The dichotomous dependent variable is *UNSC vote*. It is coded "1" if a country votes yes on the nonproliferation resolution and "0" if the country votes no or abstains.[41] The key independent variable is *US arsenal*. I control for other factors that might affect state voting on nonproliferation issues in the UNSC. We might expect militarily powerful countries to be more threatened by the spread of nuclear weapons and thus be more likely to support nonproliferation measures in the UNSC.[42] To account for military power, I include *Capabilities*, a composite index containing information on total population, urban population, energy consumption, iron and steel production, military personnel, and military expenditures. Data for this variable are drawn from the Correlates of War composite capabilities index, version 3.02, and extracted using EUGene.[43,44] I include *Regime type* to account for the possibility that democratic countries may be more likely to cooperate within international institutions, including the IAEA and the UNSC.[45] To gauge the effect of economic development on UNSC voting patterns, I include *GDP per capita*. In addition, one might expect NPT member states to be more likely to enforce violations of the NPT than nonmembers. I therefore include *NPT*, which measures whether a state was a member of the NPT at the time that the vote was taken.[46] Finally, I include *Explore*, as defined earlier, to account for the possibility that states that are actively exploring a nuclear option themselves might be less likely to support tough nonproliferation measures in the UNSC.

To test the correlates of UNSC voting behavior, I employ logistic regression. Robust standard errors are clustered by country.[47] The results are presented in Table 8.3.

Table 8.3 **Correlates of UNSC Voting on Nuclear Proliferation Issues, 1945–2010**

Independent Variable	1	2
US arsenal	–9.46e–03	–0.012
	(0.017)	(0.016)
Capabilities	5.229**	1.600
	(1.899)	(1.681)
GDP per capita	6.64e–03	
	(0.013)	
Regime type	0.014	
	(0.022)	
NPT	0.829*	1.034**
	(0.337)	(0.331)
Explore	–0.489	
	(0.280)	
Constant	1.076*	1.002*
	(0.454)	(0.433)
N	370	375
Wald chi²	33.45	17.52
Log pseudolikelihood	–50.813	–52.124
Pseudo R²	0.147	0.128

Statistically significant parameter estimators are denoted by * ($p < 0.05$), ** ($p < 0.01$), *** ($p < 0.001$). The dependent variable is UNSC voting coded from 0 (abstention or no vote) to 1 (yes vote). Robust standard errors are in parentheses and are adjusted for clustering by country. Data on regime type for Bosnia-Herzegovina in 2010 and 2011 are unavailable, resulting in five missing observations.

Turning to Table 8.3, we can see that there is no relationship between US arsenal size and state voting in the UNSC on proliferation issues. *US arsenal* does not reach statistical significance in a fully specified (model 1) or a trimmed (model 2) model. This test provides no empirical support for the idea that the maintenance of a large arsenal complicates US efforts to garner international cooperation on nuclear proliferation issues.

Turning to the other variables, we can see that, consistent with the argument of this chapter, other variables are correlated with UNSC voting. *Capabilities* is positive and statistically significant. As expected, militarily powerful states are more likely to support nonproliferation measures in the UNSC. *NPT* is also positive and statistically significant, meaning that NPT member states are more likely to vote to enforce nonproliferation measures in the UNSC. This finding supports the intuition that nonmember states, such as Israel, India, and Pakistan, might be less willing to support nonproliferation enforcement for fear that they themselves might become the targets of such measures. The other variables do not reach statistical significance. Domestic political regime type, levels of economic development, and the exploration of nuclear weapons do not appear to influence UNSC voting.

In sum, the quantitative results show that there are many statistically significant correlates of nuclear proliferation and nonproliferation, but the size of the US nuclear arsenal is not among them.

Robustness Checks

This section presents the results of a number of robustness tests.[48] First, I look for a relationship between the size of the US nuclear arsenal and other nonproliferation-related dependent variables, including the percent of countries outside the NPT that signed the treaty each year, whether a UNSC resolution vote on nuclear issues takes place, and whether states adopt the IAEA Additional Protocol (AP).[49] Next, to assess whether the findings are sensitive to conceptualizations of the key independent variable, I create a number of alternate measures of US arsenal size. I create variables that gauge the natural logarithm of the US arsenal, an ordinal categorization of the US arsenal size (<100, 100–1k, 1k–10k, >10k), annual changes in US arsenal size, whether the United States cuts the size of its arsenal in any given year, and the size of the arsenals of the P 5 nuclear powers combined.[50] I test for the possibility that US arsenal size is related to sensitive nuclear assistance, but as this finding might be obscured by counting instances of continued nuclear transfer over time, I drop dyad-years from the data set after the first instance of sensitive nuclear cooperation. I then assess whether the findings depend on historical time. It is possible that any relationship between US nuclear weapons and proliferation only came into existence after the establishment of the NPT in 1968. Similarly, it is possible that the relationship varied from the Cold War to the post–Cold War periods. To test for these possibilities, I divided my sample by historical time period and conducted regression analysis on the resulting subsamples of data. In addition, in my coding of US nuclear security guarantees, I tried excluding the 1947 Rio Pact, which never contained an explicit nuclear dimension. Finally, I reran the above tests, using a different data set of nuclear weapons proliferation from Jo and Gartzke.[51]

All of these tests produced similar results. The overall pattern revealed in this study through dozens of tests is that there are many significant correlates of proliferation and nonproliferation behavior, but scant evidence of any significant relationships between US nuclear weapons and the proliferation behavior of other states.[52]

Conclusion

This chapter examined the relationship between US nuclear weapons and nuclear proliferation. It found that there is no evidence of a relationship between the size of the US nuclear arsenal and a variety of nuclear proliferation outcomes, including whether other states engage in nuclear proliferation themselves and whether they adopt policies designed to prevent the spread of nuclear weapons to additional countries. This finding was robust in a large battery of statistical tests that included alternate conceptualizations and measures of key independent and dependent variables and in several subsamples of data. Claims that the size of the US nuclear arsenal is an important determinant of the proliferation behavior of other states, therefore, do not find empirical support. In contrast, the findings of this research lend greater support to the idea that state behavior on nuclear issues is determined by calculations about how nuclear proliferation outcomes affect their interests more narrowly defined.

In his 2016 annual report to Congress on the projected threats to the national security of the United States of America, Director of National Intelligence James R. Clapper assessed that the prospect of nuclear proliferation in various countries constitutes a major threat to US national security.[53] The United States is correct to recognize nuclear proliferation as a threat to international peace and security, but, given the findings of this research, there is reason to believe that efforts to use disarmament as a means of advancing nonproliferation goals will not be met with success. Similarly, this research suggests that if Washington were to decide to pursue a nuclear arms buildup in the future, it need not worry that this move would have the unintended consequence of spurring proliferation in other countries. Rather than focus on nuclear reductions, the United States should continue to use proven methods for preventing nuclear proliferation, such as denying states the technology required to produce nuclear weapons and addressing the threat environments that motivate states to desire nuclear weapons in the first place.

Most importantly, this chapter provides support for the central argument of this book. The United States can pursue military nuclear advantages over its rivals in order to achieve deterrent and coercive benefits, while incurring minimal downside costs to its national security. In particular, this chapter showed that America's nonproliferation goals are not a casualty of the maintenance of a robust nuclear posture.

But, in an era of shrinking defense spending and budget austerity, is a robust nuclear force simply too expensive?

9

The Defense Budget

Can the United States afford a robust nuclear posture? To this point, we have seen that US nuclear weapons provide strategic advantages and also come with minimal geopolitical costs. But what is the *financial* cost to maintaining thousands of nuclear warheads and delivery vehicles? Many of the United States' legacy systems are entering the end of their service lives and the United States will need to spend hundreds of billions of dollars over the coming decade to modernize its nuclear forces.[1] Moreover, this comes at a time of slower US growth, high budget deficits, and growing political support in some quarters for greater budget austerity. Even if strategic nuclear advantages are important, it would certainly be foolish for the United States to pursue them at the cost of undermining its very fiscal health and economic well-being. Indeed, many analysts have looked carefully at the coming "bow wave" of nuclear costs and have concluded that the US nuclear arsenal is simply "unaffordable."[2]

This chapter shows that this view incorrect. The United States can afford to maintain and modernize its nuclear forces, and, indeed, they come at a good value. While hundreds of billions of dollars over a decade is undoubtedly a large number, it actually represents a small percentage of overall US defense spending. While reasonable people may disagree, the contention of this chapter, and the prevailing logic of US nuclear strategy, is that roughly 5% of the US defense budget is not too much to spend to provide the United States and its treaty allies in Europe and Asia with a robust strategic deterrent.

This chapter continues in several parts. First, it reviews the arguments made by those in favor of reducing spending on US nuclear weapons. Second, it moves on to present the counterargument about why the US nuclear force is affordable. Finally, it offers concluding remarks.

The Unaffordable Arsenal

During the Cold War, the cost of the US nuclear weapons budget was not a subject of intense political controversy only because there was widespread political agreement about the need to maintain a deterrent against possible Soviet aggression. As former Acting Administrator of the National Nuclear Security Administration Neile Miller testified before Congress, the US government did not prioritize "understanding the cost of [nuclear weapons] because of the imperative to deliver during the Cold War."[3]

Once the Cold War ended, however, outside analysts began to more closely scrutinize US nuclear weapons spending and increasingly question the price tag. In a foundational report published in the mid-1990s, Stephen Schwartz estimated that, beginning with the Manhattan Project, the United States had spent at least $4 trillion on the nuclear weapons enterprise.[4] He detailed costs related to nuclear warheads; delivery vehicles; command and control systems; strategic defenses; warhead retirement and dismantlement; environmental cleanup and waste management; and efforts to maintain secrecy. All told, he concluded that nuclear weapons spending had accounted for "more than one-quarter of all military spending since World War II and $1 trillion more than the cost of World War II itself."[5]

Bloated US nuclear weapons spending remained a theme throughout the post–Cold War era, with many US analysts and politicians, especially on the political left, questioning why the United States was spending so much to maintain weapons capable of destroying the world when that money could be better used to construct something more positive, like schools or roads in the United States.

The argument became an even more prominent part of political discourse in the 2010s, for at least three reasons. First, in his famous Prague speech, President Barack Obama promised to rid the world of nuclear weapons, thus creating a political safe space for some mainstream foreign policy analysts, in addition to the traditional arms control and disarmament organizations, to openly criticize America's existing nuclear posture and future modernization plans.[6]

Second, Cold War systems were nearing the end of their service lives and a significant and near simultaneous set of financial outlays loomed on the horizon if the US hoped to modernize these forces. While Obama promised to rid the world of nuclear weapons, he also vowed that as long as nuclear weapons exist, the United States will maintain a "safe, secure, and effective" nuclear deterrent.[7] The Obama administration planned, therefore, to build new: factories to produce plutonium pits and uranium; ICBMs; nuclear submarines (the Ohio-Class Replacement); long-range bombers (the B21); and ALCMs (the so-called long-range standoff, or LRSO). It also had plans to upgrade the B61 nuclear gravity bombs. The Obama administration estimated the cost of these modernization programs to come to approximately $200 billion over the course of 10 years.[8] The nonpartisan Congressional Budget Office put the price tag at about $350 billion.[9] This so-called "bow wave" of major impending costs, arriving at the same time, raised legitimate questions about whether all of the modernization programs were necessary and whether some programs could be pushed into the future or canceled altogether.

Third, and finally, these developments intersected with deeper economic concerns. The United States was still in a slow recovery from the 2007 global financial crisis. There was growing bipartisan consensus that the United States needed to rein in spending to balance its budget and stave off future financial difficulties. And to deal with these problems, in 2011, Congress passed the Budget Control Act, which paved the way for the 2013 "sequester" and across-the-board spending cuts. In this financial environment, all government spending was subject to scrutiny, especially weapons systems that many regarded as little more than Cold War relics.

In 2011, the Ploughshares Fund released a report arguing that the US government was vastly underestimating the size of the nuclear weapons budget and that the true cost was closer to $700 billion over 10 years.[10] Also, in 2011, Global Zero, an organization devoted to ridding the world of nuclear weapons, launched a "cost campaign."[11] It predicted that governments around the world would spend over $1 trillion on nuclear weapons over the coming decade. It argued that, "at a time of economic crisis and austerity measures, world governments wrestle with grim choices—like cuts to education, healthcare, public safety and other essential services. But one cut is a no-brainer: nuclear weapons budgets worldwide."[12] Instead of modernizing America's nuclear forces, Global Zero advocated "cutting our bloated nuclear weapons budget" to "save hundreds of billions of dollars and help keep things we value off the chopping block."[13]

Building on this report, the aforementioned Global Zero study on nuclear posture argued that an important "reason for undertaking these illustrative next steps of [nuclear force reductions] is that the world is spending vast sums on producing and maintaining nuclear arms and on mitigating their environmental and health consequences." The presumption being that these costs could be eliminated, or greatly reduced, through nuclear cuts.[14] For this reason and others, as the reader will recall from chapter 2, the report recommended major nuclear reductions, including the elimination of the ICBM leg of the triad.

In January 2014, the James Martin Center for Nonproliferation Studies released a report that came to a similar conclusion.[15] The authors criticize the Obama administration for estimating the cost of nuclear modernization over a 10-year period, pointing out that the modernization cycles for the new bomber and ICBM would extend beyond that window. They instead argued for a 30-year time frame and estimate that the 3-decade cost of modernizing and maintaining US nuclear weapons will result in a "trillion dollar nuclear triad."[16] They raised concerns about these plans, stating, "it is an open question whether this level of investment can be sustained along with other national priorities."[17] Instead, they recommended nuclear reductions as a solution. They write, "a better strategy is one in which we choose to align the nation's deterrent with current geopolitical and fiscal realities. This will almost certainly involve a managed reduction in the number of nuclear weapons as we replace delivery systems."[18]

Similarly, in October 2014, the Arms Control Association released a report titled "The Unaffordable Arsenal: Reducing the Costs of the Bloated US Nuclear Stockpile."[19] It repeated the estimates of $355 billion over 10 years and $1 trillion over 30 years, noted the pressures on the defense budget due to the 2011 Budget Control Act, and pointed to other national security challenges, such as terrorism and Ebola, that cannot be addressed with nuclear weapons. "Fortunately," they concluded, "there is a sizable chunk of the Pentagon budget that can be safely cut back: the U.S. nuclear arsenal."[20] The report recommended delaying some modernization programs and killing off others as a means to save $70 billion over the coming decade. This can be done with little cost to US national security, the report argues, because "the U.S. nuclear force remains far larger than is necessary to deter nuclear attack against the United States or its allies."[21]

The arguments from this direction are certainly consistent in their message, but are they accurate? Are US nuclear modernization plans truly unaffordable? Can the cost savings to be had through nuclear reductions make a significant dent in America's budgetary woes? In short, is the maintenance of a robust US nuclear force simply too expensive?

Nuclear Weapons Do Not Actually Cost That Much

In 2013, then–Secretary of Defense Ashton Carter argued, "nuclear weapons don't actually cost that much . . . it is not a big swinger of the budget. You don't save a lot of money by having arms control and so forth."[22] This section demonstrates that, contrary to claims of an "unaffordable" arsenal, Secretary Carter was correct. The US nuclear arsenal and modernization plans are affordable and, to quote Secretary Carter, they "don't actually cost that much." The section shows that some of the high estimates for the cost of nuclear weapons are relying on faulty arithmetic; studies that focus on the cost of nuclear weapons fail to consider the substitution of nuclear and conventional forces; the cost of nuclear weapons is in the infrastructure, not in the level of forces; there are significant costs to drawing down, as well as to building up, strategic forces; and nuclear weapons are a small fraction of US defense and national spending and are not, in Carter's words, a "big swinger of the budget."

Funny Numbers

Many of the organizations making claims about the unaffordability of the arsenal have a clear political mission to advocate for arms control and disarmament. They release reports arguing that we should cut nuclear weapons because they are too expensive. But they also release reports arguing that we should cut nuclear weapons for many other reasons as well.[23] Just because they have an agenda does not mean we should dismiss their analysis, but it does mean we should take it with a grain of salt and examine the numbers carefully. When one does that, it is clear that they do not add up. For example, Glenn Kessler of the *Washington Post* "fact checker" found that the Ploughshares' estimate of $700 billion resulted from including items that do not obviously belong in an accounting of nuclear forces; double counting the costs of modernization programs; and employing a faulty formula to produce exaggerated estimates for the cost of overhead and support to nuclear systems. Kessler gave the Ploughshares estimate "two Pinocchios" for their inaccurate claims.[24] The US Department of Defense agreed with this critique. When asked about large estimates produced by outside organizations in congressional testimony, US defense official James Miller replied:

> I've had an opportunity to look at some of the materials that were referenced in the cost estimates just before coming over here and I—without giving this more time than it deserves—suffice it to say there was double counting and some rather curious arithmetic involved.[25]

The Relationship between Nuclear and Conventional Forces

Critics of the US nuclear arsenal often fail to recognize, or deliberately sweep under the rug, the various interrelationships between nuclear and conventional forces, leading them to overestimate the cost savings of nuclear cuts, for a variety of reasons.

First, many of the items often lumped into the "nuclear" budget are not directly relevant to the nuclear deterrence mission.[26] Some of these estimates include, for example; the cost of naval nuclear reactors used to power the Navy's conventional attack submarines; missile defenses; nuclear nonproliferation programs; and nuclear environmental cleanup and waste management.[27] These are budget items that would need to remain even if every nuclear weapon in the arsenal were eliminated tomorrow. Indeed, as we see in what follows, some of these costs would almost certainly increase if a decision were made to dispose of nuclear weapons.

Second, many of the other items counted as part of the nuclear budget are actually dual-use in nature, resulting in some degree of overcounting of nuclear spending. All estimates of nuclear modernization, for example, include the costs of a new long-range B21 bomber. But, again, even if the United States eliminated nuclear weapons tomorrow, it would almost certainly continue plans to develop the new bomber to deliver conventional munitions. Indeed, the B-2 Spirit bomber and the Tomahawk Land-Attack Cruise Missile (T-LAM) were originally designed during the Cold War with the nuclear mission in mind, but they have become features of America's conventional military missions in the post–Cold War era. Simply counting the new bomber as a conventional, instead of a nuclear, platform would remove $80 billion from the estimated cost of "nuclear" modernization.[28]

Third, nuclear reductions or a failure to modernize would confront Washington with a choice of either accepting a less capable military force, or of spending more—probably much more—to develop new conventional weapons to fill the roles and missions previously performed by nuclear weapons. The Arms Control Association acknowledges, for example, that reducing America's SLBM force according to its recommendations would result in a reduced ability to promptly hold at risk targets in Russia and China.[29] Eliminating the entire ICBM force as proposed by Global Zero's nuclear posture report would greatly reduce the US forces available for targeting an enemy's strategic weapons or other high-value targets. As a final example, complete nuclear abolition, the long-term objective of Global Zero, would gut US strategic deterrence altogether. Perhaps, some may argue, these missions are unnecessary. There is, however, a long-standing, bipartisan consensus that strategic deterrence is important. So, if the United States eliminates nukes, then it will need conventional forces to replace them.

Some may claim that, given America's overwhelming conventional military might, we already have all the capabilities we need without nuclear weapons, but this is simply not true. Despite America's awesome military power, the United States currently does not have conventional weapons that can substitute for nuclear weapons. Washington does not possess conventional weapons that can promptly hold at risk hundreds or thousands of ballistic missile silos, air bases, naval bases, command and control facilities, and other targets in Russia, China, and North Korea. It simply does not. Even if one is only interested in lower requirements for strategic deterrence, Washington also lacks the ability to promptly "assure destruction" of a major power rival, using only conventional forces. The greatest threat the US can pose with conventional forces alone is the threat to invade an enemy and fight a months- or years-long conventional war (possibly in a losing cause). This is simply not as credible or as terrifying (especially against a great power rival) as threats to unleash vast devastation in 30 minutes or less.

The United States may or may not be able to develop and field a force capable of conventional strategic deterrence over time, but the effort would be hugely expensive. Doing so would likely require developing thousands of new prompt conventional global strike forces. This could mean placing conventional warheads on SLBMs and ICBMs, developing hundreds or thousands of hypersonic glide vehicles, designing new higher-yield conventional warheads, and investing in other state-of-the-art technologies. The price tag on this endeavor is difficult to estimate, but it would certainly be much more than simply maintaining and modernizing the nuclear forces we already have. Moreover, even these massive investments might not succeed in fully replacing the capabilities of nuclear forces. The laws of physics are stubborn. The high yields required to destroy hardened ballistic missile silos and underground bunkers, for example, may simply never be achievable with conventional explosives on long-range delivery vehicles.

Indeed, it is for all of these reasons that nuclear weapons are generally thought of as cost-effective. Attempting to provide strategic deterrence against a major power competitor with conventional forces is much more expensive than relying on nuclear forces. US President Dwight Eisenhower decided to rely more heavily on nuclear weapons as part of his "New Look" policy in the early 1950s precisely as a cost-saving measure.[30] Similarly, faced with deteriorating economic conditions after the collapse of the Soviet Union, Russia was no longer able to sustain conventional forces at desired levels, and instead prioritized more cost-effective nuclear weapons in its military strategy and doctrine.[31]

Rhetoricians argue that an effective tactic of debate is to take an opponent's greatest strength and portray it as a weakness. This is precisely what disarmament advocacy organizations have done with nuclear weapons. For high-end, strategic-deterrence missions, nuclear weapons are the cheapest possible option. In other words, nuclear weapons, both literally and figuratively, provide a lot of bang for the buck.

The Cost of Nuclear Weapons is in the Infrastructure

Another reason nuclear reductions do not save money is because the cost of nuclear weapons is in the infrastructure; the warheads, in comparison, are virtually free. If the United States is going to retain even a handful of nuclear weapons, it will need national laboratories with scientists, engineers, and technicians; delivery vehicles; military units trained to handle nuclear weapons and perform nuclear missions; a national command and control system; and many other capabilities. These are substantial, fixed costs regardless of the number of delivery vehicles or warheads in the arsenal.

As the independent Government Accountability Office (GAO) concludes, "Reducing stockpile size is unlikely to significantly affect . . . costs because a sizable portion of these costs is fixed to maintain base nuclear weapons capabilities."[32] It continues, "base capability costs appear to be relatively insensitive to reductions in the stockpile."[33] In other words, reducing the size of the nuclear arsenal does not significantly reduce the cost one spends on nuclear weapons. In fact, it might even increase costs.

Nuclear Reductions Cost Money

A further consideration is that, while there are certainly costs involved with maintaining nuclear weapons, there are also costs to not maintaining them. When making a decision between two options, one must weigh the costs and benefits of each, but proponents of reductions point only to the costs of nuclear weapons and ignore the cost of their preferred solution, nuclear reductions. Nuclear reductions, however, are also costly. They require pulling missiles out of ground-based silos and launch tubes on submarines, retiring and dismantling warheads, and decommissioning and dismantling nuclear facilities. The estimated cost of implementing the New START Treaty changes in 2010 was $300 million.[34] Much of this cost was due to the need to remove SLBMs from submarines and alter submarine launch tubes. In addition, the United States currently has a 15-year backlog of thousands of retired warheads waiting to be destroyed.[35] In order to complete this process, the United States will need to build several new multibillion-dollar facilities. As another example, the US Department of Energy shut down its only plutonium-pit manufacturing plant at Rocky Flats, Colorado, in 1989 and decommissioning and decontaminating the facility cost taxpayers $7 billion.[36] Granted, these figures are less than the full estimates for modernizing US nuclear forces, but they still must be taken into account.

Moreover, if these were one-time costs, they might be palatable, but there is no guarantee the United States will not want to resurrect these capabilities in the future. And, indeed, Washington has in the past shut down facilities, regretted its decision, and then paid a premium to bring them back to life. After decommissioning Rocky Flats, for example, in 2007, the Department of Energy decided to restore its pit-manufacturing capability there at a cost of billions of dollars, and it is seeking billions more for a new facility. Given that other countries are modernizing and expanding their arsenals, any reductions the United States makes now might need to be reversed in the future. As the Rocky Flats example illustrates, it would be much cheaper to simply recapitalize the current force and infrastructure rather than pay multiple times by cutting now and rebuilding later.

In short, nuclear reductions are themselves expensive. Or, as one nuclear scientist explained to me, "if we stopped destroying weapons, we'd save a lot of money."[37]

Nuclear Weapons Are Affordable

Finally, and most importantly, nuclear weapons are affordable. The estimated cost of modernizing the US nuclear arsenal is, depending on the estimate between $20 and $30 billion per year over the coming 25 years. These numbers are unfathomably large to the average person, but so are other figures of US government spending. For example, in 2014, the US Postal Service alone lost $5 billion, mostly due to pension costs.

The US defense budget currently stands at $598.5 billion. It is, therefore, estimated that the cost of this nuclear "bow wave" of modernization will never exceed 5%–7% of US defense spending.[38] This is much lower than during the Cold War, when the nuclear forces were originally being constructed and their share of spending regularly exceeded 15% to 20% of the defense budget. When placed in comparison to national spending, the relative insignificance of nuclear costs is even starker. The 2015 US federal budget was $3.8 trillion, making the share of national spending devoted to nuclear forces less than 1% (0.008).

Is 5% of the US defense budget and 1% of the US national budget too much to spend on strategic nuclear deterrence for the United States and its more than thirty treaty allies in the most important geostrategic regions on the planet? Reasonable people may disagree, but given the benefits chronicled in the first half of the book, this seems to be a very reasonable price.

Even if one believes the US federal budget is in need of an overhaul, the idea that national debt and deficit shortfalls can be meaningfully addressed through nuclear cost savings does not stand up to scrutiny. Serious efforts to address the budget deficit have demonstrated that the savings necessary can only be found in reforms to entitlement spending.[39] The budget cannot be balanced on the back of the military and certainly not from cuts to nuclear forces. The nuclear budget is simply too insignificant a category to make a major difference to the bottom line. Indeed, as defense acquisition expert David Mosher has explained, the recurring temptation to search for cost savings through nuclear reductions, is "the hunt for small potatoes."[40]

Conclusion

This chapter analyzed the budgetary implications of American nuclear strategy. It found that the United States spends significant sums on its nuclear forces.

Washington will spend between \$20 and \$30 billion per year over the coming quarter century to modernize its nuclear forces. It also demonstrated, however, that these costs make up only a small percentage of US defense and national spending. The United States allocates only 5% and 1% of defense and national spending, respectively, on nuclear forces. The financial costs of US nuclear strategy, therefore, are quite affordable and, depending on one's perspective, a good value.

To this point, therefore, the book has demonstrated that the US nuclear arsenal provides significant strategic benefits and entails only minimal geopolitical and economic cost. We can understand, therefore, why the United States constructed a robust nuclear posture in the past and why it plans to retain and modernize it at present.

But, what does this analysis mean for the future? What kind of nuclear arsenal should the United States build as it enters a new nuclear age? And what does this analysis, which stands in sharp contrast to decades of scholarship on nuclear deterrence theory, mean for our understanding of academic international relations theory? It is to these questions that we turn in our final, concluding, chapter.

Conclusion

Why has the United States developed and maintained a robust nuclear posture for decades even though existing academic deterrence theory suggests that such behavior is illogical? This question may be among the most notable puzzles in the entire field of international security studies. In universities around the world since the beginning of the nuclear era, countless pupils have been taught the basics of nuclear deterrence theory. They have been instructed that in order to achieve nuclear deterrence, states must ensure a secure, second-strike capability. They learned further that additional nuclear capabilities beyond this point, such as those maintained by the United States, are unnecessary and wasteful overkill. Many of these students never have the occasion to think seriously about nuclear weapons again and they may go through life assuming that they and their professors know more about nuclear strategy than do the policymakers responsible for protecting them and their families.

Others continue to think about nuclear weapons. They go on to work on related issues in government, the military, or as experts themselves in think tanks and universities. And in so doing, they were continually confronted with a glaring contradiction: the United States has never been content with a mere, second-strike capability. Elements of its nuclear posture, including the maintenance of thousands of warheads, counterforce targeting and capabilities, and a recurring interest in damage limitation, do not square with notions of minimum deterrence or assured retaliation taught in the classroom. This divergence between theoretical wisdom and real-world practice has generated no small amount of mental angst and has contributed to confused and sometimes suboptimal US defense policy. As a scholar-practitioner in this field, I myself struggled for almost a decade to make sense of this confounding gap between theory and practice. In this case, however, the labors inspired by this discomfort may have proven worthwhile. I believe this book helps to square the circle between nuclear deterrence scholarship and policy.

This book explained the logic of American nuclear strategy and provided a novel, theoretical explanation for why military nuclear advantages matter.

It did so by presenting a new theory of nuclear competition: the superiority-brinkmanship synthesis theory. From the nuclear strategy literature, the theory builds on the idea that a robust nuclear posture can limit damage to a state in the event of a nuclear exchange. From the nuclear deterrence literature, it borrows the idea that competitions among nuclear-armed states are games of nuclear brinkmanship. Combining these logics, the theory maintains that nuclear superior states are, on average, willing to run greater risks in these competitions in risk taking. Since they are less vulnerable to the costs of nuclear war, they are able to push harder in a crisis. For this reason, nuclear superior states are more likely to achieve their goals in international crises and less likely to be targeted with military challenges in the first place.

This logic applies universally to competitions among nuclear powers, but it is most applicable to understanding American nuclear strategy. Indeed, one of the puzzles raised by the central argument of the book is why all countries do not mimic the United States and seek a more robust nuclear force. To be sure, other countries, including Russia and Pakistan, have demonstrated interest in warfighting postures and military nuclear advantages. In the future, perhaps other states, including China, will seek a much larger nuclear arsenal. But, there are at least two reasons why the United States has been especially attuned to the benefits of strategic superiority. First, as the world's largest and most innovative economy throughout the nuclear era, the United States has been better able than other states to afford military nuclear advantages, even over other great power rivals. As we saw in chapter 7, other nuclear powers, including Russia, have had a hard time over the years maintaining strategic parity with the United States. Second, and just as important, Washington places greater demands on its strategic forces than any other nation, and so it requires a much more capable force to fill these roles and missions. It does not merely seek to deter nuclear attack on itself, but it has provided political commitments to extend a nuclear umbrella over much of the free world. When extending deterrence to dozens of geographically distant states, the balance of resolve often favors local adversaries, so the United States has sought to counteract this stakes shortfall with a force overmatch.

The first part of the book provided systematic empirical evidence in support of the superiority brinkmanship synthesis theory. In chapter 2, a series of nuclear exchange calculations demonstrated that the nuclear balance of power matters for nuclear war outcomes. Alterations in the nuclear balance of power between the United States and its nuclear-armed adversaries (Russia, China, and North Korea) can mean the difference between whether hundreds of US cities and millions of American lives are saved or lost. This finding served a dual purpose. First, it provided the first empirical test of the theory against competing hypotheses. Limiting damage if deterrence fails is a goal of US nuclear strategy, and this chapter demonstrated that military nuclear advantages contribute to that important objective. Second, this chapter substantiated a key premise of the superiority-brinkmanship synthesis theory: the nuclear balance of power greatly shapes a state's vulnerability to nuclear war.

Chapter 3 tested the superiority-brinkmanship synthesis theory in the domain of nuclear crises. The chapter provided a quantitative test of the relationship between the nuclear balance of power and nuclear crisis outcomes. Performing statistical analysis on a data set of nuclear crises from 1945 to 2001, the chapter showed that nuclear superior states are ten times more likely than their inferior competitors to achieve their goals in high-stakes crises.

Chapter 4 stuck with the theme of nuclear crises outcomes and performed in-depth case analyses to provide further support for the superiority-brinkmanship synthesis theory. Qualitative investigations into the Cuban Missile Crisis, the Sino-Soviet Border War, the 1973 Arab-Israeli War, and the Kargil Crisis provided evidence that policymakers pay attention to the nuclear balance of power and believe that it affects their strategic position; nuclear inferior states are less willing to escalate dangerous crises; and nuclear superior states more often achieve their basic crisis objectives. The chapter thus revealed the causal processes predicted by the theory in operation in the most important crises of the nuclear era.

In chapter 5, the book turned to deterrence and compellence and found additional empirical backing of the superiority-brinkmanship synthesis theory. Conducting quantitative analysis on all militarized compellent threats (MCTs) from 1945 to 2001, the chapter demonstrated that nuclear superior states are less likely to be targeted in MCTs. Indeed, according to the MCT data set, the chapter showed that nuclear superiority is undefeated in compellent threat episodes. Since 1945, nuclear-armed states have issued forty-nine threats and, remarkably, all forty-nine of these were against states with fewer nuclear weapons. This chapter showed, therefore, that nuclear superiority deters military threats. It also demonstrated, contrary to the claims of others, that nuclear superiority greatly matters for compellence.

The book considered not only the benefits, but also the potential costs, of a robust nuclear posture. Critics argue that even if military nuclear advantages enhance deterrence, they might come with downside risks such as upsetting strategic stability, provoking unwinnable arms races, fueling nuclear proliferation, and draining the defense budget. If these costs are as severe as some might lead us to believe, however, we are back to the puzzle that prompted the investigations in this book: Why does the United States pursue military nuclear advantages if the costs are so high? Is US policy irrational? Or are these costs being exaggerated by the opponents of America's nuclear forces?

Part II of the book demonstrated that the potential downside risks of nuclear superiority are not that severe and, in some cases, are nonexistent. Contrary to the claims of critics, chapter 6 argued that nuclear superiority does not cause strategic instability and increase the risk of nuclear war. Rather, the opposite is true. Preponderance causes peace. Moreover, the chapter also showed that US nuclear superiority may increase instability that strengthens Washington's hand, but it almost certainly dampens the more threatening sources of instability. In short, on reflection, we saw that global strategic stability is better categorized as an additional benefit, not a cost, of a robust U.S. nuclear posture.

Chapter 7 turned our attention to nuclear arms races. Critics have argued that the pursuit of military nuclear advantages is both futile and foolhardy because adversaries will move quickly to close any capabilities gaps, making it impossible to gain a lasting strategic edge and will only result in costly and unnecessary arms races. This chapter reviewed the arms race literature, presented a new series of theoretical propositions about nuclear underkill, and conducted case studies of the development of the nuclear balance of power between Washington and its nuclear-armed rivals. The chapter demonstrated that (1) arms races are unlikely in most strategic situations, (2) competing in and winning arms races is sometimes necessary to secure one's interests in a dangerous international system, and (3) the United States has in fact been able to secure enduring strategic advantages over nuclear-armed rivals. In sum, it showed that unnecessary arms races are rarely a cost of the maintenance of a robust nuclear posture.

Chapter 8 considered nuclear nonproliferation. A case study of the Iranian nuclear crisis and a systematic quantitative analysis demonstrated that there is no evidence of a link between US nuclear posture and the proliferation and non-proliferation policies of other states. This nonfinding was explained with a theory of nuclear proliferation decision-making that emphasizes tangible security and economic concerns, and not the amorphous example supposedly set by US nuclear posture. The chapter demonstrated that, contrary to the claims of some, a robust US nuclear posture does not cause other countries to pursue nuclear weapons, or complicate Washington's ability to conduct a successful nonprolif-eration policy.

The final substantive chapter considered the defense budget. Chapter 9 dispelled the myth that the maintenance of a robust US nuclear arsenal is unaffordable. The United States allocates only about 5% of its defense budget to nuclear weapons. The chapter argued that, given America's strategic objectives, this is a small price to pay to deter attack against much of the free world by ensuring military nuclear advantages over nuclear-armed rivals.

Alternative explanations cannot account for the patterns of nuclear competition explored in this book. Second-strike theory outperforms others, but ultimately falls short. The theory is correct that states are hesitant to engage in conflicts with other nuclear-armed states. We also saw, consistent with the theory, that disputes between nuclear powers become games of nuclear brinkmanship and that the balance of stakes helps shape crisis outcomes. But, unlike the superiority-brinkmanship synthesis theory, second-strike theory was generally bad at explaining the outcome of nuclear crises. The balance of stakes is generally unclear because the stakes are high for both sides. Moreover, second-strike theory cannot account for the clear and enduring role of military nuclear advantages in international politics in the post-1945 era. As I have written elsewhere in this book, second-strike theory is not incorrect, but it is incomplete. Second-strike capabilities, brinkmanship, and stakes matter, but so too do military nuclear advantages. Scholars gravitate toward either/or debates, but we live in a both/and world.

The theory that proved least helpful in our investigations was nuclear irrelevance theory. This was the case for the atomic obsession, nuclear taboo, and nuclear compellence skepticism variants of this school of thought. Many people may wish that nuclear weapons were irrelevant (after all, if they were irrelevant, it would be much easier to abolish them), but the empirical evidence demonstrates that they greatly shape world events. Irrelevance theory cannot account for why nuclear weapons featured so prominently in this book's empirical chapters. Contrary to the claims of the nuclear compellence skepticism school, the role of nuclear superiority was equally profound, if not more so, in the chapter 5 study of nuclear compellence. Nuclear superiority proved to be a necessary condition for even attempting a compellent threat among nuclear-armed states. Moreover, if nuclear weapons are so useless, then why does the United States maintain a robust arsenal? Why do eight other states, including all the major powers, possess nuclear forces today? And why have many other states pursued them over time? Superiority-brinkmanship synthesis theory provides a ready-made answer to this question. Nuclear irrelevance theory does not.

Regional nuclear posture theory was considered, but the issues explored in this book were mostly beyond its scope. This theory is critical for understanding the strategies adopted by regional powers, but it simply does not have much to say about the largest nuclear powers, such as the United States; the nuclear balance of power between states and nuclear superiority; or the full range of outcomes affected by nuclear weapons, such as nuclear war and crisis outcomes. To understand these issues, a consideration of superiority-brinkmanship synthesis theory is necessary.

The book showed that conventional military power matters in international politics, but not to the exclusion of the nuclear balance. Indeed, the evidence in the book demonstrated that, among nuclear states, the nuclear balance was generally more central than the conventional balance. This is understandable. As chapter 9 explained, conventional weapons are simply not capable of performing the roles and missions expected of nuclear weapons. Margaret Thatcher is reported to have said, referring to the memorials to the victims of Europe's world wars, "there is a monument to the failures of conventional deterrence in every French village."[1] This finding also makes sense in combination with the lack of evidence in support of nuclear irrelevance theory. These theories are often used in tandem, with analysts claiming that nuclear weapons are irrelevant and it is in fact the more usable conventional forces that shape international politics. This line of argumentation has always contained an inherent tension, however, in that it attempts to maintain that powerful weapons matter, except for the most powerful weapons. The evidence in this book suggests a more commonsensical interpretation: powerful weapons matter and the most powerful weapons matter most. As former US Undersecretary of Defense for Policy Walter Slocombe and I have written elsewhere, "Nuclear weapons . . . remain the ultimate instrument of military force."[2]

A robust nuclear posture cannot be explained by bureaucratic politics. As chapter 7 demonstrated, inter-service rivalries have in recent years encouraged military services to shed, not accumulate, nuclear capabilities. Moreover, standard approaches to international relations theory tend to turn to sub-optimal, domestic-level explanations to account for phenomena that cannot be adequately explained using a state-level, rational-actor model. But this book demonstrated that, for the United States, the pursuit of military nuclear advantages is, in fact, quite logical.

Finally, democratic advantage theory found little support. The quantitative analysis shows that democratic states are neither more nor less likely than autocracies to achieve their basic goals in nuclear crises. In the case studies, we saw that democratic states often achieved their basic goals, but the mechanisms of the case were more supportive of superiority-brinkmanship synthesis theory than of democratic advantage theory. These findings point to interesting avenues for future research. They suggest either that nuclear competition may operate according to a distinct logic and that democratic advantages matter in conventional, but not nuclear, disputes. Or, it may cast even further doubt on the embattled democratic advantage theory.

Theory: Why Nuclear Superiority Matters

The primary theoretical contribution of this book was to resolve what is perhaps the most important and long-standing puzzle in the entire field of international security studies: if nuclear superiority does not matter, then why do policymakers often act as if it does? As pointed out, the academy's response to this question has been to cling to its theories and to dismiss the contrary empirical evidence.

Confusion about the role of nuclear superiority, however, is not confined to the ivory tower. Policymakers themselves are sometimes conflicted on the subject. As we saw in chapter 4, participants in the Cuban Missile Crisis disagreed about whether nuclear superiority mattered. Moreover, sometimes these debates played out within the minds of the exact same people. During the crisis, Secretary of State Dean Rusk articulated a clear argument to President Kennedy about the centrality of the nuclear balance of power with Russia, but years later he argued the contrary position.

The most prominent example of indecision on this issue, however, comes from perhaps the best-known statesman in recent history: Henry Kissinger. At a 1974 press conference, the then–secretary of state emoted, "What in the name of God is strategic superiority? What is the significance of it, politically, militarily, operationally, at these levels of numbers? What do you do with it?"[3] Kissinger's skepticism in this statement is cited as evidence that he did not believe in military nuclear advantages, but less well noted is that he fully recanted this position only 5 years later. During Senate hearings on the SALT II treaty on July 31, 1979, Kissinger explained, "After an exhausting negotiation in July 1974, I gave an answer at a press conference which I have come to regret. . . . My statement reflected fatigue and exasperation, not analysis. . . . If we opt out of the race unilaterally, we will probably be faced eventually with a younger group of Soviet leaders who will figure out what can be done with strategic superiority."[4] Not even Kissinger, a scholar-statesman who prided himself on clearly grasping the grand strategic picture, could make up his mind on the simple matter of whether the United States should seek military nuclear advantages over its opponents.

Scholars deeply familiar with the history of the nuclear age are similarly irresolute. Richard Betts concludes that "U.S. nuclear superiority . . . was neither all-important nor unimportant."[5] Similarly, drawing on his influential studies of the Cuban Missile Crisis, Philip Zelikow's takeaway is, "U.S. nuclear superiority mattered. And, at some level, it also didn't."[6]

All of this circumspection may initially appear perplexing, but the reason why so many thoughtful people were unwilling to take a clear stand on this issue is actually quite understandable. Reasonable people are unwilling to conclude that something matters if they are not quite sure why it matters. Where there is smoke there is fire, and there is more than ample evidence to suggest that the nuclear balance of power has been an influential force in international politics over the past seven decades. At the same time, there is the troubling truth that everyone, scholars and practitioners alike, struggled to articulate a clear rationale.

That is not to say that no one tried.

Some argued that a strategic advantage (even if the other state possessed an assured retaliatory capability) might allow the superior state to choose to fight and win nuclear wars. In 1968, for example, US Air Force General Curtis LeMay argued, "A war fought . . . from a base of nuclear superiority would leave the United States sorely wounded, but viable and victorious."[7] LeMay's argument and others like it, however, call into question the very definition of "victorious." If a state possessed a "splendid" first-strike capability, then LeMay's argument has merit. But once an adversary has the ability to retaliate, then the situation changes. It is doubtful that any US president would choose to intentionally launch a nuclear war in the knowledge that he or she was preparing to leave the United States "sorely wounded."

Other proponents of superiority turned the argument around to argue that even if the United States might be deterred by the prospect of retaliation from an inferior nuclear force, US adversaries might not. Then–Secretary of Defense Donald Rumsfeld testified in 1977, for example, "if the Soviet Union could emerge [from nuclear war] with superior military power, and could recuperate from the effects more rapidly than the United States, the U.S. capability for assured retaliation would be considered inadequate."[8] Similarly, Keith Payne has argued that leaders from different countries have fundamentally different mindsets and just because Americans might find a given level of damage unacceptable, its adversaries might not.[9] This is a compelling point, but these are exactly the kinds of claims that scholars in the second-strike school found unpersuasive. As long as the United States possessed the ability to inflict massive devastation on the Soviet Union (even if the United States might suffer more), then what is the rational explanation for why Moscow would choose to intentionally start a nuclear war? Proponents never provided an answer that the critics judged as persuasive.

Others suggested that the effects of nuclear superiority might not be rational at all. Snyder and Diesing conjectured that superiority might provide:

> If not a rational comfort, a visceral one . . . It may be, for example, that in the tension of a crisis there is a tendency to regress to a more primitive, naïve thinking and feeling, to tacitly set aside the esoteric calculations of the strategic theorists, and to adopt and act upon the simple and deeply ingrained idea that he who is superior in physical force is superior in bargaining power.[10]

At its core, however, this explanation is only a slightly more sophisticated version of dismissing policymaker behavior as irrational. Moreover, even if subconscious urges are at play, this is not necessarily inconsistent with a rational explanation. As recent research in cognitive psychology has shown, emotions are an inseparable part of rational decision-making.[11] Still, therefore, we were faced with the lack of a rational explanation for why nuclear superiority matters.

This book aimed to change that. It provided a rationalist theoretical explanation for why the nuclear balance of power matters. Military nuclear advantages affect deterrence and coercion even when both states possess an assured retaliatory capability, because they shape a state's willingness to run the risk of nuclear war. With this theoretical insight in hand, nuclear strategy and deterrence theory should be much easier to understand going forward. It is also my hope that future scholars can refine our theoretical understanding and develop additional empirical tests to further understand the role of the nuclear balance of power in global politics.

The Partial Nuclear Revolution

The analysis in this book also has implications for how we think about the so-called nuclear revolution. In 2005, Schelling won the Nobel Prize in Economics, in part, for his pioneering work on nuclear deterrence theory. For decades, Schelling and other leading scholars argued that nuclear weapons completely and irrevocably altered the nature of international conflict.[12] Unlike in previous eras when larger militaries translated into greater political influence, it was thought that, following the nuclear revolution, the balance of political stakes determined the outcome of disputes. International politics were transformed from a competition in military capabilities to a "competition in risk taking." Nuclear superiority was thought to be irrelevant to a state's political influence and its ability to shape international political conflicts to its advantage.

The argument and findings of this book demonstrate that previous understandings of the nuclear revolution are only half right. Consistent with previous scholarship, this book found that in the nuclear era, states are incredibly reluctant to intentionally launch major wars, but they are willing to risk them, transforming international politics into a "competition in risk taking." In sharp contrast with theories of the nuclear revolution, however, the nuclear balance of power is highly relevant to these games of nuclear brinkmanship. In this way, the nuclear age is very similar to competition in earlier eras; the balance of military power continues to shape international conflict.

Method: Bridging the Gap

This book may also prove instructive for debates about bridging the gap between international relations scholarship and US foreign policymaking. It sought to demonstrate that rigorous social science research can be policy-relevant when it studies relevant independent and dependent variables and when it is organized around a central independent variable.

In recent years, scholars have bemoaned a widening chasm between the research produced in the ivory tower and the concerns of those in the corridors of power.[13] One of the alleged culprits for the growing irrelevance of academic research is the trend toward more rigorous and hard-to-understand research methods, including statistical analysis and game theory. Among other arguments, critics hold that scholars search for research questions that permit pristine research designs and the application of advanced research methods and ignore the messiness inherent in the most important and relevant subjects.

This book, on the other hand, demonstrated that game theory and statistical analysis can be employed in policy-relevant ways if they are directed at the right issue areas. Some debates that have preoccupied international relations scholars over the past decade or so, such as audience cost theory, are simply not of much interest to US policymakers. If one applies these same methods in more salient domains, then the resulting research can have an impact.

How can one choose a policy-relevant issue? As a colleague and I have argued elsewhere, in order to be relevant, academic scholarship must examine a relevant dependent variable and an independent variable subject to manipulation.[14] As a rule of thumb, a dependent variable is relevant if there is an office in the National Security Council, the Department of Defense, or the Department of State devoted to the issue. There are many offices in the executive branch devoted to terrorism, nuclear weapons, cybersecurity, Asia, the Middle East, and other important functional and geographic issues areas. There are not offices devoted to peace, audience costs, or international stability. This is not to say these issues are unimportant, but they are policy-irrelevant. If there is not a part of the US government that is organized around an issue area, then there is unlikely to be a policy audience eager to read research published in that space.

Second, scholars must identify the independent variables that policymakers can manipulate to push or pull outcomes in one direction or another. Research can be interesting or important, but if it does not tell policymakers what they should do differently when they show up to work on Monday morning, then it is unlikely to have an impact. Research on effects of variables subject to manipulation, such as sanctions, drone strikes, development aid, or nuclear posture, instruct policymakers on factors they can control. Structural or deep historical factors, however, like the international distribution of power or patterns of colonial settlement, are often important and can permit for cleaner research designs, but these are also forces that policymakers cannot easily change.

This book attempted to be relevant to policymakers by identifying a dependent variable around which several offices in the executive branch are devoted: nuclear deterrence. In addition, it studied an independent variable, US nuclear posture, which is well within the power of US policymakers to alter.

The analysis in this book also attempted to aid policy analysis by structuring the study around a single independent variable and multiple dependent variables. Scholars often design research to examine how a single independent variable affects a single dependent variable. For example, international relations theorists debate whether democracy is associated with peace or whether nuclear weapons proliferation affects international stability.[15] But policymakers generally do not have the luxury of stopping after considering an outcome on a single issue. They must wrestle with how a single independent variable affects a range of national security interests, or dependent variables. When policymakers are considering any policy intervention (essentially, an independent variable), they need to understand how that intervention will affect a range of US interests (dependent variables). They also need to understand how not acting will affect that entire range of interests. Then, they must weigh the outcomes against one another. For example, in deciding whether to provide lethal arms to the Ukrainian government to fight Russian-backed rebels, scholars may point out that civil wars last longer when rebel groups receive arms from an outside patron.[16] This is undoubtedly useful information and may suggest that if Washington prefers peace on any terms above all else, then it should refrain from providing arms. But policymakers also want to know how providing arms will affect the prospect that Ukraine wins the conflict, Russia's decisions on whether and how to escalate, broader US-Russian relations, US-European relations, American credibility, and many other factors as well. An analysis that focuses on only one of these outcomes, therefore, only begins to address the range of questions policymakers must answer before choosing a course of action.

In contrast, this book focused on how a robust US nuclear posture affects a full range of national security interests. As discussed in chapter 5, colleagues and I have in the past debated whether nuclear superiority relates to compellent success. This is an important question, but it is only a small piece of the larger puzzle that policymakers must assemble when making decisions about nuclear posture. As this book demonstrated, policymakers must also consider how US nuclear superiority affects warfighting, crisis bargaining, deterrence, stability, arms races, nonproliferation, and the defense budget. As such, these items became the subjects for the chapters in my book. By examining how this single independent variable under the control of US policymakers affects a wide range of US foreign policy interests, it is hoped that this book can be more directly useful to US foreign policymaking.

Policy: The Ideal US Nuclear Posture

This book explained the past and present of American nuclear strategy, but it also has implications for its future. What should US nuclear posture and strategy look like going forward? What is an ideal nuclear balance of power between the United States and its adversaries?

Critics of US nuclear posture are armed with an ideal end state in mind when they enter the policy arena. Disarmament advocates aim for complete nuclear abolition. Proponents of minimum deterrence would like to see the United States reduce its nuclear forces to several hundred warheads on a monad or a dyad of delivery vehicles. These clear objectives provide a useful guide for forming positions on specific policy proposals and a clear focal point that is a useful rhetorical device in policy debates.

Defenders of deterrence, on the other hand, often lack a clear objective. In the 1960s, some called for a nuclear arsenal "second to none."[17] At the end of the Cold War, the official US nuclear force sizing construct became the amorphous "lowest possible number consistent with our national security."[18] In the Obama years, the standard became to "reduce reliance on nuclear weapons" while retaining a "safe, secure, effective, and reliable," nuclear force.[19] And Trump has called for a nuclear arsenal "at the top of the pack." But what does any of this mean in concrete terms? Unlike proponents of disarmament or minimum deterrence, defenders of a robust nuclear posture do not have a clear end state to which they are consciously driving. This impedes their ability to coordinate among themselves and weakens their case in the public square. At the end of the day, the United States has tended to retain a robust nuclear force (certainly much more robust than many critics would like), but this appears to be driven by a series of adaptive, uncoordinated, and to some degree, subconscious responses to the threat environment and defense requirements and not fully the result of deliberate intellectual planning.

In contrast to previous approaches, this book articulates a clear conceptual end state toward which defenders of deterrence can focus their efforts: strategic superiority. The goal of US nuclear strategy should be to reduce US vulnerability to nuclear war to the greatest extent possible, while simultaneously maximizing adversary vulnerability. In some sense, this is the end to which US nuclear strategy has always been geared, whether publically acknowledged or even recognized by US leaders. By making this objective more explicit, the United States may be able to improve its strategic planning and better articulate its position to sway domestic and international public opinion on the benefits of a robust nuclear force.

This concept is illustrated in Figure C.1, alongside other possible nuclear balances of power. The figure places US vulnerability to nuclear war on the Y axis and adversary vulnerability on the X axis. In the lower left-hand corner of the figure, one can see a situation in which neither state is vulnerable to nuclear war. This is the nuclear balance of power that pertains among nonnuclear states, or in the world envisioned by disarmament advocates. As we move to the upper right-hand corner of the figure, we enter the world of MAD, in which both states are

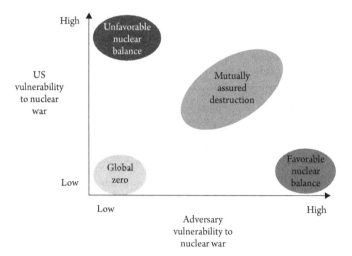

Figure C.1 Possible nuclear balances of power.

highly vulnerable to nuclear war. This is the preference of those in the minimum deterrence and assured retaliation camps.

The contention of this book, however, is that the real action in strategic competitions among nuclear powers is on the diagonal that runs from the upper left-hand corner to the lower right-hand corner of the figure. In the lower right-hand side of the figure, we see US nuclear superiority; US adversaries are highly vulnerable to nuclear exchange, but the United States is not. In the upper left-hand side of the figure, we see US nuclear inferiority. Here the situation is reversed and the United States is vulnerable, while its adversaries are not. Clearly one of these states of the world is more desirable than the other for Washington. The overriding purpose of US nuclear strategy, therefore, should be to seek to push the nuclear balance of power between the United States and its adversaries toward the lower right-hand corner. It is in this domain that the United States is safest and that its deterrent leverage is maximized.

To be sure, getting there might be difficult and, in some cases, impossible. Furthermore, in some cases there may be insurmountable costs to additional movements in this direction. This book demonstrated, however, that Washington is better positioned if it can move the nuclear balance toward reduced vulnerability even if it is not possible to eliminate it altogether. There are degrees of vulnerability and these shades of gray matter. Moreover, as was pointed out in the second half of this book, the costs to maintaining superiority are less severe than many analysts believe. In many cases, therefore, there will be additional and low-cost steps the United States can take to usefully move itself along the path to reduced vulnerability.

To understand these steps, it is helpful to begin with the somewhat abstract discussion of what an ideal nuclear posture might look like. In short, the United

States would like a strategic posture that would render itself as invulnerable as possible to nuclear attack from its three nuclear-armed rivals, Russia, China, and North Korea, while simultaneously maximizing adversary vulnerability to nuclear war. In broad terms, this means that Washington would need a survivable force. It must retain nuclear warheads in large enough numbers to cover all of the counterforce targets in each country. It would also need enough warheads not just to assure the destruction but also to guarantee the complete and utter annihilation of an enemy. It would need these warheads to possess a range of yields and capabilities so that it could destroy even difficult targets with a high degree of confidence. It must be able to get these warheads to their intended targets; this demands flexible and reliable delivery systems with various ranges and the ability to arrive promptly and penetrate enemy defense systems. It would need an advanced ISR system to track and target enemy mobile capabilities and to detect enemy preparations for nuclear attack. And it needs a nuclear command and control system to execute nuclear plans if necessary, even in inhospitable environments. Finally, it would need a robust system of active and passive defenses, including missile defenses. In other words, the ideal posture would look like a beefed-up version of America's current nuclear posture.

Putting aside the abstract discussion of an ideal posture, what are some of the concrete steps Washington can take today to usefully enhance its strategic position? There is no doubt that America's nuclear posture could be further enhanced. Washington could, for example, develop a nuclear Earth-penetrating weapon to hold at risk deeply buried and hardened targets, such as command and control bunkers in enemy states. It could improve the accuracy of its ICBMs. It could bring back retired capabilities and develop new more flexible systems that can more effectively penetrate US enemies' increasingly sophisticated air defenses. This could include new nuclear SLCMs, ALCMs and GLCMs. To enhance homeland defense, the United States could deploy a layered defense system of cruise missile and terminal phase missile defenses, including THAAD and Patriot batteries within the continental United States. It could also increase the number and sophistication of Ground Based Interceptors and erect a third missile defense site on the East Coast. To ensure that it is not outpaced by adversary technological developments, Washington should also invest in directed-energy interceptors and explore space-based defenses.

How Much Is Enough?

What about the question that often dominates nuclear policy debates: how much is enough? How many nuclear warheads does the United States need in its arsenal? As indicated previously, many opponents of America's current nuclear posture have a clear number toward which they are striving. The proper size for the US nuclear arsenal, it has been suggested in recent years, should be: 0, 311, and 1,000.[20] All of these are less than the 2,000 or so currently deployed by the United States and far below the 31,255 the United States maintained at the height of the Cold War. Many of these proposals, however, have the feeling of starting with a nice round number and then working backward to justify it.

In contrast, the superiority-brinkmanship synthesis theory provides a clear recipe for nuclear force sizing. To begin, we must first identify the relevant counterforce targets in America's potential nuclear adversaries that must be held at risk. This target list should include: missile silos, mobile missile garrisons and launch pads, nuclear submarine bases, nuclear air bases, nuclear weapons storage areas and production facilities, missile defense interceptors and strategic air defenses, and command and control sites. A proper accounting can only be performed using classified information, but by my rough count using open-source information, I estimate approximately 1,150 targets in Russia, China, and North Korea. To maximize the odds of killing each target and using the rule of thumb discussed in chapter 2, Washington should employ a double-tap targeting strategy. If the United States were to allocate two warheads to each of these enemy counterforce targets, the ideal number of US strategic warheads for the counterforce mission, given current conditions, is approximately 2,300. Furthermore, in the aftermath of a counterforce nuclear exchange, the United States would ideally like to retain additional warheads to deter other conventional or unconventional threats from these and other states. A couple of hundred warheads may be sufficient for this minimum deterrence function, raising the requirements for US nuclear force sizing to 2,500.

What this analysis also demonstrates, therefore, is that, far from overkill, the roughly 2,000 deployed strategic warheads currently in the US arsenal is a bit on the low end. The United States could usefully expand the size of its nuclear arsenal in order to enhance deterrence. At a minimum, the argument of the book explains that the "deep cuts" to the arsenal that some recommend would be unwise.

Moreover, the size of the US nuclear arsenal cannot be static, but must continue to adapt in response to changes in the security environment and enemy nuclear posture. The number of US nuclear weapons is determined by the number of targets they must be able to destroy and the primary targets of America's nuclear weapons are enemy nuclear weapons. Therefore, America's nuclear posture has historically been, and should continue to be, a direct function of enemy nuclear arsenal size. This means when the Soviet Union possessed tens of thousands of nuclear weapons at the height of the Cold War, then the United States also needed tens of thousands of nuclear weapons. Far from irrational, a US arsenal of this size was necessary for deterrence. When adversaries reduce the size of their arsenals, then the United States can afford to do the same, as

Washington has done since the conclusion of the Cold War. If, on the other hand, enemy nuclear arsenals continue to expand and modernize, then so too must the United States be prepared to build back up.

How Much Is Too Much?

So, America's nuclear force sizing construct throughout the nuclear era has been quite prudent, but what would a true overkill capability look like? As pointed out earlier, the United States pursues a pure counterforce targeting policy for moral and legal reasons and it should continue to do so. If the United States or any other state wanted to fully enhance deterrence in accordance with the above model, however, then the state would not only seek to reduce its own vulnerability to nuclear war, but it would also attempt to maximize an opponent's vulnerability. In other words, such a hypothetical country would also pursue a countervalue strategy with the intent of bringing about not just the destruction but also the complete and utter annihilation of an enemy's society. Once a state has the ability to hold at risk every possible counterforce and countervalue target in an enemy society, then any additional warheads would truly only serve to make the rubble bounce. To be sure, even a strike aimed only at counterforce targets would result in massive collateral damage and widespread destruction. As discussed earlier, however, to hold at risk 100% of Russia's population, it is estimated that as many as 140,000 nuclear weapons would be required. For a state with multiple nuclear adversaries, this already large number would then need to be multiplied according to the number and size of one's nuclear-armed rivals. Including an exhaustive countervalue element in one's nuclear strategy, therefore, would require many more warheads than the 40,000 or so possessed by the Soviet Union at the height of the Cold War. In other words, by this standard, no country has ever come close to possessing a true "overkill" capability. There were always more targets to which additional warheads could conceivably have been allocated. Again, I would strongly advocate against pursuing such a strategy, but it is useful to identify the absolute theoretical maximum level of a logically justifiable nuclear force in order to put current and historical numbers in their proper perspective. And by his standard, current and historical numbers have been quite modest.

Limited Nuclear War and Nuclear "De-Escalation" Strikes

The arguments in this book rest on the idea that a crisis among nuclear powers could result in a full-scale nuclear exchange, but currently many US policymakers are more concerned with the risks of limited nuclear war. They fear that US adversaries such as Russia or North Korea could resort to early nuclear use in a crisis in order to force Washington to sue for peace on favorable terms.[21] At first blush, this might seem like a very different set of challenges, but in fact they are intimately linked to the central themes in this book. Limited nuclear strikes are simply one means among many to raise the risk of full-scale nuclear war in games of nuclear brinkmanship. Limited nuclear strikes exert coercive leverage not primarily because they are so devastating but because they signal the possibility of further devastation to come. Adversaries see limited nuclear strikes as potentially effective because they calculate that they have a greater stake in their near abroad than does the United States. By rapidly raising the risk of nuclear war through limited nuclear strikes, therefore, they hope that Washington will prefer to back down, rather than run any additional risk of a larger catastrophe.

This is a textbook example of nuclear brinkmanship and, therefore, it is fully accounted for by the superiority-brinkmanship synthesis theory. As previously argued, therefore, the primary policy recommendation for addressing this challenge is to ensure that the United States maintains superiority at the strategic level, to reduce an adversary's willingness to run the risk of strategic exchange. Moreover, and specific to this challenge, the United States must ensure that it has available rungs to reach for at each stage of the escalation ladder. If Washington would like to continue to pursue its crisis aims even after a limited nuclear strike from an enemy, then it must have some means of further increasing the risk of nuclear war without intentionally launching a full-scale nuclear exchange. This means that the United States needs a range of "flexible" nuclear options. As I have written elsewhere, the United States has shed many of these capabilities since the end of the Cold War, but, given new challenges, it would be helpful to bring some of them back.[22]

Cross-Domain Deterrence, Emerging Technology, and Strategic Stability

Recently policymakers have begun to question how new strategic military technologies, such as cyber, space, missile defenses, and conventional prompt global strike, among others, could affect nuclear deterrence. While this set of issues presents many challenges, the foremost concern is that states might use these nonnuclear but strategic capabilities to eliminate an opponent's nuclear forces, thus contributing to first-strike incentives and nuclear instability. For example, in the future, states might conduct a massive cyber-attack to "turn off" an opponent's nuclear forces and then use conventional strikes and missile defenses to mop up any surviving nuclear weapons, thus denying the target state a secure, second-strike capability. Some argue that states, fearing that their forces may be at risk, therefore, may have incentives to use nuclear weapons early in a crisis.

Puzzling over how new technology might upend established modes of warfare is not unique to cyber weapons and 21st-century warfare. In the 1500s, for example, Machiavelli expressed bewilderment about the revolutionary success of Swiss pikemen and French artillery on battlefields in the Great Italian Wars, which rendered obsolete Spanish cavalry and medieval Italian fortifications, respectively.[23] While technology always changes, the fundamentals of strategy remain the same: a state's bargaining leverage will be enhanced to the degree it can minimize its own vulnerability and maximize an opponent's vulnerability to large-scale warfare. As it relates to emerging technologies, therefore, the United States should seek to develop and exploit new technologies and work to deny those capabilities to potential adversaries. It should invest in new strategic capabilities and cultivate an ability to employ these capabilities in a combined manner in order to blunt effectively an adversary's strategic capabilities. At the same time, it should also develop defenses to protect its own strategic forces and to reduce its own vulnerability to strategic attack. To those who worry that steps in this direction will undermine strategic stability or generate a new arms race, I simply refer them back to chapters 6 and 7 and the many myths surrounding both topics. In sum, strategic technology will continue to change, but the benefits of strategic superiority will not.

Arms Control, Disarmament, and Nonproliferation

Issues of arms control, disarmament, and nuclear nonproliferation are vital for US national security, but they are not the focus of this book. Rather, this book centered on questions of nuclear strategy and deterrence. For readers interested in my views on these other issues, I have written about them extensively elsewhere.[24] In short, the United States should continue its efforts to prevent other countries from acquiring nuclear weapons and to strengthen the institutions of the nuclear nonproliferation regime. It should view arms control not as an end in itself but rather as a useful tool that can be employed to advance US and allied interests. And, finally, the United States and all states should continue to live up to their commitments under Article VI of the NPT to make progress toward eventual worldwide disarmament. In working toward this goal, however, we should not put the cart before the horse. Reducing nuclear forces in the midst of intense and growing international security threats would be unwise and only render the United States and its allies vulnerable to nuclear coercion from its nuclear-armed rivals without resulting in corresponding reductions from others. Rather than focusing immediately on nuclear cuts, therefore, disarmament efforts should be devoted primarily toward creating a more benign international security environment. If and when the international system is fundamentally transformed in a more peaceful direction, then nuclear reductions will easily follow.

Preventing Nuclear War

Arguments about nuclear weapons may be the closest analogue foreign policy has to the contentious "culture wars" in US domestic politics. Passions run high on all sides and the dogma of devoted advocates often crowds out more sensible analysis and recommendations. Cutting through this noise is no easy task. Nevertheless, this book attempted to do just that. It aimed to provide a systematic and well-reasoned approach to thinking about nuclear strategy that ranged from, at the most abstract level, the logic of strategic deterrence, all the way down to the most practical and mundane issues, such as the numbers of nuclear warheads that should be sitting in US military bases tomorrow afternoon. For supporters of America's nuclear deterrence mission, I hope this book provided a coherent intellectual architecture for making sense of American nuclear strategy. For antinuclear advocates, even if this book did not change your mind, I hope it persuaded you that defenders of deterrence are thoughtful and well intentioned.

Indeed, debates over nuclear strategy are as intense as they are important and they will almost certainly continue for years to come. Rather than end with another argument, however, I close with a reminder of what unites us. For whether one's preferred method is nuclear abolition or the maintenance of a robust nuclear deterrent, our ultimate objective remains the same: to ensure that the world's most destructive weapons are never used again.

NOTES

Preface

1. Matthew Kroenig, "Nuclear Superiority and the Balance of Resolve: Explaining Nuclear Crisis Outcomes," *International Organization* 67, no. 1 (January 2013): 141–71; Matthew Kroenig, "US Nuclear Weapons and Non-Proliferation: Is There a Link?," *Journal of Peace Research* 53, no. 2 (March 1, 2016): 166–79; Matthew Kroenig, "Think Again: American Nuclear Disarmament," *Foreign Policy*, no. 202 (October 2013): 42–49; Matthew Kroenig, "Facing Reality: Getting NATO Ready for a New Cold War," *Survival* 57, no. 1 (January 2, 2015): 49–70.

Introduction

1. George Perkovich and James M. Acton, eds., *Abolishing Nuclear Weapons: A Debate* (Washington, DC: Carnegie Endowment for International Peace, 2009).
2. Kroenig, "Facing Reality."
3. Elbridge Colby, "Asia Goes Nuclear," *The National Interest*, no. 135 February 2015.
4. Paul J. Bracken, *The Second Nuclear Age: Strategy, Danger, and the New Power Politics*, 1st ed. (New York: Times Books, 2012).
5. Charles L. Glaser, *Analyzing Strategic Nuclear Policy* (Princeton, NJ: Princeton University Press, 1990); Robert Jervis, *The Illogic of American Nuclear Strategy*, Cornell Studies in Security Affairs (Ithaca, NY: Cornell University Press, 1984); Robert Jervis, *The Meaning of the Nuclear Revolution: Statecraft and the Prospect of Armageddon*, Cornell Studies in Security Affairs (Ithaca, NY: Cornell University Press, 1989); Robert Powell, *Nuclear Deterrence Theory: The Search for Credibility* (Cambridge; New York: Cambridge University Press, 1990); Kenneth N. Waltz, *The Spread of Nuclear Weapons: More May Be Better*, Adelphi Papers, no. 171 (London: International Institute for .Strategic Studies, 1981).
6. On US arsenal size, see, for example, William J. Broad, "Reduction of Nuclear Arsenal Has Slowed under Obama, Report Finds," *New York Times*, May 26, 2016; on US counterforce targeting, see US Department of Defense, "Report on Nuclear Employment Strategy of the United States Specified in Section 491 of 10 U.S.C.," June 12, 2013, available at https://2009-2017.state.gov/t/avc/rls/2016/263488.htm
7. John F. Kennedy, Remarks at the Hanford, Washington, Electric Generating Plant. September 26, 1963, available at https://www.jfklibrary.org/Asset-Viewer/Archives/JFKPOF-047-002.aspx.
8. For a criticism of this approach, see, for example, Jervis, *The Illogic of American Nuclear Strategy*.
9. For a perspective from the Democratic side of the aisle, see James Steinberg and Michael E. O'Hanlon, *Strategic Reassurance and Resolve: U.S.–China Relations in the Twenty-First Century* (Princeton, NJ: Princeton University Press, 2014).

10. Eli Saslow, "Top Officials Stress Country's Nuclear Strength," *Washington Post*, April 12, 2010, http://www.washingtonpost.com/wp-dyn/content/article/2010/04/11/AR2010041103344.html.

11. Steve Holland, "Trump Wants to Make Sure U.S. Nuclear Arsenal at 'Top of the Pack,'" *Reuters*, February 24, 2017, http://www.reuters.com/article/us-usa-trump-exclusive-idUSKBN16221F.

12. Jervis, *The Illogic of American Nuclear Strategy*.

13. Ibid.

14. Thomas C. Schelling, *Arms and Influence* (New Haven, CT: Yale University Press, 1966); Powell, *Nuclear Deterrence Theory*.

15. Schelling, *Arms and Influence*, p. 94.

16. Herman Kahn, *On Thermonuclear War* (Princeton, NJ: Princeton University Press, 1960).

17. For a review of these arguments, see, for example, Glaser, *Analyzing Strategic Nuclear Policy*, p. 133; Baker Spring, "Congressional Commission Should Recommend Damage Limitation Strategy," *The Heritage Foundation*, accessed July 1, 2016, http://www.heritage.org/research/reports/2008/08/congressional-commission-should-recommend-damage-limitation-strategy.

18. Stanley Hoffmann, *The State of War: Essays on the Theory and Practice of International Politics* (New York: Praeger, 1965), p. 236.

19. James Shepley, "How Dulles Averted War," *Life*, January 16, 1956, p. 78.

20. Jervis, *The Illogic of American Nuclear Strategy*, p. 31.

21. For a review of these arguments, see Michael S. Gerson, "The Origins of Strategic Stability: The United States and the Threat of Surprise Attack," in Elbridge A. Colby and Michael S. Gerson, *Strategic Stability: Contending Interpretations* (Carlisle, PA: Strategic Studies Institute, US Army War College, 2013), p. 1–46.

22. Glaser, *Analyzing Strategic Nuclear Policy*.

23. Jeffrey W. Knopf, "Nuclear Disarmament and Nonproliferation: Examining the Linkage Argument," *International Security* 37, no. 3 (December 13, 2012): 92–132.

24. Jon B. Wolfsthal, Jeffrey Lewis, and Marc Quint, "The Trillion Dollar Nuclear Triad: U.S. Strategic Nuclear Modernization over the Next Thirty Years" (James Martin Center for Nonproliferation Studies, January 2014), http://www.nonproliferation.org/wp-content/uploads/2016/04/140107_trillion_dollar_nuclear_triad.pdf.

25. Aaron Mehta, "Carter: Nuclear Triad 'Bedrock of Our Security,'" *DefenseNews*, September 26, 2016.

26. Lawrence Freedman, *The Evolution of Nuclear Strategy*, 2nd ed. (New York: St. Martin's Press, 1989).

27. For an excellent review of these arguments, see Brad Roberts, *The Case for U.S. Nuclear Weapons in the 21st Century* (Stanford, CA: Stanford Security Studies, 2015).

28. Robert Gates, "Nuclear Posture Review Report" (US Department of Defense, April 2010), available at https://www.defense.gov/Portals/1/features/defenseReviews/NPR/2010_Nuclear_Posture_Review_Report.pdf; US Department of Defense, "Report on Nuclear Employment Strategy of the United States."

29. Jervis, *The Meaning of the Nuclear Revolution*.

30. Thomas C. Schelling, *The Strategy of Conflict* (Cambridge, MA: Harvard University Press, 1960); Schelling, *Arms and Influence*; Powell *Nuclear Deterrence Theory*; Glaser, *Analyzing Strategic Nuclear Policy*; Jervis, *The Illogic of American Nuclear Strategy*; Jervis, *The Meaning of the Nuclear Revolution*.

31. Nina Tannenwald, *The Nuclear Taboo: The United States and the Non-Use of Nuclear Weapons since 1945* (Cambridge: Cambridge University Press, 2007); John E. Mueller, *Atomic Obsession: Nuclear Alarmism from Hiroshima to Al-Qaeda* (Oxford; New York: Oxford University Press, 2010).

32. Todd S. Sechser and Matthew Fuhrmann, "Crisis Bargaining and Nuclear Blackmail," *International Organization* 67, no. 1 (January 2013): 173–95; Todd S. Sechser and Matthew Fuhrmann, *Nuclear Weapons and Coercive Diplomacy*, (New York: Cambridge University Press, 2017).

33. Vipin Narang, *Nuclear Strategy in the Modern Era: Regional Powers and International Conflict* (Princeton, NJ: Princeton University Press, 2014).

34. James D. Fearon, "Domestic Political Audiences and the Escalation of International Disputes." *American Political Science Review* 88, no. 3 (1994): 577–92.
35. Marc Trachtenberg, "Audience Costs: An Historical Analysis," *Security Studies* 21, no. 1 (January 1, 2012): 3–42; Erik Gartzke and Yonatan Lupu, "Still Looking for Audience Costs," *Security Studies* 21, no. 3 (July 1, 2012): 391–97; Jack Snyder and Erica D. Borghard, "The Cost of Empty Threats: A Penny, Not a Pound," *American Political Science Review* 105, no. 3 (August 2011): 437–56.
36. Graham T. Allison, and Morton H. Halperin. "Bureaucratic Politics: A Paradigm and Some Policy Implications." *World Politics* 24 (1972): 40–79.
37. Robert Jervis, "Why Nuclear Superiority Doesn't Matter," *Political Science Quarterly* 94, no. 4 (1979): 617–33.
38. David Alan Rosenberg, "The Origins of Overkill: Nuclear Weapons and American Strategy, 1945–1960," *International Security* 7, no. 4 (1983): 3–71.
39. Glenn Herald Snyder and Paul Diesing, *Conflict among Nations: Bargaining, Decision Making, and System Structure in International Crises* (Princeton, NJ: Princeton University Press, 1977), p. 459.
40. Ibid.
41. Glaser *Analyzing Strategic Nuclear Policy*, p. 39.
42. Barry M. Blechman and Robert Powell, "What in the Name of God Is Strategic Superiority?" *Political Science Quarterly* 97, no. 4 (1982): 589–602.
43. Jervis, *The Illogic of American Nuclear Strategy*, p. 38.
44. Erik Gartzke and Matthew Kroenig, "Nukes with Numbers: Empirical Research on the Consequences of Nuclear Weapons for International Conflict," *Annual Review of Political Science* 19, no. 1 (2016): 397–412.
45. James Goldgeier and Bruce Jentleseon. "How to Bridge the Gap Between Policy and Scholarship," *War on the Rocks*, June 29, 2015.
46. An earlier version of this study was published in Kroenig, "Nuclear Superiority and the Balance of Resolve."
47. Sechser and Fuhrmann, "Crisis Bargaining and Nuclear Blackmail."
48. An earlier version of this study was published in Kroenig, "US Nuclear Weapons and Non-Proliferation."
49. Russell Rumbaugh and Nathan Cohn, "Resolving Ambiguity: Costing Nuclear Weapons," The Henry L. Stimson Center, June 2012, http://www.stimson.org/images/uploads/research-pdfs/RESOLVING_FP_4_no_crop_marks.pdf.

Chapter 1

1. Kahn, *On Thermonuclear War*. Fred M. Kaplan, *The Wizards of Armageddon* (New York: Simon and Schuster, 1983); Lawrence Freedman, *The Evolution of Nuclear Strategy*, 2nd ed. (New York: St. Martin's Press, 1989); Samuel P. Huntington, ed., *The Strategic Imperative* (Cambridge, MA: Ballinger, 1982), pp. 38–42.
2. Kahn, *On Thermonuclear War*, p. 20.
3. Ibid.
4. Mueller, *Atomic Obsession*, p. 8.
5. Jonathan Bierce and Michael Newkirk, "Nuclear Weapon Allocation Extremes," Johns Hopkins University Applied Physics Laboratory, August 2016, FPS-P-16-0245.
6. Harold Brown, "Preparedness Investigation Subcommittee of the Committee on Armed Services. Hearings on the Status of U.S. Strategic Power" (90th Congress, 2nd Session, April 30, 1968), p. 186.
7. See, for example, Glaser, *Analyzing Strategic Nuclear Policy*, pp. 211–12.
8. Information on nuclear arsenals and delivery vehicles are drawn from the 2015 "The Nuclear Notebook" series published by the *Bulletin of the Atomic Scientists*.
9. As the book was going to press, North Korea tested an ICBM, leading some to conclude that Pyongyang might possess the ability to devliver nuclear weapons to the US homeland. Neverthless, the central points about differences in adversary arsenal size and the magnitude of the threat to the United States still stand.

10. Mueller, *Atomic Obsession*, p. 17.
11. Hans M. Kristensen and Robert S. Norris, "US Nuclear Forces, 2015," *Bulletin of the Atomic Scientists* 71, no. 2 (January 1, 2015): 107–19.
12. Glaser, *Analyzing Strategic Nuclear Policy*, p. 133.
13. On the damage limitation approach to nuclear war, see also Kaplan, *Wizards of Armageddon*, pp. 201–19; and Freedman, *The Evolution of Nuclear Strategy*, pp. 117–30.
14. Brown, *Preparedness Investigation Subcommittee of the Committee on Armed Services*, p. 66.
15. US Department of Defense, "Report on Nuclear Employment Strategy of the United States Specified in Section 491 of 10 U.S.C.," June 12, 2013, http://www.defense.gov/Portals/1/Documents/pubs/ReporttoCongressonUSNuclearEmploymentStrategy_Section491.pdf.
16. See Kaplan, *Wizards of Armageddon*, pp. 201–19; Freedman, *The Evolution of Nuclear Strategy*, pp. 117–30; Glaser, *Analyzing Strategic Nuclear Policy*, pp. 133–65.
17. Narang, *Nuclear Strategy in the Modern Era*; Keir A. Lieber and Daryl G. Press, "The End of MAD? The Nuclear Dimension of U.S. Primacy," *International Security* 30, no. 4 (2006): 7–44; Austin Long and Brendan Rittenhouse Green, "Stalking the Secure Second Strike: Intelligence, Counterforce, and Nuclear Strategy," *Journal of Strategic Studies* 38, no. 1–2 (January 2, 2015): 38–73.
18. Bernard Brodie et al., *The Absolute Weapon: Atomic Power and World Order*, 1st ed. (New York: Harcourt, Brace and Company, 1946); Albert Wohlstetter, "The Delicate Balance of Terror," *Foreign Affairs* 37, no. 2 (January 1959): 211–34.
19. For the classic debate on this issue, see Scott Douglas Sagan and Kenneth Neal Waltz, *The Spread of Nuclear Weapons: A Debate*, 1st ed. (New York: Norton, 1995).
20. Schelling, *Strategy of Conflict*, pp. 187–204; Schelling, *Arms and Influence*, pp. 92–125.
21. Schelling, *Strategy of Conflict*, p. 187.
22. For the argument that nuclear war could result from accident or inadvertent escalation, see Scott Douglas Sagan, *The Limits of Safety: Organizations, Accidents, and Nuclear Weapons*, Princeton Studies in International History and Politics (Princeton, NJ: Princeton University Press, 1993); Barry R. Posen, *Inadvertent Escalation: Conventional War and Nuclear Risks*, 1st ed. (Ithaca, NY: Cornell University Press, 1991).
23. See Schelling, *Arms and Influence*, pp. 92–125; Jervis, *The Illogic of American Nuclear Strategy*, pp. 126–46; Powell, *Nuclear Deterrence Theory*, pp. 33–109.
24. Robert Powell, "Nuclear Deterrence Theory, Nuclear Proliferation, and National Missile Defense," *International Security* 27, no. 4 (April 1, 2003): 90.
25. See Powell, *Nuclear Deterrence Theory*; Snyder and Diesing, *Conflict among Nations*; Glenn H. Snyder, "'Prisoner's Dilemma' and 'Chicken' Models in International Politics," *International Studies Quarterly* 15, no. 1 (1971): 66–103; R. Harrison Wagner, "Deterrence and Bargaining," *Journal of Conflict Resolution* 26, no. 2 (1982): 329–58.
26. Schelling, *Arms and Influence*, pp. 92–125; Jervis, *The Meaning of the Nuclear Revolution*; Powell, *Nuclear Deterrence Theory*, pp. 33–109.
27. See, for example, Powell, *Nuclear Deterrence Theory*.
28. Robert Powell, "Nuclear Brinkmanship, Limited War, and Military Power," *International Organization* 69, no. 3 (Summer 2015): 589–626.
29. Jervis, "Why Nuclear Superiority Does Not Matter."
30. See, for example, Paul H. Nitze, "Deterring Our Deterrent," *Foreign Policy*, no. 25 (1976): 195–210.
31. Glaser, *Analyzing Strategic Nuclear Policy*.
32. For one exception, see Kroenig, "Nuclear Superiority and the Balance of Resolve."
33. Richard K. Betts, *Nuclear Blackmail and Nuclear Balance* (Washington, DC: Brookings Institution, 1987).
34. Dong-Joon Jo and Erik Gartzke, "Determinants of Nuclear Weapons Proliferation," *Journal of Conflict Resolution* 51, no. 1 (February 1, 2007): 167–94; Michael Horowitz, "The Spread of Nuclear Weapons and International Conflict Does Experience Matter?" *Journal of Conflict Resolution* 53, no. 2 (April 1, 2009): 234–57; Kyle Beardsley and Victor Asal, "Winning with the Bomb," *Journal of Conflict Resolution* 53, no. 2 (2009): 278–301; Mark S. Bell and Nicholas L. Miller, "Questioning the Effect of Nuclear Weapons on Conflict," *Journal of Conflict Resolution* 59, no. 1 (February 1, 2015): 74–92; Carol Atkinson, "Using

Nuclear Weapons," *Review of International Studies* 36, no. 4 (October 2010): 839–51; T. V. Paul, Patrick M. Morgan, and James J. Wirtz, eds., *Complex Deterrence: Strategy in the Global Age* (Chicago: University of Chicago Press, 2009); Powell, "Nuclear Brinkmanship Theory, Limited War, and Military Power."

35. The argument in this section is presented verbally. For those who prefer to see the formal model expressed in symbols, please consult Matthew Kroenig, "Nuclear Superiority and the Balance of Resolve."

36. For a complete description of nuclear brinkmanship models, see Robert Powell, "Nuclear Brinkmanship with Two-Sided Incomplete Information," *American Political Science Review* 82, no. 1 (March 1988): 155; Powell, "Nuclear Deterrence Theory"; Powell, *Nuclear Deterrence Theory*.

37. Steven J. Brams, *Superpower Games: Applying Game Theory to Superpower Conflict* (New Haven, CT: Yale University Press, 1985); Powell, "Nuclear Brinkmanship"; Powell, "Nuclear Deterrence Theory."

38. Powell, *Nuclear Deterrence Theory*, pp. 154–55; Powell, "Nuclear Brinkmanship," p. 95.

39. Powell, "Nuclear Brinkmanship," p. 96.

40. Scholars have identified equilibria in which states with lower levels of resolve may prevail because of bluffing strategies in games with incomplete information. See, for example, Robert Powell, "Crisis Bargaining, Escalation, and MAD," *American Political Science Review* 81, no. 3 (1987): 717–35; Powell, "Nuclear Brinkmanship"

41. Powell, "Nuclear Deterrence Theory."

42. Powell, "Nuclear Deterrence Theory," p. 94.

43. See Powell, "Nuclear Brinkmanship, Limited War, and Military Power." An exception is Powell, "Nuclear Deterrence Theory," which considers how missile defenses could reduce the costs of a nuclear disaster.

44. For a thorough review of this literature, see Kaplan, *Wizards of Armageddon*; Freedman, *Evolution of Nuclear Strategy*; Scott Douglas Sagan, *Moving Targets: Nuclear Strategy and National Security* (Princeton, NJ: Princeton University Press, 1989), pp. 10–57.

45. See also Betts, *Nuclear Blackmail*, p. 187.

46. Fearon, "Domestic Political Audiences and the Escalation of International Disputes."

47. Waltz, *The Spread of Nuclear Weapons*; Jervis, *The Meaning of the Nuclear Revolution*; Jervis, *The Illogic of American Nuclear Strategy*; Powell, *Nuclear Deterrence Theory*; Glaser, *Analyzing Strategic Nuclear Policy*.

48. Jervis, *The Meaning of the Nuclear Revolution*.

49. Jervis, *The Illogic of American Nuclear Strategy*, pp. 56–63.

50. William Burr, "The Nuclear Vault: 'How Much Is Enough?': The U.S. Navy and 'Finite Deterrence,'" *The National Security Archive*, May 1, 2009, http://nsarchive.gwu.edu/nukevault/ebb275/.

51. Jeffrey Lewis, "Minimum Deterrence," *Bulletin of the Atomic Scientists* 64, no. 3 (August 7, 2008): 38–41; Keith B. Payne and James R. Schlesinger, *Minimum Deterrence: Examining the Evidence* (New York; London: Routledge, 2015).

52. Fiona S. Cunningham and M. Taylor Fravel, "Assuring Assured Retaliation: China's Nuclear Posture and U.S.-China Strategic Stability," *International Security* 40, no. 2 (Fall 2015): 7–50.

53. Henry D. Sokolski, ed., *Getting MAD: Nuclear Mutual Assured Destruction, Its Origins and Practice* (Carlisle, PA: Strategic Studies Institute, US Army War College, 2004), p. 278.

54. Mueller, *Atomic Obsession*.

55. John Mueller, "Think Again: Nuclear Weapons," *Foreign Policy*, December 18, 2009, http://foreignpolicy.com/2009/12/18/think-again-nuclear-weapons/.

56. Tannenwald, *The Nuclear Taboo*.

57. Scott Douglas Sagan and Benjamin A. Valentino, "Revisiting Hiroshima in Iran: What Americans Really Think about Using Nuclear Weapons and Killing Noncombatants," *International Security* 42, no. 1 (July 1, 2017): 41–79.

58. Sechser and Fuhrmann, "Crisis Bargaining and Nuclear Blackmail"; Sechser and Fuhrmann, *Nuclear Weapons and Coercive Diplomacy*.

59. Schelling, *Arms and Influence*.

60. David A. Baldwin, "Power Analysis and World Politics: New Trends versus Old Tendencies," *World Politics* 31, no. 2 (1979): 188.
61. Frank Gavin, "What We Talk about When We Talk about Nuclear Weapons," *H-Diplo* Forum, No. 2 (2014): p. 25.
62. Powell, *Nuclear Deterrence Theory*.
63. Schelling, *Arms and Influence*, pp. 92–125.
64. Narang, *Nuclear Strategy in the Modern Era*.
65. Matthew Kroenig, "Posturing the Bomb," *International Studies Review* 17, no. 3 (September 1, 2015): 482–84.
66. Paul Nitze, "Atoms, Strategy, and Policy" Foreign Affairs 34, no. 2 (1956): 187–191.
67. Fearon, "Domestic Political Audiences and the Escalation of International Disputes."
68. Jessica L. P. Weeks, *Dictators at War and Peace* (Ithaca, NY: Cornell University Press, 2014).
69. Schelling, *Arms and Influence*; Jervis, *The Meaning of the Nuclear Revolution*; Powell *Nuclear Deterrence Theory*; Glaser, *Analyzing Strategic Nuclear Policy*.
70. Jonathan Kirshner, "Rationalist Explanations for War?" *Security Studies* 10, no. 1 (September 1, 2000): 143–50.
71. Trachtenberg, "Audience Costs"; Snyder and Borghard, "The Cost of Empty Threats."
72. Trachtenberg, "Audience Costs"; Snyder and Borghard, "The Cost of Empty Threats."
73. Matthew Kroenig and Dani Nedal, "Audience Costs or Superpower Patrons? Sources of Restraint in Crisis Bargaining," *American Political Science Association Annual Meeting, San Francisco, CA*, September 2015.
74. Gary King, Robert O. Keohane, and Sidney Verba, *Designing Social Inquiry: Scientific Inference in Qualitative Research* (Princeton, NJ: Princeton University Press, 1994).
75. Gartzke and Kroenig, "Nukes with Numbers."
76. Ibid.
77. Alexander L. George and Andrew Bennett, *Case Studies and Theory Development in the Social Sciences*, 4th printing ed. (Cambridge, MA: MIT Press, 2005).
78. King, Keohane, and Verba, *Designing Social Inquiry*.
79. Aaron Rapport, "Hard Thinking about Hard and Easy Cases in Security Studies," *Security Studies* 24, no. 3 (2015): 431–65.
80. Jason Seawright and John Gerring, "Case Selection Techniques in Case Study Research: A Menu of Qualitative and Quantitative Options," *Political Research Quarterly* 61, no. 2 (June 1, 2008): 294–308.

Chapter 2

1. For an exception, see Sagan, *Moving Targets*.
2. Herman Kahn, *Thinking about the Unthinkable* (New York: Horizon Press, 1962).
3. Carl von Clausewitz, *On War*, Everyman's Library (New York: Knopf, 1993).
4. Information on nuclear arsenals and delivery vehicles are drawn from the 2015 "The Nuclear Notebook" series published by the *Bulletin of the Atomic Scientists*.
5. Natural Resources Defense Council, "Chinese Nuclear Forces, 2006," *Bulletin of the Atomic Scientists* 62, no. 3 (2006): 60–63.
6. Global Zero U.S. Nuclear Policy Commission, "Global Zero U.S. Nuclear Policy Commission Report: Modernizing U.S. Nuclear Strategy, Force Structure and Posture," Global Zero, May 2012, http://www.globalzero.org/files/gz_us_nuclear_policy_commission_report.pdf.
7. For the classic text on the physical effect of nuclear weapons, see Samuel Glasstone, ed., *Effects of Nuclear Weapons* (Whitefish, MT: Literary Licensing, LLC, 2013).
8. Samuel Glasstone, ed., *Effects of Nuclear Weapons*. See also Lynn Eden, *Whole World on Fire: Organizations, Knowledge, and Nuclear Weapons Devastation*, Cornell Studies in Security Affairs (Ithaca, NY: Cornell University Press, 2004).
9. The Department of Defense has developed a computer program for estimating casualties from nuclear and radiological incidents, the Hazard Prediction and Assessment Capability (H-PAC), but this tool is best used for estimating the effects of a single incident, such as a single nuclear explosion or the release of radiological material in a dirty bomb. It is less

well equipped to estimate with any precision the effects of a large-scale nuclear exchange. Alexander Hill, "Using the Hazard Prediction and Assessment Capability (HPAC) Hazard Assessment Program for Radiological Scenarios Relevant to the Australian Defense Force," DTSO Platforms Sciences Laboratory, Victoria, Australia, March 2003, file:///C:/Users/mhk32/Downloads/ADA416823.pdf.

10. Glasstone, ed., *Effects of Nuclear Weapons*.
11. United States Census Bureau, "Annual Estimates of the Resident Population for Incorporated Places of 50,000 or More," July 1, 2015, http://factfinder.census.gov/faces/tableservices/jsf/pages/productview.xhtml?src=bkmk.
12. Alex Wallerstein, "NUKEMAP," Stevens Institute of Technology, 2012, http://nuclearsecrecy.com/nukemap/.
13. For one take on this approach to assessing nuclear war outcomes, see Carol Cohn, "Sex and Death in the Rational World of Defense Intellectuals," *Signs* 12, no. 4 (1987): 687–718.
14. For a review of the arguments in this section, see Clyde Haberman, "Global Warming Gives Science behind Nuclear Winter a New Purpose," *New York Times*, April 3, 2016.
15. See, for example, Paul R. Ehrlich et al., *The Cold and the Dark: The World after Nuclear War* (New York: Norton, 1984).
16. T. J. Raphael, "How the Threat of Nuclear Winter Changed the Cold War," *Public Radio International*, April 5, 2016, http://www.pri.org/stories/2016-04-05/how-threat-nuclear-winter-changed-cold-war.
17. T. J. Raphael, "How the Threat of Nuclear Winter Changed the Cold War"; Malcolm W. Browne, "Nuclear Winter Theorists Pull Back," *New York Times*, January 23, 1990.
18. Kate Ravilious, "Weatherwatch: Would Modern Humans Survive a Volcanic Winter?" *The Guardian*, November 30, 2012; "Doubt over 'Volcanic Winter' after Toba Super-Eruption," accessed July 12, 2016, http://phys.org/news/2013-05-volcanic-winter-toba-super-eruption.html.
19. William J. Broad, "A Volcanic Eruption That Reverberates 200 Years Later," *New York Times*, August 24, 2015.
20. Hans M. Kristensen and Robert S. Norris, "Russian Nuclear Forces, 2015," *Bulletin of the Atomic Scientists* 71, no. 3 (2015): 84–97.
21. Author interview with Russian think tank expert, January 2016.
22. Hans M. Kristensen and Robert S. Norris, "Chinese Nuclear Forces, 2015," *Bulletin of the Atomic Scientists* 71, no. 4 (2015): 77–84.
23. Narang, *Nuclear Strategy in the Modern Era*, pp. 121–152.
24. As the book was heading to press in 2017, DPRK tested an ICBM, leading some to conclude that it might now have the ability to threaten nuclear war against the United States. This development is still consistent with the basic argument of the chapter, which is that there are meaningful variations in nuclear war outcomes.
25. David Albright and Christina Walrond, "North Korea's Estimated Stocks of Plutonium and Weapon-Grade Uranium," Institute for Science and International Security, August 16, 2012, https://isis-online.org/uploads/isis-reports/documents/dprk_fissile_material_production_16Aug2012.pdf.
26. Elizabeth Philipp, "North Korea's Nuclear ICBM?" Arms Control Association, October 5, 2015, http://www.armscontrol.org/blog/armscontrolnow/2015-10-05/North-Koreas-Nuclear-ICBM.
27. Reuters, "North Korea Could Hit US Homeland with Nuclear Weapon, Says Top Admiral," *The Guardian*, October 8, 2015.
28. It is generally reported that the United States possesses 450 ICBMs, but this study relies on the numbers detailed in Kristensen and Norris, "US Nuclear Forces, 2015."
29. US Department of Defense, "Report on Nuclear Employment Strategy of the United States."
30. For the classic statement on nuclear targeting, see Theodore A. Postal, "Targeting," in Ashton B. Carter et al., eds., *Managing Nuclear Operations* (Washington, DC: Brookings Institution, 1987), pp. 373–406.
31. In a recent study considering nuclear exchanges between the United States and Russia, for example, Lieber and Press allocated up to eight warheads per target. Lieber and Press, "The End of MAD?"

32. Rebeccah Heinrichs and Baker Spring, "Deterrence and Nuclear Targeting in the 21st Century," The Heritage Foundation, November 30, 2012, http://www.heritage.org/research/reports/2012/11/deterrence-and-nuclear-targeting-in-the-21st-century.

33. The central findings of this chapter do not change under reasonable alterations to this formula, such as assigning two warheads to the most important counterforce targets.

34. Information on US nuclear sites, taken from "United States Nuclear Facilities," Atomic Archive, accessed July 9, 2016, http://www.atomicarchive.com/Almanac/USAFacilities_static.shtml.

35. Ibid.

36. Ibid.

37. These sites were taken from a selection of bases listed in "List of US Air Force Bases," accessed July 9, 2016, http://militarybases.com/air-force/.

38. Data on the largest US cities by population was drawn from the US Census Bureau. United States Census Bureau, "Annual Estimates of the Resident Population for Incorporated Places of 50,000 or More."

39. Ibid.

40. Ted Greenwood, *Making the MIRV: A Study of Defense Decision Making* (Cambridge, MA: Ballinger, 1975).

41. Ibid.

42. Cunningham and Taylor, "Assuring Assured Retaliation."

43. Lieber and Press, "The End of MAD?", p. 14.

44. Ibid., p. 26.

45. Long and Green, "Stalking the Secure Second Strike."

46. Kristensen and Norris, "Russian Nuclear Forces," p. 91.

47. Ibid.

48. Lieber and Press, "The End of MAD?, p. 15.

49. Long and Green, "Stalking the Secure Second Strike."

50. All of the information in this paragraph comes from Kristensen and Norris, "Russian Nuclear Forces."

51. Lieber and Press count 127 nuclear weapons storage and production areas alone. I estimate another 23 targets for the other areas. Lieber and Press, "The End of MAD?"

52. Kristensen and Norris, "U.S. Nuclear Forces."

53. Lieber and Press, "The End of MAD?", p. 15.

54. Kristen and Norris, "U.S. Nuclear Forces," p. 67.

55. Lieber and Press, "The End of MAD?" p. 15.

56. Lieber and Press, "The End of MAD?"

57. Bruce G. Blair, *Strategic Command and Control: Redefining the Nuclear Threat* (Washington, DC: Brookings Institution, 1985).

58. Lieber and Press, "The End of MAD?"

59. Jeffrey S. Lantis et al., "The Short Shadow of U.S. Primacy?" *International Security* 31, no. 3 (January 1, 2007): 174–93.

60. Defense Industry Daily staff, "Missile Defense: Next Steps for the USAs GMD," *Defense Industry Daily*, accessed July 11, 2016, http://www.defenseindustrydaily.com/3979m-next-step-or-last-step-for-gmd-05229/.

61. David Willman, "$40-Billion Missile Defense System Proves Unreliable," *LA Times*, June 15, 2014, http://www.latimes.com/nation/la-na-missile-defense-20140615-story.html.

62. Kristensen and Norris, "Chinese Nuclear Forces," p. 80.

63. Ibid.

64. For all information in this paragraph, see Sean O'Connor, "PLA Second Artillery Corps," Air Power Australia, December 16, 2009, http://www.ausairpower.net/APA-PLA-Second-Artillery-Corps.html.

65. Ibid.

66. Long and Green, "Stalking the Secure Second Strike."

67. Li Bin, "Tracking Chinese Strategic Mobile Missiles," *Science and Global Security* 15, no. 1 (2007): p. 8. Li discusses 20 mobile missiles. Kristensen and Norris put the number at 25 in 2015.

68. Kristensen and Norris, "Chinese Nuclear Forces."
69. See, for example, James Acton, *Low Numbers: A Practical Path to Deep Nuclear Reductions* (Washington, DC: Carnegie Endowment for International Peace, 2011).
70. Global Zero U.S. Nuclear Policy Commission, "Global Zero U.S. Nuclear Policy Commission Report."
71. Ibid.
72. Ibid., p. 1.
73. Kaplan, "Rethinking Nuclear Policy."
74. Heinrichs and Spring, "Deterrence and Nuclear Targeting in the 21st Century."

Chapter 3

1. This chapter draws heavily on Kroenig, "Nuclear Superiority and the Balance of Resolve." Readers interested in more details of the analysis, can consult this original research article.
2. Michael Brecher and Jonathan Wilkenfeld, *A Study of Crisis* (Ann Arbor: University of Michigan Press, 1997).
3. Ibid.
4. Information on nuclear weapons possession is drawn from Erik Gartzke and Matthew Kroenig, "A Strategic Approach to Nuclear Proliferation," *Journal of Conflict Resolution* 53, no. 2 (2009): 151–60. There could be disagreement about when some countries should be coded as having acquired nuclear weapons. Altering the universe of cases by employing different dates for when key countries acquired nuclear weapons did not affect the results.
5. For further discussion on this point and for the results of an analysis performed using a data set that includes nonnuclear states, see the "Robustness Tests" section of this chapter.
6. Christopher Gelpi, "Crime and Punishment: The Role of Norms in Crisis Bargaining," *American Political Science Review* 91, no. 2 (1997): 339–60; Christopher F. Gelpi and Michael Griesdorf, "Winners or Losers? Democracies in International Crisis, 1918–94," *American Political Science Review* 95, no. 3 (2001): 633–47; J. Joseph Hewitt, "Dyadic Processes and International Crises," *Journal of Conflict Resolution* 47, no. 5 (2003): 669–92; Beardsley and Asal, "Winning with the Bomb."
7. A robustness check performed on a data set structured around non-directed-dyad crises produced similar results.
8. For example, in the 1973 Arab-Israeli War, Israel is included in a crisis dyad against the Soviet Union, but not the United States. Hewitt, "Dyadic Processes and International Crises," p. 674.
9. Of course, observations of the dependent variable (crisis outcome) are not independent across all dyads within each crisis. I account for this problem by clustering the standard errors by crisis dyad, which allows for nonindependence of dyads within a crisis. I also tried clustering the robust standard errors by crisis only and then, in a separate analysis, by dyad only. The core results reported below were not affected by the choice of clusters.
10. Gelpi and Griesdorf, "Winners or Losers?"; Beardsley and Asal, "Winning with the Bomb."
11. ICB Data Codebook, available at http://www.cidcm.umd.edu/icb/dataviewer/variable.asp.
12. Creating a victory variable that includes compromise, or compromise and stalemate, in the victory category produced similar results. I also tried an ordered probit on a four-point ordinal outcome variable. It also provided support for the core hypotheses.
13. There are many advantages to employing the ICB data, but, like any data set, some of the coding could be questioned. For example, ICB codes the United States as winning the Cuban Missile Crisis, but one could plausibly argue that the crisis is better scored as a draw because the United States, while achieving its primary goal, gave in to some Soviet demands by pledging not to invade Cuba and implicitly promising to remove NATO missiles from Turkey. Recoding this, and other questionable cases, and rerunning the analysis did not alter the core results reported in this study. For a discussion of other questionable ICB coding decisions, see the online data appendix published with Kroenig, "Nuclear Superiority and the Balance of Resolve."
14. The number of participants and victors listed in the table differs slightly from the figures reported in the text of the data section because the statistical analysis employs directed dyads as the unit of analysis.

15. Kroenig, "Nuclear Superiority and the Balance of Resolve."

16. Although France became a nuclear weapon state when it conducted its first nuclear weapon test in 1960, it did not begin maintaining a nuclear stockpile until 1964. "Nuclear Notebook," *Bulletin of the Atomic Scientists*, accessed July 12, 2016, http://thebulletin.org/nuclear-notebook-multimedia. Excluding observations for France from 1960 to 1963 and rerunning the analysis did not alter the results reported in this study.

17. *Nuclear Weapons and Coercive Diplomacy*, 2017.

18. Using an alternate variable that measures a country as possessing a second-strike capability only if it possesses SLBMs produces nearly identical results.

19. For the argument that Russia and China are vulnerable to a US first strike despite the possession of a second-strike capability as defined previously, see Lieber and Press, "The End of MAD?"

20. Available online. Kroenig, "Nuclear Superiority and the Balance of Resolve."

21. Previous research on the effectiveness of extended deterrence offered by "major powers" has accounted for stakes by coding the major powers' "intrinsic interests" in the protégé state that is seeking protection. Paul K. Huth, "The Extended Deterrent Value of Nuclear Weapons," *Journal of Conflict Resolution* 34, no. 2 (1990): 270–90. This measure of stakes cannot be incorporated into this study because it examines the outcome of crises between nuclear-armed states and not on the effectiveness of extended deterrence guarantees from "major powers" to protégé states.

22. Robert Jervis, "What Do We Want to Deter and How Do We Deter It?" in Benjamin Ederington and Michael J. Mazarr, eds., *Turning Point: The Gulf War and U.S. Military Strategy* (Boulder, CO: Westview Press, 1994), p. 130; T. V. Paul, *Asymmetric Conflicts: War Initiation by Weaker Powers* (Cambridge: Cambridge University Press, 1994); Powell, "Nuclear Deterrence Theory," pp. 100–106.

23. Distance is measured in number of miles between capital cities and is extracted using EUGene. Scott D. Bennett and Allan Stam, "EUGene: A Conceptual Manual," *International Interactions* 26 (2000): 179–204.

24. Recoding the variable to score countries that share a common border as "1," or creating a continuous variable that measures the difference in the number of miles between the two countries' capital cities and the site of the crisis did not alter the core results reported in this study.

25. The ICB gravity variable is coded: (0) economic threat, (1) limited military damage, (2) political threat, (3) territorial threat, (4) threat to influence, (5) threat of grave damage, (6) threat to existence. In their analysis of crisis outcomes, Gelpi and Griesdorf, recode the variable to make threat to influence less serious than political or territorial threats. Gelpi and Griesdorf, "Winners or Losers?," p. 638. Reordering the variable in this way and rerunning the analysis did not alter the core results reported in this study.

26. I also tried a variable that gauges the difference between the gravity of the crisis for State A and State B and included separate variables measuring the gravity of the crisis for both State A and State B. These variables were not statistically significant and did not alter the results reported in this study.

27. I also tried a third variable to measure a country's political stake in a crisis, drawing on the ICB "issue" variable. The variable gauges the importance of the disputed issue in a crisis and ranges from 1 (most important) to 6 (least important). I dichotomized the variable to assess whether the country was fighting over a more important issue than its adversary in a crisis. The variable was not statistically significant and did not affect the core results in any of the models in which it was included.

28. Narang, *Nuclear Strategy in the Modern Era*.

29. Using a variety of alternate measures of conventional military capability, such as including separate measures of the power of State A and State B, did not affect the core results reported in this study. The correlations between *Capabilities* and *Superiority* and *Capabilities* and *Nuclear ratio* are 0.631 and 0.698, respectively.

30. Data on capabilities are drawn from the Correlates of War composite capabilities index, version 3.02, and extracted using EUGene. David J. Singer, Stuart Bremer, and John Stuckey, "Capability, Distribution, Uncertainty, and Major Power War, 1820–1965," in Bruce M. Russett, *Peace, War, and Numbers* (Beverly Hills, CA: Sage, 1972); Bennett and Stam, "EUGene."

31. Gelpi and Griesdorf, "Winners or Losers?" See also Dan Reiter and Allan C. Stam, *Democracies at War* (Princeton, NJ: Princeton University Press, 2010); Fearon, "Domestic Political Audiences and the Escalation of International Disputes."

32. Keith Jaggers and Ted Robert Gurr, "Tracking Democracy's Third Wave with the Polity III Data," *Journal of Peace Research* 32, no. 4 (1995): 469–82. Including variables that gauge the regime type of State B only or the joint democracy of State A and State B did not affect the results reported in this study.

33. In addition, and drawing from Beardsley and Asal, I tried a "target" variable, which measures whether State A was the target or the initiator of the crisis. Beardsley and Asal, "Winning with the Bomb." Scholars (e.g., Schelling, *Arms and Influence*, pp. 69–78) have argued that deterrence, defined as a threat aimed at defending the status quo, is easier than compellence, defined as a threat designed to change the status quo. If this is correct, we should expect that the states targeted in a crisis, that is, states defending the status quo, will be more likely to win nuclear crises. Consistent with this perspective, the sign on the target variable was positive and statistically significant. The inclusion of this variable did not alter the other core findings presented in this study. Nuclear superior states were more likely to win nuclear crises even after controlling for the initiator of the crisis. See the online data appendix, Kroenig, "Nuclear Superiority and the Balance of Resolve."

34. As an alternate test of a country's ability to absorb a nuclear attack, I also tried a variable that gauges a country's territorial size. This variable was not statistically significant and did not affect the core results reported in this study.

35. Singer, Bremer, and Stuckey, "Capability, Distribution, Uncertainty, and Major Power War"; Bennett and Stam, "EUGene." Using alternate measures that assess the difference in population size between State A and State B, whether State A is larger than State B, and separate variables for the population sizes of State A and State B, produces similar results.

36. On intractable conflicts, see Ron E. Hassner, "The Path to Intractability: Time and the Entrenchment of Territorial Disputes," *International Security* 31, no. 3 (2006): 107–38.

37. Beardsley and Asal, "Winning with the Bomb." Including other variables to assess a state's security, such as whether the state is involved in an enduring rivalry, did not affect the core results.

38. The two exceptions were the Berlin Wall Crisis and the Soviet war in Angola, both of which were coded as victories by the inferior Soviet Union. Future scholarship could consider these outlier cases in greater detail.

39. King and Zeng recommend using rare-events logistic regression (ReLogit) to correct for problems of small sample size, which they define as sample sizes below 200. Gary King and Langche Zeng, "Explaining Rare Events in International Relations," *International Organization* 55, no. 3 (2001): 693–715. Using ReLogit, instead of probit, produced similar results.

40. I also tried clustering the robust standard errors by crisis only and then, in a separate analysis, by dyad only. The results were not affected.

41. Gary King, Michael Tomz, and Jason Wittenberg, "Making the Most of Statistical Analyses: Improving Interpretation and Presentation," *American Journal of Political Science* 44, no. 2 (2000): 347–61; Michael Tomz, "Clarify: Software for Interpreting and Presenting Statistical Results," *Journal of Statistical Software* 44, no. 2 (2000): 347–61. All substantive interpretations reported here are based on Model 2 of Table 3. All variables were set at their mean.

42. The 95 percent confidence interval is 0.011 to 0.163.

43. The 95 percent confidence interval is 0.374 to 0.847.

44. The 95 percent confidence interval is 0.240 to 0.832.

45. Substantive interpretations reported here are based on Model 5 of Table 3. All variables were set at their mean. The 95 percent confidence interval is 0.485 to 0.996.

46. Tannenwald, *The Nuclear Taboo*.

47. I also tried a number of other control variables. For example, I included a variable that gauged the year in which the crisis occurred in order to assess whether time affected the likelihood of victory in crises. Asal and Beardsley argue that crises with more nuclear-armed states exhibit lower levels of violence. Victor Asal and Kyle Beardsley, "Proliferation and International Crisis Behavior," *Journal of Peace Research* 44, no. 2 (2007): 139–55. I also included variables that

counted the number of nuclear-armed actors in a crisis and a dummy that gauged whether a superpower was matched against a non-superpower opponent. None of these variables reached statistical significance or affected the core results.

48. Shifting from the lowest to the highest levels of violence increases the probability of victory by 31 percent. Substantive interpretations are based on Model 5 of Table 3. All variables were set at their mean. The 95 percent confidence interval is 0.089 to 0.489.

49. See, for example, Raymond L. Garthoff, *Soviet Military Policy: A Historical Analysis* (New York: Praeger, 1966), p. 119.

50. These tests are described in greater detail in the online data appendix. Kroenig, "Nuclear Superiority and the Balance of Resolve."

51. Fearon, "Domestic Political Audiences and the Escalation of International Disputes."

52. James J. Heckman, "Sample Selection Bias as a Specification Error," *Econometrica* 47, no. 1 (1979): 153–61.

53. Patrick Puhani, "The Heckman Correction for Sample Selection and Its Critique," *Journal of Economic Surveys* 14, no. 1 (February 1, 2000): 53–68; Beth A. Simmons and Daniel J. Hopkins, "The Constraining Power of International Treaties: Theory and Methods," *American Political Science Review* 99, no. 4 (2005): 623–31.

54. Using *Superiority* produced similar results.

55. There are thirty-eight observations that do not contain the United States and thirty-one observations that do not contain the Soviet Union.

Chapter 4

1. King, Keohane, and Verba, *Designing Social Inquiry*.

2. Rappaport, "Hard Thinking about Hard and Easy Cases in Security Studies."

3. Barbara Geddes, "How the Cases You Choose Affect the Answers You Get: Selection Bias in Comparative Politics," *Political Analysis* 2 (1990): 131–50.

4. George and Bennett, *Case Studies and Theory Development in the Social Sciences*, pp. 9, 120, 253; John Gerring, "Is There a (Viable) Crucial-Case Method?" *Comparative Political Studies* 40, no. 3 (March 1, 2007): 231–53.

5. George and Bennett, *Case Studies and Theory Development in the Social Sciences*.

6. James Mahoney, "After KKV: The New Methodology of Qualitative Research," *World Politics* 62, no. 1 (2010): 125.

7. Ibid.

8. Ibid.

9. Mahoney, "After KKV," p. 128.

10. See Tannenwald, *The Nuclear Taboo*, for a similar discussion of the role of "taboo talk" in providing evidence for the existence of a nuclear taboo.

11. There have been volumes written on this subject. For a good, recent treatment of the crisis, see Michael Dobbs, *One Minute to Midnight: Kennedy, Khrushchev, and Castro on the Brink of Nuclear War* (London: Hutchinson, 2008).

12. Theodore C. Sorensen, *Kennedy*, 1st ed. (New York: Harper & Row, 1965), p. 705.

13. "Nuclear Notebook," *Bulletin of the Atomic Scientists*, accessed July 12, 2016, http://thebulletin.org/nuclear-notebook-multimedia.

14. Robert S. Norris and Hans M. Kristensen, "The Cuban Missile Crisis: A Nuclear Order of Battle, October and November 1962," *Bulletin of the Atomic Scientists* 68, no. 6 (November 1, 2012): 85–91.

15. Norris and Kristensen, "The Cuban Missile Crisis."

16. Ibid.

17. A. I. Gribkov, William Y. Smith, and Alfred Friendly, *Operation ANADYR: U.S. and Soviet Generals Recount the Cuban Missile Crisis* (Chicago: Edition q, 1994), p. 10–11.

18. Scott Douglas Sagan, "SIOP-62: The Nuclear War Plan Briefing to President Kennedy," *International Security* 12, no. 1 (1987): 22–51.

19. Ibid., p. 30.

20. Ibid., p. 24.

21. Brecher and Wilkenfeld, *A Study of Crisis*; Kroenig, "Nuclear Superiority and the Balance of Resolve"; Sechser and Fuhrmann, "Nuclear Blackmail and Crisis Bargaining."
22. Gavin, "What We Talk about When We Talk about Nuclear Weapons."
23. Matthew Fuhrmann, Matthew Kroenig, and Todd Sechser, "The Case for Using Statistics to Study Nuclear Security," *H-Diplo* Forum, No. 2 (2014): 37–54.
24. As quoted in Dobbs, *One Minute to Midnight*, p. 322.
25. Dobbs, *One Minute to Midnight*, p. 88.
26. As cited in Marc Trachtenberg, "The Influence of Nuclear Weapons in the Cuban Missile Crisis," *International Security* 10, no. 1 (Summer 1985), p. 157.
27. Ibid., pp. 142–43, 158.
28. Dobbs, *One Minute to Midnight*, pp. 194–95.
29. Colonel-General Victor Yesin, interview with the author, Washington, DC, November 2012; Norris and Kristensen, "The Cuban Missile Crisis."
30. Dobbs, *One Minute to Midnight*, p. 249.
31. Ibid., pp. 157, 161.
32. Betts, *Nuclear Blackmail and Nuclear Balance*, p. 120.
33. Trachtenberg, "The Influence of Nuclear Weapons in the Cuban Missile Crisis." p. 161.
34. "Documentation: White House Tapes and Minutes of the Cuban Missile Crisis," *International Security* 10, no. 1 (1985): 164–203.
35. Trachtenberg, "The Influence of Nuclear Weapons in the Cuban Missile Crisis," p. 141.
36. Warren Kozak, *LeMay: The Life and Wars of General Curtis LeMay*, 1st ed. (Washington, DC; New York: Regnery Publishing, 2009).
37. David Talbot, *Brothers: The Hidden History of the Kennedy Years*, 1st ed. (New York: Free Press, 2007), p. 13.
38. Dillon, quoted in James G. Blight and David A. Welch, *On the Brink: Americans and Soviets Reexamine the Cuban Missile Crisis*, 2nd ed., Noonday Press ed. (New York: Noonday, 1990), p. 153.
39. Jack Snyder, "Active Citation: In Search of Smoking Guns or Meaningful Context?" *Security Studies* 23, no. 4 (October 2, 2014): 708–14.
40. Charles E. Bohlen, *Witness to History, 1929–1969*, 1st ed. (New York: Norton, 1973), p. 523.
41. Tad Szulc, *Fidel: A Critical Portrait*, 1st ed. (New York: Morrow, 1986), pp. 582–85.
42. Rachel Dobbs, "What Was at Stake in 1962?" *ForeignPolicy.com*, July 10, 2012, http://foreign-policy.com/2012/07/10/what-was-at-stake-in-1962/.
43. Quoted in Marc Trachtenberg, *History and Strategy* (Princeton, NJ: Princeton University Press, 1991), p. 235.
44. Dean Rusk et al., "The Lessons of the Cuban Missile Crisis," *Time* 120, no. 13 (September 27, 1982): 89.
45. Betts, *Nuclear Blackmail and Nuclear Balance*, p. 179.
46. Ibid.
47. Francis J. Gavin, "Lessons from the Cuban Missile Crisis." *The National Interest Online*. October 26, 2012.
48. Betts, *Nuclear Blackmail and Nuclear Balance*, p. 115.
49. For a more detailed discussion of the effect of the missiles on the balance of power, see Trachtenberg, "The Influence of Nuclear Weapons in the Cuban Missile Crisis."
50. Gavin, "What We Talk about When We Talk about Nuclear Weapons," p. 17.
51. Sechser and Fuhrmann, "Crisis Bargaining and Nuclear Weapons."
52. Trachtenberg, "The Influence of Nuclear Weapons in the Cuban Missile Crisis," p. 143.
53. See, for example, Daryl G. Press, *Calculating Credibility: How Leaders Assess Military Threats*, Cornell Studies in Security Affairs (Ithaca, NY: Cornell University Press, 2007), pp. 117–41.
54. Ibid.
55. Robert McNamara, as quoted in Trachtenberg, "The Influence of Nuclear Weapons in the Cuban Missile Crisis."
56. Bernard Brodie, "What Price Conventional Capabilities in Europe?" Rand Paper P-2696 (Santa Monica, CA: Rand Corporation, February 1963), pp. 24–25.
57. Trachtenberg, "Audience Costs: An Historical Analysis;" Snyder and Borghard. "The Cost of Empty Threats."

220   NOTES

58. Gavin, "What We Talk about When We Talk about Nuclear Weapons," p. 26. See also, Marc Trachtenberg, *A Constructed Peace* (Princeton, NJ: Princeton University Press, 1999).
59. Clausewitz, *On War*.
60. For a thorough treatment of the conflict, see Michael S. Gerson, "The Sino-Soviet Border Conflict: Deterrence, Escalation, and the Threat of Nuclear War in 1969," Center for Naval Analyses, November 2010, https://www.cna.org/CNA_files/PDF/D0022974.A2.pdf.
61. Allen S. Whiting, "China's Use of Force," *International Security* 26, no. 2 (Fall, 2001): 103–31; M. Taylor Fravel, *Strong Borders, Secure Nation: Cooperation and Conflict in China's Territorial Disputes*, p. 212.
62. CIA, Directorate of Intelligence, "Intelligence Memorandum: Sino-Soviet Border Talks, Problems and Prospects," 10 November 1969, p. 8, available at http://www.foia.cia.gov/sites/default/files/document_conversions/89801/DOC_0000326154.pdf; James R. Holmes and Toshi Yoshihara, "Mao's 'Active Defense' Is Turning Offensive," *United States Naval Institute. Proceedings* 137, no. 4 (April 2011): 24–29.
63. Hans M. Kristensen and Robert S. Norris, "Nuclear Notebook," *Bulletin of the Atomic Scientists*, accessed July 12, 2016, http://thebulletin.org/nuclear-notebook-multimedia.
64. Raymond L. Garthoff, US Department of State Bureau of Politico-Military Affairs to Deputy Under Secretary for Political Affairs Foy Kohler, "Subjective and Objective Strategic Balances," 31 March 1967, Top Secret, excised copy.
65. Central Intelligence Agency, "Communist China's Weapons Program for Strategic Attack, NIE 13-8-71," October 28, 1971.
66. Ibid.
67. Gerson, "The Sino-Soviet Border Conflict," p. iii.
68. Sechser and Fuhrmann, *Nuclear Weapons and Coercive Diplomacy*, p. 210–218.
69. Kissinger, *The White House Years*, p. 186.
70. Central Intelligence Agency, "The Evolution of Soviet Policy in the Sino-Soviet Border Dispute," April 28, 1970, available at https://www.cia.gov/library/readingroom/docs/esau-44.pdf.
71. Gerson, "The Sino-Soviet Border Conflict."
72. Raymond L. Garthoff, *Détente and Confrontation: American-Soviet Relations from Nixon to Reagan* (Washington, DC: Brookings Institution, 1985).
73. Gerson, "The Sino-Soviet Border Conflict," pp. 32–33.
74. Central Intelligence Agency, Directorate of Intelligence, "The Evolution of Soviet Policy in the Sino-Soviet Border Dispute," p. 55, available at http://www.foia.cia.gov/sites/default/files/document_conversions/14/esau-44.pdf.
75. "Memorandum of Conversation between William L. Stearman and Boris N. Davydov," August 18, 1969.
76. Gerson, "The Sino-Soviet Border Conflict," p. 34.
77. Ibid.
78. Victor Louis, "Will Russia Czech-Mate China?" *London Evening News*, September 16, 1969.
79. Ibid.
80. Gerson, "The Sino-Soviet Border Conflict," p. 47.
81. Sydney H. Schanberg, "China Said to Be Moving Nuclear Plant to Tibet: Reported Leaving Sinkiang in Wake of Soviet Dispute India Says Pace of Transfer Has Recently Accelerated," *New York Times*, September 13, 1969.
82. Gerson, "The Sino-Soviet Border Conflict," p. 50.
83. Yang Kuisong, "The Sino-Soviet Border Clash of 1969: From Zhenbao Island to Sino-American Rapprochement," *Cold War History* 1, no. 1 (August 2000), p. 40; John Wilson Lewis and Litai Xue, *Imagined Enemies: China Prepares for Uncertain War* (Stanford, CA: Stanford University Press, 2006), pp. 61–66.
84. Yang Kuisong, *The Sino-Soviet Border Clash of 1969*, p. 38; Gerson, "The Sino-Soviet Border Conflict," p. 50.
85. Lewis and Xue, *Imagined Enemies*, p. 65.
86. Gerson, "The Sino-Soviet Border Conflict," p. 44.
87. Gerald Segal, *Defending China* (Oxford; New York: Oxford University Press, 1985), p. 182.

88. As cited in Richard Wich, *Sino-Soviet Crisis Politics: A Study of Political Change and Communication*, Harvard East Asian Monographs 96 (Cambridge, MA: Harvard University, 1980), p. 106.
89. As cited in Gerson, "The Sino-Soviet Border Conflict," p. 29.
90. Gerson, "The Sino-Soviet Border Conflict," p. 43.
91. Gerson, "The Sino-Soviet Border Conflict," p. 52.
92. Gerson, "The Sino-Soviet Border Conflict," p. iv.
93. Gerson, "The Sino-Soviet Border Conflict."
94. Arkady N. Shevchenko and Russell J. Bowen, *Breaking with Moscow*, 1st ed. (New York: Knopf, 1985), pp. 164–65.
95. Gerson, "The Sino-Soviet Border Conflict," p. 44.
96. Weeks, *Dictators at War and Peace*.
97. US Department of State. "Milestones: 1969–1976," Office of the Historian, accessed August 1, 2016, https://history.state.gov/milestones/1969-1976/arab-israeli-war-1973. For detailed studies of this crisis, including the nuclear element, see Barry M. Blechman and Douglas M. Hart, "The Political Utility of Nuclear Weapons: The 1973 Middle East Crisis," *International Security* 7, no. 1 (1982): 132–56; and Betts, *Nuclear Blackmail and Nuclear Balance*, pp. 123–29.
98. Kristensen and Norris, "Nuclear Notebook."
99. James R. Schlesinger, "Report of the Secretary of Defense to the Congress on the FY 1975 Defense Budget and FY 1975–1979 Defense Program," March 9, 1974.
100. Betts, *Nuclear Blackmail and Nuclear Balance*, p. 123.
101. Betts, *Nuclear Blackmail and Nuclear Balance*, p. 123.
102. "Memorandum of Conversation between U.S. Secretary of State, Henry Kissinger and Chinese Ambassador Huang Chen, Thursday October 25, 1973," available at http://nsarchive.gwu.edu/NSAEBB/NSAEBB98/octwar-72.pdf.
103. Betts, *Nuclear Blackmail and Nuclear Balance*, p. 129.
104. Leonid Brezhnev, "Letter from Soviet Premier to U.S. President Richard Nixon," October 24, 1973, available at http://nsarchive.gwu.edu/NSAEBB/NSAEBB98/octwar-71.pdf.
105. Betts, *Nuclear Blackmail and Nuclear Balance*, p. 129.
106. Brecher and Wilkenfeld, *A Study of Crisis*.
107. Richard M. Nixon, *The Memoirs of Richard Nixon*, vol. 2 (New York: Grosset & Dunlap, 1978), pp. 498–99.
108. Henry Kissinger, as quoted in Bernard Gwertzman, "Kissinger Speaks," *New York Times*, October 26, 1973.
109. Betts, *Nuclear Blackmail and Nuclear Balance*, p. 125.
110. As quoted in Betts, *Nuclear Blackmail and Nuclear Balance*, p. 125.
111. Blechman and Hart, "*Political Utility of Nuclear Weapons*," p. 129.
112. Blechman and Hart, "The Political Utility of Nuclear Weapons," p. 139.
113. As quoted in ibid., p. 139.
114. Ibid., p. 149.
115. As quoted in Sechser and Fuhrmann 2017, 224.
116. Ibid.
117. Ibid.
118. On the Kargil War, see, for example, P. R. Chari, Pervaiz Iqbal Cheema, and Stephen P. Cohen, *Four Crises and a Peace Process: American Engagement in South Asia* (Washington DC: Brookings Institution Press, 2007); P. R. Chari, "Reflections on the Kargil War," *Strategic Analysis* 33, no. 3 (April 9, 2009): 360–64; V. P. Malik, "Kargil War: Reflections on the Tenth Anniversary," *Strategic Analysis* 33, no. 3 (April 9, 2009): 349–56; B. G. Verghese, "Kargil War: Reflections on the Tenth Anniversary," *Strategic Analysis* 33, no. 3 (April 9, 2009): 357–59.
119. Robert S. Norris and Hans M. Kristensen, "Global Nuclear Weapons Inventories, 1945–2010," *Bulletin of the Atomic Scientists*, May 30, 2013.
120. David Albright, "India's and Pakistan's Fissile Material and Nuclear Weapons Inventories, End of 1999," October 11, 2000, http://www.isis-online.org/publications/southasia/stocks1000.html.

121. Author interview, Former US defense official, July 2017.
122. Brecher and Wilkenfeld, *A Study of Crisis.*
123. Ibid.
124. Chari et al., *Four Crises and a Peace Process,* p. 139.
125. Alexander Chancellor and Yascha Mounk, "Kissinger's Dream Comes True," *Slate,* June 3, 1999, http://www.slate.com/articles/news_and_politics/international_papers/1999/06/kissingers_dream_comes_true.html.
126. See, for example, S. Paul Kapur, *Dangerous Deterrent: Nuclear Weapons Proliferation and Conflict in South Asia,* Studies in Asian Security (Stanford, CA: Stanford University Press: Sponsored by the East-West Center, 2007).
127. Chari, Cheema, and Cohen, *Four Crises and a Peace Process,* p. 139.
128. Strobe Talbott, *Engaging India: Diplomacy, Democracy, and the Bomb* (Washington, DC: Brookings Institution Press, 2004); Feroz Khan, *Eating Grass: The Making of the Pakistani Bomb* (Stanford, CA: Stanford Security Studies, 2012).
129. Kapur, *Dangerous Deterrent,* p. 133.
130. Sumit Ganguly and S. Paul Kapur, *India, Pakistan, and the Bomb: Debating Nuclear Stability in South Asia* (New York: Columbia University Press, 2010).
131. "India's Draft Nuclear Doctrine," Arms Control Association, accessed January 5, 2017, https://www.armscontrol.org/act/1999_07-08/ffja99.
132. Talbott, *Engaging India.*
133. Narang, *Nuclear Strategy in the Modern Era.*
134. According to Freedom House, Pakistan was only "partly free" at the time of the Kargil Crisis. "Pakistan, Country Report," *Freedom in the World 1999,* accessed January 5, 2017, https://freedomhouse.org/report/freedom-world/1999/pakistan.

Chapter 5

1. Sechser and Fuhrmann, "Crisis Bargaining and Nuclear Blackmail."
2. Todd S. Sechser, "Militarized Compellent Threats, 1918–2001," *Conflict Management and Peace Science* 28, no. 4 (2011): 377–401.
3. Schelling, *Arms and Influence.*
4. Richard Ned Lebow and Janice Gross Stein, "Deterrence: The Elusive Dependent Variable," *World Politics* 42, no. 3 (April 1990): 336–69.
5. Paul Huth and Bruce Russett, "Testing Deterrence Theory: Rigor Makes a Difference," *World Politics* 42, no. 4 (July 1990): 466–501.
6. Sechser and Fuhrmann, "Crisis Bargaining and Nuclear Blackmail"; Sechser and Fuhrmann, *Nuclear Weapons and Coercive Diplomacy.*
7. Baldwin, "Power Analysis and World Politics."
8. Sechser and Fuhrmann try a "nuclear superiority" variable as a robustness test in a single regression model reported in a data appendix, but it is not at the center of their theoretical or empirical analysis. Sechser and Fuhrmann, "Crisis Bargaining and Nuclear Blackmail."
9. Fearon, "Domestic Political Audiences and the Escalation of International Disputes."
10. Simmons and Hopkins, "The Constraining Power of International Treaties."
11. Christopher H. Achen, "Let's Put Garbage-Can Regressions and Garbage-Can Probits Where They Belong." *Conflict Management and Peace Science* 22 (2005): p. 337.
12. Sechser, "Militarized Compellent Threats."
13. The findings are robust to the inclusion of data from the pre-1945 period. I focus on the post-1945 period because one cannot draw meaningful insights about the correlation between two variables from observations in which variation on the key explanatory variable was not even possible.
14. Since 26 percent of all international conflicts occur among "politically irrelevant" dyads I include all dyads, not just the so-called politically relevant dyads in our analysis. Bear F. Braumoeller and Austin Carson, "Political Irrelevance, Democracy, and the Limits of Militarized Conflict," *Journal of Conflict Resolution* 55, no. 2 (2011): 292–320.
15. Sechser and Fuhrmann, "Crisis Bargaining and Nuclear Blackmail."

16. Matthew Kroenig, Miriam Krieger, and Hans Noel, "Dare to Fail: Nuclear Superiority, Threat Initiation, and Compellent Success." Working Paper. Georgetown University.

17. Narang, "Nuclear Strategy in the Modern Era."

18. See, for example, Sechser and Fuhrmann, "Crisis Bargaining and Nuclear Blackmail."

19. Alexander B. Downes and Todd S. Sechser, "The Illusion of Democratic Credibility," *International Organization* 66, no. 3 (July 2012): 457–89.

Chapter 6

1. For many perspectives on this subject, see Colby and Gerson, *Strategic Stability*. See also, Caitlin Talmadge, "Would China Go Nuclear? Assessing the Risk of Chinese Nuclear Escalation in a Conventional War with the United States," *International Security* 41, no. 4 (April 1, 2017): 50–92 and Michael S. Gerson, "No First Use: The Next Step for U.S. Nuclear Policy," *International Security* 35, no. 2 (September 17, 2010): 7–47.

2. Thomas Schelling, "Foreword," in Colby and Gerson, *Strategic Stability*, 2013.

3. See, for example, David E. Sanger and William J. Broad, "Trump Forges Ahead on Costly Nuclear Overhaul," *The New York Times*, August 27, 2017, sec. Politics, https://www.nytimes.com/2017/08/27/us/politics/trump-nuclear-overhaul.html.

4. Waltz, *Theory of International Politics*.

5. Glenn A. Kent, Randall James DeValk, and David E. Thaler, *A Calculus of First-Strike Stability: A Criterion for Evaluating Strategic Forces* (Washington, D.C: Rand, 1988).

6. Bernard Brodie et al., *The Absolute Weapon*.

7. Wohlstetter, "The Delicate Balance of Terror."

8. Gerson, "The Origins of Strategic Stability."

9. See, for example, "The Rise and Fall of MIRV," *New York Times*, January 27, 1992.

10. Gerson, "No First Use."

11. Charles L. Glaser and Steve Fetter, "Should the United States Reject MAD? Damage Limitation and U.S. Nuclear Strategy toward China," *International Security* 41, no. 1 (July 1, 2016): 49–98.

12. Talmadge, "Would China Go Nuclear?"

13. Sanger and Broad, "Trump Forges Ahead."

14. William J. Broad and David E. Sanger, "Race for Latest Class of Nuclear Arms Threatens to Revive Cold War," *New York Times*, April 16, 2016.

15. Stephen Biddle, "Seeing Baghdad, Thinking Saigon," *Foreign Affairs* 85, no. 2 (April 2006): 2–14.

16. Quoted in Randall L. Schweller, "The Balance of Power in World Politics," *Oxford Research Encyclopedia of Politics*, May 9, 2016.

17. Waltz, *Theory of International Politics*.

18. Geoffrey Blainey, *The Causes of War* (New York: Free Press, 1973).

19. James D. Fearon, "Rationalist Explanations for War," *International Organization* 49, no. 3 (1995): 379–414; Dan Reiter, "Exploring the Bargaining Model of War," *Perspectives on Politics* 1, no. 1 (2003): 27–43.

20. Jacek Kugler and Douglas Lemke, *Parity and War: Evaluations and Extensions of The War Ledger* (Ann Arbor: University of Michigan Press, 1996). William Reed, "A Unified Statistical Model of Conflict Onset and Escalation," *American Journal of Political Science* 44, no. 1 (2000): 84–93; Douglas Lemke and Suzanne Werner, "Power Parity, Commitment to Change, and War," *International Studies Quarterly* 40, no. 2 (June 1, 1996): 235–60. William Reed et al., "War, Power, and Bargaining," *Journal of Politics* 70, no. 4 (October 2008): 1203–16.

21. Douglas Gibler, "State Development, Parity, and International Conflict," *American Political Science Review* 110, no. 4 (November 2016): 1–18.

22. Colin S. Gray and Keith Payne, "Victory Is Possible," *Foreign Policy*, no. 39 (1980): 14–27.

23. Matthew Kroenig, "The History of Proliferation Optimism: Does It Have a Future?" *Journal of Strategic Studies* 38, no. 1–2 (January 2, 2015): 98–125.

24. Sagan and Waltz, *The Spread of Nuclear Weapons*.

25. Gates, "Nuclear Posture Review Report."

26. Elliott Negin, "Let's Take U.S. Nukes off Hair-Trigger Alert before We Blow up the Planet," *Huffington Post*, 02:36 400AD, http://www.huffingtonpost.com/elliott-negin/lets-take-us-nukes-off-ha_b_7174346.html.

27. Keir A. Lieber and Daryl G. Press, "The Nukes We Need: Preserving the American Deterrent," *Foreign Affairs* 88, No. 6 (November/December 2009): 39–51.

28. Roberts, *The Case for U.S. Nuclear Weapons in the 21st Century*.

29. Nitze, "Deterring Our Deterrent."

Chapter 7

1. See, for example, Glaser, *Analyzing Strategic Nuclear Policy*.

2. Ibid.

3. Charles L. Glaser, *Rational Theory of International Politics: The Logic of Competition and Cooperation* (Princeton, NJ: Princeton University Press, 2010); Robert Jervis, "Cooperation under the Security Dilemma," *World Politics* 30, no. 2 (1978): 167–214.

4. Glaser, *Rational Theory of International Politics*; Jervis, "Cooperation under the Security Dilemma."

5. See Glaser, *Rational Theory of International Politics*, esp. chapters 3 and 9; Jervis, "Cooperation under the Security Dilemma," esp. pp. 206–211.

6. Glaser, *Analyzing Strategic Nuclear Policy*, p. 136.

7. Glaser and Fetter, "Should the United States Reject MAD?"

8. Broad and Sanger, "Race for Latest Class of Nuclear Arms Threatens to Revive Cold War."

9. Joseph Cirincione, "Testimony to the Democratic Party 2016 National Convention Platform Committee," Washington, DC, June 9, 2016.

10. Aaron Mehta, "Former SecDef Perry: US on 'Brink' of New Nuclear Arms Race," *DefenseNews*, December 3, 2015, http://www.defensenews.com/story/defense/policy-budget/2015/12/03/former-secdef-perry-us-brink-new-nuclear-arms-race/76721640/.

11. Barack Obama, "Press Conference," *Whitehouse.gov*, April 1, 2016, https://www.whitehouse.gov/the-press-office/2016/04/01/press-conference-president-obama-412016.

12. Rosenberg, "The Origins of Overkill."

13. Bruno Tetrais, "Destruction Assuree: The Origins and Development of French Nuclear Strategy, 1945–1982," in Sokolski, ed., *Getting MAD*, p. 95.

14. Ibid., p. 86.

15. Ibid., p. 96.

16. M. Taylor Fravel and Evan S. Medeiros, "China's Search for Assured Retaliation: The Evolution of Chinese Nuclear Strategy and Force Structure," *International Security* 35, no. 2 (2010): 48–87.

17. Bill Gertz, "Pentagon Confirms Patrols of Chinese Nuclear Missile Submarines," *Washington Times*, December 9, 2015, http://www.washingtontimes.com/news/2015/dec/9/inside-the-ring-chinas-nuclear-missile-submarine-p/.

18. Reuters, "Gates: China Confirms Stealth Jet Test-Flight," accessed August 27, 2016, http://www.reuters.com/article/us-china-defence-fighter-idUSTRE70A19B20110111.

19. Graham T. Allison and Morton H. Halperin, "Bureaucratic Politics: A Paradigm and Some Policy Implications": 40–79; Graham T. Allison and Frederic A. Morris, "Armaments and Arms Control: Exploring the Determinants of Military Weapons," *Daedalus* 104, no. 3 (Summer 1975): 99–129.

20. Susan J. Koch, "The Presidential Nuclear Initiatives of 1991–1992," Center for the Study of Weapons of Mass Destruction, September 2012, http://permanent.access.gpo.gov/gpo60870/CSWMD-Case-Study-5-for-web.pdf.

21. Editorial Board, "Russia's New Underwater Nuclear Drone Should Raise Alarm Bells," *Washington Post*, December 27, 2015, https://www.washingtonpost.com/opinions/russias-ship-of-terror/2015/12/27/b2085ee0-a9bb-11e5-bff5-905b92f5f94b_story.html?utm_term=.96a01ee8cd7f.

22. Anonymous official, US Navy, Interview with the author, November 2015.

23. For more on this argument, see Mahnken, Maiolo, and Stevenson, eds., *Arms Races in International Politics*.

24. Ibid.
25. Fravel and Medeiros, "China's Search for Assured Retaliation."
26. Luke Harding, "We Will Dump Nuclear Treaty, Putin Warns," *The Guardian*, October 13, 2007, sec. World news, https://www.theguardian.com/world/2007/oct/13/russia.international.
27. Michael R. Gordon, "U.S. Says Russia Tested Cruise Missile, Violating Treaty," *New York Times*, July 28, 2014, http://www.nytimes.com/2014/07/29/world/europe/us-says-russia-tested-cruise-missile-in-violation-of-treaty.html.
28. Albert Wohlstetter, "Nuclear Sharing: NATO and the N+1 Country," *Foreign Affairs* 39, no. 3 (April 1961): 355.
29. Michael D. Wallace, "Arms Race and Escalation: Some New Evidence," *Journal of Conflict Resolution* 23, no. 1 (March 1979): 3–16; Paul F. Diehl, "Arms Races and Escalation: A Closer Look," *Journal of Peace Research* 20, no. 3 (September 1983): 205–12; Susan G. Sample, "Arms Race and Dispute Escalation: Resolving the Debate," *Journal of Peace Research* 30, no. 1 (February 1997): 7–22; Susan G. Sample, "Furthering the Investigation into the Effects of Arms Buildups," *Journal of Peace Research* 35, no. 1 (January 1998): 122–26; Susan G. Sample, "The Outcomes of Military Buildups: Minor States vs. Major Powers," *Journal of Peace Research* 39, no. 6 (November 2002): 669–91; Paul F. Diehl and Mark J. C. Crescenzi, "Reconfiguring the Arms Race-War Debate," *Journal of Peace Research* 35, no. 1 (January 1998): 111–18; Douglas M. Gibler et al., "Taking Arms against a Sea of Trouble: Conventional Arms Races during Periods of Rivalry," *Journal of Peace Research* 42, no. 2 (2005): 131–47; Toby J. Rider, "Understanding Arms Race Onset: Rivalry, Threat, and Territorial Competition," *Journal of Politic* 71, no. 2 (April 2009), 693–703; Rider et al., "Just Part of the Game? Arms Races, Rivalry, and War," *Journal of Peace Research* 48, no. 1 (2011): 85–100; Toby J. Rider, "Uncertainty, Salient Stakes, and the Causes of Conventional Arms Races," *International Studies Quarterly* 57, no. 3 (September 2013): 580–91.
30. Diehl, "Arms Races and Escalation."
31. Rider et al., "Just Part of the Game?"
32. See replication data for Rider et al., "Just Part of the Game?"
33. Nuclear weapons are not discussed directly in most of this work, but Charles Glaser helpfully draws the connection between doctrine and procurement policy. See Charles Glaser, "The Causes and Consequences of Arms Races," *Annual Review of Political Science*, no. 3 (2000): 251–76. While some action-reaction dynamics are present in this model of arms racing, the prime cause is domestic. Barry Posen, *The Sources of Military Doctrine: France, Britain, and Germany between the World Wars*, Cornell Studies in Security Affairs (Ithaca, NY: Cornell University Press, 1984); Jack L. Snyder, *The Ideology of the Offensive: Military Decision Making and the Disasters of 1914*, Cornell Studies in Security Affairs (Ithaca, NY: Cornell University Press, 1984); Jack L. Snyder, *Myths of Empire: Domestic Politics and International Ambition*, Cornell Studies in Security Affairs (Ithaca, NY: Cornell University Press, 1993).
34. Harvey Brooks, "The Military Innovation System and the Qualitative Arms Race," *Daedalus* 104, no. 3 (1975): 75–97; Deborah Shapley, "Technology Creep and the Arms Race: ICBM Problem a Sleeper," *Science* 201, no. 4361 (1978): 1102–5; Deborah Shapley, "Technology Creep and the Arms Race: Two Future Arms Control Problems," *Science* 202, no. 4365 (1978): 289–92.
35. Mary Kaldor, *The Baroque Arsenal* (New York: Hill and Wang, 1981); James R. Kurth, "The Political Economy of Weapons Procurement: The Follow-on Imperative," *American Economic Review* 62, no. 1/2 (1972): 304–11.
36. Matthew Evangelista, *Innovation and the Arms Race: How the United States and the Soviet Union Develop New Military Technologies*, Cornell Studies in Security Affairs (Ithaca, NY: Cornell University Press, 1988); Barry Buzan and Eric Herring, *The Arms Dynamic in World Politics* (London: Lynne Rienner, 1998).
37. Ernest R. May, John D. Steinbruner, and Thomas W. Wolfe, *History of the Strategic Arms Competition, 1945–1972* (Washington, DC: Historical Office, Office of the Secretary of Defense, 1981). Also discussed in Thomas Mahnken, Joseph Maiolo, and David Stevenson, *Arms Races in International Politics: From the Nineteenth to the Twenty-First Century* (New York: Oxford University Press, 2016).

38. Quoted in Alexander T. Lennon, *Contemporary Nuclear Debates: Missile Defense, Arms Control, and Arms Races in the Twenty-First Century* (Cambridge, MA: MIT Press, 2002), p. 204.

39. Roberts, *The Case for U.S. Nuclear Weapons in the 21st Century*, p. 238.

40. Ashton Carter, "Remarks on 'Sustaining Nuclear Deterrence,'" US Department of Defense, accessed June 21, 2017, https://www.defense.gov/News/Speeches/Speech-View/Article/956630/remarks-on-sustaining-nuclear-deterrence/.

41. Kroenig, "Trump Said the U.S. Should Expand Nuclear Weapons."

42. Colin S. Gray, "Social Science and the Arms Race," *Bulletin of the Atomic Scientists* 29, no. 6 (June 1973): 23–26. Colin S. Gray, "The Arms Race Phenomenon," *World Politics* 24, no. 1 (1971): 39–79.

43. Andrew Kydd, "Arms Races and Arms Control: Modeling the Hawk Perspective," *American Journal of Political Science* 44, no. 2 (2000): 228–44; Robert Powell, "Guns, Butter, and Anarchy," *American Political Science Review* 87, no. 1 (1993): 115–32.

44. Kennan, "The Sources of Soviet Conduct."

45. Roberts, "The Case for U.S. Nuclear Weapons in the 21st Century," p. 244.

46. Matthew Kroenig, "Approaching Critical Mass: Asia's Multipolar Nuclear Future," National Bureau of Asia Research, June 2016, http://www.nbr.org/publications/specialreport/pdf/free/083116/SR58_Approaching_Critical_Mass_June2016.pdf.

47. Ibid., p. 21.

48. Victor D. Cha, *The Impossible State: North Korea, Past and Future*, 1st ed. (New York: Ecco, 2012).

49. Charles L. Glaser, "Political Consequences of Military Strategy: Expanding and Refining the Spiral and Deterrence Models," *World Politics* 44, no. 4 (July 1992): 497–538; Robert Legvold, "Managing the New Cold War," *Foreign Affairs* (July/August 2014); see William Perry comments cited previously.

50. Paul C. Warnke, "Apes on a Treadmill," *Foreign Policy*, no. 18 (1975): 12–29.

51. John Lewis Gaddis, *We Now Know: Rethinking Cold War History* (Oxford; New York: Oxford University Press, 1997).

52. Kennan, "The Sources of Soviet Conduct."

53. Daniel Deudney and G. John Ikenberry, "Who Won the Cold War?" *Foreign Policy*, no. 87 (1992): 123–38.

54. Steven Pifer et al., "Forum: NATO and Russia," *Survival* 57, no. 2 (March 4, 2015): 119–44.

55. Ibid.

Chapter 8

1. This chapter draws heavily on Kroenig, "U.S. Nuclear Weapons and Nonproliferation." The author thanks the *Journal of Peace Research* for the right to reprint this material.

2. Deepti Choubey, "Are New Nuclear Bargains Obtainable?," Carnegie Endowment for International Peace, 2008, p. 1.

3. For the exception, see Knopf, "Nuclear Disarmament and Nonproliferation". For research on nuclear proliferation, see Erik Gartzke and Matthew Kroenig, "Nuclear Posture, Nonproliferation Policy, and the Spread of Nuclear Weapons," *Journal of Conflict Resolution* 58, no. 3 (April 1, 2014): 395–401.

4. Treaty on the Nonproliferation of Nuclear Weapons, April 22, 1970, available at http://www.iaea.org/Publications/Documents/Infcircs/Others/infcirc140.pdf.

5. Ibid.

6. Choubey, "Are New Nuclear Bargains Obtainable?," p. 22.

7. Orlando Ribeiro, "A Better NPR," speech at the conference, International Perspectives on the Nuclear Posture Review, Carnegie Endowment for International Peace, Washington, DC, April 21, 2010, quoted in Irma Argüello, "The Position of an Emerging Global Power," *Nonproliferation Review* 18, no. 1 (March 1, 2011): 183–200.

8. Knopf, "Nuclear Disarmament and Nonproliferation."

9. Ibid., p. 94.

10. Ibid., p. 132.

11. Christopher F. Chyba, "Time for a Systematic Analysis: U.S. Nuclear Weapons and Nuclear Proliferation," *Arms Control Today* 38, no. 10 (2008): p. 27.
12. Gartzke and Kroenig, "Nuclear Posture, Nonproliferation Policy, and the Spread of Nuclear Weapons."
13. Scott Douglas Sagan, "Why Do States Build Nuclear Weapons? Three Models in Search of a Bomb," *International Security* 21, no. 3 (1996): 54–86; Sonali Singh and Christopher R. Way, "The Correlates of Nuclear Proliferation: A Quantitative Test," *Journal of Conflict Resolution* 48, no. 6 (2004): 859–85; Jo and Gartzke, "Determinants of Nuclear Weapons Proliferation"; Matthew Kroenig, "Importing the Bomb: Sensitive Nuclear Assistance and Nuclear Proliferation," *Journal of Conflict Resolution* 53, no. 2 (2009): 161–80; Christoph Bluth et al., "Civilian Nuclear Cooperation and the Proliferation of Nuclear Weapons," *International Security* 35, no. 1 (July 1, 2010): 184–200; Matthew Fuhrmann, "Spreading Temptation: Proliferation and Peaceful Nuclear Cooperation Agreements," *International Security* 34, no. 1 (2009): 7–41; Maria Rost Rublee, *Nonproliferation Norms: Why States Choose Nuclear Restraint* (Athens: University of Georgia Press, 2009); Etel Solingen, *Nuclear Logics: Contrasting Paths in East Asia and the Middle East*, Princeton Studies in International History and Politics (Princeton, NJ: Princeton University Press, 2007); Chaim Braun and Christopher F. Chyba, "Proliferation Rings: New Challenges to the Nuclear Nonproliferation Regime," *International Security* 29, no. 2 (October 1, 2004): 5–49; Jacques E. C. Hymans, *Achieving Nuclear Ambitions: Scientists, Politicians and Proliferation* (New York: Cambridge University Press, 2012); Jacques E. C. Hymans, *The Psychology of Nuclear Proliferation: Identity, Emotions, and Foreign Policy* (Cambridge, UK; New York: Cambridge University Press, 2006).
14. Sagan, "Why Do States Build Nuclear Weapons?"
15. Chyba, "Time for a Systemic Analysis."
16. Vesna Danilovic, "The Sources of Threat Credibility in Extended Deterrence," *Journal of Conflict Resolution* 45, no. 3 (June 2001): 341–69.
17. Matthew Kroenig, "Force or Friendship? Explaining Great Power Nonproliferation Policy," *Security Studies* 23, no. 1 (January 1, 2014): 1–32; Matthew Fuhrmann and Sarah E. Kreps, "Targeting Nuclear Programs in War and Peace: A Quantitative Empirical Analysis, 1941–2000," *Journal of Conflict Resolution* 54, no. 6 (2010): 831–59.
18. Kroenig, "Force or Friendship;" Fuhrmann and Kreps, "Targeting Nuclear Programs in War and Peace;" Peter D. Feaver and Emerson M. S. Niou, "Managing Nuclear Proliferation: Condemn, Strike, or Assist?" *International Studies Quarterly* 40, no. 2 (1996): 209–33; Matthew Kroenig, *Exporting the Bomb: Technology Transfer and the Spread of Nuclear Weapons* (Ithaca, NY: Cornell University Press, 2010).
19. Matthew Kroenig, "Exporting the Bomb: Why States Provide Sensitive Nuclear Assistance," *American Political Science Review* 103, no. 1 (February 2009): 113–33.
20. Matthew Kroenig, *A Time to Attack: The Looming Iranian Nuclear Threat*, 1st ed. (New York: St. Martin's Press, 2014). For a complete list of sources, see the online data appendix for this chapter, which can be found at http://www.prio.org/jpr/datasets.
21. For a detailed list of sources for this section, see the online data appendix for this chapter, which can be found at http://www.prio.org/jpr/datasets.
22. Interview with the author, July 9, 2015.
23. I begin the analysis in 1945 to examine the hypotheses in the full universe of possible cases. It is conceivable, however, that any relationship between US nuclear weapons and nonproliferation only emerged after the opening for signature of the NPT in 1968 and I test for this idea in the "Robustness Test" section.
24. Singh and Way, "The Correlates of Nuclear Proliferation."
25. A list of states engaged in these various levels of proliferation behavior is available in the online data appendix, which can be found at http://www.prio.org/jpr/datasets.
26. See http://www.defense.gov/npr/docs/10-05-03_fact_sheet_us_nuclear_transparency__final_w_date.pdf. In order for numbers of US nuclear weapons to affect proliferation decisions in other states, of course, leaders in other states must have a rough idea about the size of the US nuclear arsenal and, although the precise number of US nuclear weapons was classified

until recently, there is good reason to believe that foreign leaders possessed information about the approximate size of the US arsenal. In addition, the statistical results presented below are robust to alternate measures of US nuclear arsenal size, including publicly available estimates provided by the National Resources Defense Council.

27. Aggregate stockpile counts provide the best indicator of US nuclear arsenal size. Moreover, due to data limitations, it is not possible to produce separate counts of tactical and strategic weapons, or of deployed and nondeployed weapons, for each year.

28. Choubey, "Are New Nuclear Bargains Obtainable?"

29. While the hazard analysis employed in this study calculates time at risk it does not account for historical time, which varies from time at risk for countries that did not yet exist or were not independent at the beginning of the nuclear era. The statistical tests demonstrate that historical time has a significant effect on proliferation behavior.

30. Singh and Way, "The Correlates of Nuclear Proliferation."

31. Kroenig, *Exporting the Bomb*.

32. Censoring observations according to whether the state engaged in lower levels of proliferation as a prerequisite for engaging in higher levels of proliferation and rerunning the analysis produced similar results.

33. I drop *Security guarantee* from these tests because it is highly collinear with *US guarantee*. The correlation coefficient is 0.85.

34. The results of the statistical analysis are presented in the online data appendix, which can be found at http://www.prio.org/jpr/datasets.

35. Kroenig, *Exporting the Bomb*.

36. One might expect that the nuclear posture of the United States might not affect the proliferation policies of other nuclear weapons states recognized by the NPT, such as Russia and China, and only affect the proliferation behavior of nonnuclear weapon states or nuclear states outside the NPT. I, therefore, conduct a robustness test in which I include only nuclear suppliers that lack nuclear weapons or are not members of the NPT. In other words, for these tests, I exclude from my analysis nuclear suppliers that joined the NPT as recognized nuclear weapon states. The results were nearly identical.

37. Kroenig, *Exporting the Bomb*.

38. For more information on each of these variables, see Kroenig, *Exporting the Bomb*.

39. Kroenig, *Exporting the Bomb*.

40. The online data appendix can be found at http://www.prio.org/jpr/datasets.

41. Estimating a multinomial logit on a trichotomous variable (1 = yes; 2 = abstain; 3 = no) and rerunning the analysis produced nearly identical results.

42. Kroenig, "Force or Friendship?"

43. Bennett and Stam, "EUGene;"

44. Data on this variable are currently available through 2007. I extrapolated the 2007 score for each country through 2010 to prevent listwise deletion of observations due to missing data. While the capabilities scores from 2008 to 2010 are not exact, they provide a more than adequate proxy of each state's military power at the time of each vote.

45. Data on regime type for Bosnia-Herzegovina in 2010 and 2011 are unavailable, resulting in five missing observations.

46. Information on membership in the NPT is from the Institute for Defense and Disarmament Studies, accessed online at www.idds.org/issNucTreatiesNPT.html.

47. Clustering by UNSC resolution did not change the core findings.

48. More detail on each of these tests is available in the online data appendix, which can be found at http://www.prio.org/jpr/datasets.

49. Shannon Carcelli et al., "The Nuclear Regime Complex: A New Dataset," International Studies Association Annual Convention, Toronto, Canada, 2014.

50. I also tested models that included separate variables for US and P5 arsenal sizes. The variables did not reach statistical significance.

51. Jo and Gartzke, "Determinants of Nuclear Weapons Proliferation."

52. More details can be found in the data appendix, available at http://www.prio.org/jpr/datasets.

53. James R. Clapper, "Worldwide Threat Assessment of the U.S. Intelligence Community for the Senate Select Committee on Intelligence," February 9, 2016, unclassified Statement for the Record.

Chapter 9

1. Congressional Budget Office, "Projected Costs of U.S. Nuclear Forces, 2015 to 2024," January 22, 2015, https://www.cbo.gov/publication/49870.
2. Tom Z. Collina, "The Unaffordable Arsenal: Reducing the Costs of the Bloated U.S. Nuclear Stockpile," Arms Control Association, October 2014; Wolfsthal, Lewis, and Quint, "The Trillion Dollar Nuclear Triad."
3. Neile Miller, "Budget Hearing: National Nuclear Security Administration Weapons Activities," Washington, DC, 2013, sec. the US House of Representatives Committee on Appropriations.
4. Stephen I. Schwartz, ed., *Atomic Audit: The Costs and Consequences of U.S. Nuclear Weapons since 1940* (Washington, DC: Brookings Institution Press, 1998).
5. Stephen I. Schwartz, "Atomic Audit," *Brookings Review* 13, no. 4 (Fall 1995): 14.
6. Barack Obama, "Remarks by President Barack Obama in Prague as Delivered," *Whitehouse.gov*, April 5, 2009, https://www.whitehouse.gov/the-press-office/remarks-president-barack-obama-prague-delivered.
7. Obama, "Remarks by President Barack Obama in Prague as Delivered."
8. James Miller, "Testimony before the House Committee on Armed Services, Subcommittee on Strategic Forces," 2011.
9. Congressional Budget Office, "Projected Costs of U.S. Nuclear Forces, 2015 to 2024."
10. Ploughshares Fund, "What We Spend on Nuclear Weapons," Working Paper, Ver. 2, September 27, 2011, http://www.ploughshares.org/sites/default/files/resources/What%20We%20Spend%20on%20Nuclear%20Weapons%20092811.pdf.
11. Global Zero, "$1 Trillion per Decade," *Global Zero*, accessed August 13, 2016, http://www.globalzero.org/get-the-facts/cost-of-nukes.
12. Ibid.
13. Ibid.
14. Global Zero, "Global Zero U.S. Nuclear Policy Commission Report." p. 4.
15. Wolfstahl, Lewis, and Quint, "The Trillion Dollar Nuclear Triad."
16. Ibid.
17. Ibid., p. 4.
18. Ibid., p. 9.
19. Collina, "The Unaffordable Arsenal."
20. Ibid., p. 2.
21. Ibid., p. 2.
22. Ashton B. Carter, "Remarks by Deputy Secretary of Defense Carter at the Aspen Security Forum at Aspen, Colorado," Aspen Institute, July 18, 2013.
23. Deep Cuts Commission, "Bank from the Brink: Toward Restraint and Dialogue between Russia and the West," June 2016, https://www.armscontrol.org/files/Third_Report_of_the_Deep_Cuts_Commission_English.pdf.
24. Glenn Kessler, "Will the United States Really Spend $700 Billion in the Next Decade on Nuclear Weapons Programs?" *Washington Post*, November 30, 2011, https://www.washingtonpost.com/blogs/fact-checker/post/will-the-united-states-really-spend-700-billion-in-the-next-decade-on-nuclear-weapons-programs/2011/11/29/gIQAbEAtBO_blog.html.
25. Ibid.
26. Rumbaugh and Cohn, "Resolving Ambiguity."
27. Ibid.
28. Collina, "The Unaffordable Arsenal," p. 8.
29. Collina, "The Unaffordable Arsenal," p. 10.
30. Saki Dockrill, *Eisenhower's New-Look National Security Policy, 1953–61* (Houndmills, Basingstoke, Hampshire: Macmillan Press; New York: St. Martin's Press, 1996).

31. Stephen J. Blank, ed., *Russian Nuclear Weapons: Past, Present, and Future* (Carlisle, PA: Strategic Studies Institute, US Army War College, 2011).

32. United States Government Accountability Office, "Nuclear Weapons: Actions Needed to Identify Total Costs of Weapons Complex Infrastructure and Research and Production Capabilities," Washington, DC, June 2010, http://www.gao.gov/products/GAO-10-582, p. 21.

33. Ibid.

34. Associated Press, "US to Reduce Nuke Missile Force as Part of START Treaty," *Associated Press*, April 8, 2014, http://www.foxnews.com/us/2014/04/08/us-to-reduce-nuke-missile-force-as-part-start-treaty.html.

35. Peter Eisler, "U.S. Warhead Disposal in 15-Year Backlog," *USA Today*, May 13, 2009, http://usatoday30.usatoday.com/news/military/2009-05-12-nukes_N.htm.

36. Kroenig, "Think Again," p. 47.

37. Interview with the author, November 2013.

38. Todd Harrison and Evan B. Montgomery, "The Cost of U.S. Nuclear Forces: From BCA to Bow Wave and Beyond," Center for Strategic and Budgetary Assessments, 2015.

39. The White House, "The Moment of Truth: Report of the National Commission on Fiscal Responsibility and Reform," Washington, DC, December 2010, https://www.fiscalcommission.gov/sites/fiscalcommission.gov/files/documents/TheMomentofTruth12_1_2010.pdf.

40. David Mosher, "The Hunt for Small Potatoes: Savings in Nuclear Deterrent Forces," in Cindy Williams, ed., *Holding the Line: U.S. Defense Alternatives for the Early 21st Century*, BCSIA Studies in International Security (Cambridge, MA: MIT Press, 2001).

Conclusion

1. Quoted in Thomas M. Nichols, *No Use: Nuclear Weapons and U.S. National Security* (Philadelphia: University of Pennsylvania Press, 2013), p. 73.

2. Matthew Kroenig and Walter Slocombe, "Why Nuclear Deterrence Still Matters to NATO," Atlantic Council, August 2014, http://www.atlanticcouncil.org/images/publications/Why_Nuclear_Deterrence_Still_Matters_to_NATO.pdf.

3. Quoted in Thérèse Delpech, *Nuclear Deterrence in the 21st Century: Lessons from the Cold War for a New Era of Strategic Piracy* (Santa Monica, CA: RAND, 2012), p. 42.

4. Quoted in ibid.

5. Betts, *Nuclear Blackmail and Nuclear Balance*, p. 175.

6. Philip Zelikow, "Review of Francis J. Gavin's Nuclear Statecraft: History and Strategy in America's Atomic Age," *H-Diplo* 15, no. 1 (2013): p. 29.

7. Quoted in Robert W. Malcolmson, *Nuclear Fallacies: How We Have Been Misguided since Hiroshima* (Montreal: McGill-Queen's University Press, 1985), p. 53.

8. Donald Rumsfeld, "Annual Report for FY1978," Washington, DC: Government Printing Office, 1977.

9. Keith B. Payne, *The Great American Gamble: Deterrence Theory and Practice from the Cold War to the Twenty-First Century*, 1st ed. (Fairfax, VA: National Institute Press, 2008).

10. Snyder and Diesing, *Conflict among Nations*, p. 459.

11. Eyal Winter, *Feeling Smart* (New York: Public Affairs, 2014).

12. See, for example, Schelling, *Arms and Influence*.

13. See, for example, Michael Desch, "Technique Trumps Relevance: The Professionalization of Political Science and the Marginalization of Security Studies," *Perspectives on Politics* 13, no. 2 (June 2015): 377–93.

14. Daniel Byman and Matthew Kroenig, "Reaching Beyond the Ivory Tower: A How to Manual," *Security Studies* 25, no. 2 (2016): 289–319.

15. Sagan and Waltz, *The Spread of Nuclear Weapons*.

16. Patrick M. Regan, "Third-Party Interventions and the Duration of Intrastate Conflicts," *Journal of Conflict Resolution* 46, no. 1 (February 1, 2002): 55–73.

17. John F. Kennedy, "Remarks at the Hanford, Washington, Electric Generating Plant," September 26, 1963.

18. "The 2000 Campaign; Excerpts from Bush's Remarks on National Security and Arms Policy," *New York Times*, May 24, 2000.
19. Gates, "Nuclear Posture Review Report."
20. Gary Schaub Jr. and James Forsyth Jr., "An Arsenal We Can All Live With," *New York Times*, May 23, 2010.
21. Roberts, *The Case for U.S. Nuclear Weapons in the 21st Century*.
22. Kroenig, "Facing Reality: Getting NATO Ready for a New Cold War."
23. Niccolò Machiavelli and Ellis Farneworth, *The Art of War*, rev. ed. (New York: Da Capo Press, 2001).
24. See, for example, Matthew Kroenig, *Exporting the Bomb: Technology Transfer and the Spread of Nuclear Weapons* (Ithaca, NY: Cornell University Press, 2010); Matthew Kroenig, "Think Again: American Nuclear Disarmament," *Foreign Policy*, no. 202 (October 2013): 42, 44–49. Matthew Kroenig, "How to Approach Nuclear Modernization?," *Bulletin of the Atomic Scientists* 71, no. 3 (January 1, 2015): 16–18.

BIBLIOGRAPHY

Achen, Christopher H. "Let's Put Garbage-Can Regressions and Garbage-Can Probits Where They Belong." *Conflict Management and Peace Science* 22 (2005): 327–39.

Acton, James M. *Low Numbers: A Practical Path to Deep Nuclear Reductions.* Washington, DC: Carnegie Endowment for International Peace, 2011.

Albright, David. "India's and Pakistan's Fissile Material and Nuclear Weapons Inventories, End of 1999." Institute for Science and International Security, October 11, 2000. http://www.isis-online.org/publications/southasia/stocks1000.html.

Albright, David, and Christina Walrond. "North Korea's Estimated Stocks of Plutonium and Weapon-Grade Uranium." Institute for Science and International Security, August 16, 2012. https://isis-online.org/uploads/isis-reports/documents/dprk_fissile_material_production_16Aug2012.pdf.

Allison, Graham T., and Morton H. Halperin, "Bureaucratic Politics: A Paradigm and Some Policy Implications." *World Politics* 24 (Spring 1972): 40–79.

Allison, Graham T., and Frederic A. Morris, "Armaments and Arms Control: Exploring the Determinants of Military Weapons." *Daedalus* 104, no. 3 (Summer 1975): 99–129.

Argüello, Irma. "The Position of an Emerging Global Power." *Nonproliferation Review* 18, no. 1 (March 1, 2011): 183–200.

Asal, Victor, and Kyle Beardsley. "Proliferation and International Crisis Behavior." *Journal of Peace Research* 44, no. 2 (2007): 139–55.

Associated Press. "US to Reduce Nuke Missile Force as Part of START Treaty." *Associated Press,* April 8, 2014. http://www.foxnews.com/us/2014/04/08/us-to-reduce-nuke-missile-force-as-part-start-treaty.html.

Atkinson, Carol. "Using Nuclear Weapons." *Review of International Studies* 36, no. 4 (October 2010): 839–51.

Baldwin, David A. "Power Analysis and World Politics: New Trends versus Old Tendencies." *World Politics* 31, no. 2 (1979): 161–94.

Beardsley, Kyle, and Victor Asal. "Winning with the Bomb." *Journal of Conflict Resolution* 53, no. 2 (2009): 278–301.

Bell, Mark S., and Nicholas L. Miller. "Questioning the Effect of Nuclear Weapons on Conflict." *Journal of Conflict Resolution* 59, no. 1 (February 1, 2015): 74–92.

Bennett, Scott D., and Allan Stam. "EUGene: A Conceptual Manual." *International Interactions* 26 (2000): 179–204.

Betts, Richard K. *Nuclear Blackmail and Nuclear Balance.* Washington, DC: Brookings Institution, 1987.

Biddle, Stephen. "Seeing Baghdad, Thinking Saigon." *Foreign Affairs* 85, no. 2 (April 2006): 2–14.

Bierce, Jonathan, and Michael Newkirk. "Nuclear Weapon Allocation Extremes." Johns Hopkins University Applied Physics Laboratory, August 2016, FPS-P-16-0245.

Bin, Li. "Tracking Chinese Strategic Mobile Missiles." *Science and Global Security* 15, no. 1 (2007): 1–30.

Blainey, Geoffrey. *The Causes of War*. New York: Free Press, 1973.

Blair, Bruce G. *Strategic Command and Control: Redefining the Nuclear Threat*. Washington, DC: Brookings Institution, 1985.

Blank, Stephen J., ed. *Russian Nuclear Weapons: Past, Present, and Future*. Carlisle, PA: Strategic Studies Institute, US Army War College, 2011.

Blechman, Barry M., and Douglas M. Hart. "The Political Utility of Nuclear Weapons: The 1973 Middle East Crisis." *International Security* 7, no. 1 (1982): 132–56.

Blechman, Barry M., and Robert Powell. "What in the Name of God Is Strategic Superiority?" *Political Science Quarterly* 97, no. 4 (1982): 589–602.

Blight, James G., and David A. Welch. *On the Brink: Americans and Soviets Reexamine the Cuban Missile Crisis*. 2nd ed. New York: Noonday, 1990.

Bluth, Christoph, Matthew Kroenig, Rensselaer Lee, William C. Sailor, and Matthew Fuhrmann. "Civilian Nuclear Cooperation and the Proliferation of Nuclear Weapons." *International Security* 35, no. 1 (2010): 184–200.

Bohlen, Charles E. *Witness to History, 1929–1969*. 1st ed. New York: Norton, 1973.

Bracken, Paul J. *The Second Nuclear Age: Strategy, Danger, and the New Power Politics*. 1st ed. New York: Times Books, 2012.

Brams, Steven J. *Superpower Games: Applying Game Theory to Superpower Conflict*. New Haven, CT: Yale University Press, 1985.

Braumoeller, Bear F., and Austin Carson. "Political Irrelevance, Democracy, and the Limits of Militarized Conflict." *Journal of Conflict Resolution* 55, no. 2 (2011): 292–320.

Braun, Chaim, and Christopher F. Chyba. "Proliferation Rings: New Challenges to the Nuclear Nonproliferation Regime." *International Security* 29, no. 2 (October 1, 2004): 5–49.

Brecher, Michael, and Jonathan Wilkenfeld. *A Study of Crisis*. Ann Arbor: University of Michigan Press, 1997.

Brezhnev, Leonid. "Letter from Soviet Premier to U.S. President Richard Nixon." October 24, 1973. http://nsarchive.gwu.edu/NSAEBB/NSAEBB98/octwar-71.pdf.

Broad, William J. "Reduction of Nuclear Arsenal Has Slowed under Obama, Report Finds." *New York Times*, May 26, 2016.

———. "A Volcanic Eruption That Reverberates 200 Years Later." *New York Times*, August 24, 2015.

Broad, William J., and David E. Sanger. "Race for Latest Class of Nuclear Arms Threatens to Revive Cold War." *New York Times*, April 16, 2016.

Brodie, Bernard. "What Price Conventional Capabilities in Europe?" Rand Paper P-2696 Santa Monica, CA: Rand Corporation, February 1963.

Brodie, Bernard, Frederick Sherwood Dunn, Arnold Wolfers, Percy Ellwood Corbett, and William T. R. Fox. *The Absolute Weapon: Atomic Power and World Order*. 1st ed. New York: Harcourt, Brace and Company, 1946.

Brooks, Harvey. "The Military Innovation System and the Qualitative Arms Race." *Daedalus* 104, no. 3 (1975): 75–97.

Brown, Harold. "Preparedness Investigation Subcommittee of the Committee on Armed Services. Hearings on the Status of U.S. Strategic Power." 90th Congress. 2nd Session, April 30, 1968.

Browne, Malcolm W. "Nuclear Winter Theorists Pull Back." *New York Times*, January 23, 1990.

Burr, William. "The Nuclear Vault: 'How Much Is Enough?': The U.S. Navy and 'Finite Deterrence.'" *National Security Archive*, May 1, 2009. http://nsarchive.gwu.edu/nukevault/ebb275/.

Buzan, Barry, and Eric Herring, *The Arms Dynamic in World Politics*. London: Lynne Rienner, 1998.

Byman, Daniel, and Matthew Kroenig. "Reaching beyond the Ivory Tower: A How to Manual." *Security Studies* 25, no. 2 (2016): 289–319.

Carcelli, Shannon, Erik Gartzke, Rebecca Gibbons, and Jeffrey M. Kaplow. "The Nuclear Regime Complex: A New Dataset." International Studies Association Annual Convention, Toronto, Canada, 2014.

Carter, Ashton B. "Remarks by Deputy Secretary of Defense Carter at the Aspen Security Forum at Aspen, Colorado." Aspen Institute, July 18, 2013. http://archive.defense.gov/transcripts/transcript.aspx?transcriptid=5277.

———. "Remarks on 'Sustaining Nuclear Deterrence.'" U.S. Department of Defense. Accessed June 21, 2017. https://www.defense.gov/News/Speeches/Speech-View/Article/956630/remarks-on-sustaining-nuclear-deterrence/.

Carter, Ashton B., John D. Steinbruner, Charles A. Zraket, Brookings Institution, and John F. Kennedy School of Government, eds. *Managing Nuclear Operations*. Washington, DC: Brookings Institution, 1987.

Carter, David B., and Curtis S. Signorino. "Back to the Future: Modeling Time Dependence in Binary Data." *Political Analysis* 18, no. 3 (2010): 271–92.

Central Intelligence Agency. Directorate of Intelligence. "Intelligence Memorandum: Sino-Soviet Border Talks, Problems and Prospects." November 10, 1969. http://www.foia.cia.gov/sites/default/files/document_conversions/89801/DOC_0000326154.pdf.

———. "Communist China's Weapons Program for Strategic Attack, National Intelligence Estimate 13-8-71." October 28, 1971, available at: https://www.cia.gov/library/reading-room/docs/DOC_0001098170.pdf

———. "The Evolution of Soviet Policy in the Sino-Soviet Border Dispute." April 28, 1970, Ahttp://www.foia.cia.gov/sites/default/files/document_conversions/14/esau-44.pdf.

Cha, Victor D. *The Impossible State: North Korea, Past and Future*. 1st ed. New York: Ecco, 2012.

Chancellor, Alexander, and Yascha Mounk. "Kissinger's Dream Comes True." *Slate*, June 3, 1999.

Chari, P. R. "Reflections on the Kargil War." *Strategic Analysis* 33, no. 3 (April 9, 2009): 360–64.

Chari, P. R., Pervaiz Iqbal Cheema, and Stephen P. Cohen. *Four Crises and a Peace Process: American Engagement in South Asia*.Washington DC: Brookings Institution Press, 2007.

Choubey, Deepti. "Are New Nuclear Bargains Obtainable?" Carnegie Endowment for International Peace, 2008.

Chyba, Christopher F. "Time for a Systematic Analysis: U.S. Nuclear Weapons and Nuclear Proliferation." *Arms Control Today* 38, no. 10 (2008): 24–29.

Cirincione, Joseph. "Testimony to the Democratic Party 2016 National Convention Platform Committee." Washington DC, June 9, 2016. http://www.ploughshares.org/sites/default/files/Cirincione%20Testimony%20to%20DNC.pdf.

Clapper, James R. "Worldwide Threat Assessment of the U.S. Intelligence Community for the Senate Select Committee on Intelligence," February 9, 2016, unclassified Statement for the Record.

Clausewitz, Carl von. *On War*. Everyman's Library. New York: Knopf, 1993.

Cohn, Carol. "Sex and Death in the Rational World of Defense Intellectuals." *Signs* 12, no. 4 (1987): 687–718.

Colby, Elbridge A. "Asia Goes Nuclear." *The National Interest*, February 2015.

Colby, Elbridge A., and Michael S. Gerson. *Strategic Stability: Contending Interpretations*. Carlisle, PA: Strategic Studies Institute, US Army War College, 2013.

Collina, Tom Z. "The Unaffordable Arsenal: Reducing the Costs of the Bloated U.S. Nuclear Stockpile." Arms Control Association, October 2014. https://www.armscontrol.org/files/The-Unaffordable-Arsenal-2014.pdf.

Congressional Budget Office. "Projected Costs of U.S. Nuclear Forces, 2015 to 2024." January 22, 2015. https://www.cbo.gov/publication/49870.

Cunningham, Fiona S., and M. Taylor Fravel. "Assuring Assured Retaliation: China's Nuclear Posture and U.S.-China Strategic Stability." *International Security* 40, no. 2 (Fall 2015): 7–50.

Danilovic, Vesna. "The Sources of Threat Credibility in Extended Deterrence." *Journal of Conflict Resolution* 45, no. 3 (June 2001): 341–69.

Deep Cuts Commission. "Back from the Brink: Toward Restraint and Dialogue between Russia and the West." Arms Control Association, June 2016. https://www.armscontrol.org/files/Third_Report_of_the_Deep_Cuts_Commission_English.pdf.

Delpech, Thérèse. *Nuclear Deterrence in the 21st Century: Lessons from the Cold War for a New Era of Strategic Piracy.* Santa Monica, CA: RAND, 2012.

Desch, Michael. "Technique Trumps Relevance: The Professionalization of Political Science and the Marginalization of Security Studies." *Perspectives on Politics* 13, no. 2 (June 2015): 377–93.

Deudney, Daniel, and G. John Ikenberry. "Who Won the Cold War?" *Foreign Policy*, no. 87 (1992): 123–38.

Diehl, Paul F. "Arms Races and Escalation: A Closer Look." *Journal of Peace Research* 20, no. 3 (September 1983): 205–12.

Diehl, Paul F., and Mark J.C. Crescenzi. "Reconfiguring the Arms Race-War Debate," *Journal of Peace Research* 35, no. 1 (January 1998): 111–18.

Dobbs, Michael. *One Minute to Midnight: Kennedy, Khrushchev, and Castro on the Brink of Nuclear War.* London: Hutchinson, 2008.

Dobbs, Rachel. "What Was at Stake in 1962?" *ForeignPolicy.com*, July 10, 2012. http://foreign-policy.com/2012/07/10/what-was-at-stake-in-1962/.

Dockrill, Saki. *Eisenhower's New-Look National Security Policy, 1953–61.* Houndmills, Basingstoke, Hampshire: New York: Macmillan Press; St. Martin's Press, 1996.

"Documentation: White House Tapes and Minutes of the Cuban Missile Crisis." *International Security* 10, no. 1 (1985): 164–203.

"Doubt over 'Volcanic Winter' after Toba Super-Eruption." Accessed July 12, 2016. http://phys.org/news/2013-05-volcanic-winter-toba-super-eruption.html.

Downes, Alexander B., and Todd S. Sechser. "The Illusion of Democratic Credibility." *International Organization* 66, no. 3 (July 2012): 457–89.

Eden, Lynn. *Whole World on Fire: Organizations, Knowledge, and Nuclear Weapons Devastation.* Cornell Studies in Security Affairs. Ithaca, NY: Cornell University Press, 2004.

Ederington, Benjamin, and Michael J. Mazarr, eds. *Turning Point: The Gulf War and U.S. Military Strategy.* Boulder: Westview Press, 1994.

Editorial Board. "Russia's New Underwater Nuclear Drone Should Raise Alarm Bells." *Washington Post*, December 27, 2015.

Ehrlich, Paul R., Carl Sagan, Donald Kennedy, and Walter Orr Roberts. *The Cold and the Dark: The World after Nuclear War.* New York: Norton, 1984.

Eisler, Peter. "U.S. Warhead Disposal in 15-Year Backlog." *USA Today*, May 13, 2009. http://usatoday30.usatoday.com/news/military/2009-05-12-nukes_N.htm.

Evangelista, Matthew. *Innovation and the Arms Race: How the United States and the Soviet Union Develop New Military Technologies.* Cornell Studies in Security Affairs. Ithaca, NY: Cornell University Press, 1988.

Fearon, James D. "Rationalist Explanations for War." *International Organization* 49, no. 3 (1995): 379–414.

———. "Domestic Political Audiences and the Escalation of International Disputes." *American Political Science Review* 88, no. 3 (1994): 577–592.

Feaver, Peter D., and Emerson M. S. Niou. "Managing Nuclear Proliferation: Condemn, Strike, or Assist?" *International Studies Quarterly* 40, no. 2 (1996): 209–33.

Fravel, M. Taylor, and Evan S. Medeiros. "China's Search for Assured Retaliation: The Evolution of Chinese Nuclear Strategy and Force Structure." *International Security* 35, no. 2 (2010): 48–87.

Freedom House. "Pakistan, Country Report." *Freedom in the World 1999.* Accessed January 5, 2017. https://freedomhouse.org/report/freedom-world/1999/pakistan.

Freedman, Lawrence. *The Evolution of Nuclear Strategy.* 2nd ed. New York: St. Martin's Press, 1989.

Fuhrmann, Matthew. "Spreading Temptation: Proliferation and Peaceful Nuclear Cooperation Agreements." *International Security* 34, no. 1 (2009): 7–41.

Fuhrmann, Matthew, and Sarah E. Kreps. "Targeting Nuclear Programs in War and Peace: A Quantitative Empirical Analysis, 1941–2000." *Journal of Conflict Resolution* 54, no. 6 (2010): 831–59.

Fuhrmann, Matthew, Matthew Kroenig, and Todd S. Sechser. "The Case for Using Statistics to Study Nuclear Security." *H-Diplo Forum*, no. 2 (2014): 37–54.

Gaddis, John Lewis. *We Now Know: Rethinking Cold War History.* 1st ed. Oxford; New York: Oxford University Press, 1997.

Ganguly, Sumit, and S. Paul Kapur. *India, Pakistan, and the Bomb: Debating Nuclear Stability in South Asia.* New York: Columbia University Press, 2010.

Garthoff, Raymond L. *Détente and Confrontation: American-Soviet Relations from Nixon to Reagan.* Washington, DC: Brookings Institution, 1985.

———. *Soviet Military Policy: A Historical Analysis.* New York: Praeger, 1966.

———. US Department of State Bureau of Politico-Military Affairs to Deputy Under Secretary for Political Affairs Foy Kohler. "Subjective and Objective Strategic Balances." March 31, 1967, Top Secret, excised copy, available at http://nsarchive2.gwu.edu/NSAEBB/NSAEBB197/nd%203%20garthoff-strategic%20balance.pdf.

Gartzke, Erik, and Matthew Kroenig. "Nukes with Numbers: Empirical Research on the Consequences of Nuclear Weapons for International Conflict." *Annual Review of Political Science* 19, no. 1 (2016): 397–412.

———. "Nuclear Posture, Nonproliferation Policy, and the Spread of Nuclear Weapons." *Journal of Conflict Resolution* 58, no. 3 (2014): 395–401.

———. "A Strategic Approach to Nuclear Proliferation." *Journal of Conflict Resolution* 53, no. 2 (2009): 151–60.

Gartzke, Erik, and Yonatan Lupu. "Still Looking for Audience Costs." *Security Studies* 21, no. 3 (2012): 391–97.

Gates, Robert. "Nuclear Posture Review Report." US Department of Defense, April 2010.

Gavin, Francis J. *Nuclear Statecraft: History and Strategy in America's Atomic Age.* Ithaca: Cornell University Press, 2012.

———. Lessons from the Cuban Missile Crisis. *The National Interest Online.* October 26, 2012.

Gavin, Frank. "What We Talk about When We Talk about Nuclear Weapons." *H-Diplo Forum*, no. 2 (2014): 11–36.

Geddes, Barbara. "How the Cases You Choose Affect the Answers You Get: Selection Bias in Comparative Politics." *Political Analysis* 2 (1990): 131–50.

Gelpi, Christopher. "Crime and Punishment: The Role of Norms in Crisis Bargaining." *American Political Science Review* 91, no. 2 (1997): 339–60.

Gelpi, Christopher F., and Michael Griesdorf. "Winners or Losers? Democracies in International Crisis, 1918–94." *American Political Science Review* 95, no. 3 (2001): 633–47.

George, Alexander L., and Andrew Bennett. *Case Studies and Theory Development in the Social Sciences.* 4th printing edition. Cambridge, MA: MIT Press, 2005.

Gerring, John. "Is There a (Viable) Crucial-Case Method?" *Comparative Political Studies* 40, no. 3 (March 1, 2007): 231–53.

Gerson, Michael S. "The Origins of Strategic Stability: The United States and the Threat of Surprise Attack," in Elbridge A. Colby and Michael S. Gerson, *Strategic Stability: Contending Interpretations* (Carlisle, PA: Strategic Studies Institute, U.S. Army War College, 2013).

———. "The Sino-Soviet Border Conflict: Deterrence, Escalation, and the Threat of Nuclear War in 1969." Center for Naval Analyses, November 2010. https://www.cna.org/CNA_files/PDF/D0022974.A2.pdf.

———. "No First Use: The Next Step for U.S. Nuclear Policy." *International Security* 35, no. 2 (September 17, 2010): 7–47. doi:10.1162/ISEC_a_00018.

Gertz, Bill. "Pentagon Confirms Patrols of Chinese Nuclear Missile Submarines." *Washington Times*, December 9, 2015.

Gibler, Douglas. "State Development, Parity, and International Conflict." *American Political Science Review* 110, no. 4 (November 2016): 1–18.

Gibler, Douglas M., Toby J. Rider, and Marc L. Hutchison. "Taking Arms Against a Sea of Trouble: Conventional Arms Races during Periods of Rivalry." *Journal of Peace Research* 42, no. 2 (2005): 131–47.

Glaser, Charles L. *Rational Theory of International Politics: The Logic of Competition and Cooperation.* Princeton, NJ: Princeton University Press, 2010.

———. "Political Consequences of Military Strategy: Expanding and Refining the Spiral and Deterrence Models." *World Politics* 44, no. 4 (July 1992): 497–538.

———. *Analyzing Strategic Nuclear Policy.* Princeton, NJ: Princeton University Press, 1990.

Glaser, Charles L., and Steve Fetter. "Should the United States Reject MAD? Damage Limitation and U.S. Nuclear Strategy toward China." *International Security* 41, no. 1 (2016): 49–98.

Glasstone, Samuel, ed. *Effects of Nuclear Weapons.* Literary Licensing, LLC, 2013.

Global Zero. "$1 Trillion per Decade." *Global Zero.* Accessed August 13, 2016. http://www.global-zero.org/get-the-facts/cost-of-nukes.

Global Zero U.S. Nuclear Policy Commission. "Global Zero U.S. Nuclear Policy Commission Report: Modernizing U.S. Nuclear Strategy, Force Structure and Posture." Global Zero, May 2012. http://www.globalzero.org/files/gz_us_nuclear_policy_commission_report.pdf.

Goldberg, Jeffrey. "Obama's Crystal-Clear Promise to Stop Iran from Getting a Nuclear Weapon." *The Atlantic,* October 2, 2012.

Goldgeier, James, and Bruce Jentleson. "How to Bridge the Gap between Policy and Scholarship." *War on the Rocks,* June 29, 2015.

Gordon, Michael R. "U.S. Says Russia Tested Cruise Missile, Violating Treaty." *New York Times,* July 28, 2014.

Gray, Colin S. "Social Science and the Arms Race." *Bulletin of the Atomic Scientists* 29, no. 6 (June 1973): 23–26.

———. "The Arms Race Phenomenon." *World Politics* 24, no. 1 (1971): 39–79.

Gray, Colin S., and Keith Payne. "Victory Is Possible." *Foreign Policy,* no. 39 (1980): 14–27.

Greenwood, Ted. *Making the MIRV: A Study of Defense Decision Making.* Cambridge, MA: Ballinger, 1975.

Gribkov, A. I., William Y. Smith, and Alfred Friendly. *Operation ANADYR: U.S. and Soviet Generals Recount the Cuban Missile Crisis.* Chicago: Edition q, 1994.

Gwertzman, Bernard. "Kissinger Speaks." *New York Times,* October 26, 1973.

Haberman, Clyde. "Global Warming Gives Science behind Nuclear Winter a New Purpose." *New York Times,* April 3, 2016.

Harding, Luke. "We Will Dump Nuclear Treaty, Putin Warns." *The Guardian,* October 13, 2007, sec. World news.

Harrison, Todd, and Evan B. Montgomery. "The Cost of U.S. Nuclear Forces: From BCA to Bow Wave and Beyond." Washington DC: Center for Strategic and Budgetary Assessments, 2015.

Hassner, Ron E. "The Path to Intractability: Time and the Entrenchment of Territorial Disputes." *International Security* 31, no. 3 (2006): 107–38.

Heckman, James J. "Sample Selection Bias as a Specification Error." *Econometrica* 47, no. 1 (1979): 153–61.

Heinrichs, Rebeccah, and Baker Spring. "Deterrence and Nuclear Targeting in the 21st Century." The Heritage Foundation, November 30, 2012. http://www.heritage.org/research/reports/2012/11/deterrence-and-nuclear-targeting-in-the-21st-century.

Hewitt, J. Joseph. "Dyadic Processes and International Crises." *Journal of Conflict Resolution* 47, no. 5 (2003): 669–92.

Hill, Alexander. "Using the Hazard Prediction and Assessment Capability (HPAC) Hazard Assessment Program for Radiological Scenarios Relevant to the Australian Defense Force." DTSO Platforms Sciences Laboratory, Victoria, Australia, March 2003. file:///C:/Users/mhk32/Downloads/ADA416823.pdf.

Hoffmann, Stanley. *The State of War: Essays on the Theory and Practice of International Politics.* New York: Praeger, 1965.

Steve Holland, "Trump Wants to Make Sure U.S. Nuclear Arsenal at 'Top of the Pack,'" *Reuters*, February 24, 2017, https://www.reuters.com/article/us-usa-trump-exclusive/trump-wants-to-expand-u-s-nuclear-arsenal-make-it-top-of-the-pack-reuters-interview-idUSKBN1622IF.

Holmes, James R., and Toshi Yoshihara. "Mao's 'Active Defense' Is Turning Offensive." *United States Naval Institute. Proceedings* 137, no. 4 (April 2011): 24–29.

Horowitz, Michael. "The Spread of Nuclear Weapons and International Conflict Does Experience Matter?" *Journal of Conflict Resolution* 53, no. 2 (2009): 234–57.

Huntington, Samuel P., ed. *The Strategic Imperative*. Cambridge, MA: Ballinger, 1982.

Huth, Paul K. "The Extended Deterrent Value of Nuclear Weapons." *Journal of Conflict Resolution* 34, no. 2 (1990): 270–90.

Huth, Paul, and Bruce Russett. "Testing Deterrence Theory: Rigor Makes a Difference." *World Politics* 42, no. 4 (July 1990): 466–501.

Hymans, Jacques E. C. *Achieving Nuclear Ambitions: Scientists, Politicians and Proliferation*. New York: Cambridge University Press, 2012.

———. *The Psychology of Nuclear Proliferation: Identity, Emotions, and Foreign Policy*. Cambridge, UK; New York: Cambridge University Press, 2006.

IIP Digital. "Clinton, Gates Interview on ABC's 'This Week.'" Transcript, April 11, 2010. http://iip-digital.usembassy.gov/st/english/texttrans/2010/04/20100412144956eaifas0.9577295.xml.

Jaggers, Keith, and Ted Robert Gurr. "Tracking Democracy's Third Wave with the Polity III Data." *Journal of Peace Research* 32, no. 4 (1995): 469–82.

Jervis, Robert. *The Meaning of the Nuclear Revolution: Statecraft and the Prospect of Armageddon*. Cornell Studies in Security Affairs. Ithaca: Cornell University Press, 1989.

———. *The Illogic of American Nuclear Strategy*. Cornell Studies in Security Affairs. Ithaca: Cornell University Press, 1984.

———. "Why Nuclear Superiority Doesn't Matter." *Political Science Quarterly* 94, no. 4 (1979): 617–33.

———. "Cooperation under the Security Dilemma," *World Politics* 30, no. 2 (1978): 167–214.

Jo, Dong-Joon, and Erik Gartzke. "Determinants of Nuclear Weapons Proliferation." *Journal of Conflict Resolution* 51, no. 1 (2007): 167–94.

Kahn, Herman. *Thinking about the Unthinkable*. New York: Horizon Press, 1962.

———. *On Thermonuclear War*. Princeton, NJ: Princeton University Press, 1960.

Kaldor, Mary. *The Baroque Arsenal*. New York: Hill and Wang, 1981.

Kaplan, Fred M. "Rethinking Nuclear Policy," *Foreign Affairs* 95, no. 5 (2016), p. 18–25.

———. *The Wizards of Armageddon*. New York: Simon and Schuster, 1983.

Kapur, S. Paul. *Dangerous Deterrent: Nuclear Weapons Proliferation and Conflict in South Asia*. Studies in Asian Security. Stanford, CA: Stanford University Press, 2007.

Kennan, George F. "The Sources of Soviet Conduct." *Foreign Affairs* 25, no. 4 (1947): 566–82.

Kennedy, John F. "Remarks at the Hanford, Washington, Electric Generating Plant." September 26, 1963, available at https://www.jfklibrary.org/Asset-Viewer/Archives/JFKWHA-225-001.aspx.

Kessler, Glenn. "Will the United States Really Spend $700 Billion in the next Decade on Nuclear Weapons Programs?" *Washington Post*, November 30, 2011.

Khan, Feroz. *Eating Grass: The Making of the Pakistani Bomb*. Stanford, CA: Stanford Security Studies, 2012.

King, Gary, Robert O. Keohane, and Sidney Verba. *Designing Social Inquiry: Scientific Inference in Qualitative Research*. Princeton, NJ: Princeton University Press, 1994.

King, Gary, Michael Tomz, and Jason Wittenberg. "Making the Most of Statistical Analyses: Improving Interpretation and Presentation." *American Journal of Political Science* 44, no. 2 (2000): 347–61.

King, Gary, and Langche Zeng. "Explaining Rare Events in International Relations." *International Organization* 55, no. 3 (2001): 693–715.

Kirshner, Jonathan. "Rationalist Explanations for War?" *Security Studies* 10, no. 1 (September 1, 2000): 143–50.

Kissinger, Henry. *White House Years*. Boston: Little, Brown and Co, 1979.

Knopf, Jeffrey W. "Nuclear Disarmament and Nonproliferation: Examining the Linkage Argument." *International Security* 37, no. 3 (2012): 92–132.

Koch, Susan J. "The Presidential Nuclear Initiatives of 1991–1992." Center for the Study of Weapons of Mass Destruction, September 2012. http://permanent.access.gpo.gov/gpo60870/CSWMD-Case-Study-5-for-web.pdf.

Kozak, Warren. *LeMay: The Life and Wars of General Curtis LeMay*. 1st ed. Washington, DC: New York: Regnery Publishing, 2009.

Kristensen, Hans M., and Robert S. Norris. "Nuclear Notebook." *Bulletin of the Atomic Scientists*. Accessed July 12, 2016. http://thebulletin.org/nuclear-notebook-multimedia.

———. "Chinese Nuclear Forces, 2015." *Bulletin of the Atomic Scientists* 71, no. 4 (2015): 77–84.

———. "Russian Nuclear Forces, 2015." *Bulletin of the Atomic Scientists* 71, no. 3 (2015): 84–97.

———. "US Nuclear Forces, 2015." *Bulletin of the Atomic Scientists* 71, no. 2 (2015): 107–19.

Kroenig, Matthew. "Trump Said the U.S. Should Expand Nuclear Weapons. He's Right." *POLITICO Magazine*, December 23, 2016.

———. "Approaching Critical Mass: Asia's Multipolar Nuclear Future." National Bureau of Asia Research, June 2016. http://www.nbr.org/publications/specialreport/pdf/free/083116/SR58_Approaching_Critical_Mass_June2016.pdf.

———. "US Nuclear Weapons and Non-Proliferation Is There a Link?" *Journal of Peace Research* 53, no. 2 (2016): 166–79.

———. "Facing Reality: Getting NATO Ready for a New Cold War." *Survival* 57, no. 1 (2015): 49–70.

———. "The History of Proliferation Optimism: Does It Have a Future?" *Journal of Strategic Studies* 38, no. 1–2 (2015): 98–125.

———. "Posturing the Bomb." *International Studies Review* 17, no. 3 (2015): 482–84.

———. "Force or Friendship? Explaining Great Power Nonproliferation Policy." *Security Studies* 23, no. 1 (2014): 1–32.

———. *A Time to Attack: The Looming Iranian Nuclear Threat*. 1st ed. New York: St. Martin's Press, 2014.

———. "Think Again: American Nuclear Disarmament." *Foreign Policy*, no. 202 (October 2013): 42, 44–49.

———. "Nuclear Superiority and the Balance of Resolve: Explaining Nuclear Crisis Outcomes." *International Organization* 67, no. 1 (January 2013): 141–71.

———. *Exporting the Bomb: Technology Transfer and the Spread of Nuclear Weapons*. Cornell Studies in Security Affairs. Ithaca, NY: Cornell University Press, 2010.

———. "Exporting the Bomb: Why States Provide Sensitive Nuclear Assistance." *American Political Science Review* 103, no. 1 (2009): 113–33.

———. "Importing the Bomb: Sensitive Nuclear Assistance and Nuclear Proliferation." *Journal of Conflict Resolution* 53, no. 2 (2009): 161–80.

Kroenig, Matthew, Miriam Krieger, and Hans Noel, "Dare to Fail: Nuclear Superiority, Threat Initiation, and Compellent Success." Working Paper. Georgetown University.

Kroenig, Matthew, and Dani Nedal. "Audience Costs or Superpower Patrons? Sources of Restraint in Crisis Bargaining." American Political Science Association Annual Meeting, San Francisco, CA, September 2015.

Kroenig, Matthew, and Walter B. Slocombe. "Why Nuclear Deterrence Still Matters to NATO." The Atlantic Council, August 2014. http://www.atlanticcouncil.org/images/publications/Why_Nuclear_Deterrence_Still_Matters_to_NATO.pdf.

Kugler, Jacek, and Douglas Lemke. *Parity and War: Evaluations and Extensions of The War Ledger*. Ann Arbor: University of Michigan Press, 1996.

Kuisong, Yang. "The Sino-Soviet Border Clash of 1969: From Zhenbao Island to Sino-American Rapprochement." *Cold War History* 1, no. 1 (August 2000): 21.

Kurth, James R. "The Political Economy of Weapons Procurement: The Follow-on Imperative." *American Economic Review* 62, no. 1/2 (1972): 304–11.

Kydd, Andrew. "Arms Races and Arms Control: Modeling the Hawk Perspective." *American Journal of Political Science* 44, no. 2 (2000): 228–44.

Lantis, Jeffrey S., Tom Sauer, James J. Wirtz, Keir A. Lieber, and Daryl G. Press. "The Short Shadow of U.S. Primacy?" *International Security* 31, no. 3 (2007): 174–93.

Lebow, Richard Ned, and Janice Gross Stein. "Deterrence: The Elusive Dependent Variable." *World Politics* 42, no. 3 (April 1990): 336–69.

Lemke, Douglas, and Suzanne Werner. "Power Parity, Commitment to Change, and War." *International Studies Quarterly* 40, no. 2 (1996): 235–60.

Lennon, Alexander T. *Contemporary Nuclear Debates: Missile Defense, Arms Control, and Arms Races in the Twenty-First Century*. Cambridge, MA: MIT Press, 2002.

Lewis, Jeffrey. "Minimum Deterrence." *Bulletin of the Atomic Scientists* 64, no. 3 (2008): 38–41.

Lewis, John Wilson, and Litai Xue. *Imagined Enemies: China Prepares for Uncertain War*. Stanford, CA: Stanford University Press, 2006.

Legvold, Robert. "Managing the New Cold War." *Foreign Affairs* 93, no. 4 (July/August 2014): 74–84.

Lieber, Keir A., and Daryl G. Press. "The End of MAD? The Nuclear Dimension of U.S. Primacy." *International Security* 30, no. 4 (2006): 7–44.

———. "The Nukes We Need: Preserving the American Deterrent." *Foreign Affairs* 88, no. 6 (November/December 2009): 39–51.

Long, Austin, and Brendan Rittenhouse Green. "Stalking the Secure Second Strike: Intelligence, Counterforce, and Nuclear Strategy." *Journal of Strategic Studies* 38, no. 1–2 (2015): 38–73.

Louis, Victor. "Will Russia Czech-Mate China?" *London Evening News*, September 16, 1969.

Machiavelli, Niccolo, and Ellis Farneworth. *The Art of War*. Rev. ed. New York: Da Capo Press, 2001.

Mahoney, James. "After KKV: The New Methodology of Qualitative Research." Edited by Henry E. Brady, David Collier, Alexander L. George, Andrew Bennett, John Gerring, Gary Goertz, and Charles Ragin. *World Politics* 62, no. 1 (2010): 120–47.

Mahnken, Thomas, Joseph Maiolo, and David Stevenson. *Arms Races in International Politics: From the Nineteenth to the Twenty-First Century*. New York: Oxford University Press, 2016.

Malcolmson, Robert W. *Nuclear Fallacies: How We Have Been Misguided since Hiroshima*. McGill-Queen's University Press, 1985.

Malik, V. P. "Kargil War: Reflections on the Tenth Anniversary." *Strategic Analysis* 33, no. 3 (April 9, 2009): 349–56.

May, Ernest R., John D. Steinbruner, and Thomas W. Wolfe. *History of the Strategic Arms Competition, 1945–1972*. Washington, DC: Historical Office, Office of the Secretary of Defense, 1981.

Mehta, Aaron. "Former SecDef Perry: US on 'Brink' of New Nuclear Arms Race." *DefenseNews*, December 3, 2015. http://www.defensenews.com/story/defense/policy-budget/2015/12/03/former-secdef-perry-us-brink-new-nuclear-arms-race/76721640/.

———. "Carter: Nuclear Triad 'Bedrock of Our Security.'" *DefenseNews*, September 26, 2016.

"Memorandum of Conversation between U.S. Secretary of State, Henry Kissinger and Chinese Ambassador Huang Chen, Thursday October 25, 1973." http://nsarchive.gwu.edu/NSAEBB/NSAEBB98/octwar-72.pdf

"Memorandum of Conversation between William L. Stearman and Boris N. Davydov," August 18, 1969.

Miller, James. "Testimony before the House Committee on Armed Services, Subcommittee on Strategic Forces." Washington DC, 2011.

Miller, Neile. "Budget Hearing: National Nuclear Security Administration Weapons Activities." Washington, DC, 2013.

Morgan, Patrick M. *International Security: Problems and Solutions*. Washington DC: CQ Press, 2006.

Mueller, John. "Think Again: Nuclear Weapons." *Foreign Policy*, December 18, 2009. http://for-eignpolicy.com/2009/12/18/think-again-nuclear-weapons/.

Mueller, John E. *Atomic Obsession: Nuclear Alarmism from Hiroshima to Al-Qaeda*. Oxford; New York: Oxford University Press, 2010.

Narang, Vipin. *Nuclear Strategy in the Modern Era: Regional Powers and International Conflict*. Princeton, NJ: Princeton University Press, 2014.

Natural Resources Defense Council. "Chinese Nuclear Forces, 2006." *Bulletin of the Atomic Scientists* 62, no. 3 (2006): 60–63.

Negin, Elliott. "Let's Take U.S. Nukes off Hair-Trigger Alert before We Blow up the Planet." *Huffington Post*, 02:36 400AD. http://www.huffingtonpost.com/elliott-negin/lets-take-us-nukes-off-ha_b_7174346.html.

Nichols, Thomas M. *No Use: Nuclear Weapons and U.S. National Security*. Philadelphia: University of Pennsylvania Press, 2013.

Nitze, Paul H. "Deterring Our Deterrent." *Foreign Policy*, no. 25 (1976): 195–210.

———. "Atoms, Strategy, and Policy." *Foreign Affairs* 34, no. 2 (1956): 187–191.

Nixon, Richard M. *The Memoirs of Richard Nixon*. New York: Grosset & Dunlap, 1978.

Norris, Robert S., and Hans M. Kristensen. "Global Nuclear Weapons Inventories, 1945–2010." *Bulletin of the Atomic Scientists*, May 30, 2013.

———. "The Cuban Missile Crisis: A Nuclear Order of Battle, October and November 1962." *Bulletin of the Atomic Scientists* 68, no. 6 (2012): 85–91.

Obama, Barack. "Press Conference," *Whitehouse.gov*, April 1, 2016. https://www.whitehouse.gov/the-press-office/2016/04/01/press-conference-president-obama-412016.

———. "Remarks by President Barack Obama in Prague as Delivered." *Whitehouse.gov*, April 5, 2009. https://www.whitehouse.gov/the-press-office/remarks-president-barack-obama-prague-delivered.

O'Connor, Sean. "PLA Second Artillery Corps." Air Power Australia, December 16, 2009. http://www.ausairpower.net/APA-PLA-Second-Artillery-Corps.html.

Paul, T. V. *Asymmetric Conflicts: War Initiation by Weaker Powers*. Cambridge: Cambridge University Press, 1994.

Paul, T. V., Patrick M. Morgan, and James J. Wirtz, eds. *Complex Deterrence: Strategy in the Global Age*. Chicago: University of Chicago Press, 2009.

Payne, Keith B. *The Great American Gamble: Deterrence Theory and Practice from the Cold War to the Twenty-First Century*. 1st ed. Fairfax, VA: National Institute Press, 2008.

Payne, Keith B., and James R. Schlesinger. *Minimum Deterrence: Examining the Evidence*. New York; London: Routledge, 2015.

Perkovich, George, and James M. Acton, eds. *Abolishing Nuclear Weapons: A Debate* Washington DC: Carnegie Endowment for International Peace, 2009.

Philipp, Elizabeth. "North Korea's Nuclear ICBM?"Arms Control Association, October 5, 2015. http://www.armscontrol.org/blog/armscontrolnow/2015-10-05/North-Koreas-Nuclear-ICBM.

Pifer, Steven, Lukasz Kulesa, Egon Bahr, Götz Neuneck, Mikhail Troitskiy, and Matthew Kroenig. "Forum: NATO and Russia." *Survival* 57, no. 2 (2015): 119–44.

Ploughshares Fund. "What We Spend on Nuclear Weapons." Working Paper, Ver. 2, September 27, 2011.

Podvig, Pavel. "The Window of Vulnerability That Wasn't: Soviet Military Buildup in the 1970s—A Research Note." *International Security* 33, no. 1 (Summer 2008): 118–38.

Posen, Barry R. *Inadvertent Escalation: Conventional War and Nuclear Risks*. 1st ed. Ithaca, NY: Cornell University Press, 2013.

———. *The Sources of Military Doctrine: France, Britain, and Germany between the World Wars*. Cornell Studies in Security Affairs. Ithaca, NY: Cornell University Press, 1984.

Powell, Robert. "Nuclear Brinkmanship, Limited War, and Military Power." *International Organization* 69, no. 3 (Summer 2015): 589–626.

———. "Nuclear Deterrence Theory, Nuclear Proliferation, and National Missile Defense." *International Security* 27, no. 4 (2003): 86–118.

———. "Guns, Butter, and Anarchy." *American Political Science Review* 87, no. 1 (1993): 115–32.

———. *Nuclear Deterrence Theory: The Search for Credibility*. Cambridge; New York: Cambridge University Press, 1990.

———. "Nuclear Brinkmanship with Two-Sided Incomplete Information." *American Political Science Review* 82, no. 1 (March 1988): 155.

———. "Crisis Bargaining, Escalation, and MAD." *American Political Science Review* 81, no. 3 (1987): 717–35.

Press, Daryl G. *Calculating Credibility: How Leaders Assess Military Threats*. Cornell Studies in Security Affairs. Ithaca, NY: Cornell University Press, 2007.

Puhani, Patrick. "The Heckman Correction for Sample Selection and Its Critique." *Journal of Economic Surveys* 14, no. 1 (2000): 53–68.

Raphael, T. J. "How the Threat of Nuclear Winter Changed the Cold War." *Public Radio International*, April 5, 2016. http://www.pri.org/stories/2016-04-05/how-threat-nuclear-winter-changed-cold-war.

Rapport, Aaron. "Hard Thinking about Hard and Easy Cases in Security Studies." *Security Studies* 24, no. 3 (2015): 431–65.

Ravilious, Kate. "Weatherwatch: Would Modern Humans Survive a Volcanic Winter?" *The Guardian*, November 30, 2012.

Reed, William. "A Unified Statistical Model of Conflict Onset and Escalation." *American Journal of Political Science* 44, no. 1 (2000): 84–93.

Reed, William, David H. Clark, Timothy Nordstrom, and Wonjae Hwang. "War, Power, and Bargaining." *Journal of Politics* 70, no. 4 (October 2008): 1203–16.

Regan, Patrick M. "Third-Party Interventions and the Duration of Intrastate Conflicts." *Journal of Conflict Resolution* 46, no. 1 (2002): 55–73.

Reiter, Dan. "Exploring the Bargaining Model of War." *Perspectives on Politics* 1, no. 1 (2003): 27–43.

Reiter, Dan, and Allan C. Stam. *Democracies at War*. Princeton, NJ: Princeton University Press, 2010.

Reuters. "Gates: China Confirms Stealth Jet Test-Flight." Accessed August 27, 2016. http://www.reuters.com/article/us-china-defence-fighter-idUSTRE70A19B20110111.

———. "North Korea Could Hit US Homeland with Nuclear Weapon, Says Top Admiral." *The Guardian*, October 8, 2015.

Rider, Toby J. "Uncertainty, Salient Stakes, and the Causes of Conventional Arms Races." *International Studies Quarterly* 57, no. 3 (September 2013): 580–91.

———. "Understanding Arms Race Onset: Rivalry, Threat, and Territorial Competition." *Journal of Politics* 71, no. 2 (April 2009): 693–703.

Rider, Toby J., Michael G. Findley, and Paul F. Diehl. "Just Part of the Game? Arms Races, Rivalry, and War." *Journal of Peace Research* 48, no. 1 (2011): 85–100.

Roberts, Brad. *The Case for U.S. Nuclear Weapons in the 21st Century*. Stanford, CA: Stanford Security Studies, 2015.

Rosenberg, David Alan. "The Origins of Overkill: Nuclear Weapons and American Strategy, 1945–1960." *International Security* 7, no. 4 (1983): 3–71.

Rublee, Maria Rost. *Nonproliferation Norms: Why States Choose Nuclear Restraint*. Athens: University of Georgia Press, 2009.

Rumbaugh, Russell, and Nathan Cohn. "Resolving Ambiguity: Costing Nuclear Weapons." The Henry L. Stimson Center, June 2012.

Rumsfeld, Donald. "Annual Report for FY1978." Washington, DC: Government Printing Office, 1977.

Rusk, Dean, Robert McNamara, George W. Ball, and Roswell Gilpatrick. "The Lessons of the Cuban Missile Crisis." *Time* 120, no. 13 (September 27, 1982): 89.

Russett, Bruce M. *Peace, War, and Numbers*. Beverly Hills, CA: Sage Publications, 1972.

Sagan, Scott Douglas. "Why Do States Build Nuclear Weapons? Three Models in Search of a Bomb." *International Security* 21, no. 3 (1996): 54–86.

———. *The Limits of Safety: Organizations, Accidents, and Nuclear Weapons*. Princeton Studies in International History and Politics. Princeton, NJ: Princeton University Press, 1993.

———. *Moving Targets: Nuclear Strategy and National Security*. Princeton, NJ: Princeton University Press, 1989.

———. "SIOP-62: The Nuclear War Plan Briefing to President Kennedy." *International Security* 12, no. 1 (1987): 22–51.

Sagan, Scott Douglas and Benjamin A. Valentino, "Revisiting Hiroshima in Iran: What Americans Really Think about Using Nuclear Weapons and Killing Noncombatants," *International Security* 42, no. 1 (2017): 41–79.

Sagan, Scott Douglas, and Kenneth N. Waltz. *The Spread of Nuclear Weapons: An Enduring Debate*. 3rd ed. New York: Norton, 2013.

Sample, Susan G. "Arms Race and Dispute Escalation: Resolving the Debate." *Journal of Peace Research* 30, no. 1, (February 1997): 7–22.

———. "Furthering the Investigation into the Effects of Arms Buildups." *Journal of Peace Research* 35, no. 1 (January 1998): 122–26.

———. "The Outcomes of Military Buildups: Minor States vs. Major Powers." *Journal of Peace Research* 39, no. 6 (November 2002): 669–91.

Sanger, David E., and William J. Broad. "Trump Forges Ahead on Costly Nuclear Overhaul." *The New York Times*, August 27, 2017, sec. Politics. https://www.nytimes.com/2017/08/27/us/politics/trump-nuclear-overhaul.html.

Schanberg, Sydney H. "China Said to Be Moving Nuclear Plant to Tibet: Reported Leaving Sinkiang in Wake of Soviet Dispute India Says Pace of Transfer Has Recently Accelerated." *New York Times*, September 13, 1969.

Schaub, Gary, and James Forsyth Jr. "An Arsenal We Can All Live With." *New York Times*, May 23, 2010.

Schelling, Thomas C. *Arms and Influence*. New Haven, CT: Yale University Press, 1966.

———. *The Strategy of Conflict*. Cambridge, MA: Harvard University Press, 1960.

Schlesinger, James R. "Report of the Secretary of Defense to the Congress on the FY 1975 Defense Budget and FY 1975–1979 Defense Program." March 9, 1974.

Schwartz, Stephen I. "Atomic Audit." *Brookings Review* 13, no. 4 (Fall 1995): 14.

———, ed. *Atomic Audit: The Costs and Consequences of U.S. Nuclear Weapons since 1940*. Washington, DC: Brookings Institution Press, 1998.

Schweller, Randall L. "The Balance of Power in World Politics," *Oxford Research Encyclopedia of Politics*, May 9, 2016.

Seawright, Jason, and John Gerring. "Case Selection Techniques in Case Study Research A Menu of Qualitative and Quantitative Options." *Political Research Quarterly* 61, no. 2 (June 1, 2008): 294–308.

Sechser, Todd S. "Militarized Compellent Threats, 1918–2001." *Conflict Management and Peace Science* 28, no. 4 (2011): 377–401.

Sechser, Todd S., and Matthew Fuhrmann. "Crisis Bargaining and Nuclear Blackmail." *International Organization* 67, no. 1 (January 2013): 173–95.

———. *Nuclear Weapons and Coercive Diplomacy*. New York: Cambridge University Press, 2017.

Segal, Gerald. *Defending China*. Oxford; New York: Oxford University Press, 1985.

Shapley, Deborah. "Technology Creep and the Arms Race: ICBM Problem a Sleeper." *Science* 201, no. 4361 (1978): 1102–5.

———. "Technology Creep and the Arms Race: Two Future Arms Control Problems." *Science* 202, no. 4365 (1978): 289–92.

Shepley, James. "How Dulles Averted War." *Life*, January 16, 1956.

Shevchenko, Arkady N., and Russell J. Bowen. *Breaking with Moscow*. 1st ed. New York: Knopf, 1985.

Simmons, Beth A., and Daniel J. Hopkins. "The Constraining Power of International Treaties: Theory and Methods." *American Political Science Review* 99, no. 4 (2005): 623–31.

Singh, Sonali, and Christopher R. Way. "The Correlates of Nuclear Proliferation: A Quantitative Test." *Journal of Conflict Resolution* 48, no. 6 (2004): 859–85.

Snyder, Glenn H. "'Prisoner's Dilemma' and 'Chicken' Models in International Politics." *International Studies Quarterly* 15, no. 1 (1971): 66–103.

Snyder, Glenn Herald, and Paul Diesing. *Conflict among Nations: Bargaining, Decision Making, and System Structure in International Crises*. Princeton, NJ: Princeton University Press, 1977.

Snyder, Jack L. "Active Citation: In Search of Smoking Guns or Meaningful Context?" *Security Studies* 23, no. 4 (2014): 708–14.

———. *The Ideology of the Offensive: Military Decision Making and the Disasters of 1914*. Cornell Studies in Security Affairs. Ithaca, NY: Cornell University Press, 1984.

Snyder, Jack, and Erica D. Borghard. "The Cost of Empty Threats: A Penny, Not a Pound." *American Political Science Review* 105, no. 3 (August 2011): 437–56.

Sokolski, Henry D., ed. *Getting MAD: Nuclear Mutual Assured Destruction, Its Origins and Practice*. Carlisle, PA: Strategic Studies Institute, US Army War College, 2004.

Solingen, Etel. *Nuclear Logics: Contrasting Paths in East Asia and the Middle East*. Princeton Studies in International History and Politics. Princeton, NJ: Princeton University Press, 2007.

Sorensen, Theodore C. *Kennedy*. 1st ed. New York: Harper & Row, 1965.

Spring, Baker. "Congressional Commission Should Recommend Damage Limitation Strategy." *The Heritage Foundation*. Accessed July 1, 2016. http://www.heritage.org/research/reports/2008/08/congressional-commission-should-recommend-damage-limitation-strategy.

Steinberg, James, and Michael E. O'Hanlon. *Strategic Reassurance and Resolve: U.S.—China Relations in the Twenty-First Century*. Princeton, NJ: Princeton University Press, 2014.

Szulc, Tad. *Fidel: A Critical Portrait*. 1st ed. New York: Morrow, 1986.

Talbot, David. *Brothers: The Hidden History of the Kennedy Years*. 1st ed. New York: Free Press, 2007.

Talbott, Strobe. *Engaging India: Diplomacy, Democracy, and the Bomb*. Washington, DC: Brookings Institution Press, 2004.

Talmadge, Caitlin. "Would China Go Nuclear? Assessing the Risk of Chinese Nuclear Escalation in a Conventional War with the United States." *International Security* 41, no. 4 (2017): 50–92.

Tannenwald, Nina. *The Nuclear Taboo: The United States and the Non-Use of Nuclear Weapons since 1945*. Cambridge Studies in International Relations 87. Cambridge: Cambridge University Press, 2007.

Tetrais, Bruno. "Destruction Assuree: The Origins and Development of French Nuclear Strategy, 1945–1982." In *Getting MAD: Nuclear Mutual Assured Destruction, Its Origins and Practice*, 2004, 51–122.

"The Rise and Fall of MIRV." *The New York Times*, January 27, 1992.

The White House. "The Moment of Truth: Report of the National Commission on Fiscal Responsibility and Reform." Washington, DC, December 2010. https://www.fiscalcommission.gov/sites/fiscalcommission.gov/files/documents/TheMomentofTruth12_1_2010.pdf.

Tomz, Michael. "Clarify: Software for Interpreting and Presenting Statistical Results." *Journal of Statistical Software* 44, no. 2 (2000): 347–61.

Trachtenberg, Marc. "Audience Costs: An Historical Analysis." *Security Studies* 21, no. 1 (2012): 3–42.

———. *A Constructed Peace*. Princeton, NJ: Princeton University Press, 1999.

———. *History and Strategy*. Princeton, NJ: Princeton University Press, 1991.

———. "The Influence of Nuclear Weapons in the Cuban Missile Crisis." *International Security* 10, no. 1 (1985): 137–63.

United States Census Bureau. "Annual Estimates of the Resident Population for Incorporated Places of 50,000 or More," July 1, 2015. http://factfinder.census.gov/faces/tableservices/jsf/pages/productview.xhtml?src=bkmk.

United States Government Accountability Office. "Nuclear Weapons: Actions Needed to Identify Total Costs of Weapons Complex Infrastructure and Research and Production Capabilities." Washington, DC, June 2010. http://www.gao.gov/products/GAO-10-582.

United States Department of Defense. "Report on Nuclear Employment Strategy of the United States Specified in Section 491 of 10 U.S.C.," June 12, 2013. http://www.defense.gov/ Portals/1/Documents/pubs/ReporttoCongressonUSNuclearEmploymentStrategy_ Section491.pdf.

United States Department of State. "Milestones: 1969–1976—Office of the Historian." Accessed August 1, 2016, https://history.state.gov/milestones/1969-1976/arab-israeli-war-1973.

Verghese, B. G. "Kargil War: Reflections on the Tenth Anniversary." *Strategic Analysis* 33, no. 3 (April 9, 2009): 357–59.

Wagner, R. Harrison. "Deterrence and Bargaining." *Journal of Conflict Resolution* 26, no. 2 (1982): 329–58.

Wallace, Michael D. "Arms Race and Escalation: Some New Evidence." *Journal of Conflict Resolution* 23, no. 1 (March 1979): 3–16.

Wallerstein, Alex. "NUKEMAP." Stevens Institute of Technology, 2012. http://nuclearsecrecy. com/nukemap/.

Waltz, Kenneth N. *The Spread of Nuclear Weapons: More May Be Better.* Adelphi Papers, no. 171. London: International Institute for Strategic Studies, 1981.

———. *Theory of International Politics,* Addison-Wesley Series in Political Science. Reading, MA: Addison-Wesley, 1979.

Warnke, Paul C. "Apes on a Treadmill." *Foreign Policy,* no. 18 (1975): 12–29.

Weeks, Jessica L. P. *Dictators at War and Peace.* Ithaca, NY: Cornell University Press, 2014.

Weinberger, Caspar. "Secretary of Defense Testimony before the Senate Foreign Relations Committee," April 29, 1982.

Whiting, Allen S. "China's Use of Force," *International Security* 26, no. 2 (Fall 2001): 103–131.

Wich, Richard. *Sino-Soviet Crisis Politics: A Study of Political Change and Communication.* Cambridge, MA: Harvard University Press, 1980.

Williams, Cindy, ed. *Holding the Line: U.S. Defense Alternatives for the Early 21st Century.* BCSIA Studies in International Security. Cambridge, MA: MIT Press, 2001.

Willman, David. "$40-Billion Missile Defense System Proves Unreliable." *LA Times,* June 15, 2014.

Winter, Eyal. *Feeling Smart.* New York: Public Affairs, 2014.

Wolfsthal, Jon B., Jeffrey Lewis, and Marc Quint. "The Trillion Dollar Nuclear Triad: U.S. Strategic Nuclear Modernization Over the Next Thirty Years." James Martin Center for Nonproliferation Studies, January 2014. http://www.nonproliferation.org/wp-content/ uploads/2016/04/140107_trillion_dollar_nuclear_triad.pdf.

Wohlstetter, Albert. "Nuclear Sharing: NATO and the N+1 Country." *Foreign Affairs* 39, no. 3 (April 1961): 355.

———. "The Delicate Balance of Terror." *Foreign Affairs* 37, no. 2 (January 1959): 211–34.

Zelikow, Philip. "Review of Francis J. Gavin's Nuclear Statecraft: History and Strategy in America's Atomic Age." *H-Diplo* 15, no. 1 (2013): 27–29.

INDEX

Note: Page numbers in *italics* indicate tables and charts.